Transactions of the Royal Historical Society

SIXTH SERIES

XXVII

CAMBRIDGE
UNIVERSITY PRESS

Published by the Press Syndicate of the University of Cambridge
University Printing House, Shaftesbury Road, Cambridge CB2 8BS,
United Kingdom
1 Liberty Plaza, Floor 20, New York, NY 10006, USA
477 Williamstown Road, Port Melbourne, VIC 3207, Australia
C/Orense, 4, Planta 13, 28020 Madrid, Spain
Lower Ground Floor, Nautica Building, The Water Club,
Beach Road, Granger Bay, 8005 Cape Town, South Africa

First published 2017

A catalogue record for this book is available from the British Library

ISBN 9781108427036 hardback

SUBSCRIPTIONS. The serial publications of the Royal Historical Society, *Royal Historical Society Transactions* (ISSN 0080–4401) and Camden Fifth Series (ISSN 0960–1163) volumes, may be purchased together on annual subscription. The 2017 subscription price, which includes print and electronic access (but not VAT), is £185 (US $309 in the USA, Canada, and Mexico) and includes Camden Fifth Series, volumes 52 and 53 and Transactions Sixth Series, volume 27 (published in December). The electronic-only price available to institutional subscribers is £155 (US $259 in the USA, Canada, and Mexico). Japanese prices are available from Kinokuniya Company Ltd, P.O. Box 55, Chitose, Tokyo 156, Japan. EU subscribers (outside the UK) who are not registered for VAT should add VAT at their country's rate. VAT registered subscribers should provide their VAT registration number. Prices include delivery by air.

Subscription orders, which must be accompanied by payment, may be sent to a bookseller, subscription agent, or direct to the publisher: Cambridge University Press, University Printing House, Shaftesbury Road, Cambridge CB2 8BS, UK; or in the USA, Canada, and Mexico: Cambridge University Press, Journals Fulfillment Department, 1 Liberty Plaza, Floor 20, New York, NY 10006, USA.

SINGLE VOLUMES AND BACK VOLUMES. A list of Royal Historical Society volumes available from Cambridge University Press may be obtained from the Humanities Marketing Department at the address above.

Printed in the UK by Bell & Bain Ltd, Glasgow

CONTENTS

Transactions of the RHS 27 (2017), pp. 1–27 © Royal Historical Society 2017
doi:10.1017/S0080440117000020

TRANSACTIONS OF THE

ROYAL HISTORICAL SOCIETY

PRESIDENTIAL ADDRESS

By Peter Mandler

EDUCATING THE NATION: IV. SUBJECT CHOICE*

READ 25 NOVEMBER 2016

ABSTRACT. This address tracks the choices made by students at English schools
(O-Level, GCSE and A-Level) and at British universities (undergraduate degree)
of what subjects to study over the whole of the period since the Second World
War. There are marked long-term trends towards a greater diversity in subjects
studied, especially at A-Level and degree level, and this tended to reduce over time
the dominance of science, to the advantage of a range of subjects including social
studies, traditional humanities and latterly creative arts. These trends reflect (most of
all) the growing size and diversity of the student body staying on to further study, but
also the broadening of the labour market which this more diverse body of students is
entering, and social and cultural changes favouring creativity and self-expression in
education. The address closes with a reflection on the possible significance of a very
recent halting and even a reversal of these trends in subject choice, to the apparent
benefit of the sciences.

In these four addresses, I have been assessing the causes and some
consequences of Britain's transition to mass education at both secondary
and tertiary levels since the Second World War. Against the run of
the literature, which has focused on elite, expert and activist discourses
(politicians, psychological and sociological critics of selection, economists,
teachers, campaigning groups), I have attributed the rush to mass
education to the rising aspiration among the majority of parents and
children for more and better education that was apparent across the
developed (and now the developing) world throughout the second half of
the twentieth century. In Britain's specifically democratic and welfarist
context, the demand for a high-quality education for all, that is, a
democratic discourse of education, parallel to the demand for high-
quality health care, overwhelmed a relatively new and fragile meritocratic

* I am grateful to Celia Phillips and Anna Vignoles for helping me navigate through
this technical subject, to Gary McCulloch and David Edgerton for discussing with me their
work on science education, and to Laura Carter for discussing with me her work on history
education.

discourse which focused energies and resources on an elite. To put it another way, mass demand elicited mass supply. In plumbing the consequences of mass education, I have also tried to give voice to parents and children, making use of economists' and sociologists' data to track their behaviours and experiences whether or not these were articulated in popular discourse. Thus, in my third address I placed, alongside the limited evidence we have about ordinary citizens' aspirations for social mobility, the vast body of sometimes inscrutable data that testifies to the impact that educational opportunity had – or did not have – on the realities of social mobility. In this final address, I turn to the impact of mass participation on the *content* of education – what in the technical literature is called 'subject choice'. Just as access to education had a lot more to do with demand for it than expert discourse would suggest, so the content of education was very largely determined by shifting demand for particular subjects, probably more so in Britain than many of its comparators because of the lack of central curricular control, and the wide range of choices facing parents and children at points as early as age 13 and continuing past compulsory education to ages 16 and 18.

For this purpose, I have assembled from educational statistics data about subject uptake at O-Level and GCSE, A-Level and undergraduate degree level from the 1950s to the present, and once again I have turned to data, argument and theory supplied by the social sciences to seek to augment and interpret these statistics and to explain changes in subject choice over time. Once again, I encounter the familiar problem that each of these social-scientific disciplines is siloed in its own favoured data series and corresponding explanatory framework. Empirical studies of subject choice based on student surveys invariably find a mix of factors – interest, enjoyment, ability, earnings potential, career choice – but are relatively uninquisitive about what might generate these evaluations and how and why they change over time. Driven as they often are by the interests of guidance counsellors, they tend to conclude with homilies about the need for more information and better guidance.[1] Psychologists pin subject choice to personality type; in one famous study of the 1960s, dividing 'clever schoolboys' into conformist 'convergers' who favoured Physics and Classics and dissenting 'divergers' who leant towards the Arts and Biology.[2] Sociologists, especially in their stern 1970s phase, have tended to see subject choice as a myth, given the determinative role of

---

[1] For example, Margaret I. Reid, Bernard R. Barnett and Helen A. Rosenberg, *A Matter of Choice: A Study of Guidance and Subject Options* (Windsor, 1974); Andrew Stables, *Subjects of Choice: The Process and Management of Pupil and Student Choice* (1996); Kate Purcell *et al.*, *Applying for Higher Education: The Diversity of Career Choices, Plans and Expectations* (Warwick, 2008).

[2] Liam Hudson, *Contrary Imaginations: A Psychological Study of the English Schoolboy* (1966); Liam Hudson, *Frames of Mind: Ability, Perception and Self-Perception in the Arts and Sciences* (1968).

the habitus in sorting children by gender and social class, a role they give a twist by identifying teachers as the agents who steer children into their socially specified paths.[3] Economists for their part tend to attribute subject choice to rational behaviours based on future earnings.[4] Historians, insofar as they are tempted to address subject choice at all, have their own favoured cultural and political explanations – favoured in part because anthropologists and political scientists are not competing in this field, but also because these explanations draw on the evidence and actors with which we are most comfortable; this is what causes us to tend towards elite, expert and activist explanations, for which the evidence is textual and archival. We should, of course, try to combine *all* of these sources and their accompanying explanatory frameworks – giving due weight to the otherwise muted majority of our fellow-citizens who speak mostly through surveys and quantitative data, however rebarbative we find those sources of evidence – and that is what I will try to do.

One further interpretive wrinkle is worth ironing out at the outset. Insofar as there is an articulated public discourse about subject choice, it has been almost entirely – again – an elite, politicians' and policymakers' discourse, in all parties, about the choice for science. Especially from the late 1950s, when economists and industrialists began to bear down on educational policy, the public discourse about subject choice has been dominated by the alleged insufficiency of science (or what we now call STEM) and policy has been aimed almost exclusively at remedying that insufficiency. How misleading this discourse is as a guide to actual behaviours is clear from the brute fact that there has been a nearly continuous swing *away* from science from the early to mid-1960s up until the last few years. This you would never guess from the public discourse, which at every step of the way is always detecting (as a way of advocating for) a swing *towards* science, undaunted by repeated waves of evidence to the contrary. But as a result we have a great deal more writing about why students choose the sciences than about why they do not, and choose instead other subjects in the humanities and social sciences. It is not only local patriotism, therefore, that will cause me to dwell upon the choice of

---

[3] Michael F. D. Young, 'An Approach to the Study of Curricula as Socially Organized Knowledge', in *Knowledge and Control: New Directions for the Sociology of Education*, ed. Michael F. D. Young (1971); Peter Woods, 'The Myth of Subject Choice', *British Journal of Sociology*, 27 (1976), 130–49; cf. Martyn Hammersley, 'A Myth of a Myth? An Assessment of Two Ethnographic Studies of Option Choice Schemes', *British Journal of Sociology*, 42 (1991), 61–94.

[4] This literature focuses on the choice to enter post-compulsory education rather than the particular path through it, though the emphasis on 'immediate earning prospects' ought to apply to choice of course as well: see e.g. Christopher A. Pissarides, 'An Overview of the Demand for Post-Compulsory Education by British Men, 1955–77', in *Human Resources, Employment and Development*, III: *The Problems of Developed Countries and the International Economy*, ed. Burton Weisbrod and Helen Hughes (1983), 147–56.

other subjects – with the choice of History of course always in the back of my mind – but also the need to rectify a glaring omission in the literature.[5] As in previous addresses, I will proceed chronologically, starting with the immediate post-war period, and then identifying the distinctive features of the 1960s, a period of expansion in post-compulsory education; the 1970s and 1980s, a period of almost complete stasis; and the period since the late 1980s, a period of very rapid expansion; the last few years, since the slump of 2008, may form a distinctive period of its own, though, as we historians like to say, it is too soon to tell. As this chronology suggests, *what* students choose to study is closely linked to the question of *who* the students are studying at any given point – what the social scientists might call cohort effects.

I

Despite the impression given by C. P. Snow's 'two cultures' controversy at the end of the 1950s, post-compulsory education in the decade or so after the war was led by the sciences – and this was very largely a cohort effect. When the Robbins Committee looked into the matter in 1963, it found that 57 per cent of full-time undergraduate students were on science, technology and medical courses against only 43 per cent in the arts, a rough division which had remained nearly unchanged since 1938, when the balance was 55 per cent to 45 per cent, although there had been a marked swing within the science subjects away from medicine and towards pure science. If there *was* a 'two cultures' problem, it was not a higher education problem in general, but rather an Oxbridge problem, where the proportion of arts students was much higher than elsewhere – more than twice as high as at London and the larger civic institutions – and indeed the 'two cultures' controversy took place very largely on Oxbridge ground (another example of an elite discourse fixing determinedly on an elite).[6] But in the secondary schools and universities of the nation at large, science was king. Maths and Physics were the most popular subjects at A-Level and Chemistry had as many passes as English and History, which

---

[5] For some preliminary work on this subject, on which I draw here, see my 'The Two Cultures Revisited: The Humanities in British Universities since 1945', *Twentieth-Century British History*, 26 (2015), 400–23, abridged and revised as 'The Humanities in British Universities since 1945', *American Historical Review*, 120 (2015), 1299–310; and, for comparisons between US, UK and Australian experiences, 'Rise of the Humanities', *Aeon*, 17 Dec. 2015, https://aeon.co/essays/the-humanities-are-booming-only-the-professors-can-t-see-it.

[6] Committee on Higher Education, *Report* (1963) (hereafter, *Robbins Report*), Appendix II (A): Students and their Education, Cmnd 2154-II, 21–4. Because science education was more expensive, even in 1938 the arts accounted for only 28 per cent of the University Grants Committee's (UGC) funding for departmental maintenance, vs. 72 per cent for the sciences. *Report of the Committee on the Provision for Social and Economic Research* (1945–6) (i.e. the Clapham Report), Cmd 6868, 15.

were the leading Arts subjects.[7] At university, the 'Arts' were occasionally described as 'the most popular group of subjects' but this conclusion was reached only by treating science, medicine and technology as separate groups.[8] In reality, Britain had one of the highest proportions of science and technology graduates in Europe.[9]

Why should this have been? Britain, England especially, had then a very academically focused and selective secondary education system, and also one, though Scotland less so, that channelled pupils narrowly from exams at 16 to exams at 18 to university. It was also, in common with most European systems, a post-compulsory education dominated by boys and by traditionally male occupations.[10] For grammar school leavers at 16, for example, the single most common destination was an engineering apprenticeship.[11] After 16, schooling was closely linked to the graduate labour market and that labour market was itself led by a few overwhelmingly male professions that favoured the sciences: medicine above all, but also engineering and management.[12] Law would not be a majority graduate profession until the 1960s and accountancy not until the 1970s.[13] Accordingly, a majority of boys specialised in science at A-Level, and boys with science at A-Level were the most likely of all 18-year-olds to apply to and to be accepted at university.[14] The saving grace for the arts was teaching, which was the single largest graduate recruiter – about a third of all graduates ended up in teaching – and, although of course schools required science as well as arts teachers, in fact more trained as arts teachers, especially women. As late as 1961, 80 per cent

---

[7] Based on the data for 1962 from DES, *Statistics of Education*, II (1961–79).

[8] Sir Frederick Ogilvie, *British Universities* (1948), 8, 13.

[9] This was the case as early as 1950 and remained so through the 1950s and 1960s, and applies not only to universities but also to other tertiary education: OECD, *Development of Higher Education 1950–1967* (Paris, 1971), 125–6, 147; Celia M. Phillips, *Changes in Subject Choice at School and University* (1969), 110–11.

[10] See Carol Dyhouse, *Students: A Gendered History* (Abingdon, 2006), ch. 4, on the persistence of male dominance in the post-war British university.

[11] Ross McKibbin, *Classes and Cultures: England 1918–1951* (Oxford, 1998), 46–7.

[12] Olive Banks, *Parity and Prestige in English Secondary Education: A Study in Educational Sociology* (1955), 178–82; Gary McCulloch, Edgar Jenkins and David Layton, *Technological Revolution? The Politics of School Science and Technology in England and Wales since 1945* (1985), 17–19. For a slightly earlier period, Carol Dyhouse's survey of graduates from the 1930s found that the vast majority of those who claimed to have had vocational goals on entering university identified medicine, engineering and science; this was, however, a retrospective survey from the 1990s. Dyhouse, *Students*, 36.

[13] Leonard Schwarz, 'Professions, Elites, and Universities in England, 1870–1970', *Historical Journal*, 47 (2004), 951–2, 955–6.

[14] Phillips, *Changes in Subject Choice*, 11, 32–4; *Robbins Report*, Appendix II (B): Students and their Education, Cmnd 2154-II-I, 27.

of female arts graduates ended up as teachers.[15] Although the situation was quite other at Oxbridge – 86 per cent of Oxford undergraduates in 1950 were doing arts degrees, vs. 45 per cent nationally, the kind of thing that aroused C. P. Snow's very Oxbridge-centred ire in the two cultures controversy[16] – across the country in grammar schools, independent schools and universities the tone was set by serious young men beavering away at Maths, Physics and Chemistry.

In these circumstances, it is a little surprising that government and punditry spent so much time and effort trying to produce *more* scientists at all levels. But in the immediate post-war period – especially from the mid-1950s when fears of 'relative decline' were building – all parties converged on investment in education for economic growth, and economic growth was widely held to mean technology-fuelled industry. This line of thinking took two different forms. The earlier but persisting form, associated largely but not exclusively with socialists, was manpower planning. The Attlee government explicitly set targets for the production of graduate scientists and technologists in the name of 'national needs' and these targets were regularly re-set and monitored by the Committee on Scientific Manpower throughout the 1950s and into the 1960s.[17] At the end of the 1950s, a vaguer but more powerful current emerged, amongst economic theorists and politicians alike, which saw education more generally as an investment in 'human-capital'. 'Human-capital' theory had the attraction to Conservatives that it did not require too much government intervention – neither strong-arming the universities nor pressurising employers – and it had the attraction to all politicians that it did not require making forecasts and setting targets which were

---

[15] Political and Economic Planning, *Graduate Employment: A Sample Survey* (1956), 59, 71; *Robbins Report*, Appendix I: The Demand for Places in Higher Education, Cmnd 2154-I, 302–4, Appendix II (B): Students and their Education, Cmnd 2154-II-I, 151–2. Below graduate level, at teacher training colleges, the gender bias was even more marked.

[16] 86 per cent in Oxford but only 71 per cent in Cambridge: Political and Economic Planning, *Graduate Employment*, 29. Science at Oxbridge rose over the course of the 1950s to 40 per cent in 1963, but this was still well below the national average which Robbins calculated at 57 per cent. *Robbins Report*, Appendix II (A): Students and their Education, Cmnd 2154-II, 24.

[17] This story is well known: it runs from the Barlow Report on Scientific Manpower, 1946, to the Advisory Council on Scientific Policy which first reported in 1948, to the targets set by its Committee on Scientific Manpower in 1956 and 1961. See, for example, McCulloch, Jenkins and Layton, *Technological Revolution?*, 27; Brian Simon, *Education and the Social Order 1940–1990* (1991), 83–95; cf. the argument in David Edgerton, *Warfare State: Britain, 1920–1970* (Cambridge, 2006), rooting this trend in the demands of war; and the important empirical survey by C. A. Moser and P. R. G. Layard, 'Estimating the Need for Qualified Manpower in Britain', in *Economics of Education*, I: *Selected Readings*, ed. M. Blaug (Harmondsworth, 1968), 287–317.

too easily foiled by events.[18] It did require throwing money at education – which the Conservative governments of the late 1950s did – and trusting to supply and demand, and the promises of human-capital theory, that such investments would yield growth.[19] Until the end of the 1950s, this policy seemed to be working – as educational participation began to extend, first at GCE and then at degree level, there was a distinct swing to science at A-Level (though less so at degree level), and it was assumed that this build-up would translate automatically into growth.[20] But then, around 1960, just when anxieties about economic decline were peaking – the two cultures controversy, which was then raging, a case in point – it stopped working. The famous 'swing away from science' had begun.

II

I say the 'famous' swing away from science, but it is not as famous as it should be; it has not been the subject of any historical research and it rarely if ever appears in histories of the 1960s, or even of education in the 1960s.[21] Yet it is one of those telling markers of great social and cultural change in 'the Sixties', and like other such markers – including educational expansion itself, to which it is closely linked – it is fascinatingly determined by a number of possibly independent yet simultaneous changes in the fabric of society.

The 'swing from science' was first brought to wide public attention by the Robbins Committee in its October 1963 report. Robbins had commissioned a number of surveys of the flow from schools to universities to labour market and had appreciated that, at the very least, the 'gradual swing towards science' at A-Level in the 1950s was 'no longer in evidence'. The Robbins Report itself was moderately sanguine about this; Lionel Robbins, a Conservative economist, was no friend of manpower planning, and neither really was his left-leaning adjutant Claus Moser. 'The majority of graduates will, we hope, be sufficiently versatile to be capable of

---

[18] For economic thought and research, see Mark Blaug, 'The Empirical Status of Human Capital Theory: A Slightly Jaundiced Survey', *Journal of Economic Literature*, 14 (1976), 827–55; for a contemporary appreciation of the rise of human-capital theory, John Vaizey and Michael Debeauvais, 'Economic Aspects of Educational Development', in *Education, Economy, and Society*, ed. A. H. Halsey, Jean Floud and C. Arnold Anderson (New York, 1961), 37–49.

[19] Human-capital thinking was already evident in the Crowther Report of 1959 and it found a champion in government in Lord Hailsham, minister of science from 1959, who deplored 'the techniques of the Party Chairman' required to do manpower planning and advocated investment in general education as more compatible with Conservative advocacy of free choice: see the discussion in McCulloch, Jenkins and Layton, *Technological Revolution?*, 64–6, 71.

[20] Phillips, *Changes in Subject Choice*, 37–44.

[21] McCulloch, Jenkins and Layton, *Technological Revolution?*, 165–6, provides an early and brief exception.

varied employment', they wrote mildly in the main report.[22] But the swing continued – 42 per cent of A-Level candidates followed a primarily scientific course in 1962 and only 31 per cent in 1967.[23] With the advent of C. P. Snow as minister of technology and a Labour government red-hot for science and technology, more susceptible than most to the siren song of manpower planning, in the mid-1960s the 'swing from science' became a major public issue and a political problem.[24] An enquiry was set afoot in 1964 with Sir Fred Dainton, chemist and vice-chancellor of Nottingham, in the chair. Just as Claus Moser had done much of the footwork for Robbins, so a student of Moser's, Celia Phillips, did much of the footwork for Dainton.[25] Dainton's final report in 1968 essentially extended the 'two cultures controversy' into the late 1960s by arguing for vigorous action against the swing on both economic and cultural grounds. The 'Dainton swing', as it was sometimes now known, gave Dainton

> cause for concern not only in relation to a future supply of qualified manpower which in consequence might possibly prove inadequate to the nation's needs, but also as a symptom of a condition in which science may be losing the esteem which its importance as an element in education deserves.[26]

Dainton was not so interested in the causes of his swing as in the levers to reverse it, mostly drawn from manpower planning.[27] For explanations, we have to turn elsewhere. These varied greatly depending on the vested interests but also on the disciplinary preferences of the commentators.

One explanation – the one most prevalent at the time, and Dainton's favourite – we can discard pretty readily. This attributed the swing to the English system's exceptionally early specialisation. Early specialisation had become a bugbear in the 'two cultures' controversy, and criticised (as 'subject-mindedness') in the wake of the 1959 Crowther Report on

---

[22] *Robbins Report*, Cmnd 2154 (1963), 166–8; Kenneth Gannicott and Mark Blaug, 'Scientists and Engineers in Britain' (1973), in *Economics and Education Policy: A Reader*, ed. Carolyn Baxter, P. J. O'Leary and Adam Westoby (1977), 128. Nevertheless, Robbins still predicted a further mild swing towards science in the near future.

[23] Council for Scientific Policy, *Enquiry into the Flow of Candidates in Science and Technology into Higher Education*, Cmnd 3541 (1967–8) (hereafter *2nd Dainton Report*), 8.

[24] John Carswell, *Government and the Universities in Britain: Programme and Performance 1960– 1980* (Cambridge, 1985), 65–9; McCulloch, Jenkins and Layton, *Technological Revolution?*, 165. There was also the particular logistical problem that universities – under government pressure and UGC guidance – had been planning for a big influx of scientists and building new labs and research facilities to accommodate them, which were now beginning to look like white elephants, unless something was done. Universities raised the alarm after the admissions round of 1964: Phillips, *Changes in Subject Choice*, 1.

[25] See Phillips, *Changes in Subject Choice*, xxi–xxii, for Moser's preface.

[26] *2nd Dainton Report*, preface.

[27] Phillips, *Changes in Subject Choice*, though it offered scrupulous documentation of the swing, doubted the possibility of a coherent explanation for it, and was also closely focused on reversing it: 2–4, 45, 116–19.

secondary education.[28] As the swing had not then begun, the argument focused on the need for a good general education in both arts and sciences at least through 18 if not beyond. Once the swing began, the same fault could be blamed for the 'English disease' of cultural backwardness and economic decline. But even Dainton admitted the swing was an international phenomenon of the 1960s unrelated to school specialisation.[29] The clinching evidence came from Scotland, which saw a similar swing despite its much delayed subject specialisation. In the end, Dainton could not explain why being forced to study science or maths to 16 or 18 would make pupils more likely to choose to study it at university. As Scotland showed, it did not.[30]

As awareness of the transnational nature of the swing grew – with evidence from the Organisation for Economic Co-operation and Development (OECD) emerging that Britain had a relatively high level of science take-up at university, and that it was hardly alone in experiencing the swing – cultural explanations gained purchase, and these were no longer solely in the doom-laden 'two cultures' vein.[31] At least from the mid-1960s, a general disillusionment with science and technology amongst the young was detected, which could be put in positive as well as negative terms, as 'a concern for people rather than things', or, as the social psychologist G. M. Carstairs noted, a move

> away from doing and towards feeling. The young seem less interested in science, factual knowledge and cognitive mastery in general – the very skills which underlie technical efficiency. Instead they seem to express a mood of irrationality; they delight in fantasy . . . the exaltation of inner freedom, of the exploration of subjective experiences, the fullest possible realisation of one's personality. Self-discovery and self-fulfilment are seen as the supreme good and anything which cramps these endeavours is deplored.

[28] Ministry of Education, *15 to 18. A Report of the Central Advisory Council for Education (England)* (1959) (i.e. the Crowther Report), I, 223–5, 262–3. Crowther was not so bothered by 'subject-mindedness', but the issue was taken up by A. D. C. Peterson of the Oxford Department of Education – an early champion of the less specialised International Baccalaureat – and injected into the debate over the 'Dainton swing'. See A. D. C. Peterson, 'The Myth of Subject-Mindedness', *Universities Quarterly*, 14 (1959–60), 223–32; A. D. C. Peterson, 'Britain's Missing Scientists', *New Statesman*, 5 Mar. 1965, 358; F. S. Dainton to G. J. Spence, 25 Feb. 1965: The National Archive (TNA), ED 189/12; H. J. Butcher, 'An Investigation of the "Swing from Science"', *Research in Education*, 1 (1969), 38–40.

[29] *2nd Dainton Report*, 2, 68–70, 74–5.

[30] On Scotland, Dainton's optimism about the benefits of later specialisation was polemically rebutted by Andrew McPherson: 'The Dainton Report – A Scottish Dissent', *Universities Quarterly*, 22 (1967–8), 261–70; '"Swing from Science" or Retreat from Reason?', *Universities Quarterly*, 24 (1969–70), 30–6; cf. *2nd Dainton Report*, 52, 64. For a study broadly supportive of Dainton, but no clearer about causes, see G. A. Barnard and M. D. McCreath, 'Subject Commitments and the Demand for Higher Education', *Journal of the Royal Statistical Society*, Series A (General), 133 (1970), 358–408.

[31] OECD, Directorate for Scientific Affairs, 'Development of Higher Education in OECD Member Countries: Quantitative Trends', 3 Apr. 1969: TNA, UGC 7/1245; UGC, *University Development 1967–1972*, Cmnd 5728 (1974), 25; McPherson, 'Dainton Report', 273nn42–3.

Surveys of schools in the late 1960s confirmed this vague presentiment, more prosaically.

> Heads felt that some of the glamour had left science careers, whereas it was becoming known that interesting careers were available to arts graduates. Many heads had observed the attraction of the socio-economic group of subjects for an increasing number of pupils, and it is possible that there is a reaction against a society dominated by technology.[32]

Most intriguingly, an A-Level General Studies examination in 1969 actually asked students (as an exam question) to 'Try to account for the fact that the number of students wishing to study arts and social sciences is increasing more rapidly than the numbers wishing to study the natural sciences.' The answers came back that the sciences were boring, had a bad public image and lacked opportunities for self-expression, whereas the arts, at least for girls, reflected 'their desire to help the community directly through social action'.[33]

This shift in atittudes, cited by Derek Duckworth who did the most thorough studies of the 'swing' in the 1970s, connects to two other explanations which dovetail with and perhaps lie behind the cultural explanation. The first is a strong cohort effect. When A-Level and higher education expand rapidly, as they did in the 1960s, a new demographic comes into play. Less academically qualified pupils, from families with no previous exposure to post-compulsory education, enter the cohort. In Duckworth's sample of Lancashire grammar school pupils in the early 1970s, Maths, Physics and Chemistry were regarded as the hardest subjects (English, Geography and History were the easiest). Though the sciences did somewhat better in terms of interest, freedom and social benefit, their difficulty proved a great sticking point to new entrants (Latin and French did poorly on all scores) (Figure 1).[34] A second cohort effect, not yet so marked but progressively growing in significance, was gender.[35] Within the sciences, girls were more likely to prefer Biology to Chemistry on nearly all grounds. 'People rather than things' could thus favour softer sciences rather than the arts, but as a result both cohort effects had a marked effect on the swing away from Maths, Physics and Chemistry at both A-Level and degree level.[36]

[32] N. J. Entwistle and D. Duckworth, 'Choice of Science Courses in Secondary School: Trends and Explanations', *Studies in Science Education*, 4 (1977), 68; Derek Duckworth, *The Continuing Swing? Pupils' Reluctance to Study Science* (Windsor, 1978), 10–13; and see also Alan Smithers, 'Occupational Values of Students', *Nature*, 24 May 1969, 725–6.

[33] Duckworth, *The Continuing Swing?*, 32.

[34] D. Duckworth and N. J. Entwistle, 'The Swing from Science: A Perspective from Hindsight', *Educational Research*, 17 (1974), 52.

[35] Dyhouse, *Students*, 97–102.

[36] Duckworth and Entwistle, 'The Swing from Science', 52; and on girls' choices for Biology, see Phillips, *Changes in Subject Choice*, 11–12.

Table 3: Rank orders of school subjects for four attitude dimensions

	INTEREST		EASINESS		FREEDOM		SOCIAL BENEFIT	
	Year 2	Year 5	Year 2	Year 5	Year 2	Year 5	Year 2	Year 5
Boys	Chemistry	Geography	English	English	English	English	English	English
	History	Biology	Geography	Geography	Chemistry	Geography	Maths	Geography
	Geography	Chemistry	History	Biology	Geography	Chemistry	Geography	Biology
	Biology	History	Chemistry	History	Physics	Maths	Biology	Maths
	English	English	Biology	French	Biology	Biology	Physics	Physics
	Physics	Maths	Latin	Maths	History	Physics	Chemistry	Chemistry
	Maths	Physics	Maths	Latin	Maths	History	French	History
	Latin	French	Physics	Chemistry	French	French	History	French
	French	Latin	French	Physics	Latin	Latin	Latin	Latin
Girls	Biology	Biology	Geography	English	English	English	Geography	Biology
	Geography	Geography	English	Geography	Geography	Biology	Maths	English
	Chemistry	English	Biology	History	Chemistry	Geography	Biology	Geography
	History	History	History	French	Biology	Chemistry	English	Maths
	English	Chemistry	Maths	Biology	Maths	Maths	Physics	Chemistry
	Maths	Physics	Chemistry	Maths	History	Physics	Chemistry	French
	Physics	Maths	French	Latin	Physics	History	French	Physics
	French	French	Physics	Chemistry	French	French	History	History
	Latin	Latin	Latin	Physics	Latin	Latin	Latin	Latin

Figure 1 Attitudes to subjects among Lancashire grammar school students in the early 1970s
Source: D. Duckworth and N. J. Entwistle, 'The Swing from Science: A Perspective from Hindsight', *Educational Research*, 17 (1974), 52. Reprinted by permission of the publisher (Taylor & Francis Ltd, www.tandfonline.com).

Another effect which dovetailed with culture and demography was the changing labour market. As we have seen, the graduate labour market in the 1950s was led by science-oriented professions, especially medicine and engineering, though teaching (which favoured the arts) was the single most common graduate destination. When the 1960s expansion took place, it not only changed the demographic makeup, it also changed the nature of the graduate labour market. A wider range of professions and employers were now fishing in a graduate pool where previously they could fish their top candidates out of school at 16 or 18.[37] There was also at the end of the 1960s the beginning of a pronounced post-industrial shift away from technologically oriented employment – the over-supply of graduate engineers was particularly obvious[38] – and towards expansion in the public sector, in the helping professions, and in retail and management.[39] It was not so much that these new graduate

[37] Schwarz, 'Professions, Elites, and Universities', 951, 955–6, 961–2. Accordingly, both medicine and teaching began a long decline in their share of career destinations for graduates.
[38] OECD, *The Educational Situation in OECD Countries* (Paris, 1974), 36–7; Gannicott and Blaug, 'Scientists and Engineers'; G. C. G. Wilkinson and J. D. Mace, 'Shortage or Surplus of Engineers: A Review of Recent U.K. Evidence', *British Journal of Industrial Relations*, 11 (1973), 105–23. There remains doubt as to whether the demand for engineers was slackening or whether manpower planning had over-supplied.
[39] OECD, *Employment Prospects for Higher Education Graduates* (Paris, 1981), 15–16, 26–9; UGC, *University Development 1967–1972*, 27–8.

occupations disfavoured science – to the contrary, many science graduates were now gravitating towards management[40] – but rather that they were more neutral as to subject choice, and thus in concert with the cultural and demographic shifts students could swing away from science without losing ground in the labour market. Evidence for this lies, for example, in the growing tendency of employers to advertise for graduates without specifying degree subject,[41] and the growing tendency of graduates to badge a wider variety of subjects (beyond science) as 'vocational'.[42] These trends had the effect of causing the University Grants Committee to back off from 'manpower planning' as early as 1968.[43] They also gave the economists pause. 'Human-capital' arguments for investment in higher education became less targeted on science and technology and focused rather on widening participation in higher education more generally. In some circles, a new light was shed on the 'human-capital' value of investment in education by the 'screening hypothesis', which argued that employers chose graduates not for their particular skills but for general qualities of mind or behaviour (or for their class background), confident that they could train up such people on the job in whatever specific skills were needed.[44] Though governments never entirely lost their taste for manpower planning – and indeed this appetite would revive again in the 1980s under most unlikely auspices – nevertheless the whole university system went into the 1970s much more oriented to student demand, which allowed students to swing away from science unmolested, whatever the reasons that were truly driving them, interest, ability or vocation.

[40] *2nd Dainton Report*, 81, and cf. 'Chemists Hit Out at Dainton', *Times Educational Supplement*, 15 Mar. 1968, 876; Eric Esnault and Jean Le Pas, 'New Relations between Post-Secondary Education and Employment', in OECD, *Towards Mass Higher Education: Issues and Dilemmas* (Paris, 1974), 133–5, 140.

[41] Andrew Jenkins and Alison Wolf, 'Employers' Selection Decisions: The Role of Qualifications and Tests', in *What's the Good of Education? The Economics of Education in the UK*, ed. Stephen Machin and Anna Vignoles (Princeton, 2005), 164; UGC, *University Development 1967–1972*, 27–8.

[42] New entrants were always more likely to be vocational, but in the 1950s and 1960s, this still allowed them considerable scope for subject choice, as teaching (both arts and science subjects) was their principal vocational goal; later in the century, new entrants gave vocational rationales for a wider range of choices. Kate Purcell and Jane Pitcher, *Great Expectations: The New Diversity of Graduate Skills and Aspirations* (Warwick, 1996), 6–7.

[43] Carswell, *Government and Universities*, 104–5; Gannicott and Blaug, 'Scientists and Engineers', 142–3; and see UGC, *University Development 1967–1972*, 25–6, a bold reversal of the views it had held at the end of the previous quinquennium.

[44] Blaug, 'Human Capital Theory', 846–8; Gareth Williams, 'The Economic Approach', in *Perspectives on Higher Education: Eight Disciplinary and Comparative Views*, ed. Burton R. Clark (Berkeley, 1984), 81–2; Mark Blaug, 'Where Are We Now in the Economics of Education?', *Economics of Education Review*, 4 (1985), 18–26; Jenkins and Wolf, 'Employers' Selection Decisions', 152–3, 156. In different versions, this could be a form of human-capital argument – 'screening' recognised the value of higher education – or an argument against it – 'screening' was about reproduction of the social order.

Even Margaret Thatcher's 1972 White Paper on Education granted that widening participation entailed a wider range of motives for education and thus a wider range of subjects, providing 'a stimulating opportunity to come to terms with themselves . . . to discover where their real interests and abilities lie' and catering not only to vocationalism but also 'personal and social action'.[45] (This is, perhaps, Thatcher's hippie moment.)

Before we consider what students were swinging *to*, let me just extend my analysis of the swing away from science into the 1980s, which will allow us to say something further about the causes of the swing, because the period from around 1970 to the late 1980s was a period of considerable stability in participation. Cohort effects, therefore, may have been reduced. And yet the swing away from science continued, and in certain respects accelerated. To 1976, at least, the swing away from Maths and Chemistry continued, the swing away from Physics slowed (after a very sharp early decline), while Biology surged ahead.[46] A great deal of this must have owed to the slow but remorseless rise in A-Level and degree participation amongst women. After about 1976, the swing halted. Both at A-Level and degree level, science held its share steady, even in Physics and Chemistry (Figures 2, 3).[47] Contemporaries prided themselves that this halting of the swing showed finally that pressure 'from above', from government, business and punditry, was telling on student demand. After 1976, the year of James Callaghan's Ruskin speech calling for a return to basics, and more particularly after 1979 with the advent of an even more furiously pro-science Conservative government, standards were seen to be holding and the 'difficult' subjects coming back into vogue.[48]

But even this may have been to some degree a cohort effect. Although higher education participation rates were holding level, more students were enrolling not in universities but in the new polytechnics. The polys had been the brainchild of the 1964 Labour government and especially

[45] *Education: A Framework for Expansion*, Cmnd 5174 (1972–3), 30–1.

[46] Duckworth, *The Continuing Swing?*, 43.

[47] Duckworth's studies halted just at the point when the swing halted too. I have calculated myself the changing shares of A-Level subjects from *Statistics of Education*, II, and *Statistics of School Leavers, CSE and GCE* (1980–5), and for degree subjects from *Education Statistics of the United Kingdom* (to 1978); *Statistics of Education*, VI: *Universities* (1979); and Universities' Statistical Record, *University Statistics*, I: *Students and Staff* (1980–5).

[48] For the imagined swing back to science, one of many false dawns, see, e.g., McCulloch, Jenkins and Layton, *Technological Revolution?*, 194–200; Michael L. Shattock and Robert O. Berdahl, 'The British University Grants Committee 1919–83: Changing Relationships with Government and the Universities', *Higher Education*, 13 (1984), 491–2; Michael Sanderson, *Educational Opportunity and Social Change in England* (1987), 14–15; W. A. C. Stewart, *Higher Education in Postwar Britain* (Basingstoke, 1989), 147. This delusion was particularly prevalent in the early 1980s during Keith Joseph's tenure as education secretary, when university administrators, civil servants and businesspeople tumbled over each other to assure the minister that his dreams were coming true.

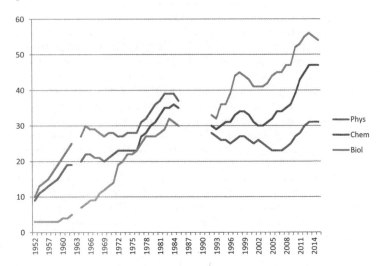

Figure 2 (Colour online) Science A-Levels, England (in thousands)
Sources: Statistics of Education, II (1961–79); *Statistics of School Leavers, CSE and GCE* (1980–5); *Statistics of Education: Public Examinations GCSE and GCE (England)* (1992–2000); GCE/Applied GCE A/AS and Equivalent Examination Results in England, 2009/10 (Revised): http://webarchive. nationalarchives.gov.uk/20110907100731/http://education.gov.uk/ rsgateway/DB/SFR/s000986/index.shtml, accessed 7 Sept. 2016 (2000–10); Subject Time Series Tables, https://www.gov.uk/government/statistics/ a-level-and-other-level-3-results-2014-to-2015-revised, accessed 7 Sept. 2016 (2011–15). There do not appear to be equivalent data for 1986–91.

of Education Secretary Tony Crosland, part of the master plan to reverse the swing away from science in the name of manpower planning. The degrees they awarded through the Council for National Academic Awards (CNAA) were at first *only* awarded in science subjects. But as demand pressures told, the swing away from science registered in the polys too. Science's share of CNAA degrees gave way steadily throughout the 1970s to social studies and humanities courses.[49] Contemporaries decried this as 'academic drift', polys losing their distinctive sense of mission and apeing the older universities.[50] But the polys were much

---

[49] For subjects' share of CNAA degrees, *Statistics of Education*, III: *Further Education* (1971–80). Although CNAA's share of total degrees awarded was modest at first, by 1980 it was awarding about 20 per cent of all first degrees nationally.

[50] On academic drift, see Stewart, *Higher Education*, 140–1, 203–10; Michael Sanderson, 'Education and the Labour Market', in *Work and Pay in Twentieth-Century Britain*, ed. Nicholas

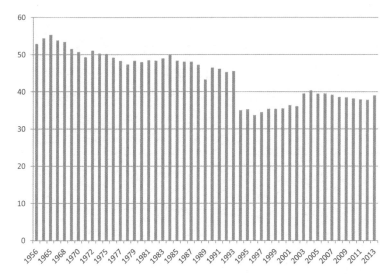

Figure 3 (Colour online) Science degrees as percentage of all first degrees in universities, UK
Sources: *Education Statistics of the United Kingdom* (to 1978); *Statistics of Education,* VI: *Universities,* GB only (1979); *Universities' Statistical Record, University Statistics,* I: *Students and Staff* (1980–5); *Higher Education Statistics for the United Kingdom,* GB only 1993–5 (1993–7); Higher Education Statistical Agency online (1998–). Values for 1994–2002 anomalous due to statisticians' problems in amalgamating polytechnic with university data.

more sensitive to demand pressures than universities – their true mission was to widen participation rather than to steer new entrants towards science and technology courses in which they had no interest.[51] So these new entrants to polys in the 1970s, like the new entrants to universities in the 1960s, swung away from 'difficult' courses and no doubt towards the 'self-discovery' and 'self-fulfilment' held to be characteristic of the period. As polys sopped up new entrants, universities in turn could afford to become more selective, attracting more traditional students back to the

Crafts, Ian Gazeley and Andrew Newell (Oxford, 2007), 287–9. Roy Lowe, *Schooling and Social Change 1964–1990* (1997), 30–42, sees academic drift as beginning in comprehensives.

[51] For an unusually robust defence of the polytechnics' response to student demand, rather than manpower planning from the centre, see the account of Christopher Ball's 14 July 1982 speech and its endorsement by the National Union of Students, in memorandum submitted by the NUS, 'Transbinary Co-operation', 14 Mar. 1983: Education, Science and Arts Committee, *Higher Education Funding. Minutes of Evidence Together with Appendices Monday, 28 March 1983,* HC293 (1982–3), 69–70. Ball was chair of the National Advisory Body, which had been set up to provide a coordinating body for the polytechnics.

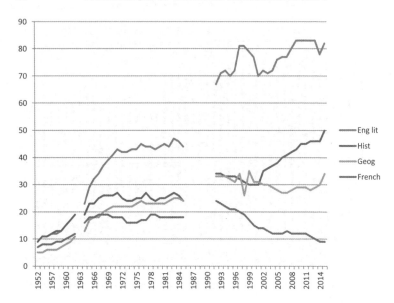

Figure 4 (Colour online) Humanities A-Levels, England (in thousands)
Sources: As Fig. 2.

sciences; thus, the swing away from science was halted in universities but continued at the polytechnics.

What, then, were students swinging to, in universities through the mid-1970s and in polytechnics through the mid-1980s? Initially, the swing appeared to go (and perhaps inevitably was) to what were then the only alternatives, the humanities. Although languages were already beginning their long-term tumble in the 1960s, English literature enjoyed robust growth in the 1960s – in part a gender effect, as English literature was the A-Level subject by far the most skewed to girls, 2–1 (whereas both History and Geography were mildly skewed to boys). But History and Geography both grew steadily during the most rapid phase of the swing to 1972.[52] After 1972, arts subjects including English Literature level off in absolute numbers and experience a mild decline in share at A-Level, much as the sciences do (Figure 4). This relative decline of almost all the established subjects, arts and sciences alike, marks a trend towards the introduction of new subjects at A-Level that had begun in the 1960s and developed further in the 1970s. The introduction of new subjects itself

[52] Duckworth, *The Continuing Swing?*, 43; Phillips, *Changes in Subject Choice*, 13.

reflects a growing sensitivity to student demand and *what* subjects are introduced (and popular) tells us more about what demand was for.

There was no popular new subject that could be counted as a science[53] and only one – Art – that could be counted as a humanities subject. By the 1980s, Art was a more popular subject at O-Level than History.[54] Most of the popular new subjects fell in an entirely new area, allegedly between arts and sciences, which became known as 'social studies', including Economics, Sociology and Business. Economics had been offered at both O- and A-Level in the 1950s but had very limited take-up (only 1,000 or 2,000 passes a year at A-Level); by 1972, it had overtaken History, with 27,000 passes. An entirely new subject, Sociology, gained growing numbers of candidates even at O-Level – where it had overtaken German by 1984.[55] A similar pattern naturally registered at university. Science and especially Engineering lost share; humanities generally retained their share (History lost a little ground); while social studies grew, with a peak share of degrees at 26 per cent in 1977. As we have seen, however, it was in the polytechnic sector that the swing away from science was benefiting the wider range of courses. At degree level in the polys, there was a big swing not only towards social studies, but also towards Creative Arts, humanities and Education (now migrating from teacher-training colleges to polytechnics as its own degree subject). By 1980, science and technology held only about the same share as social studies, 25 per cent, with Creative Arts, humanities and Education all still growing.

We can ask the same set of questions about the swing to social studies (and, to a lesser extent, to Creative Arts) that we asked about the swing away from science: what caused it, and what relative weights can we assign to the influences of interest, enjoyment, ability, earnings potential, career choice? We have already seen a number of cohort effects that help to explain this swing. A widening range of achievement and rising uptake of non-compulsory education by girls devalued Physics and Maths and favoured Geography, History, English and Biology, all seen by girls as easy and interesting. Pupils' judgement of the freedom and social benefit afforded by the various subjects had the same effects, though less so for History. Creativity was a newly professed goal, evident in the rise of Art as an A-Level subject and, from the late 1970s, at degree level in the polytechnics. Pupils of both sexes were more explicit about seeking

---

[53] Botany and Zoology were popular new subjects at A-Level but in 1972 they were amalgamated with Biology.

[54] There were 82,000 good O-Level passes in Art in 1984 vs. 74,000 in History. *Statistics of School Leavers, CSE and GCE.*

[55] See also Cyril S. Smith, 'The Research Function in the Social Sciences', in *The Future of Research*, ed. Geoffrey Oldham (Guildford, 1982), 152.

fulfilment and self-development through their academic studies, and girls about social service.[56]

Structural effects also benefited social studies. Unlike the sciences or even the humanities, degree courses in social studies had no or few A-Level requirements, so they recruited from specialists in both.[57] The loosening of the link between school subjects, degree subjects and occupation encouraged freedom of choice. And as we have also seen, this did open up subject choice to more cultural influences, not only negative influences pushing young people away from science but also positive influences pushing them towards social studies. Girls were particularly apt to voice these positive impressions. Girls' subject choices had always exhibited a traditional bent towards social service, which owed much to the fact that girls unlike boys had to find some selfless rationale to justify further education and vocationalism, and before the 1970s this usually ended up as a choice for teacher training. In the 1970s and 1980s, as women entered a wider variety of occupations, at a time when teacher training was being severely cut back, social studies seemed to combine social service with a number of the most popular new careers, in social work, personnel, commerce and local government.[58] Biology led to another new set of graduate professions in subjects related to medicine – pharmacy, ophthalmology, nursing – none of which expected a background in Physics or Chemistry.[59] Men, too, of course, were entering a widening array of occupations after university, notably business and management, and social studies were as useful a preparation for these careers as science. There is even some evidence that the traditional graduate premium attaching to science degrees – resulting from higher incomes for the science-based professions in medicine, engineering and industry – was receding, and that social studies degrees were producing a premium of their own.[60] Thus, cohort effects, cultural effects, changes in the labour market and employers' growing need for graduates of any kind were all virtuously combining to favour social studies. As by 1980 social studies had become

[56] See above, pp. 10–12.

[57] Phillips, *Changes in Subject Choice*, 29–30.

[58] Dyhouse, *Students*, 115–16; Laurence C. Hunter, 'Employers' Perceptions of Demand', in *Higher Education and the Labour Market*, ed. Robert Lindley (Guildford, 1981), 12–13, 20–2, 38–9.

[59] Phillips, *Changes in Subject Choice*, 30–1; Duckworth, *The Continuing Swing?*, 48.

[60] Vera Morris, 'Investment in Higher Education in England and Wales: A Subject Analysis' (1973), in *Economics and Education Policy: A Reader*, ed. Carolyn Baxter, P.J. O'Leary and Adam Westoby (1977), 76–9, 86; G. L. Williams, 'The Events of 1973–1974 in a Long-Term Planning Perspective' (1974), in *ibid.*, 54–5. This kind of research was through the 1980s only in its infancy. See E. Rudd, 'The Right Balance of Subjects?', in Education, Science and Arts Committee, 5th Report, *The Funding and Organisation of Courses in Higher Education*, HC787 (1979–80), 625–6.

share) of A-Level candidates in Physics dropped continuously from 1984 to a low in 2007, losing a third of its candidates.[68]

In the continuing swing away from science, 'social studies' remained the principal beneficiary, though within social studies the social sciences had stopped growing while business and commerce boomed, the latter overtaking the former in 1996. Other boom subjects were increasingly hard to categorise, reflecting the diversification of the disciplines, a growing tendency for candidates to take A-Levels in both science and arts subjects (encouraged by the introduction of AS-Level in 2000), and the ever-widening extension of the graduate labour market. One new subject lies on the borderland between science and social studies – Psychology – which now matches Biology in numbers of A-Level candidates, benefiting from the gender swing, presumed applicability to a wide range of jobs in the welfare and helping professions, and probably also from a cultural shift towards questions of social and personal identity. Another new subject group lies on the borderland between social studies and humanities – Communications, which includes both business-related and humanities-related subjects, including Media Studies and Cultural Studies. Education, now an all-graduate profession, with its own degrees as well as graduates in other subjects, also leans towards the humanities. And the Creative Arts, which had hardly figured at all as degree-level subjects at universities, grew robustly in share through the 2000s, reaching a peak in 2012 at 11 per cent of all degrees granted, matching the levels of the traditional humanities. Indeed, if one were to seek to measure the relative fortunes of the sciences and humanities, broadly construed, the humanities did much better in the period of rapid expansion since the late 1980s, largely because the Creative Arts did so much better than the only new science degree subjects, those subjects allied with medicine such as pharmacy and nursing (Figure 5). But even some traditional humanities subjects have benefited from expansion. Though languages have suffered a long decline, A-Level passes in History have doubled since 1985, a faster rate of growth than Biology, Business, Art or indeed any traditional subject. English, a compulsory examined subject for all secondary school pupils for the first time after GCSE was introduced in the late 1980s, benefited most; it had always been the most popular humanities subject at 16, but it was now even more so at 16 and 18. (Figure 4).

[68]For an unusual observation of the continuing swing in this later period of expansion, see Emma Smith, 'Is There a Crisis in School Science Education in the UK?', *Educational Review*, 62 (2010), 189–202. For a puzzling assertion of a swing to science in the early part of this period, see Susan Harkness and Stephen Machin, 'Graduate Earnings in Britain, 1974–95', Department for Education and Employment, Research Brief No. 95 (Feb. 1999).

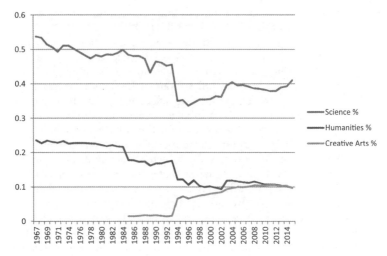

Figure 5 (Colour online) Science, Humanities and Creative Arts degrees as percentage of all first degrees in universities, UK
Sources: As Fig. 3.

If we stand back and survey the entire trajectory from the 1950s nearly up to the present, the overall trends in subject choice are clear enough, though the multiple factors behind those trends remain hard to disentangle. Expansion of post-compulsory education meant a long and sustained swing away from science, despite repeated insistence by policymakers and industrial employers that 'national needs' required a swing in the other direction. Within the sciences, there is a marked swing to female-friendly subjects, principally Biology and Psychology. The greatest beneficiary of the swing was the odd ragbag of subjects that get categorised as 'social studies' – initially, social sciences; increasingly, Business and Commerce; but also humanities-leaning subjects such as Communications and Education. While the traditional humanities experience a swing similar to (but not as sharp as) the swing away from science, they are fortified by the recruitment of new subjects in the Creative Arts, greater than the recruitment by science of subjects allied to medicine.

I have shown that many of these trends can be traced back to the democratisation of education itself, as new entrants – women, students from less academic backgrounds or fewer academic qualifications, and latterly ethnic minorities – prefer social studies and humanities to science. These cohort effects, however, interact subtly with economic and cultural effects. Whatever industrial employers claim, the graduate labour market, as it expands, has less need for science graduates specifically and more for 'graduateness' unconnected to subject, thus facilitating freer choice. Employers in the growing sectors – retail, clerical and for much of our period the public sector – need supervisory skills and analytical skills, but not technical skills, and in their employing behaviours (rather than in industrial employers' propaganda) are 'screening' candidates either for 'graduateness' or for other cognitive and behavioural characteristics, rather than seeking job-specific skills from education. Both the cohort effects and the widening of the graduate labour market chime with students' higher prioritisation since the 1960s of self-understanding, self-development and creativity. What is interesting to consider, therefore, is the possibility that the sheer fact of democratisation – widening participation in post-compulsory education – is itself driving *all* these factors. A more diverse cohort necessarily brings a wider range of motivations into higher education, and as it is dominated by students with less academic background it is likely to introduce less academic considerations into subject choice. Their inexperience with the graduate labour market also suggests that they will be less purposefully vocational in their choices, even though they are *more* likely to badge their choices as vocational, to justify (mainly to their parents) staying on in the first place.[69] The graduate labour market then ratifies this decision by not placing very much weight on the subject of the degree. And the diversification of subject choice may even be responsible for, rather than simply reactive to, cultural values, as the average graduate – less technically oriented, more female, open to a wider range of occupations – is now more likely to appear as a 'seeker' than as a young, upper- or middle-class man hell bent on one of the few traditional graduate professions.[70]

[69]Purcell *et al.*, *Applying for Higher Education*, 162–3, suggests the opposite – that new entrants (both ethnic minorities and students from lower socio-economic classes) are more purposefully vocational in subject choice. But in fact the differences between stated reasons for subject choice by class are small, and as the differences in actual subject choice are small too there is reason to think these differences arise from attempts to justify rather than from actual knowledge of the graduate labour market. There is more evidence of purposeful vocational choice among ethnic minorities. Cf. *ibid.*, 35, 38, 39, 60–6. See also Kate Purcell *et al.*, *Futuretrack Stage 4: Transitions into Employment, Further Study and Other Outcomes* (Warwick, 2012), 11–14.

[70]Though cast in a rather different language, there are some parallels between my argument and that of Michael Gibbons, Camille Limoges, Helga Nowotny, Simon Schwartzman, Peter Scott and Martin Trow, *The New Production of Knowledge: The Dynamics of Science and Research in Contemporary Society* (1994), 3–8, 11, 76–80, 83–4, 94–9, 105, 110. On the 'new diversity of graduate skills and aspirations', see Purcell and Pitcher, *Great Expectations*.

IV

But this story has a sting in its tail. Three factors in the last decade have (or could have) suddenly changed the calculus lying behind subject choice. Most important is probably the slump of 2008 and its aftermath, which is widely held to have disadvantaged especially the bottom end of the graduate pool, seen increasingly to be 'overeducated' and thus doomed to 'graduate' careers as baristas and shelf-stackers. In fact, the graduate premium has not shown much sign of declining – employers still favour graduates over non-graduates. Still, the slump might well have raised future earnings in the hierarchy of students' subject-choice calculations. Then, in 2012, tuition fees were trebled to £9,000 a year. Funded primarily through income-contingent loans, high tuition fees might not have focused students' minds further on future earnings but they have certainly focused ministers' minds: for the first time, the lower the graduate's earnings, the higher the payout from the Treasury. Finally, as a result of both these factors as well as the well-documented politicians' propensity to do this anyway (with as ever help from the engineering employers), a more explicit campaign is now under way to steer students towards science. Perhaps the most egregious illustration of this came in a speech (in the offices of Google, no less) by the education secretary, Nicky Morgan, in November 2014 which decried the last generation of careers advice as steering pupils towards the arts and humanities when, she claimed, 'now we know . . . that the subjects that keep young people's options open and unlock doors to all sorts of careers are the STEM subjects'.[71] No wonder some people have taken to calling the current period 'the age of STEM'.[72]

This rhetoric, I hope you will recognise, is terribly familiar; politicians of all parties have been trying to reverse the swing away from science since it began in the early 1960s (while often also trumpeting 'student choice'). But under the triple-whammy of slump, fees and a concerted propaganda campaign, who is to say that this time it might not work? Since 2008, the biggest growth subject at A-Level has been Maths, though the curve for other major subjects has been pretty flat (Figure 2). Since 2012, the first year of full-fees graduates, the swing away from science has for the first time in fifty years halted and gone into reverse. The humanities have not gone into sharp decline, but their historic slow decline in relative share has continued as science's has not, and for the first time the traditional humanities' decline has not been compensated for by a growth in the Creative Arts, which have levelled off since 2011 (Figure 5).

---

[71] www.gov.uk/government/speeches/nicky-morgan-speaks-at-launch-of-your-life-campaign, accessed 20 Nov. 2016.
[72] *The Age of STEM: Educational Policy and Practice Across the World in Science, Technology, Engineering and Mathematics*, ed. Brigid Freeman, Simon Marginson and Russell Tytler (2015).

This trend may continue; it may not; it *is* too soon to tell, and it is not for an historian to predict the future. Still, I want to conclude with a warning from history. The swing to STEM may be built on false promises, if students are being persuaded to choose subjects against their natural inclinations based on the prospect of higher future earnings. A recent study by a team of economists for the Institute of Fiscal Studies (IFS) has begun to track the correlation between choice of subject and subsequent earnings. It demonstrates considerable variation in mean earnings between subjects, with Creative Arts and Communications at the low end and Medicine, Economics, Engineering, Law and Physics at the high end. This would seem to confirm the rewards to many STEM subjects and the low returns for some of the fastest-growing non-STEM subjects, and to justify a swing to STEM as serving employers' and perhaps thus national needs. The same study, however, also controls these returns for student characteristics, including age, region, prior attainment and parental income. Once you control for student characteristics, the disparities are much reduced – what appears to be a clear hierarchy at the median now dissolves into a pretty flat picture where subject choice does not seem to make that much difference to returns to education (with the clear exception of medicine). (Interestingly, choice of university seems to remain more important than choice of subject, even after controls for student characteristics are applied.)[73]

From this, we might conclude, as we have concluded from some historical evidence that I have presented in my third and fourth addresses, that the economic rewards to education may not be so much rewards to specific skills or subjects as rewards to other characteristics, notably the generic analytic skills associated with 'graduateness' and the behavioural characteristics associated with class. Employers do not make much distinction between degree subjects, but they do make a distinction between graduates and non-graduates, and among graduates between those who share certain other characteristics – age, region, prior attainment, parental income – and those who do not. They use degree subject and institution, in other words, to screen for candidates who share more generically valued characteristics.[74]

[73] Jack Britton, Lorraine Dearden, Neil Shephard and Anna Vignoles, 'How English Domiciled Graduate Earnings Vary with Gender, Institution Attended, Subject and Socio–Economic Background', IFS Working Paper W16/06 (Apr. 2016), esp. Figs. 3, 4, 5. For some earlier attempts based on British Household Panel and Labour Force Survey data, see Ian Walker and Yu Zhu, 'Differences by Degree: Evidence of the Net Financial Rates of Return to Undergraduate Study for England and Wales', *Economics of Education Review*, 30 (2011), 1177–86; Ian Walker and Yu Zhu, 'The Impact of University Degrees on the Lifecycle of Earnings: Some Further Analysis', BIS Research Paper 112 (Aug. 2013).

[74] This was very much the conclusion drawn fifteen years earlier by Wolf, *Does Education Matter?*, 27–33, 37, 45, 196–7. For a counter-argument, see Arnaud Chevalier and Ian Walker,

If this is true, then driving more students to STEM may have a series of perverse and unintended consequences. It may lead to more failure amongst lower-income students whose prior attainment and whose own preferences would have led them elsewhere, a result which Andrew Hacker has already documented as a result of ludicrously high Maths requirements in US high schools.[75] One government aim – more STEM students – is thus likely to frustrate another aim – widening participation. Or it may lead to an over-supply of STEM graduates, as those graduates find that their artificially generated STEM skills do not help them much in the labour market, when really employers had been using STEM skills to screen for something else, which these new STEM graduates lack – favoured background and prior attainment. It will of course please the engineering employers, who, as Hacker again suggests, will now be in a position possibly to spend less on training and certainly to spend less on wages.[76] Above all, it seems to me, seeking to override traditional student preferences for subjects that they enjoy and are good at, in favour of possibly illusory effects on the labour market and on economic growth, is likely to make education less fulfilling and more frustrating.

The degree of specificity in the IFS study about the returns to particular kinds of student, particular universities and particular subjects is only possible because of access to information about parental income and graduate income newly available from tax records and the Student Loan Company. Government has facilitated this access because it wishes itself to measure the degree of subsidy that it is providing through the student loan regime to specific courses at specific universities. That might be all to the good, if the goal is to show that courses chosen by less advantaged students – Creative Arts at post-1992 universities, for example – are being subsidised more, much as the pupil premium subsidises less advantaged students in schools. It is doubtful that that is the government's goal, however. It seems more likely that its aim will be to put pressure on the more subsidised courses as part of a broader campaign to push less advantaged students towards STEM. I have suggested some reasons why

'United Kingdom', in *Education and Earnings in Europe: A Cross Country Analysis of the Returns to Education*, ed. Colm Harmon, Ian Walker and Niels Westergaard-Nielsen (Cheltenham, 2001), 315–16. It is of course possible that 'graduateness' adds value but not specific subjects. For some sociologists' arguments for the screening or 'allocative' role of education, see Yujia Liu and David B. Grusky, 'The Payoff to Skill in the Third Industrial Revolution', *American Journal of Sociology*, 118 (2013), 1330–74; John H. Goldthorpe, 'The Role of Education in Intergenerational Social Mobility: Problems from Empirical Research in Sociology and Some Theoretical Pointers from Economics', *Rationality and Society*, 26 (2014), 265–89.

[75] Hacker, *Math Myth*, 16, 21.

[76] As it is, engineering employers complain that STEM graduates do not often linger in engineering jobs, but move on to management and finance, which are better paid. *SET for Success*, 107, 165–8; Hacker, *Math Myth*, 33–4; and see also Liu and Grusky, 'Payoff to Skill', 1349–51.

that will not work, or if it does work might have perverse consequences. The threat of new league tables based on graduate income – or the reality of a new Teaching Excellence Framework based on alleged 'value added' by subject – will be among the greatest challenges my successors will have to face. I hope in this address to have added some arguments to their armamentarium. And I end with confidence that they will be more than up to the task.

Transactions of the RHS 27 (2017), pp. 29–64 © Royal Historical Society 2017
doi:10.1017/S0080440117000032

THE CLEOPATRAS AND THE JEWS

By Sarah Pearce

READ 23 SEPTEMBER 2016

ABSTRACT. This paper explores a variety of evidence for relations between Cleopatra VII, the last Ptolemaic ruler of Egypt, and her Jewish subjects. In the first part of the paper, the focus is on the profoundly negative portrait of the queen in the works of Josephus, with particular attention to Cleopatra's alleged antipathy to Alexandrian Jews in Josephus's *Against Apion*. Analysis of Josephus's evidence confirms, I argue, that his case against the queen does not stand up. The second part of the paper offers a detailed consideration of other evidence, epigraphic and literary, which, I suggest, confirms a picture of the queen as continuing the policy of her predecessors with regard to the Jews of the Ptolemaic kingdom, by participating in the long-established practice of extending royal support and protection to Jewish *proseuchai* (places of prayer). While the evidence does not permit definitive conclusions, it suggests that Cleopatra looked to particular Jewish groups – as to others – within Egypt for support and in this, followed a path taken by Cleopatra II and Cleopatra III. Finally, a few details in Plutarch's *Life of Antony* may also suggest the queen's political and personal alliances with individual Jews, in Egypt and Judea.

Little has come down to us from antiquity by way of detailed reports of the life of Cleopatra VII. This is not surprising in view of the tendency of ancient authors to neglect the lives of women,[1] and, in particular, a life that was subjected to the relentlessly negative propaganda of the Augustan house.[2] Our most substantial literary source is the biographer and philosopher Plutarch (*c.* 45–*c.* 125 CE), whose moralising accounts of famous Greek and Roman men, as presented in the *Parallel Lives*, deal with Cleopatra's role in the lives of Julius Caesar and Mark Antony. Our most complete narrative of the period context of Cleopatra's reign comes from Cassius Dio's *Roman History*; writing long after the Roman victory over Cleopatra, Dio (*c.* 164 CE – after 229) is nevertheless our most substantial source for the preservation of Augustan propaganda against the queen. Otherwise, our most important literary account of Cleopatra is provided by the Jewish historian Josephus, writing towards the end of the first century CE, in the aftermath of the Jewish War against Rome

[1] Mary R. Lefkowitz, *Heroines and Hysterics* (Bristol, 1981), vii: 'No great ancient writer devoted himself or herself to the task of writing a woman's biography.'

[2] Maria Wyke, *The Roman Mistress: Ancient and Modern Representations* ('Meretrix regina: Augustan Cleopatras') (Oxford, 2002), 195–243.

and the fall of Jerusalem in the year 70. Josephus represents Cleopatra as a significant figure in two distinct contexts: first, in her relations with her close neighbour, Herod, the king of Judaea; and, secondly, as an enemy of the Jews of her capital, Alexandria. In both contexts, the queen is painted as a monster.[3]

The testimony of Josephus has long served to define the rule of Cleopatra as profoundly negative for Jews, and it forms the basis for later judgements that Jews responded by betraying Cleopatra and rejoiced at her downfall.[4] In the case of the Jews of Egypt, there is no evidence for either contention. If Cleopatra's rule was indeed a negative experience for the Jews of her kingdom, this would mark her out as following a very different path from that taken by her predecessors with regard to the large and important Jewish community that prospered in Ptolemaic Egypt from the times of Ptolemy II Philadelphus onwards. A golden age of Jewish literature flourished in Ptolemaic Egypt, from the translation of the Hebrew Scriptures into Greek to tales of Jewish triumphs and happy relationships with Ptolemaic monarchs who valued their Jewish subjects and honoured the Jewish God. Inscriptions from Jewish prayer-houses record the loyalty of Jewish communities in Egypt to their Ptolemaic rulers, while the corpus of Jewish papyri from Egypt illuminates the lives of Jewish settlers, serving in the Ptolemaic army and administration.[5] Against this background, Josephus's testimony presents Cleopatra as an aberration. In so doing, he applied to the Jews the more general tendency of the Augustan literature to present the queen as a 'singular stain' on her

---

[3] The subject of Josephus's treatment of Cleopatra is rarely studied in detail: notable exceptions include Ilse Becher, *Das Bild der Kleopatra in der griechischen und lateinischen Literatur* (Berlin, 1966), 63–8; Jan Willem van Henten, 'Cleopatra in Josephus: From Herod's Rival to the Wise Ruler's Opposite', in *The Wisdom of Egypt: Jewish, Early Christian, and Gnostic Essays in Honour of Gerard P. Luttikhuizen*, ed. Anthony Hillhorst and George H. van Kooten (Leiden, 2006), 115–34; Aryeh Kasher, *King Herod: A Persecuted Persecutor: A Case Study in Psychohistory and Psychobiography* (Berlin, 2007), 126–54.

[4] See, for example, *Encyclopaedia Judaica* (Jerusalem, 1971), s.v. 'Cleopatra'; Louis H. Feldman, 'Pro-Jewish Intimations in Anti-Jewish Remarks', in Louis H. Feldman, *Studies in Hellenistic Judaism* (Leiden, 1996), 177–236 (214–16); Werner Huß, *Ägypten in hellenistischer Zeit 332–30 v. Chr.* (Munich, 2001), 754–5; and the more detailed attempt to show Cleopatra's antipathy towards Jews in Livia Capponi, *Il Tempio di Leontopoli in Egitto: Identità Politica e Religiosa dei Giudei di Onia (c. 150 a.C.–73 d.C.)* (Pisa, 2007), 115–19. Against the construction of Cleopatra as anti-Jewish, see, for example, brief remarks in Victor A. Tcherikover, 'Prolegomena', in *Corpus Papyrorum Judaicarum*, I, ed. Victor A. Tcherikover in collaboration with Alexander Fuks (Cambridge, MA, 1957), 55; Joseph Mélèze-Modrzejewski, 'La dernière chance des Juifs d'Egypte', *L'Histoire*, 238 (Dec. 1999), 48–9 (49); Sandra Gambetti, *The Alexandrian Riots of 38 C.E. and the Persecution of the Jews: A Historical Reconstruction* (Leiden, 2009), 55 n. 121; Duane W. Roller, *Cleopatra: A Biography* (Oxford, 2010), 103–4.

[5] For an authoritative overview, see Joseph Mélèze-Modrzejewski, *The Jews of Egypt: From Rameses II to Emperor Hadrian* (Princeton, 1995).

Macedonian heritage;[6] the last, and worst, of Ptolemaic rulers. In what follows, I attempt to open up Josephus's evidence for closer scrutiny to see what lies beneath, together with an examination of other evidence that may offer alternative perspectives.

I begin with Josephus on Cleopatra and the Alexandrian Jews. Josephus's treatment of this subject forms part of an extended attack on Cleopatra in his work known as the *Against Apion*. Among ancient sources, this attack may be considered, as Duane Roller observes in his recent biography of the queen, 'perhaps the most complete and concise polemic' directed against Cleopatra's reputation.[7] As Josephus constructs her in the *Against Apion*, Cleopatra committed every possible crime: against her family, her husbands and her 'benefactors', the Roman people and their leaders; she murdered her siblings; desecrated the temples and tombs of her ancestors; her 'husband' Antony she made a traitor to Rome, and then betrayed him herself. In this great catalogue of monstrous crimes, the final place is given to Cleopatra's alleged hostility to the Jews of Alexandria.[8]

As with all our literary sources for the representation of Cleopatra, the context is complicated. Indeed, in the case of Josephus's *Against Apion*, we are dealing with the polemical use of the figure of Cleopatra in different contexts over more than a century, and a brief look at that background is essential for understanding what Josephus is about. First, the *Against Apion* is a work of the late first/early second centuries CE (*c.* 94–*c.* 105 CE), in which Josephus sets out to defend the reputation of the Jewish people against their detractors and to promote a vision of Judaism as compatible with Roman values and loyalty to the Roman Empire.[9] A member of the ruling class of Judaea before the war, Josephus played a leading role on the rebel side before his imprisonment by the Romans in 67 CE; in the freedom awarded by the victors, Vespasian and Titus, Josephus dedicated his life to writing in defence of the Jewish people. Older studies often portrayed Josephus as traitor to the Jewish cause; the Roman lackey, living a life of ease in the household of the emperors who made their name with the destruction of Jerusalem. A very different and more complex portrait of Josephus emerges in modern scholarship: a courageous and loyal Jew, working in a context deeply hostile towards Jews. As a matter of imperial policy, all Jews of the Roman Empire were punished for the revolt in Judaea (66–73/4 CE) through the imposition of

---

[6] Propertius, *Elegies* Book 3.11, 40: 'una Phillipeo sanguine adusta nota'.

[7] Roller, *Cleopatra*, 131.

[8] Josephus, *Apion* 2.56–61.

[9] The *Against Apion* must post-date the publication of Josephus's *Antiquities*, referred to at *Apion* 1.1; 2.287, and known to have been completed in 93/94 CE (Josephus, *Antiquities* (*Ant.*) 20.267): for detailed discussion, see John M. G. Barclay, *Against Apion: Translation and Commentary* (*Flavius Josephus: Translation and Commentary*, X, ed. Steve Mason; Leiden, 2007), xxvi–viii.

the *fiscus iudaicus*; the propaganda of the emperors promoted their own role as saviours of the Roman people by emphasising the magnitude of the Jewish threat that they had crushed. In the decades after the destruction of Jerusalem, the Roman world was not a comfortable place for Jews – not at all – and Josephus's work is a powerful witness to that fact.[10]

The *Against Apion* is a deeply apologetic work, explicitly formulated as a response to specific accusations against the Jews and Jewish customs, and filled with features that look designed to appeal to Roman readers – with an emphasis on the venerable antiquity of the Jews and the harmonious relationship between the authentic Jewish way of life and loyalty to Rome and traditional Roman values.[11] At the heart of this work is a long, sustained refutation of hostile statements made by Greek-writing authors against Jews and Judaism.[12] Among these, the final example is represented by the figure of Apion of Alexandria, the eponymous villain of the book's best-known title.[13] It is Apion, according to Josephus, who was apparently the source for the allegation that Cleopatra VII treated the Jews of Alexandria badly.[14] Josephus aims to turn this charge around to benefit the reputation of the Jews, assuming his readers' familiarity with the deeply negative reputation of Cleopatra in Rome: if the Roman people and its government were Cleopatra's deadly enemies, then 'we' Jews should be glorified, not maligned, for finding 'ourselves' also abused by this monstrous queen.[15] In fact, the strength of Josephus's argument is unimpressive on this point: the list of murders, sacrilege and betrayals attributed to the queen climaxes in her omission of the Jews from a distribution of grain in time of famine.[16]

The charge that Cleopatra was hostile to the Jews of Alexandria has often been accepted at face value. The great Thackeray, editor of the 1926 Loeb edition of the *Against Apion*, still a great standard in scholarship,

---

[10] Tessa Rajak, *Josephus: The Historian and his Society* (2nd edn; Oxford, 2002), 226–9. On the Roman context of Flavian propaganda: Fergus Millar, 'Last Year in Jerusalem: Monuments of the Jewish War in Rome', in *Flavius Josephus and Flavian Rome*, ed. Jonathan Edmondson, Steve Mason and James Rives (Oxford, 2008), 101–28; Steve Mason, *A History of the Jewish War*, A.D. 66–74 (New York, 2016), 3–43; and, in relation to the *Against Apion*, Barclay, *Against Apion*, xxxvi–xliv.

[11] On the alignment of the *Against Apion* with Roman values, political and cultural: Martin Goodman, 'Josephus' Treatise *Against Apion*', in *Apologetics in the Roman Empire: Pagans, Jews, and Christians*, ed. Mark J. Edwards, Martin Goodman, Simon Price and Christopher Rowland (Oxford, 1999), 45–58; Barclay, *Against Apion*, 167–9, 362–9. On the apologetic character of the work: Barclay, *Against Apion*, xxx–vi.

[12] Josephus, *Apion* 1.219–2.286; as 'refutation', cf. 2.1, ἀντίρρησις, 'counter-statement'; on his purpose in writing, cf. especially 1.1–5; 2.1–7, 287–96.

[13] *Ibid.* 2.2–144, cf. 148, 295.

[14] *Ibid.* 2.56.

[15] *Ibid.* 2.56: 'Is (Apion) autem etiam ultimae Cleopatrae Alexandrinorum reginae meminit, ueluti nobis improperans quoniam circa *nos* fuit ingrata' (my emphasis).

[16] *Ibid.* 2.60.

entitles this section 'Persecution by the infamous Cleopatra'.[17] However, there are good reasons to be cautious about the reliability of this allegation against the queen. First of all, it relies on the testimony of Apion, as mediated through Josephus. A contemporary of neither Cleopatra nor Josephus, Apion was an Alexandrian scholar of the first half of the first century CE, famous for his commentaries on the classics of Greek literature but also with a mixed reputation, based on his publishing some manifestly outlandish lies.[18] Apion's many works are all lost, preserved only in fragments in the works of authors like Josephus, who uses them to his own end.[19] As his source for Apion's statements on the Jews, Josephus drew on Apion's five-volume work on Egyptian topics, the *Aigyptiaka*.[20] This was no systematic treatise against the Jews, but, in the extracts preserved by Josephus, Apion had created a hostile and unflattering portrait of the Jews and their ancestors. A major part of this material dealt with Apion's contempt for the idea that Jews could be called 'Alexandrians', even though Jews did not worship the gods of the city.[21] It is in this broader context that Josephus locates Apion's remarks about Cleopatra and the Jews. We also know from Josephus that Apion played a leading role in the politics surrounding the crisis of 38 CE, when a faction of the Greek elite in Alexandria led an attack on Jewish civic rights in that city, culminating in an outbreak of extreme violence against the Jews. Apion led an embassy to the emperor Gaius Caligula to put the case for the Greeks; Philo, the outstanding Jewish scholar of the time, headed up the delegation to speak for the Jews of Alexandria.[22] The precise nature and cause of the dispute is impossible to determine from the evidence available.[23] Philo, our chief source for events, emphasises the wholly unprecedented character of the

---

[17] Henry St J. Thackeray, *Josephus*, I: *The Life. Against Apion* (London and Cambridge, MA, 1926), 315.

[18] A notorious example involves the claim that Apion's expositions of Homer owed their authority to a tutorial with the spirit of Homer in the underworld (Pliny, *H.N.* 30.18). On the figure of Apion: Barclay, *Against Apion*, 170–1, with detailed bibliography.

[19] The remains of Apion's works are collected in *FGrHist.* 616.

[20] Josephus, *Apion* 2.10, cites a passage about Moses from the third book of Apion's *Aigyptiaka*. Following Aulus Gellius (*Attic Nights* 5.14.4), Apion's *Aigyptiaka* comprised 5 volumes; Tatian (*Discourse to the Greeks* 38) refers to volume IV of the same work.

[21] Josephus, *Apion* 2.32–78.

[22] Josephus, *Ant.* 18.257–60. Philo wrote an extended account of his embassy to Gaius, but does not name Apion among the members of the opposing Alexandrian embassy: Philo, *Embassy to Gaius*, esp. 178–206, 349–73.

[23] On the crisis of 38 CE and its wider context, important recent studies include John M. G. Barclay, *Jews in the Mediterranean Diaspora: From Alexander to Trajan (323 BCE–117 CE)* (Edinburgh, 1996), 48–71; Erich S. Gruen, *Diaspora: Jews Amidst Greeks and Romans* (Cambridge, MA, and London, 2002), 54–83; Pieter van der Horst, *Philo's Flaccus: The First Pogrom. Introduction, Translation and Commentary* (Leiden, 2003); Gottfried Schimanowski, *Juden und Nichtjuden in Alexandrien: Koexistenz und Konflikte bis zum Pogrom unter Trajan (117 n.Chr.)* (Berlin, 2006); Gambetti, *Alexandrian Riots*.

attempt to destroy the civic privileges of the Jewish community, above all the right of Jews to observe their ancestral customs without compromising the fundamental Jewish prohibition of worshipping other gods.[24] The matters brought before Gaius, so Philo states, had not been brought up for 400 years;[25] in other words, at no time since the conquest of Egypt by Alexander the Great and his foundation of the city of Alexandria. Under all the Ptolemaic monarchs, Philo declares, Jews were permitted to show their loyalty to the crown by making offerings to God on behalf of the monarchs, a way of honouring their rulers without taking part in the city's cults of the deified Ptolemies.[26] Philo leaves us in no doubt that this was also the situation under Cleopatra VII and that the policy continued under the rule of Roman emperors until the accession of the lunatic Gaius Caligula, who declared himself a god. It was only then that a certain faction in Alexandria, among whom we should include Apion (not named by Philo), stirred up accusations against the Jews that their refusal to worship the emperor was, in effect, treason. Against this background, it seems that part of Apion's argument was that Cleopatra's treatment of the Jews confirmed that they lacked civic privileges and that this state of affairs was also reflected in later Roman policy towards the Jews.[27]

But what did Apion really say? We only have access to his words on these matters through Josephus; and we have access to Josephus's Greek original only through a sixth-century Latin translation (of variable reliability).[28] In this context, the introduction to Apion's statement about Cleopatra reads as follows: '(Apion) also mentioned Cleopatra, the last queen of the Alexandrians, as if it were a matter of reproach against us that she was ungracious (or ungrateful) towards us (*nos fuit ingrata*), instead of using his energy to indict her.'[29] Since Apion failed to condemn the queen, as (Josephus implies) he should have done, Josephus lists her alleged crimes at length – against her family and her ancestors, her husbands (Ptolemies XIII, XIV and Mark Antony), the gods and the Roman state – thus setting the scene for her alleged *ingratia* towards the Jews.[30] The task of interpreting Josephus is not helped by the Latin, in which textual

---

[24] On which, see, for example, Philo, *On the Decalogue* 58–81.

[25] Philo, *Embassy to Gaius* 350.

[26] *Ibid.* 138–40.

[27] Cf. Barclay, *Against Apion*, 188–9, 202 n. 214.

[28] On the Latin translation of Josephus's *Apion* (and *Antiquities*), commissioned by Cassiodorus, see the summary overview, with key bibliography, in Barclay, *Against Apion*, lxii. Critical edition: Karl Boysen, *Flavii Iosephi Opera ex Versione Latina Antiqua*, VI: *De Iudaeorum Vetustate sive Contra Apionem* (Vienna, 1898).

[29] Josephus, *Apion* 2.56 (tr. Barclay, adapted).

[30] *Ibid.* 2.57–9.

corruption seems to have greatly augmented the queen's alleged offence against the Jews:

> Finally, when Alexandria had been captured by Caesar (Octavian), she was reduced to such straits that she judged she could hope for salvation if, by her own hand, she could kill the Jews, after the cruelty and treachery which she had practised towards all. Would you not think it something to be proud of if, as Apion says, she did not distribute grain rations to Jews in a time of famine?[31]

The suspect text belongs to Josephus's own formulation of the queen's crimes: that, after Octavian's conquest of Alexandria, Cleopatra was 'reduced to such straits' 'ut salutem hinc sperare se iudicaret, si posset ipsa manu sua Iudaeos perimere'. Almost all critics take the Latin as hopelessly corrupt. Thus, for example, Thackeray: 'The Latin is manifestly absurd'; the Greek original probably read something like 'if she could kill herself (Greek: αὐτὴν) by her own hand'; αὐτὴν was corrupted to αὐτοὺς, 'them', and thence to Ἰουδαίους, 'Jews'.[32] Cleopatra's hope for *salus* is surely for her deliverance from the fate of being paraded in Octavian's Roman triumph, an escape she secures 'by her own hand', through suicide.[33] This interpretation matches Josephus's emphasis in this same context on Cleopatra's death as a fitting punishment for her crimes against others.[34] It is hard to see how even the most hostile enemy of the queen could plausibly argue that Cleopatra sought escape from Octavian by killing Jews.[35] That proposition, in my view, can be safely set aside.[36] This leaves

[31] *Ibid.* 2.60 (tr. Barclay, adapted).

[32] Thackeray, *Josephus*, I, 316 n. 2.

[33] Thus, the Blum/Reinach rendering of *Apion* 2.60: 'elle ne vit plus d'espoir pour elle que dans le suicide': *Flavius Josèphe, Contre Apion*, Texte Établi et Annoté par Théodore Reinach et Traduit par Léon Blum (Paris, 1930), 69; cf. Siegert's rendering of the same lines: 'Zuletzt aber . . . ist sie so weit gegangen, ihr Heil davon zu erwarten, dass sie sich mit eigener Hand selbst . . . umbrächte': *Flavius Josephus, Über die Ursprünglichkeit des Judentums: Contra Apionem*, I, ed. Folker Siegert (Göttingen, 2008), 169. With regard to the Latin, Siegert justly notes (*ibid.*) that 'Das wäre für die königliche Hand viel Arbeit gewesen'!

[34] Josephus, *Apion* 2.61.

[35] Contra the attempt by Volkmann to read Josephus's paraphrase of Apion as the words of Cleopatra herself, interpreted psychologically: '"I would have conquered, if I had been able to destroy all the Jews". These despairing words of Cleopatra's show that she felt she was surrounded by difficulties and treachery'; cf. Hans Volkmann, *Cleopatra: A Study in Politics and Propaganda* (1958), 199.

[36] Barclay (*Against Apion*, 202, n. 213; cf. lxiv, the reading *Iudaeos* is 'just possible') offers an interpretation of the text as it stands, suggesting the possibility that some (but certainly not *all*) Jews may have been killed in the purge (reported in Cassius Dio 51.5.4–5) directed against some leading citizens in Alexandria, after the Battle of Actium and news of the defection of Herod and other client kings to Octavian. Plutarch, on the other hand, observes that the news of defections did not much disturb Antony (*Antony* 71.1–2). If there was a purge in Alexandria at this time, following Dio, there is no evidence that it specifically targeted Jews, let alone 'the Jews' as a collective. No mention is made of such an event in Herod's post-Actium speech before Octavian (30 BCE), in which, as king of Judaea, he claims to have proved himself a loyal ally to Antony in advising him to kill Cleopatra (Josephus,

us with the allegation, based on Apion's words, that 'in a time of famine, Cleopatra did not distribute grain rations to Jews (*triticum non est mensa*)'.[37] Josephus does not give the context, but instead focuses on Apion's allegedly astounding ignorance of written Roman testimony to the loyalty of the Jewish people towards Rome and, before the time of Roman rule, 'under Alexander and under all the Ptolemies'.[38] Clearly, however, the real heart of the problem addressed by Josephus is the situation in the Roman administration of Egypt, since he follows the denunciation of Cleopatra with special pleading about the similar treatment of Jews by Germanicus, nephew of the emperor Tiberius, on his visit to Alexandria in the year 19 CE: 'If (says Josephus) Germanicus was unable to distribute grain to all the inhabitants of Alexandria, that is an indication of the failure of the crops and the shortage of grain, not grounds for an indictment of the Jews.'[39] Josephus thus tries to dispose of what, presumably, were further claims made by Apion about the status of Jews in Alexandria under Roman rule. In response, Josephus seeks to show that Roman rule did not single out Jews for discriminatory purposes, while implying, on the other hand, that – if Cleopatra did indeed leave Jews out of a grain distribution – her policy was manifestly part of her appalling portfolio of evil acts committed against all those who deserved much better. What, we might ask, was Apion's purpose in mentioning Cleopatra's distribution of grain? In the context of a dispute over Jewish civic rights, the topic might well serve to underline the inferior status of those rights in relation to those of

War 1.389–90; Josephus, *Ant.* 15.191–2). Given the various claims attributed to Herod about Cleopatra's hostility to himself and to Judaea, one would expect that his account of her atrocities would include reference to a massacre of Alexandrian Jews, but it does not.

[37] Josephus, *Apion* 2.60.

[38] *Ibid.* 2.62: 'omnibus Ptolomaeis'; cf. *Apion* 2.48, on the exceptional kindness of almost all the Macedonian kings towards the Jews, as a fact ignored by Apion.

[39] Josephus, *Apion* 2.63–4 (tr. Barclay, adapted). Josephus's brief treatment of this episode gives no sense of how problematic it in fact was in the context of imperial politics. According to Tacitus (*Annals* 2.59), Germanicus visited Egypt without the permission of the emperor Tiberius, and, while there, lowered the price of corn by opening the state granaries; his entry into Egypt transgressed the strict Augustan prohibition of entry into Egypt, without the emperor's permission, by senators and equestrians of the higher rank, and earned Germanicus a severe rebuke from Tiberius. See further Francis R. D. Goodyear, *The Annals of Tacitus Books 1–6*, II: *Annals 1.55–81 and Annals 2* (Cambridge, 1981), 372–80. Suetonius (*Tiberius* 52.2) gives a severe famine as the motive for Germanicus's visit, an explanation that probably derives from the supporters of Germanicus in defence of his reputation, and against Tiberius. In the papyrus record of Germanicus's speech in Alexandria on the reasons for his visit, no reference is made to a famine (*P. Oxy.* 2435), perhaps because the measures he took in the grain distribution may have benefited only the citizen body, a small part of the population to be addressed. On the other hand, a distribution given only to a small minority is not likely to have lowered the price of grain, and might suggest that a much larger part of the population benefited; cf. Dieter Georg Weingärtner, *Die Ägyptenreise des Germanicus* (Bonn, 1969), 94. In that case, the exclusion of the Jews would indeed appear as a deliberately hostile act in the time of Germanicus.

the Alexandrian citizen body. Nevertheless, the evidence is very unclear
in this case, with no sense of why this distribution was made, and no
clear identification of the recipients of the grain from the queen. Apion's
argument seems to have presented this case as a one-off event rather
than a regular occurrence. If, as seems likely, Cleopatra was engaged
in the distribution of a grain dole, and that privilege was, as in other
Greek cities,[40] reserved for the citizen class, it should be noted that the
Alexandria's citizen body is likely to have included some Jews as well
as others of non-Greek background, though certainly not the Jews of
Alexandria as a whole.[41] As to a date for this episode, we know that
serious famine struck Egypt following the failure of the Nile flood at the
time of Cleopatra's co-rule with her young brother Ptolemy XIII (51/50
BCE) and again in the years 43–41 BCE, when she ruled with her infant
son Ptolemy XV Caesar.[42] From October 50 BCE, a royal decree prohibits
the transport of grain supplies to anywhere other than Alexandria.[43]
Its significance is best understood, as Dorothy Thompson suggests, as
exemplifying 'the Queen at work in Egypt', concerned, in a time of
crisis, to ensure political stability in the capital by ensuring sufficient
food for its population; or perhaps specifically to benefit the wealthy
landowners and elite of Alexandria, as a pitch for their support.[44] The
queen's concern for the welfare of the landowning class of Alexandria is
explicit in another decree of 41 BCE, guaranteeing their fiscal privileges.[45]
Both in 51, her first year as ruler, and in 41, following the defeat of the
assassins of Julius Caesar at Philippi, Cleopatra faced turbulent times in
which it was essential to do all she could to preserve stability and win
support, particularly among the elite of Alexandria. If she restricted the
distribution of grain to Alexandria's citizen class in time of famine, this

[40] In the Hellenistic context, cf. the grain law of Samos (*Syll.*[3] 976 = Bagnall and Derow
no. 75; *c.* 250 BCE).
[41] Ulrich Wilcken, 'Zum Germanicus Papyrus', *Hermes*, 63 (1928), 48–65 (52–3); cf.
Reinach, *Contre Apion*, 69 n. 3; Aryeh Kasher, *The Jews in Hellenistic and Roman Egypt* (Tübingen,
1985), 341; Barclay, *Against Apion*, 202 n. 214; Gambetti, *Alexandrian Riots*, 55. An alternative
view speculates that Cleopatra's grain distribution took place on the Sabbath, thereby
excluding observant Jews: Schimanowski, *Juden*, 155; cf. Philo's praise for Augustus who
ensured that Jews entitled to the monthly corn doles at Rome might receive them on a
day other than the Sabbath (*Embassy to Gaius* 158). We do not know, however, whether a
similar right existed at Alexandria: cf. Miriam Pucci ben Zeev, *Jewish Rights in the Roman
World* (Tübingen, 1998), 439.
[42] Seneca, *Natural Questions* 4.2.16; Appian, *Civil Wars* 4.61; OGIS 194.14–20 (39 BCE,
Thebes).
[43] *C. Ord. Ptol.* 73 = *BGU* 1730 (27 Oct. 50 BCE).
[44] Dorothy J. Thompson, 'Cleopatra VII: The Queen in Egypt', in *Cleopatra Reassessed*,
ed. Susan Walker and Sally-Ann Ashton (2003), 31–4 (32).
[45] *C. Ord. Ptol.* 75–6 (12 Apr. 41 BCE), cf. Jean Bingen, 'Les ordonnances royales *C. Ord.
Ptol.* 75–76 (Héracléopolis, 41 avant J.-C.)', *Chronique d'Égypte*, 70 (1995), 206–18; Thompson,
'Cleopatra VII', 32–3.

was hardly a policy of discriminating against the Jews or anyone else, but a tried and tested means of keeping the powerful among the Alexandrian population on side.

Thus far, several factors emerge as shaping the image of Cleopatra in the *Against Apion*: the Augustan perspective on Cleopatra, adapted by Josephus for apologetic purposes after the Jewish War, to stress the alignment of loyal Jews with Roman values;[46] and the perspective of Apion, who seems to have appealed to Cleopatra as a precedent for his own times, under Gaius Caligula, in upholding status distinctions that put the Jews of Alexandria in their place, outside the Alexandrian citizen body.

Another element in the mix, I suggest, is the influence of Cleopatra's contemporary, Herod, king of Judaea (*c.* 73–4 BCE), and his role in constructing the queen's negative reputation. In the *Jewish War* and the *Antiquities*, Josephus provides detailed reports of Herod's reign, including accounts of Herod's thoughts on Cleopatra.[47] Josephus gained access to those thoughts primarily through the work of Nicolaus of Damascus. Sometime tutor to the children of Antony and Cleopatra, Nicolaus later became Herod's courtier and historian: his account of Herod's reign, part of a massive work of world history, draws on the king's *Memoirs* as well as Nicolaus's knowledge of events in which he himself played a leading part, notably as Herod's ambassador to Augustus.[48] By the time that Nicolaus joined Herod's retinue (no later than 14 BCE), Cleopatra was certainly a figure of the past; in Nicolaus's construction, however, she plays a vital role as one of several female figures portrayed as threatening Herod's kingship.[49]

Of non-royal stock, Herod was a king made in Rome. Pompey's Roman settlement of Syria in 63 BCE ended the rule of the Hasmonean monarchy in Judea (revived temporarily 40–37 BCE, see below), while retaining the Hasmonean Hyrcanus II as high priest and ethnarch – but not king – of a country now under the control of the Roman governor of the newly created province of Syria. In this role, Hyrcanus was assisted by the powerful figure of Antipater of Ascalon, the father of the future Herod the Great, and Hyrcanus's long-time supporter in the inner-dynastic

---

[46] Barclay, *Against Apion*, 200 n. 194.

[47] The reign of Herod: Josephus, *War* 1.203–673; Josephus, *Ant.* 14.158–17.208.

[48] Tutor to the children of Antony and Cleopatra: *FGrHist.* 90, T2. Herod's Memoirs: Josephus, *Ant.* 15.174; *FGrHist.* 90 Fr. 135. On the life and works of Nicolaus of Damascus: Emil Schürer (revised by Geza Vermes, Fergus Millar and Matthew Black), *The History of the Jewish People in the Age of Jesus Christ*, I (Edinburgh, 1973), 28–32; cf. 50–2 on Josephus's use of Nicolaus in the *War* and the *Antiquities*.

[49] Tal Ilan, '"Things Unbecoming a Woman" (Josephus, *Ant.* 13.431): Josephus and Nicolaus on Women', in Tal Ilan, *Integrating Women into Second Temple History* (Tübingen, 1999), 85–125 (111, 113).

Hasmonean conflict that had led to Pompey's intervention in Jerusalem.[50] Following the demise of Pompey (killed in Egypt on the authority of Ptolemy XIII, 48 BCE), Julius Caesar confirmed Hyrcanus as high priest, in recognition of the assistance received by Caesar from Antipater and Hyrcanus in the course of the Alexandrian War in which Ptolemy XIII was eliminated (47 BCE); in the same year, Antipater's rewards included the prize of Roman citizenship and the position of procurator (*epitropos*) of Judea.[51] Early in the Second Triumvirate, following the assassinations of Caesar (44 BCE) and Antipater (43 BCE), Antony's settlement of the East (41 BCE) promoted Antipater's sons, including Herod, as local governors (*tetrarchs*) within the Jewish territory.[52] In the following year, the Parthians invaded Roman Syria, taking Jerusalem and installing as its high priest and king Antigonus, who, as nephew of Hyrcanus II, was to be the last of the Hasmonean monarchs (40–37 BCE).[53] Herod fled – via Cleopatra's Alexandria – to Antony in Rome, where, with the support of the triumvirs, he received from the Senate the kingship of Judea (40 BCE); [54] and, in time, the might of Roman military backing to exterminate the pro-Parthian Antigonus, executed on the order of Antony, and to install Herod as king in Judea (37 BCE).[55]

Any evaluation of Herod must take into account the fundamental insecurity that dominated much of his reign. Internally, surviving Hasmoneans remained a powerful threat, not at all diminished by Herod's marriage to Mariamme, Hasmonean granddaughter of Hyrcanus II.[56] Josephus records Cleopatra's support for Alexandra and Aristobulus,

---

[50] Hyrcanus II: Schürer, *History* I, 267–80.

[51] Josephus, *War* 1.187–94; Josephus, *Ant.* 14.127–55.

[52] Josephus, *War* 1.242–7; Josephus, *Ant.* 14.324–6. Josephus places the appointment, it should be noted, in the context of the beginning of Antony's relationship with Cleopatra: at Daphne by Antioch, with Antony 'already enslaved to love for Cleopatra' (Josephus, *War* 1.243); or at Tarsus, when Antony 'was taken prisoner through love' (Josephus, *Ant.* 14.324). On the assassination of Antipater by Malichus, a supporter of Hyrcanus: Josephus, *War* 1.226–37; Josephus, *Ant.* 14.277–93.

[53] Antigonus: Schürer, *History*, I, 281–6. A prisoner of the Parthians, Hyrcanus II's position as high priest was terminated following his deliberate mutilation, performed by Antigonus in order to disqualify Hyrcanus from resuming the high priesthood (Josephus, *War* 1.270; Josephus, *Ant.* 14.366).

[54] Josephus, *War* 1.277–85; Josephus, *Ant.* 14.370–89; Tacitus, *History* 5.9 (Herod receives his throne from Antony); cf. the accounts of Herod's appointment as king in Strabo, *Geography* 16.2.46; Appian, *Civil Wars* 5.75. Cleopatra received Herod in Alexandria as he sought refuge from the Parthian invaders: Josephus, *War* 1. 278–9; Josephus, *Ant.* 14.374–6. Her positive reception of Herod reflects loyalty to Antony, but also contrasts with the rebuff given to Herod by Malchus, the Nabatean king, who refused Herod assistance (allegedly for financial motives) at this time: Josephus, *War* 1.274–7; Josephus, *Ant.* 14.370–3.

[55] Josephus, *War* 1.328–57; Josephus, *Ant.* 14.394–491.

[56] Marriage to Mariamme proved a source of terrible division in Herod's household (so Josephus, *War* 1.432–3), and fatal for its Hasmonean members: in addition to the assassination of Aristobulus, Herod ordered the execution of Hyrcanus II (30 BCE),

Mariamme's mother and brother, promoting to Antony their claim to the right of Aristobulus to the high priesthood, and, on behalf of the old monarchy, challenging the legitimacy of Herod as commoner turned king.[57] Confined to house arrest by Herod, Alexandra appealed to Cleopatra for help.[58] The queen offered sanctuary to Alexandra and Aristobulus in Egypt, but their plan to escape was betrayed to Herod; Aristobulus, the last Hasmonean high priest, was dead within the year, drowned in Herod's swimming pool at Jericho (35 BCE).[59] Alexandra again appealed to Cleopatra, hoping that the queen's influence with Antony would lead to Herod's punishment for the killing; while Josephus portrays Cleopatra's promotion of Alexandra's cause as the pursuit of her supposed long-term policy to make Antony the enemy of Herod, the power of the queen's hold over Antony was not proved on this occasion as Antony, bribed by Herod, dismissed the challenge to his client king.[60] In another episode, of uncertain date, Josephus reports the attempt by Costobarus, the Idumean husband of Herod's sister Salome and governor of Idumea, to persuade Cleopatra to collaborate with him against Herod. In this case, Costobarus allegedly appealed explicitly to Cleopatra's ancestral claims on Idumea as the basis on which she should ask Antony for the return of the land. The motive of Costobarus, we are told, involved another kind of ancestral claim: to free Idumea of subjection to Jewish laws and to promote his own rule of the country.[61] With Antony's refusal of Cleopatra's request, the plan came to nothing, but the story is striking for its explicit articulation of Cleopatra's ambition for the restoration of the empire of her ancestors.

Externally, Herod saw Cleopatra as his greatest threat, driven by her ambition for his territory. Josephus tells us that Herod fortified Masada as a refuge from his enemies, specifically pro-Hasmonean Jews, aiming to

---

Mariamme (29 BCE), Alexandra (28 BCE?), and his own sons by Mariamme (7 BCE). On Herod's suspicions, encouraged by his mother and sister, of Cleopatra's involvement in the breakdown of his relations with Mariamme: Josephus, *War* 1.439–40. Given that Herod had recently ordered the killing of Mariamme's brother, she already had good grounds for 'hatred' of Herod. Contrary to Herod's supposed thoughts, Cleopatra is hardly likely to have encouraged Antony's involvement with the beautiful Mariamme.

[57] Josephus, *Ant.* 15.23–32. Alexandra's challenge to the legitimacy of Herod and promotion of the Hasmonean cause through Mariamme, after the killing of Aristobulus: Josephus, *Ant.* 15.63, 73.

[58] Josephus, *Ant.* 15.45–8.

[59] Josephus, *War* 1.437; Josephus, *Ant.* 15.23–79.

[60] Josephus, *Ant.* 15.62–5, 75–7, 79.

[61] Josephus, *Ant.* 15.254–8; cf. Jan Willem van Henten, *Judean Antiquities*, XV: *Translation and Commentary* (*Flavius Josephus: Translation and Commentary*, VIIb, ed. Steve Mason; Leiden, 2014), 177–80. The continuation of the narrative, in which Salome denounces Costobarus to Herod for a further act of treason, makes clear Costobarus's alliance with pro-Hasmonean sympathisers: Josephus, *Ant.* 15.259–66.

restore the old dynasty to power, and the even greater danger of Cleopatra, who allegedly sought the throne of Judea for herself.[62] A client king of Rome, Herod owed loyalty to Antony as commander in the East; after Antony's defeat at Actium (at which Herod was not present),[63] Herod presented himself to Octavian as always a loyal servant to Rome but an enemy of Cleopatra from the beginning.[64] Herod benefited greatly from Cleopatra's fall, and played a major role in promoting Octavian's victory as the salvation of the Roman state.[65]

In Josephus's portrait of Cleopatra in the *Against Apion*, the influence of Herod's perspective may be seen in two respects, beginning with the condemnation of Cleopatra as 'ingrata (circa nos fuit ingrata)'.[66] What does this mean here? The question goes back to Müller's commentary of 1877, in which he states that Josephus knew no reason why Cleopatra should be grateful to the Jews; rather, *ingrata* should be read as 'ungracious', a symptom of the queen's malevolence.[67] Müller's interpretation is widely adopted. But I would like to speak up for the 'ungrateful' reading of Cleopatra.[68] This, I suggest, reflects the view that

---

[62] Josephus, *War* 7.300–3.

[63] Herod blamed his absence from the battle on Cleopatra, who was allegedly behind Antony's commissioning of Herod with a campaign against Malchus, king of the Nabateans: Josephus, *War* 1.364–5, 440; Josephus, *Ant.* 15.108–60, esp. 110. Antony's motive for the campaign was the disloyalty of Malchus, as reported to him by both Herod and Cleopatra: Josephus, *Ant.* 15.110. In the case of Herod, Malchus owed him huge sums in arrears for the tribute owed to Cleopatra for the lease of their lands: Josephus, *Ant.* 15.106–8 (on Herod's earlier plans to attack Malchus on this account), 132–3. Herod also seems to have considered Cleopatra responsible for the demise of Malchus (Josephus, *War* 1.440), though the latter's fate after 30 BCE is unknown. The role of Malchus in a plan to give refuge from Herod to the aged Hyrcanus II led to the latter's execution after the Battle of Actium (Josephus, *Ant.* 15.167–78; spring 30 BCE).

[64] Josephus, *War* 1.388–91; Josephus, *Ant.* 15.187–201.

[65] On Herod's acquisitions, resulting from Cleopatra's fall (territory and men, comprising 400 Gauls who had served as Cleopatra's bodyguards): Josephus, *War* 1.396–7; Josephus, *Ant.* 15.217; cf. Tacitus's brief note confirming that, post-Actium, Augustus extended Herod's territory (*History* 5.9.2). At the site of Nicopolis, founded by Octavian near Actium to celebrate his victory over Antony and Cleopatra, Herod funded the construction of most of the public buildings (Josephus, *Ant.* 16.147). On the site of Strato's Tower, added to Herod's kingdom by Octavian (Josephus, *War* 1.396; Josephus, *Ant.* 15.217), Herod founded the city of Caesarea Maritima in honour of his patron (Josephus, *Ant.* 16.136–41). The flattering note on Roman approval of Herod's generosity in this venture no doubt reflects Herod's own propaganda and the reality that the extension of his territory resulted, at least in part, from the loss of Cleopatra's: 'And they say that Caesar himself and Agrippa often remarked that the extent of Herod's realm was not equal to his magnanimity, for he deserved to be king of all Syria and Egypt' (Josephus, *Ant.* 16.141).

[66] Josephus, *Apion* 2.56.

[67] J. G. Müller, *Des Flavius Josephus Schrift gegen den Apion: Text und Erklärung* (Basel, 1877), 251; cf. Thackeray, *Josephus* 1, 315; Barclay, *Against Apion*, 200 and n. 193.

[68] *Oxford Latin Dictionary* (2nd edn, Oxford, 2012), I, 997–8, s.v. '*ingratus*'; cf. *Flavius Josephus*, ed. Siegert, 169 ('dass sie undankbar zu uns war').

Cleopatra should have counted the Jews, especially the family of Herod, among her benefactors. As Josephus reports it, Herod's father Antipater played a crucial military role in Roman efforts to restore Cleopatra's father to power in Alexandria (55 BCE), while Antipater's support for Julius Caesar in Egypt (48/47 BCE) brought Jewish troops to assist the restoration of Cleopatra.[69] Herod's actions in 40 BCE, after the Parthian takeover in Judea, assume the strength of this connection, heading for Alexandria as his first source of refuge, and received 'magnificently (λαμπρῶς)' by Cleopatra as an ally.[70] Cleopatra did indeed have reason to be grateful.[71]

Secondly, the list of crimes attributed to Cleopatra in the *Against Apion* matches very closely the account of her atrocities as given in Josephus's details of Herod's reign in Book 15 of the *Jewish Antiquities*.[72] In that context, Cleopatra's insatiable greed is repeatedly given as the root cause of all her other evil acts, with particular focus on her greed (πλεονεξία) for Herod's kingdom.[73] This idea is at the heart of Herod's construction of Cleopatra and exploits a powerful theme of the Augustan propaganda which justified going to war on the grounds that Antony was giving Cleopatra lands that belonged to the Roman people.[74] To this familiar theme, the Herodian perspective adds the further, specific charge – that Cleopatra sought to obtain his lands, either by seduction or by plotting to kill him.[75]

Certainly, Herod's fear of Cleopatra centred on the threat to his newly acquired kingdom posed by Antony's policy of expanding the queen's lands outside Egypt in the period from 37 to 34 BCE. Antony's organisation

[69]Restoration of Ptolemy XII/assistance to Gabinius and Mark Antony: Josephus, *War* 1.175; Josephus, *Ant.* 14.99. Restoration of Cleopatra VII/assistance to Mithridates of Pergamum, ally of Julius Caesar: Josephus, *War* 1.187–90; Josephus, *Ant.* 14.127–39, cf. 14.139, citing Strabo.

[70]Josephus, *War* 1.279; cf. Josephus, *Ant.* 14.375–6.

[71] In Josephus's account of the reception of Herod in Rome in 40 BCE, he reports that Octavian, even more than Antony, was in favour of Herod's promotion to kingship because of the loyalty shown by Herod's father to Julius Caesar, the 'father' of Octavian, in the course of the Egyptian campaign (Josephus, *War* 1.283; Josephus, *Ant.* 14.383). Antony, too, is said to have supported Herod because (among other things) of the memory of Antipater's hospitality (*xenia*) in Judaea in the course of the Judaean campaign led by Gabinius (Josephus, *War* 1.244, 282; Josephus, *Ant.* 14. 381, cf. 14.84–6, 326).

[72]Josephus, *Ant.* 15.88–103, expanding Josephus, *War* 1.359–61; cf. van Henten, 'Cleopatra in Josephus', 126–30; *idem, Judean Antiquities*, XV, 59–103.

[73]Josephus, *Ant.* 15.89–95.

[74]Cassius Dio 50.25.4–5; 50.26.2.

[75]Josephus, *War* 1.360; Josephus, *Ant.* 15.97–103. The *Antiquities* account of Cleopatra's supposed attempt at seducing Herod, in the context of Cleopatra's visit to Judaea, follows the model of Octavian's vilification of Cleopatra as arch-seductress; in any case, her dependence on Antony, by whom she was then pregnant with a third son, makes such a scenario implausible: cf. Roller, *Cleopatra*, 121.

of the East involved the gradual redistribution of territories among rulers friendly to Rome. Herod benefited. But Cleopatra benefited most, her proven loyalty to Julius Caesar and Antony rewarded with Antony's enlargement of Cleopatra's territories and the extension of the Ptolemaic Empire in the East almost to its glory days at the beginning of the third century BCE. In 37/36 BCE, Antony's dispositions granted Cleopatra a vast extension to her territory: Chalcis (in Lebanon), parts of Judea and the Nabatean kingdom, together with the city of Cyrene and estates on Crete.[76] For Cleopatra, 37/36 BCE marked the official beginning of a new era of her rule, 'Year 16 which is also Year 1'.[77] In the East, coins of the new territories, with portraits of Antony (reverse), and Cleopatra (obverse), mark the new era and a new titulature for the queen: 'Thea Neotera (the New Goddess)' or 'Queen Cleopatra Thea Neotera'.[78] The title promotes Cleopatra VII as successor to Cleopatra Thea (c. 164–c. 121 BCE), daughter of Ptolemy VI and Cleopatra II; as queen of three Seleucid kings in turn, Cleopatra Thea had represented the Ptolemies' ancestral claims over large parts of the Seleucid empire.[79]

The expansion of Ptolemaic-controlled lands had already begun, in fact, under the Egyptian settlement of Julius Caesar, who in 48 BCE restored Roman Cyprus to Ptolemaic rule (first acquired under Ptolemy I Soter); and, apparently with no objection raised by Octavian, Roman Cilicia (under Ptolemaic rule in the third century BCE) was placed by Antony under Ptolemaic control c. 40 BCE.[80] As tensions increased between Octavian and Antony, however, the further extension of Cleopatra's territories from 37 BCE became a focus of Octavian's negative propaganda against his rival. These gifts, as Plutarch puts it, 'particularly annoyed the Romans', even though – as Plutarch justly notes – Antony had also distributed lands to others, including commoners who received the lands of former monarchs, the Hasmonean Antigonus

---

[76] Josephus, *War* 1.361; Josephus, *Ant.* 15.94–6 (with wrong chronology); Plutarch, *Antony* 36.3–4; Cassius Dio 49.32.4–5; Porphyry in *FGrHist.* 260, Fr. 2.17; Günther Hölbl, *A History of the Ptolemaic Empire* (London and New York, 2001), 241–4; Roller, *Cleopatra*, 90–101.

[77] Porphyry in *FGrHist.* 260 Fr. 2.17; *BGU* 14.2376 (35 BCE; Year 2).

[78] *Cleopatra of Egypt: From History to Myth*, ed. Susan Walker and Peter Higgs (2001), 233–4, nos. 214–17 (Chalcis), 221–2 (?), 232–4 (Cyrene?).

[79] Thompson, 'Cleopatra VII', 31. Cleopatra Thea: John Whitehorne, *Cleopatras* (London and New York, 1994), 149–63.

[80] Hölbl, *History*, 241; Jean Pouilloux, 'Deux amis: le stratège Diogénès fils de Nouménios et le gymnasiarque Stasicratès fils de Stasicratès', in *Praktika tou Protou Diethnous Kyprologikou Synedriou*, I (Leukosia, 1972), 141–50; Edmond Van't Dack, 'Notices Cypriotes', in *Studia Paulo Naster Oblata II: Orientalia Antiqua*, ed. Jan Quaegebeur (Louvain, 1982), 321–6 (323); Thomas Schrapel, *Das Reich der Kleopatra: Quellenkritische Untersuchungen zu den 'Landschenkungen' Mark Antons* (Trierer Historische Forschungen; Trier, 1996), 259.

among them.[81] The propaganda of Octavian, matched by Herod, makes Antony's land distributions to Cleopatra the product of his passion for the Egyptian queen. That view does not stand up to historical scrutiny. As Günther Hölbl observes in his *History of the Ptolemaic Empire*, 'It is no longer the opinion of modern scholarship that these so-called gifts to Cleopatra were the acts of an unrestrained lover. Instead, they are now seen as a "balanced and clear-sighted reorganisation of the administration of the east which won over to Antony's cause capable figures and powerful dominions"'.[82]

From Herod's perspective, outrage was particularly directed at Cleopatra's acquisition – as part of Antony's reorganisation of the East – of parts of Judaea, including Jericho, rich in balsam and date groves, and sections of the coastal area.[83] From then on, Herod leased from Cleopatra the lands 'detached from his kingdom' at 200 talents a year (at least a fifth of his annual income).[84] For Cleopatra, the deal could be seen as the restoration of ancestral territory, first won under Ptolemy I Soter in 301 BCE; Palestine later came under the rule of Seleucid Syria with the conquests of Antiochus the Great in 201, but the marriage of his daughter Cleopatra I to Ptolemy V served to fuel Ptolemaic ambitions to reclaim sovereignty in this region. According to pro-Ptolemaic sources, including the Jewish 'Tales of the Tobiads', Cleopatra I, 'the Syrian', the first Cleopatra to rule Egypt, brought Palestine to the Ptolemies as part of her dowry, employing loyal Jews to collect the tax revenues.[85] In a sense, her descendant Cleopatra VII was continuing the practice of her ancestors.

From the testimony of Josephus and the world of Herod, I now turn to explore other sources of evidence bearing on the relationship between

---

[81] Plutarch, *Antony* 36.3–4; cf. Cassius Dio 49.32.4–5; Christopher B. R. Pelling, *Plutarch, Life of Antony* (Cambridge, 1988), 217–18; Meyer Reinhold, *From Republic to Principate: An Historical Commentary on Cassius Dio's Roman History Books 49–52 (36–29 B.C.)* (Atlanta, GA, 1988), 63–5.

[82] Hölbl, *History*, 242, citing Karl Christ, *Krise und Untergang der römischen Republik* (2nd edn; Darmstadt, 1984), 448; cf. Pelling, *Life of Antony*, 217.

[83] Josephus, *War* 1.360–3; Josephus, *Ant.* 15.93–6; Plutarch, *Antony* 36.3. On Cleopatra's alleged ambition for the whole of Herod's kingdom or for Malchus's kingdom of Nabatea, by fomenting conflict between the two: Josephus, *War* 1.365, 367; Josephus, *Ant.* 15.115–16.

[84] Josephus, *War* 1.362–3; Josephus, *Ant.* 15.106, 132. Herod's annual income is estimated at 1,050–2,000 talents: Samuel Rocca, *Herod's Judaea: A Mediterranean State in the Classical World* (Tübingen, 2008), 208.

[85] Cleopatra's dowry: Josephus, *Ant.* 12.154; cf. Polybius 28.20.9; Appian, *Syrian Wars* 5; see further Daniel R. Schwartz, 'Josephus' Tobiads: Back to the Second Century?', in *Jews in a Graeco-Roman World*, ed. Martin Goodman (Oxford, 1998), 47–61. The Tobiads as tax-collectors for the Ptolemaic monarchy: Josephus, *Ant.* 12.160–223.

Cleopatra and Jews, based on documentary evidence from the Ptolemaic era and the testimony of Plutarch's biography of Mark Antony.[86]

I An asylum decree for a Jewish place of prayer

Rare material evidence bearing on our subject appears in the form of a bilingual (Greek and Latin) marble plaque, on which is inscribed the grant of asylum by a Ptolemaic monarch to a Jewish place of prayer (Greek, *proseuche*) and the renewal of the grant ordered by 'the queen and king', who are almost certainly to be identified with Cleopatra VII and a co-ruler, probably her son Ptolemy XV Caesarion.[87] The royal grant of asylum to temples in Egypt represents a distinctive part of Ptolemaic domestic policy from the beginning of the first century BCE until the fall of Cleopatra.[88] As Kent Rigsby shows in his comprehensive treatment of *asylia* documents from the Hellenistic world, Ptolemaic asylum decrees served to honour certain temples with the privilege of 'religious immunity from the civil law',[89] and at least in some cases to show royal favour towards powerful institutions that could promote crucial support for the monarchy. Judging by the number of decrees extant, the grant of *asylia* to religious institutions in Ptolemaic Egypt was a rather rare privilege.[90] Most of the extant evidence concerns temples of Egyptian gods, including institutions of 'first rank', such as the temple of Horus at Athribis in the southern Delta, distinguished by its fame and antiquity,[91] as well as the more modest temples of the Fayum.[92] From the reign of Cleopatra VII, we have the latest known example of the grant of asylum made

---

[86]Some scholars identify evidence for Jewish representation of Cleopatra VII, including Jewish support for the queen against Rome, in the *Third Sibylline Oracle*. On this question, I follow Erich Gruen's analysis of the evidence which finds no reference to Cleopatra here: 'Jews, Greeks, and Romans in the Third Sibylline Oracle', in *Jews in a Graeco-Roman World*, ed. Goodman, 15–36 (25–7). Relevant to the history of Jewish reception of Cleopatra, but not considered here, are references to the queen in rabbinic literature; see further Joseph Geiger, 'Cleopatra the Physician', in *Zutot: Perspectives on Jewish Culture*, ed. Shlomo Berger, Michael Brocke and Irene Zwiep (Dodrecht, Boston and London, 2001), 28–32; Rivka Ulmer, 'Cleopatra, Isis, and Serapis', in Rivka Ulmer, *Egyptian Cultural Icons in Midrash* (Berlin, 2009), 215–43.

[87]*CIL* III Suppl. no. 6583 = *OGIS* no. 129 = *JIGRE* no. 125 = Kent J. Rigsby, *Asylia: Territorial Inviolability in the Hellenistic World* (Berkeley, Los Angeles and London, 1996) no. 228.

[88]Rigsby *Asylia*, 540–73.

[89]*Ibid.* 540.

[90]*Ibid.* nos. 219–28, a corpus of eleven grants of *asylia* from Ptolemaic Egypt; additional evidence for such grants is supplied by references to other temples already in possession of the grant of *asylia* (e.g. Rigsby, *Asylia* no. 219).

[91]Rigsby, *Asylia* no. 19, Temple of Horus (Ptolemy X, 96 BCE).

[92]E.g. Rigsby, *Asylia* no. 221, Temple of Isis Sachypsis (Theadelphia; Ptolemy X, 93 BCE). In addition to temples of Egyptian gods (Horus, Isis, Ammon and various manifestations of the crocodile god Sobek), grants of *asylia* are also known for Magdola's temple of Heron, a Thracian god whose cult was probably founded in Egypt by military settlers under the early

to the temple of an Egyptian deity, the temple of Isis south of the city of Ptolemais in Upper Egypt.[93] Dated to year 6 of Cleopatra's rule (46 BCE), following Julius Caesar's departure from Egypt and the birth of Cleopatra's son by Caesar, Caesarion (47 BCE), the grant was issued at a very significant moment in the queen's political life: her first year in charge after the elimination of her brother Ptolemy XIII in the Alexandrian War, and a crucial period for building alliances for the future. As part of that strategy, the royal decree gives protection to a new Isis temple, built for the monarchy by Cleopatra's powerful ally Callimachos, close to Ptolemais, the Greek city founded by Ptolemy I to support the monarchy's interests in Upper Egypt.[94] By promoting the worship of the traditional gods of Egypt, Cleopatra continued the policies of her father, following a strategy of embracing Egyptian religion that goes back to the beginning of the Ptolemaic dynasty.

Much more unusual, based on what we know of Ptolemaic policy, is the grant of asylum for a Jewish *proseuche*, a 'place of prayer', preserved in a bilingual inscription of uncertain date and provenance, but which may, with good reason, be placed in the reign of Cleopatra VII. The royal command is given as follows:

> (Greek). On the orders of the queen and king.
> In place of the previous plaque concerning the dedication of the *proseuche*
> (προσευχή) let the following be inscribed. King Ptolemy Euergetes
> (proclaimed) the *proseuche* inviolate (ἄσυλον).
> (Latin). The queen and king gave the order.[95]

That the decree concerns a Jewish institution is not in doubt. The term *proseuche* means 'prayer', and by extension 'place of prayer', and in the latter sense, in ancient literary and documentary evidence, normally designates a Jewish place of worship.[96] The use of *proseuche* in this sense

---

Ptolemies (Rigsby, *Asylia* no. 220), and for Theadelphia's temple of the Greek god Heracles Callinicus (no. 222).

[93] *C. Ord. Ptol.* 67 = Rigsby, *Asylia* no. 226.

[94] Thompson, 'Cleopatra VII', 33.

[95] Βασιλίσσης καὶ βασιλέως προσταξάντων ἀντὶ τῆς προανακειμένης περὶ τῆς ἀναθέσεως τῆς προσευχῆς πλακὸς ἡ ὑπογεγραμμένη ἐπιγραφήτω· [*vacat*] βασιλεὺς Πτολεμαῖος Εὐεργέτης τὴν προσευχὴν ἄσυλον. *Regina et rex iusser(un)t* (text follows *JIGRE* no. 125, based on *CIJ* 2, no. 126).

[96] On the Jewish significance of *proseuche*: William Horbury and David Noy, *Jewish Inscriptions of Graeco-Roman Egypt: With an Index of the Jewish Inscriptions of Egypt and Cyrenaica* (Cambridge, 1992), 14; David Noy, 'A Jewish Place of Prayer in Roman Egypt', *Journal of Theological Studies*, 43 (1992), 118–22; Irina Levinskaya, *The Book of Acts in its First Century Setting*, V: *Diaspora Setting* (Grand Rapids, MI, and Carlisle, 1996), 213–25, correcting LSJ s.v. προσευχή.

gives way only gradually in later centuries to the use of Greek *synagoge*, 'place of assembly', in Jewish communal contexts.[97] In the context of our evidence for Ptolemaic grants of *asylia*, this is the only known example of such a grant to a Jewish institution.

The decree is unique in another respect, as the only known witness to the renewal of an asylum decree in Ptolemaic Egypt. The royal order commands the renewal of an asylum grant made originally for a *proseuche* at the time of its dedication under 'King Ptolemy Euergetes'. Two different monarchs may be in view here: Ptolemy III Euergetes (r. 246–221 BCE) or Ptolemy VIII Euergetes II (r. 170–163, 145–116 BCE). Since the dated evidence for the use of asylum decrees as an instrument of royal policy belongs to the later period of Ptolemaic rule, however, we are almost certainly dealing with Ptolemy VIII Euergetes II and therefore a latest possible date of 116 BCE for the initial grant of asylum.[98] On this basis, the renewal may be seen as supplying rare and precious evidence for the continuity of a particular Jewish community in Egypt over a significant

[97] *A Greek–English Lexicon of the New Testament and Other Early Christian Literature*, revised and edited by Frederick William Danker (3rd edn (BDAG); Chicago and London, 2000), 963, s.v. συναγωγή; cf. Steven Fine, *This Holy Place: On the Sanctity of the Synagogue during the Greco-Roman Period* (Eugene, OR, 1997), 25–33; Anders Runesson, *The Origins of the Synagogue: A Socio-Historical Study* (Stockholm, 2001), 436–59.

[98] See, however, Rigsby's doubts about the authenticity of the claim that asylum was originally granted to the *proseuche* at the time of its dedication, because (1) this is the only example known from Ptolemaic Egypt in which royal permission is given for the renewal of a grant of asylum (though Rigsby notes the not wholly dissimilar example from Nysa in modern Turkey of the restoration of a temple's documents to the record office (Rigsby, *Asylia* no. 186); and (2) based on the fact that a date of 116 BCE or earlier would make this the first known example of an asylum decree in Ptolemaic Egypt (but not necessarily by more than twenty years), with the suggestion that it is unlikely that the first known grant should be for a Jewish institution rather than an Egyptian temple; and (3) on the supposed improbability of a scenario in which any religious institution might be granted asylum from the time of its original dedication: Rigsby, *Asylia*, 572; *idem*, 'A Jewish Asylum in Greco-Roman Egypt', in *Das Antike Asyl: kultische Grundlagen, rechtliche Ausgestaltung und politische Funktion*, ed. Martin Dreher (Cologne, Weimar and Vienna, 2003), 127–41 (135–8). These points do not, in my view, prove the inauthenticity of the grant of asylum under Ptolemy Euergetes. On the early date, it is clear from the Amnesty Decree issued by Ptolemy VIII, Cleopatra II and Cleopatra III that certain temples in Egypt already enjoyed the privilege of asylum, which the Decree aims to protect (*C. Ord. Ptol.* 53=*P. Tebt.* I 5, ll. 84–5; 118 BCE). The grant of asylum to a new temple is exemplified in the case of the temple of Isis near Ptolemais (Rigsby, *Asylia* no. 226, see above), which received from Cleopatra VII the grant of asylum at a time close to its foundation. Rejecting the claim that the *proseuche* received a grant of asylum under Ptolemy VIII, Rigsby argues that 'the claim of Euergetes's grant of asylum to the synagogue will be a fabrication of the first century B.C., in imitation of the report about the Temple in I Maccabees' (Rigsby, *Asylia*, 572, referring to I Maccabees 10:31). This seems an unnecessarily complicated hypothesis.

period of time.[99] Frustratingly, the identity or location of this community is not stated, a point to which we will return.

As for the date of the renewal of the grant of asylum, the decree is issued by order (προτάσσω/ *iusserunt*) of 'the queen and king', βασίλισσα καὶ βασιλεὺς, *regina et rex*. No names are given, but the unusual order of the royal titles, giving precedence to the queen, is matched in some of the official documents of powerful Ptolemaic queens as co-rulers with their children or siblings: in particular, Cleopatra III, widow of Ptolemy VIII, who ruled jointly with both her sons (Ptolemy IX and Ptolemy X) at different times until her assassination in 101 BCE;[100] and Cleopatra VII, as co-ruler and official wife successively to her younger brothers Ptolemy XIII and XIV and from 44 to 30 BCE as co-ruler with her son Ptolemy XV Caesarion.[101] Our inscription supplies no dates, but the use of Latin clearly points to the reign of Cleopatra VII, and the substantial presence in her kingdom from 47 BCE onwards of a Latin-speaking, Roman military force to protect the queen and the interests of Rome as represented by Julius Caesar and, from 41 BCE, by Mark Antony.[102]

Of course, our decree relates to just one, unnamed *proseuche*, rather than to Jews in general. Theoretically, the decree could belong to any one of the multiple Jewish places of prayer known to have existed throughout

[99] Gideon Bohak, 'Ethnic Continuity in the Jewish Diaspora in Antiquity', in *Jews in the Hellenistic and Roman Cities*, ed. John R. Bartlett (London and New York, 2002), 175–92 (186).

[100] Cleopatra III: e.g. *I. Alex. Ptol.* no. 30 (112 BCE). For the brief period of co-rule of Cleopatra II, Cleopatra III and Ptolemy IX, with both queens given precedence in the naming sequence: Hölbl, *History*, 205, with reference to *P. Rylands dem.* III.20 (116 BCE). Cleopatra I: for evidence of her preeminence, as regent with her son Ptolemy VI, in official documents: Whitehorne, *Cleopatras*, 86–7.

[101] E.g. *P. Bon.* 10 (46/45 BCE); *P. Oxy.* 14.1629 (45/44 BCE); *P. Ryl.* IV.582 (42 BCE); *C. Ord. Ptol.* 75–6 (41 BCE); *OGIS* 194 (39 BCE); *P. Cair. Dem.* 31232 (37/36 BCE?); *BGU* XIV.2376 (35 BCE). See further Jean Bingen, *Hellenistic Egypt: Monarchy, Society, Economy, Culture. Edited with an Introduction by Roger S. Bagnall* (Berkeley, 2007), 63–79, esp. 67–71; originally published as 'La politique dynastique de Cléopâtre VII', *Comptes Rendus de l'Académie des Inscriptions et Belles-Lettres* (1999), 49–66; Linda M. Ricketts, 'A Chronological Problem in the Reign of Cleopatra VII', *Bulletin of the American Society of Papyrologists*, 16.3 (1979), 213–17; Linda M. Ricketts, 'The Administration of Ptolemaic Egypt under Cleopatra VII' (Ph.D., Minnesota, 1980), 11–44.

[102] Identification with Cleopatra VII: Hermann Dessau in *Inscriptiones Latinae Selectae*, 3.2 (1916), clxxi; Jean Bingen, 'L'asylie pour une synagogue CIL III *Suppl.* 6583–CIJ 1449', in *Studio Paulo Naster Oblata II*, ed. Quaegebeur, 11–16 (with a decisive refutation of Mommsen's influential argument (1881), predating the publication of most of the relevant documentary evidence for Ptolemaic Egypt, in which he identified the queen and king with Zenobia and Vallabath of Palmyra during their brief period of control in Egypt (270–2 CE)); Laura Boffo, *Iscrizione Greche e Latine per lo Studio della Bibbia* (Brescia, 1994), 113–20; Rigsby, 'A Jewish Asylum', 131–3. Cf. the attempted revival of Mommsen's theory by Glen Bowersock ('The Miracle of Memnon', *Bulletin of the American Society of Papyrologists*, 21 (1984), 21–32), dismissed in Bingen, *Hellenistic Egypt*, 71 (originally published as 'Cléopâtre VII Philopatris', *Chronique d'Égypte*, 74 (1999), 118–23).

Alexandria and the Egyptian countryside.[103] The exceptional character of the decree in its application to a Jewish *proseuche*, however, suggests the likelihood that this was no ordinary institution.[104] Might this then be identified with the 'great *proseuche*' of Alexandria, so large and prominent in Philo's time that the Alexandrian mob failed to destroy it?[105] A different place of origin is, however, indicated by the fact that the plaque turned up for sale in Cairo, not Alexandria, and that it was reportedly found in Lower Egypt.[106] In that context, Kent Rigsby makes a strong case for identifying the unnamed *proseuche* of the asylum decree with the Jewish temple of Onias at Leontopolis near Heliopolis in the Nile Delta, founded under the patronage of Ptolemy VI and Cleopatra II, the older siblings of Ptolemy VIII, the likely author of the original grant of asylum to the *proseuche*.[107] When dealing with a world that must be reconstructed from the survival of fragments and chance finds, great caution must of course be exercised in any attempt to draw conclusions based on linking one rare piece of evidence to another. But the hypothesis that Cleopatra VII singled out the temple of Onias for exceptional privileges has much to commend it. In scale, judging by Josephus's account(s), the Jewish foundation at Leontopolis might well have been considered a great temple, not only in size and importance,[108] but also in the prestige of its founder, Onias IV,

---

[103] The documentary evidence is listed in Zsuzsanna Szántó, 'The Jews of Ptolemaic Egypt in the Light of the Papyri' (Ph.D., Eötvös Loránd University, Budapest, 2016), 180, which adds *PSI Congr.* XVII 22 (Fayum, 114 or 78 BCE) to Tcherikover's earlier summary of the documentary evidence for Egyptian *proseuchai* ('Prolegomena', *Corpus Papyrorum Judaicarum*, I, 8). *CPJ* I, no. 138, a fragmentary papyrus record of unknown provenance, deals with a resolution agreed at 'a meeting in the *proseuche* (συναγωγῆς ἐν τῆι προσευχῆι)', dated on palaeographical grounds to the reign of Cleopatra VII (cf. Noy, 'A Jewish Place', 119 n. 9). On the literary evidence, including rabbinic literature: Lee I. Levine, *The Ancient Synagogue: The First Thousand Years* (New Haven and London, 2005), 82–96.

[104] Rigsby, *Asylia*, 572.

[105] Philo, *Embassy to Gaius* 134–5, on the violations perpetrated by Alexandrian enemies of the Jews within the 'largest and most distinguished (ἐν τῇ μεγίστῃ καὶ περισημοτάτῃ)' of the Alexandrian prayer-houses (38 CE); on the colossal size of the 'great synagogue' of Alexandria, cf. the later rabbinic traditions recorded in *t. Sukkah* 4.6; *y. Sukkah* 5,1, 55a–b; *b. Sukkah* 51b.

[106] On the discovery of the inscription: Rigsby, 'A Jewish Asylum', 127.

[107] Rigsby, *Asylia*, 571–3; idem, 'A Jewish Asylum'.

[108] Josephus gives conflicting accounts of the appearance of the temple: (1) as modelled on the Jerusalem temple (Josephus, *War* 1.33; 7.428, 431–2 (intended as a rival to the Jerusalem temple); cf. Josephus, *Ant.* 12.388; 13.63, 67; 20.236); (2) as 'not like that in Jerusalem' (Josephus, *War* 7.427). Other signs of the magnitude of the temple include reference to its similarity to a tower built of massive stones, sixty cubits high (Josephus, *War* 7.427); its extensive lands, donated by Ptolemy VI and Cleopatra II (Josephus, *War* 7.430); the foundation of a fortress or small town (πολίχνη) associated with the temple (Josephus, *War* 1.33). Josephus varies the terminology for the temple, using, apparently without significant distinction in meaning: (1) ναός (e.g. Josephus, *War* 7.427; Josephus, *Ant.* 13.63; 20.236); (2) ἱερόν, 'holy place' (e.g. Josephus, *War* 7.431; Josephus, *Ant.* 12.388; 13.70–3). Josephus

descendant of the old Jerusalem high priesthood and a powerful supporter of the Ptolemaic monarchy.[109] From its beginnings, the Jewish settlement at Leontopolis repeatedly demonstrated its loyalty to the crown.[110] The founder Onias was probably one of the two Jewish commanders (Onias and Dositheos) to whom Ptolemy VI and Cleopatra II entrusted their army, as Josephus proudly reports in the *Against Apion*.[111] After the death of Ptolemy VI, the same Onias fought on the side of Cleopatra II in her military struggle against Ptolemy VIII to retain power.[112] In the next generation, Cleopatra III, daughter of Cleopatra II, relied on the military leadership of the sons of Onias IV in her war against her elder son, Ptolemy IX. Josephus quotes Strabo (a source with privileged access to information in Egypt in the first decade after the fall of Cleopatra) as confirming that 'only the Jews of the district named for Onias remained faithful to her' because of the queen's favour to her Jewish generals, 'Chelkias and Ananias, sons of the Onias who had built the temple in the nome of Heliopolis'.[113] In the lifetime of Cleopatra VII, according to Josephus, the support of 'the Jews from the so-called land of Onias'

---

locates the temple at Leontopolis in the nome of Heliopolis, *c.* 20 miles from Memphis (Josephus, *War* 7.426; Josephus, *Ant.* 13.65, 70), known as 'the temple (νεώς) of the Jews in the so-called district of Onias' (Josephus, *War* 7.421); but the exact site of the temple, following its destruction by Roman forces in the aftermath of the Jewish Revolt (Josephus, *War* 7.420–1, 433–6; 73/74 CE), has not been found. That territory within the Heliopolite nome was identified as 'the land of Onias' is known not only from Josephus's sources, including Strabo (Josephus, *War* 1.190; Josephus, *Ant.* 13.287, citing Strabo), but also from the epitaph of Arsinoe, associated with the cemeteries at Tell el-Yehoudieh (*c.* 20 miles north-east of Cairo), who names 'the land of Onias' as her birth-place (*JIGRE* no. 38). The archaeological site of Tell el-Yehoudieh has yielded a large corpus of Greek epitaphs, of which more than 50 per cent may be judged to include distinctively Jewish names; this site of Jewish settlement corresponds to at least part of Onias's foundation; cf. Horbury and Noy, *Jewish Inscriptions*, xvi–xix; Capponi, *Il Tempio di Leontopoli*, 207–11.

[109] On Onias IV as founder of the temple of Leontopolis under Ptolemy VI and Cleopatra II: Josephus, *Ant.* 12.387; 13.62–73 (contra Josephus, *War* 7.423, which attributes the foundation to Onias III, father of Onias IV); cf. Gideon Bohak, *Joseph and Aseneth and the Jewish Temple in Heliopolis* (Atlanta, GA, 1996), 19–27; Erich S. Gruen, 'The Origins and Objectives of Onias' Temple', *Scripta Classica Israelica*, 16 (1997), 47–70 (55); Capponi, *Il Tempio di Leontopoli*, 39–59. Against the current majority view, Meron M. Piotrkowski argues for Onias III as the founder of Leontopolis, against the background of political crisis in Judaea and the Maccabean Revolt against the Seleucid Antiochus IV, who had deposed Onias III as Jerusalem High Priest (175 BCE; cf. Josephus, *War* 1.33; 7.423): 'Priests in Exile: The History of the Temple of Onias and Its Community in the Hellenistic Period' (Ph.D., Hebrew University, Jerusalem, 2014).

[110] See Whitehorne, *Cleopatras*, 101–3 (Onias IV), 106–7 (on Josephus, *Apion* 2.53–6); 139–46 (Chelkias and Ananias).

[111] Josephus, *Apion* 2.49.

[112] *Ibid.* 2.50–2.

[113] Josephus, *Ant.* 13.285–7; cf. 13.351–5; Edmond Van't Dack, 'Les armées en cause', in *The Judean–Syrian–Egyptian Conflict of 103–101 B.C. A Multilingual Dossier concerning a 'War of Sceptres'*, ed. Edmond Van't Dack, Willy Clarysse *et al.* (Brussels, 1989), 127–36 (129–31).

(persuaded by Antipater, father of the future Herod the Great, and the authority of the Jerusalem high priest Hyrcanus) played an important role in the victory of Julius Caesar over the forces of Cleopatra's rival, Ptolemy XIII, in the course of the Alexandrian War (spring 47 BCE).[114] Though Josephus does not say so, it follows that Jews from 'the land of Onias' played an important part in events that led to the restoration of Cleopatra VII as queen of Egypt.[115] The asylum decree may well reflect that context of a special relationship between the crown and the Jews of Leontopolis, and perhaps of Cleopatra's hopes of continued reliance on this powerful base of support outside Alexandria, as in the case of her patronage of the Isis temple near Ptolemais in the south.[116]

Whether this decree originates with the Jews of Leontopolis or belongs to another Jewish place of worship in Egypt, other evidence points to the conclusion that the rule of Cleopatra VII did not deviate from the long-established practice of the Ptolemaic monarchs with regard to their official, publicly stated support for Jewish *proseuchai*. From the third century BCE on, the Jews of Egypt dedicated their *proseuchai* 'on behalf of (ὑπέρ)' the royal family.[117] This custom, attested in diverse inscriptions and literary sources, adapted the practice known from non-Jewish temples in Egypt in using such dedications as a means of honouring the monarchs, promoting their image as pious rulers by associating them in the worship of the deity/ies, while refraining from any explicit ascription of divinity

---

[114] Josephus, *Ant.* 14.127–39. According to Josephus, *Ant.* 14.127, Antipater acted under orders from the Jerusalem high priest Hyrcanus. Somewhat different is the account in Josephus's *War* (1.187–94), in which Antipater receives the credit for persuading the Egyptian Jews to cooperate in assisting Julius Caesar and his allies. Neither Jewish leader is mentioned in the Caesarian account of the Alexandrian War, though reference is made there to the post-victory rewards made by Caesar to his allies; cf. *Alexandrian War* 26–8, 65, 78; Schürer, *History*, I, 270–1.

[115] Caesar's restoration of Cleopatra with her second brother, Ptolemy XIV, in Alexandria: *Alexandrian War*, 33.

[116] Thompson, 'Cleopatra VII', 33.

[117] The earliest dated examples are from the reign of Ptolemy III Euergetes (r. 246–221 BCE) and his wife Berenike II: e.g. 'On behalf of king Ptolemy, son of Ptolemy, and queen Berenice his wife and sister and their children, the Jews in Crocodilopolis (dedicated) the proseuche' (*JIGRE* no. 117; cf. no. 22). A century later, the same formula is used in dedications made 'on behalf of' Ptolemy VIII Euergetes II and his co-rulers, Cleopatra II ('the sister') and Cleopatra III ('the wife') (co-rule, 124–116 BCE) (*JIGRE* nos. 24, 25). In other cases, dedications made 'on behalf of king Ptolemy and queen Cleopatra' leave unclear the exact identification of the rulers (*JIGRE* nos. 27, 28; and cf. the fragmentary remains of *JIGRE* nos. 9, 14). The honorific dedication is a distinctive phenomenon of Egyptian Jewry under Ptolemaic rule, reflected, for example, in the petition presented to Ptolemy VI and Cleopatra II for the building of a Jewish temple at Leontopolis (Josephus, *Ant.* 13.67). On the unusual character, in the context of the practice of the Jews of antiquity, of making dedications on behalf of the ruler: Levine, *The Ancient Synagogue*, 84.

to the Ptolemies themselves.[118] Within the temples of Greek (non-Jewish) communities, the honorific dedication served, as Peter Fraser explains, as 'a formula of loyalty, expressing the fact that the Greeks had a personal relationship with, and were therefore under the protection of the sovereign'.[119] Among Jews, the honorific dedication of a *proseuche* permitted public expression of loyalty towards the monarchy,[120] while at the same time not compromising their exclusive, ancestral commitment to the God of Israel, which permitted the worship of no other god.

The reign of Cleopatra VII is very likely the setting for the last known *proseuche* inscription of this kind.[121] Found among rubbish in modern Gabbari, a suburb in the south-west of Alexandria, a badly damaged plaque preserves the following words:

[On behalf] of the queen and king, for the great God who listens to prayer, Alyp[os (made) the] *prose[uche]* in the 15th year, Me[cheir...]

[ὑπὲρ] βασ[ιλίσση]ς καὶ β[ασι]λέως θεῶι [με]γάλωι ἐ[πηκό]ωι (?) Ἄλυπ[ος τὴν] προσε[υχὴν] ἐπόει [?vacat] (ἔτους) ιε΄ Με[χείρ...][122]

A date of 37 BCE, the fifteenth year of Cleopatra's rule, is suggested by the sequence of royal titles, giving precedence to the queen (over Caesarion).[123] If this identification is correct, it offers a striking example

[118] On the use of the dedicatory formula in dedications to Greek and Egyptian deities: Peter M. Fraser, *Ptolemaic Alexandria* (3 vols.,Oxford, 1972), I, 226–7. The practice implies recognition that, though the cult of the Ptolemies was introduced under Ptolemy II Philadelphus alongside that of Alexander, the 'divine' rulers were not 'fully gods': Dorothy J. Thompson, *Memphis under the Ptolemies* (2nd edn; Princeton and Oxford, 2012), 125–6.

[119] Fraser, *Ptolemaic Alexandria*, I, 116. In the case of non-Jewish Greek dedications, Fraser notes that the dedicatory formula, known from other Hellenistic kingdoms, was especially prominent in Ptolemaic Egypt, particularly in Alexandria. In the time of Cleopatra, see *I. Fay.* 3, 205 = Rowlandson no. 12 (Arsinoite nome, 51 BCE): 'On behalf of (ὑπέρ) Queen Cleopatra the goddess Philopator, the place of the association of (Isis) Snonaitiake, of whom the president is the chief priest Onnophris. Year 1, Epeiph' (the Greek inscription accompanies traditional, Egyptian religious iconography).

[120] Fraser, *Ptolemaic Alexandria*, I, 282–3.

[121] The absence of a dedication to the Ptolemaic ruler is seen (among other data) as confirming a Roman date for the dedication by Papous of a *proseuche* 'on behalf of (ὑπέρ) himself and his wife and children' (*JIGRE* no. 126).

[122] *Ibid.* 13, based on the reconstruction by David M. Lewis (*CPJ* 3, no. 1432), here adapted, with my underline in the English translation of letters too damaged to read in the Greek equivalent (with damaged letters in square brackets). The final letters, designating the Egyptian month, here identified as Mecheir, allow for the alternative reading of the month Mesore (Adam Łajtar, Review of Horbury and Noy, *Jewish Inscriptions*, in *The Journal of Juristic Papyrology*, 24 (1994), 57–70).

[123] An impressively strong consensus dates *JIGRE* no. 13 to 37 BCE: M. L. Strack, 'Inschriften aus ptolemäischer Zeit', *Archiv für Papyrusforschung*, 2 (1903), 559 n. 41; Evaristo Breccia, *Iscrizioni Greche e Latine* (Cairo, 1911), no. 41; *CIJ* 2, no. 1432; *CPJ* 3, no. 1432; Mélèze-Modrzejewski, *The Jews of Egypt*, 91; Horbury and Noy, *Jewish Inscriptions*, 19 (a 'tentative date' of 37 BCE); *I. Alex. Ptol.* no. 35. Alternatively, 36 BCE: Giuseppe Botti, 'Bulletin Épigraphique', *Bulletin de la Société archéologique d'Alexandrie*, 4 (1902), 85–107 (86); Fraser, *Ptolemaic Alexandria*,

of the declaration of loyalty to the monarchs by at least one group of Jews within the royal capital, in a momentous year for the politics of the Ptolemaic kingdom. At the same time, the dedication suggests the confidence of the Jews of this Alexandrian *proseuche* in the patronage and support of the queen and her co-ruler.[124] This was no doubt one of the many *proseuchai* which Philo describes as scattered throughout the city in the 30s CE.[125] Many, if not all, of those buildings will have been part of the landscape of Cleopatra's Alexandria. In his powerful denunciation of those who violated the *proseuchai* of Alexandria in 38 CE, Philo emphasises that no such violation ever took place in the Ptolemaic era. In the context of Roman-ruled Egypt, more than sixty years after the death of Cleopatra VII, Philo reflects on the stark contrast between the respectful treatment of the *proseuchai* under all the Ptolemaic monarchs and the disastrous situation in his own Alexandria. According to Philo, the *proseuchai* of Alexandria's Jews became the target for accusations of Jewish disloyalty and impiety towards the emperor Gaius; in 38 CE, as Philo reports, most of the *proseuchai* were destroyed with great violence or transformed, with images of Gaius 'the god', into shrines for the worship of the emperor. Philo condemns these actions as an illegal innovation, designed only to inflict suffering on the Jews by their enemies in Alexandria. In this perspective, the rule of Cleopatra and her predecessors provides the model of appropriate monarchic piety with regard to the *proseuchai*. Philo's testimony serves to confirm the continuation of Ptolemaic policy under Cleopatra VII in permitting Jews to dedicate their places of prayer 'on

---

I, 282, II, 2, 441, n. 766. An identification with the fifteenth year of Cleopatra III (as proposed by Ulrich Willamowitz-Möllendorf, 'Alexandrinische Inschriften', *Sitzungberichte der kgl. Preussischen Akademie der Wissenschaft zu Berlin*, 49 (1902), 1093–9 (1094)) puts the dedication just prior to the year of the queen's assassination (101 BCE). The inscription, however, lacks the double date expected for the era of Cleopatra III and Ptolemy X Alexander, i.e. 'the thirteenth year' of Ptolemy X, as noted by Strack, 'Inschriften aus ptolemäischer Zeit'.

[124] In terms of the identification of the group behind the *proseuche*, the extant letters of the inscription suggest the name Alypos as the benefactor responsible for the building of the *proseuche*. The name is not otherwise known to have been used by Jews in Egypt, though the Greek epithet *alypos*, 'without pain', 'one who causes no pain', is associated with Jews buried in the necropolis at Leontopolis (Tell el-Yehoudieh) (*JIGRE* nos. 74 (Marion) and 98 (Sabbataios), both probably of the Augustan period). Variants of the name (Alypis, Alypius) are known to have been used by Palestinian Jews of a later period (Beth She'arim 196; *CIJ* 2, no. 502). Alypios has been proposed as a possible alternative reading for the name in *JIGRE* no. 13: see, for example, Greg H. R. Horsley, 'Towards a New Corpus Inscriptionum Iudaicarum? A propos W. Horbury and D. Noy, *Jewish Inscriptions of Graeco-Roman Egypt*', *Jewish Studies Quarterly*, 2.1 (1995), 77–101 (89); against, Étienne Bernand, *Inscriptions Grecques d'Alexandrie Ptolémaïque* (Cairo, 2001), 101, commentary on l. 5. The inscription represents the only example from Ptolemaic Egypt of the patronage of a *proseuche* by an individual benefactor: Carsten Claussen, *Versammlung, Gemeinde, Synagoge: das hellenistisch-jüdische Umfeld der frühchristlichen Gemeinden* (Göttingen, 2002), 91.

[125] Philo, *Embassy to Gaius* 132.

behalf of the monarchs, without imposing on the Jews the worship of the Ptolemaic rulers themselves as gods.[126]

II Plutarch, Cleopatra and the Jews

The final group of evidence to be considered comes from Plutarch's *Life of Antony*. A younger contemporary of Josephus, Plutarch is of first importance as a source for many details of the life of Cleopatra VII, including some intriguing passages bearing on the question of the queen's relations with individual Jews. The task of interpreting this version of Cleopatra is by no means straightforward. In his account of Mark Antony, Plutarch's portrait of Cleopatra as enslaving and bewitching Antony is clearly shaped by the hostile perspective of Octavian's propaganda. Plutarch's *Antony* is the story of a great man who went wrong through lack of self-discipline and submission to the control of others, including his wife Fulvia, whose unwomanly desire 'to rule a ruler' helped Cleopatra by establishing 'the female domination (γυναικοκρατία)' of Antony.[127] According to Plutarch, Antony's passion for Cleopatra represents the 'final evil (τελευταῖον κακόν)' in the story of the Roman's downfall.[128] Plutarch's account is nevertheless valuable not only for confirming the enduring power of the negative propaganda against Antony and Cleopatra, but also for what it offers by way of alternative viewpoints, including reports by those who apparently witnessed first-hand the activities and appearance of the queen.[129] To the last category belongs the following well-known anecdote about Cleopatra's multi-lingual skills, which, among other things, are said to have included her ability to speak to 'Hebrews' without an interpreter:[130]

> There was pleasure even in the sound of her voice, and her tongue, like an instrument of many strings, she could easily turn to whatever kind of language she wished, so that with barbarians she very rarely conversed through an interpreter, but gave her answers to most of them herself and in her own person, whether Ethiopians, Trôgodytes, Hebrews (*Hebraioi*), Arabians, Syrians, Medes or Parthians. It is said that she knew the languages of many other peoples too, though the monarchs before her did not

[126] *Ibid.* 138. In the confrontation between Gaius and Philo's embassy over Gaius's plans to put a statue of himself as a god in the Jerusalem temple, Gaius (so Philo) rejected the value of the Jews' offerings to God (in the Jerusalem temple) 'on behalf' of the emperor, 'For you have not sacrificed to me (οὐ γὰρ ἐμοὶ τεθύκατε)!' (*Embassy to Gaius* 356–7).

[127] Plutarch, *Antony* 10.6.

[128] *Ibid.* 25.1.

[129] Pelling, *Life of Antony*, 16–18, 26–31; Frederick E. Brenk, 'Plutarch's Life "Markos Antonios": A Literary and Cultural Study', in *Aufstieg und Niedergang der römischen Welt*, Part II: *Principat*, vol. XXXIII: *Sprache und Literatur*, VI (Berlin and New York, 1992), 4348–4469, indices 4895–915.

[130] Roller suggests that the source for this anecdote 'was presumably someone in regular contact with the queen and her court, perhaps Nikolaos of Damascus or Sokrates of Rhodes': *Cleopatra*, 169.

even trouble themselves to learn the Egyptian language, and some of them had even abandoned speaking Macedonian.[131]

This statement finds its place within Plutarch's spectacular description of Antony's first meeting with Cleopatra at Tarsus (41 BCE), to which the triumvir had summoned the queen to test her loyalties in the context of the struggle for power in Rome after the assassination of Julius Caesar.[132] Here, however, Plutarch's interest is less in the politics than the impact of Cleopatra on Antony's mental state. Thus, according to Plutarch, this meeting serves to explain how Antony was 'taken prisoner (ἁλίσκεται)';[133] how Cleopatra 'overpowered (ἥρπασεν)' him, hurrying him away from Tarsus and his duties in Rome to join her in Alexandria.[134]

How then to explain this captivating power over Antony? In our passage, Plutarch's rationale appeals to the testimony of those who saw and heard Cleopatra. In terms of the queen's appearance, Plutarch cites others as confirming ('as they say') that Cleopatra's beauty was not wholly 'incomparable (οὐ πάνυ δυσπαράβλητον)';[135] on the other hand, he reports ('it is said') that her overpowering attractiveness lay rather in her remarkable interaction with all those she encountered.[136] While Plutarch's primary purpose in this context is to explain Cleopatra's power over Antony, the description of the queen, from unnamed sources, may offer a rare insight into the 'real' Cleopatra, at work in her personal diplomacy with Egypt's neighbouring peoples; it also offers significant evidence about Cleopatra's identification with Egypt, with the strong suggestion that she was fluent in Egyptian, the language of the vast majority of her subjects.[137]

In Plutarch's report, the list of 'barbarians' (non-Greek-speaking peoples) with whom the queen is said to have spoken corresponds to regions in which the Ptolemaic monarchy had long-standing interests; these peoples represent the importance of diplomacy for the queen,

---

[131] Plutarch, *Antony* 27.4–5.

[132] *Ibid.* 25.2.

[133] *Ibid.* 25.2.

[134] *Ibid.* 28.1.

[135] *Ibid.* 27.3. The adjective appears only here in the Thesaurus Linguae Graecae corpus, perhaps a sign of the influence of an oral tradition? Other sources contradict Plutarch's testimony in emphasising Cleopatra's beauty as part of her fatal attractiveness: cf. Cassius Dio 42.34.5. On Plutarch's use of λέγεται ('it is said'), and similar impersonal expressions: Brad L. Cook, 'Plutarch's Use of λέγεται: Narrative Design and Source in *Alexander*', *Greek, Roman, and Byzantine Studies*, 42 (2001), 329–60.

[136] Plutarch, *Antony* 27.4–5; cf. Plutarch, *Caesar* 49.2 on the supposed power of Cleopatra's presence over Julius Caesar in Alexandria.

[137] Wolfgang Schuller, *Kleopatra: Königin in drei Kulturen. Eine Biographie* (Hamburg, 2006), 40–1.

particularly on behalf of Antony and his campaigns in the East.[138] As Duane Roller observes, the details may also be indicative of Cleopatra's intellectual interests: the learned ruler represents an ideal of Hellenistic monarchy (male),[139] and one that Cleopatra seems to have embraced if we follow Roller's carefully constructed evaluation of the young queen as 'a remarkably educated person'.[140]

That Cleopatra is said to have spoken with '*Hebraioi* (Hebrews)' in their own language has been interpreted as a sign of her favour towards Jews.[141] That judgement goes beyond the evidence of Plutarch's text, which confirms (if we believe the report) only that the queen had taken the trouble to learn enough of their language to speak directly with 'Hebrews' and a number of other barbarian peoples. It does not prove the queen's favour or particular friendship towards any particular group, though it at least suggests that she sought alliances with these peoples.

What Plutarch means here by *Hebraioi* is not clear-cut and deserves brief comment.[142] Elsewhere in Plutarch's writings, he refers only once to the *Hebraioi*, their 'secret rituals' a topic of one of several questions about the practices and beliefs of the Jews, discussed at a symposium (narrated by Plutarch, who presents himself as participant) whose participants appear neither positive nor particularly well informed about the culture of the Jews.[143] Elements of their description of Jewish practices are clearly derived from a source, and that same source may be responsible for the

[138] See the useful discussion in Roller, *Cleopatra*, 46–50. Antony's alliance with the Median king, Artavasdes, included the betrothal of their children (Plutarch, *Antony* 53.12; Cassius Dio 49.40.2).

[139] Cleopatra's supposed linguistic skills are comparable (given the 'many other' languages she is credited with) to those attributed to Mithradates VI of Pontus (120–63 BCE), whose ability as king of twenty-two tribes to give judgements in as many languages, without an interpreter, earned him the admiration of Pliny for such remarkable powers of memory: Pliny, *Natural History* 7.88; 25.6; cf. variations on this tradition in Valerius Maximus, *Memorable Deeds and Sayings* 8.7.16; Aulus Gellius, *Attic Nights* 17.17.1–2; cf. Anika Strobach, *Plutarch und die Sprachen: ein Beitrag zur Fremdsprachenproblematik in der Antike* (Stuttgart, 1997), 160 ('Solche Berichte über Sprachgenies gab es öfter in der antiken Literatur'). It is not impossible that Cleopatra and her supporters promoted her linguistic skills in deliberate emulation of Mithradates, cf. Roller, *Cleopatra*, 3, 49–50; for a more sceptical view, Pelling, *Life of Antony*, 191.

[140] Roller, *Cleopatra*, 43–51.

[141] Cleopatra's ability to speak directly with 'Hebrews' is treated as positive evidence of her relationship with Jews in, for example, Heinz Heinen, 'Onomastisches zu Eiras, Kammerzofe Kleopatras VII', *Zeitschrift für Papyrologie und Epigraphik*, 79 (1989), 243–7; republished in Heinen, *Kleopatra-Studien: Gesammelte Schriften zur ausgehenden Ptolemäerzeit* (Konstanz, 2009), 176–81 (181); note Stern's comment on Plutarch, *Antony* 27 that, despite the testimony of Apion in Josephus, 'there is no reason to assume that she was consistently anti-semitic': Menahem Stern, *Greek and Latin Authors on Jews and Judaism* (3 vols., Jerusalem, 1974–84), I, 568.

[142] Roller, *Cleopatra*, 47.

[143] Plutarch, *Convivial Questions* 671c.

use of the term *Hebraioi*.[144] In the same context, Plutarch's symposiasts also refer to the *Ioudaioi* and their customs,[145] and it is clear that both terms are used here interchangeably to refer to a people (*Hebraioi* or *Ioudaioi*) defined by religious practices and beliefs, though not by territory.[146]

In the case of Cleopatra's 'Hebrews', the geographical shape of Plutarch's report (almost a half circle around Egypt) probably points to Jews from Herod's kingdom. A good number of the Jews of Judea, including Herod and his courtiers, would have spoken Greek. But since Plutarch specifies Cleopatra's prowess in speaking with 'barbarians', conversation with 'Hebrews' must mean Aramaic or Hebrew. As other evidence confirms, the language of the 'Hebrews' in the Graeco-Roman period could include Hebrew or Aramaic, and the context does not usually reveal which language is meant. Aramaic and Hebrew were both spoken in first-century Judea and the wider Palestinian region.[147] If Aramaic was the language in which Cleopatra addressed certain 'Hebrews', it was also the language in which she likely spoke with others including Syrians. And if Cleopatra really could speak to 'Hebrews' in their own language, she could do more than is usually presumed for most of the Jews of Ptolemaic Egypt in which few traces of the use of Hebrew or Aramaic survive. In any case, Plutarch's evidence for Cleopatra's conversations with *Hebraioi* adds to the broader picture of what we know of Cleopatra's personal interactions with Herod, as ally of Mark Antony,[148] and with Hasmonaean members of his family by marriage.

Eiras and Cleopatra

Plutarch also supplies important evidence that allows at least for the possibility that one of Cleopatra's most trusted companions was a Jew. The issue rests on the question of the identity of Eiras, one of the two

[144] On Plutarch's source for the description of the Jerusalem temple in this context: Stern, *Greek and Latin Authors*, I, 546.

[145] Plutarch, *Convivial Questions* 669d,e; 670d; 671c.

[146] Stern, *Greek and Latin Authors*, I, 559: 'Plutarch belongs to the generation of writers who started to use "Hebrews" instead of or together with "Jews"' (see references on 559). From the early Hellenistic period on, the term *Hebraios/oi* is used by Greek-speaking Jews to designate both themselves and their ancestors; cf. BDAG, s.v. Ἑβραῖος; Graham Harvey, *The True Israel: Uses of the Names Jew, Hebrew, and Israel in Ancient Jewish and Early Christian Literature* (Leiden, 1996), 104–47. In some contexts, 'Hebrew/s' clearly refers to a particular territory (e.g. Tacitus, *Histories* 5.2; Pausanias, *Description of Greece* 5.7.4); or to the speakers of a specific language (e.g. Philo, *Moses* 2.32; Josephus, *War* 6.97; Lucian, *Alexander the False Prophet* 13).

[147] On whether Josephus spoke Hebrew as well as Aramaic: Rajak, *Josephus*, 230–2.

[148] Plutarch refers to 'Herod the Jew' as part of the alliance that sent forces to Antony at Actium: Plutarch, *Antony* 61.3.

women who, according to Plutarch's *Antony*, accompanied Cleopatra in her last days after the Battle of Actium and who died with the queen.[149] Plutarch first mentions Eiras in words attributed directly to Octavian:

> Caesar (Octavian) said in addition that Antony had been drugged and was not even master of himself, and that the Romans were carrying on war with Mardion the eunuch, and Potheinos, and Eiras, Cleopatra's hairdresser, and Charmion, by (all of whom) the principal affairs of the government were managed.[150]

Octavian's reported words stress the humiliation of Antony, no longer a man, no longer in control of himself, but the slave of a foreign government under the misrule of eunuchs and women. There is good reason to think that such images of Antony and his relationship to Cleopatra's court indeed originated with Octavian and his supporters, in the context of the campaign from the mid-30s BCE onwards to justify the elimination of Antony. A strong emphasis on Antony as the 'slave' of the 'Egyptian woman' and the unmanly, female character of Egypt's government, whose destruction is the duty of loyal Romans, pervades the sources for Octavian's war of words against Antony and Cleopatra. We see this powerfully exemplified in Dio's report of Octavian's arguments for war on the eve of the Battle of Actium,[151] or in the celebration of Octavian's victory by the poet Horace who makes Antony 'a Roman (you future generations will refuse to believe it!) enslaved to a woman (*emancipatus feminae*)', a soldier who 'can bear to serve a lot of shrivelled eunuchs (*spadonibus servire rugosis potest*)'.[152] Writing as a friend of the prefect of Roman Egypt in the 20s BCE, the geographer Strabo writes approvingly of the fact that, in contrast with the years of Antony's subservience to Cleopatra, Egypt is now ruled 'by prudent men (ὑπὸ σωφρόνων ἀνδρῶν)'.[153] Certainly, Plutarch reflects the influence of Octavian's propaganda when he places the description of Cleopatra's unmanly court in prime position within the arguments presented by Octavian in Rome for war against Cleopatra (32 BCE), with the goal of removing from Antony 'the authority which he had surrendered to a

---

[149] Eiras: *Prosopographia Ptolemaica* 14720. Other ancient sources that name Eiras with Charmion as among Cleopatra's companions: Pseudo-Plutarch, *Proverbs of the Alexandrians* Fr. 45, l. 1 (Eiras was tasked with the care of Cleopatra's hair while Charmion dealt with the queen's nails; the same in Zenobius, *Epitome of Didymus' and Lucillus Tarrhaeus' Collections of Proverbs* 5.24 who, however, gives the name Naera instead of Eiras); Zonaras, *Epitome of Histories* 2.432, l. 30 (closely follows Plutarch, *Antony* 85.7). Naera (Νάηρα) and Charmion: Zenobius, *Epitome* 5.24. Naeira (Νάειρα) and Charmion: Galen, 14.235–6.

[150] Plutarch, *Antony* 60.1 (tr. Bernadotte Perrin, adapted).

[151] Cassius Dio 50.24.1–30.4; cf. also the articulation of the theme of Antony as 'slave' to 'the Egyptian woman' (48.24.2), and of Antony's own effeminacy (γυναικίζει, 50.27.6).

[152] Horace, *Epode* 9, 11–16 (tr. Niall Rudd).

[153] Strabo 17.1.12.

woman'.[154] Whether Octavian is also Plutarch's source for identifying Eiras and the other names of Cleopatra's retinue we do not know; it is more likely that Plutarch drew such details from a different source with close knowledge of the Alexandrian court.[155]

The description of Eiras as 'hairdresser (κουρεύτρια)' is suggestive of low status, marked by a job associated with slaves or freedwomen. For Ptolemaic queens, with their power hair and melon coiffures, the hairdresser was an essential and influential role.[156] But in this context, 'hairdresser' might be intended as a term of abuse, not a real job description,[157] – serving to underline the construction of the unmanly, servile character of Cleopatra's followers, a rabble that has turned the natural order of male-led government upside down.

Eiras is also named by Plutarch as one of the 'two women' who accompanied Cleopatra in her imprisonment in Alexandria, under Roman guard, and who joined the queen in a self-inflicted death in her tomb in August 30 BCE.[158] In Plutarch's account of those final days, Eiras and Charmion play a crucial role in helping Cleopatra to avoid humiliation in Octavian's triumph, and to die a noble death of her own making. The high status of these women is indicated by Plutarch's

[154] Plutarch, *Antony* 60.1.

[155] Pelling, *Life of Antony*, 264. Reference to Potheinos seems to be either an error or a deliberate confusion with the courtier of Ptolemy XIII. The eunuch Potheinos was a figure remembered as hostile to Rome; influential in promoting the cause of Ptolemy XIII against his sister Cleopatra, Potheinos was executed on the orders of Julius Caesar, 48 BCE (Plutarch, *Caesar* 49.2–3; Cassius Dio 42.36.1–3).

[156] Cf. Diana E. E. Kleiner, *Cleopatra and Rome* (Cambridge, MA, and London, 2005), 242–50. Evidence for female 'hairdressers' is relatively rare, cf. LSJ s.v. κουρεύτρια, which lists Plutarch, *Antony* 60, as the source for this feminine form. In the context of early Ptolemaic Egypt, a tax-register for the Fayum village of Lysimachis includes a woman named Kleopatra, listed as a (masculine) 'hairdresser (κουρεύς)' (*P. Count.* 26.320 (254–231 BCE)); cf. Willy Clarysse and Dorothy J. Thompson, *Counting the People in Hellenistic Egypt*, II: *Historical Studies* (Cambridge, 2006), 203. Plutarch nearly always refers to the (male) hairdresser as a prime example of the purveyor of gossip through their ability to mix with the powerful and the servant class: *Nicias* 30.2; *On Talkativeness* 508f–509b. In the same context, Plutarch mentions Julius Caesar's barber (κουρεύς), a slave (οἰκέτης), who served as Caesar's spy in Ptolemy XIII's Alexandria (*Caesar* 49.2). The tradition transmitted in Pseudo-Plutarch, *Proverbs of the Alexandrians* 45, also makes Charmion the queen's manicurist.

[157] Contra ancient and modern acceptance of this role for Eiras: Pseudo-Plutarch, *Proverbs of the Alexandrians* Fr. 45, l. 1; *Wörterbuch der griechischen Eigennamen*, 336, s.v. Εἰράς, 'Haarkräuslerin der Kleopatra'.

[158] Plutarch, *Antony* 85.7; cf. Cassius Dio 51.14.3, who does not name the two θεράπαιναι who die with Cleopatra. Plutarch's narrative of Cleopatra's death does not make clear until the end that the two women who alone accompanied the queen in her mausoleum were Charmion and Eiras (Plutarch, *Antony* 77.2; 79.2–3; 84.3). Furthermore, Eiras and Charmion are almost certainly to be identified with the unnamed female companions of Cleopatra who accompanied Cleopatra and served to reconcile the queen with Antony on the voyage home after the Battle of Actium (Plutarch, *Antony* 67.6); cf. Pelling, *Life of Antony*, 307.

note that their bodies received 'honourable interment' on the orders of Octavian.[159] If we follow Plutarch, Eiras and Charmion were Cleopatra's most trusted and devoted people. Their loyalty is enshrined in the words of the dying Charmion, as she responds defiantly to the Roman soldiers of Octavian: that the queen's death was 'excellently done (κάλλιστα) and befitting the woman who was the descendant of so many kings'.[160]

As for the possible association of Eiras with Jewish identity, the issue rests on the significance of her name.[161] The volumes of the *Lexicon of Greek Personal Names* published thus far do not include Εἰρᾶς as a female name.[162] Most of the (currently meagre) evidence for parallels comes from Egypt, to the extent that Εἰρᾶς may be designated a 'Graeco-Egyptian' name,[163] attested by the following examples:

(i) The genitive form Εἰρᾶτος in a Herakleopolis papyrus of CE 224.[164]

(ii) A possible variant of the name in Εἴρα (or Εἰρᾶ?) Εἰκαβαθίου, documented in the Fayum in the sixth–seventh centuries CE.[165]

(iii) Closer to the era of Cleopatra VII, the epitaph of Εἰρᾶς θυγάτηρ, 'Eiras the daughter', from the necropolis at Tell el-Yehoudieh,

[159] Plutarch, *Antony* 86.7: ἐντίμου δὲ καὶ τὰ γύναια κηδείας ἔτυχεν αὐτοῦ προστάξαντος. Eiras and Charmion belong among the 'Dames du Cour' (otherwise mostly represented by courtesans of the Ptolemaic kings) in the *Prosopographia Ptolemaica*, ed. Willy Peremans, Edmond Van't Dack, Willy Clarysse, Loe de Meulemeester-Swinnen and Hans Hauben (Leuven, 1950–81); cf. Daniel Ogden, *Polygamy, Prostitutes and Death: The Hellenistic Dynasties* (1999), 217, who notes that the trade of hairdresser is also abusively associated by Tlepolemus with the courtesans of Ptolemy IV Philopator (Polybius 15.25).

[160] Plutarch, *Antony* 85.8.

[161] In some post-Plutarchian versions of Cleopatra's death, the name Eiras is replaced by other names: Νάηρα, 'Naera' (Zenobius, *Epitome* 5.24), or Νάειρα, 'Naeira' (Galen 14.235). Pseudo-Plutarch (*Proverbs of the Alexandrians* 45) and Zonaras (*Epitome of Histories* 10.31), however, follow Plutarch in preserving the name Eiras. The name Charmion, by contrast, remains fairly stable in the tradition (cf. Καρμιόνη in Galen etc.). Nevertheless, Charmion is another rare female name; cf. *P. Mich.* 4.223 (Valeria Charmion; CE 172, Karanis).

[162] The closest female parallel is Εἰραῖς from fourth/third century BCE Anthedon in Boeotia (IIIb, no. 24690; noted in Hannah M. Cotton *et al.*, *Corpus Inscriptionum Iudaeae/Palaestinae*, I: *Jerusalem. Part 1, 1–704* (henceforth, *CIIP*) (Berlin and New York, 2010)), 314. Two second-century BCE inscriptions from Pamphylia attest Εἴρας (in the genitive Εἴραυ) as a male name (*Lexicon of Greek Personal Names* Vb, s.v. Εἴρας).

[163] David Noy and Hanswulf Bloedhorn, *Inscriptiones Judaicae Orientis*, III: *Syria and Cyprus* (henceforth *IJO*) (Tübingen, 2004), 115–16, commenting on *Syr*72ⁿ = *CIIP* I, 1, no. 291.

[164] *Stud. Pal.* 20.26, an example of the name Eiras in a non-Jewish context, cf. Horbury and Noy, *Jewish Inscriptions*, 121. In other evidence, the name Eiras is no longer read in the revised edition of *Stud Pal.* 22.101 (second century CE; Fayum); and from the graffito carved on the Memnonion at Abydos (332 BCE – CE 284?), 'Eiras and Helene were here!', Eiras is taken to be male (*I. Memnonion* 131.1).

[165] *P. Vindob. Sal.* 19; see Heinen ('Onomastisches zu Eiras', 179) on the possibility of reading Εἰρᾶ as a variant of Εἰρᾶς.

associated with the Jewish settlement of Onias at Leontopolis.[166] Though the inscription includes no date, it must belong to the period of settlement between Onias's foundation in the mid-second century BCE to the presumed end of the settlement as a consequence of the revolt under Trajan (CE 115–117).[167] Here, Eiras the daughter is commemorated in a modest epitaph, together with 'Tryphaina the mother', placed over two burial niches.

(iv) Finally, from the Akeldama burial caves, south of Jerusalem, an ossuary of the first centuries BCE/CE contains the bones of a woman commemorated by two brief lines: ΕΙΡΑΤΟΣ | ΣΕΛΕΥΚ , 'EIRAS' | '(daughter of?) SELEUK[OS]', or 'from SELEUK[IA]'.[168] As indicated by the inscriptions, Akeldama's burial caves seem to have been used by interrelated families, with most names recorded in Greek, others in a Jewish script or in bilingual records.[169] In the case of Eiras, it is not certain whether the second, incomplete word refers to her *patris*, or (as is more likely, based on the use of patronymics in the associated ossuaries) to her father.[170] If Seleuk- does not refer to Seleucia in Syria (there are two candidates for this location), a Syrian origin for Eiras and other family members buried at Akeldama is suggested but not proved by a reference to Apamea as the home of one of the deceased,[171] and by the predominant use of Greek in the inscriptions, characteristic of other Jewish inscriptions from Syria but not generally of Jerusalem ossuaries.[172] Certainly, the Eiras buried at Akeldama is likely to have come originally from outside

[166] *JIGRE* no. 52. The epitaph was recorded in situ in 1887; cf. Edouard Naville, 'The Mound of the Jew and the City of Onias', *Egypt Exploration Fund*, 7th Memoir (1890), 14, pl. IV N.

[167] On the Jewish context of the burials at Tell el-Yehoudieh, cf. Horbury and Noy, *Jewish Inscriptions*, xviii: more than 50 per cent of the names given in the epitaphs are 'distinctively Jewish'; others include many names (including Eirene) known to have been much used by Jews without being distinctively Jewish; the same family can include members with Jewish, Egyptian and Greek names; while 'the community may not have been exclusively Jewish . . . there are no reliable grounds for identifying any non-Jewish minority which may have been buried at the site'.

[168] *CIIP* I, 1, no. 291 = *IJO*, *Syr*72ⁿ; cf. Tal Ilan, 'The Ossuary and Sarcophagus Inscriptions', in *The Akeldama Tombs: Three Burial Caves in the Kidron Valley, Jerusalem*, ed. Gideon Avni and Zvi Greenhut (Jerusalem, 1996), 57–72 (59, no. 3); Tamar Shadmi, 'The Ossuaries and the Sarcophagus', *ibid.*, 41–55 (43, Fig. 2.7; Ossuary 11; ed. pr.); P.-L. Gatier, in *Bulletin Épigraphique*, 654 (1997), 596–7, no. 654. My thanks to Meron Piotrkowski for advice on this topic.

[169] Cotton *et al.*, *CIIP* I, 1, nos. 309–10; cf. their observation that the family buried with Eiras in Cave 2 'seems to have had a predilection for names based on Eros', and that Eiras is similar sounding.

[170] *IJO* 116; *CIIP* I, 1, no. 314.

[171] *CIIP* I, 1, no. 304, 'Ariston from Apamea'.

[172] On the basis of new readings, *CIIP* I, 1, 310, revise the arguments for the inscriptions' Syrian origin as given in the *editio princeps*, cf. Ilan, 'The Ossuary'.

Judaea; whether she lived at some point in Jerusalem or simply had her bones transported to Judaea is unknown.[173]

On the basis of this evidence, the case for identifying Εἰρᾶς as a name strongly suggestive of Jewish origins depends on several factors. First, while the name is rarely documented in the ancient world, Εἰρᾶς is attested in two contexts associated with Jews, in Egypt at Tell el-Yehoudieh, and in Judaea, apparently as part of a diaspora Jewish burial site in the vicinity of Jerusalem. Furthermore, a distinctively Jewish association with the name Εἰρᾶς is also indicated by the likelihood, as demonstrated in the authoritative analysis of Heinz Heinen, that Εἰρᾶς is a hypocoristic form (the short form of a name, typically used in intimate circles) of Eirene, a name generally widespread from the Hellenistic period on, and well documented among the Jews of Egypt and elsewhere.[174] As Heinen puts it, 'The popularity of the name Eirene among the Jewish population of Ptolemaic Egypt is a fact.'[175] In the Jewish context, Eirene (Greek: εἰρήνη, 'peace') may have been used as the equivalent of the Hellenised Hebrew name Salome (Hebrew: *Shalom*, 'Peace'), the most popular female name in Graeco-Roman Palestine.[176] The strongest case for identifying Cleopatra's companion Eiras as a Jew

---

[173] Cotton *et al.*, *CIIP* I, 1, 310.

[174] Εἰρᾶς as hypocoristic form: suggested by David M. Lewis, in *Corpus Papyrorum Judaicarum*, III, ed. Victor Tcherikover, Alexander Fuks and Menahem Stern, with an Epigraphical Contribution by David M. Lewis (Cambridge, MA, 1964), 148; argued in detail by Heinen, 'Onomastisches zu Eiras', 176–81. Heinen (178–9) notes the use of hypocoristic name forms of other individuals within Cleopatra's court or administration (e.g. the queen's male servant Saras (Sarapion) mentioned in Cicero, *Atticus* 15.15.2), while rare hypocoristic forms of feminine names ending in -ᾶς appear, for example, in the names Κλεοπᾶς/Κλεοπᾶτος (Kleopas) (*I. Philae* 1.29; Philae, first century BCE) and Κλευπᾶς (Kleupas) (*CPJ* 3, no. 1530b = *JIGRE* no. 99; Tell el-Yehudieh; mid-second century BCE – early second century CE; 7 BCE?), both derived from the name Κλεοπάτρα (Kleopatra). In the same context, one should also note Heinen's decisive refutation of earlier attempts to interpret the significance of the name Eiras, including his critique of the entry in the standard lexicon by W. Pape (G. E. Benseler), *Wörterbuch der grischischen Eigennamen* (3rd edn; Braunschweig, 1911), s.v. Εἰρᾶς = 'Wollkopf' ('Woolhead', based on τὸ εἶρος = 'wool').

[175] Heinen, 'Onomastisches zu Eiras', 181 (my tr.).

[176] *Ibid.*, 179; Horbury and Noy, *Jewish Inscriptions*, 138 (noting, on the basis of the evidence available before 1992, that Salome is not attested in Greek transliteration in Egypt with the possible exception of treating the name Salamis as a variant form (*JIGRE* no. 48)). Gerard Mussies treats Eirene as an example of 'foreign names used by Jews', and specifically of names translated from the Hebrew: 'Jewish Personal Names in Some Non-Literary Sources', in *Studies in Early Jewish Epigraphy*, ed. Jan Willem van Henten and Pieter W. van der Horst (Leiden, 1994), 242–76 (245). The fact that Eirene is a well-established Greek (non-Jewish) name does not render unlikely the adoption by Jews of the name as equivalent to Salome, despite the doubts expressed by Tal Ilan, *Lexicon of Jewish Names in Late Antiquity. Part III. The Western Diaspora 330 BCE–650 CE* (Tübingen, 2008), 416. On the extreme popularity of the name Salome, cf. Tal Ilan, 'Notes on the Distribution of Jewish Women's Names in Palestine in the Second Temple and Mishnaic Periods', *Journal of Jewish Studies*, 40 (1989), 186–200.

is based on the rarity of this name formation, probably a hypocoristic form of Eirene, and its appearance, despite that rarity, in distinctively Jewish contexts. New evidence may transform that picture. Following Heinen's cautious findings, the evidence does not prove that Cleopatra's Eiras was a Jew,[177] but her name is certainly suggestive of Jewish origins,[178] and this suggestion is further strengthened by the Akeldama inscription not yet available at the time of Heinen's study. Certainly, the context of Cleopatra's rule, her connections to the Hasmoneans of Judaea, and the evidence for her good relations with Jewish groups within Egypt, allows for the possibility that one of her most trusted companions might have been a Jew. Was Eiras perhaps a Jew from a high-ranking family in the Jewish colony of Leontopolis? The presence of Jews in the Ptolemaic court is not so unusual in the context of the practice of Cleopatra's predecessors, particularly from the time of the earlier Cleopatras, when the bond of loyalty was forged between the Jewish priest Onias IV and his followers with Ptolemy VI Philometor and Cleopatra II, and with their daughter, Cleopatra III, the great-grandmother of Cleopatra VII.[179]

III Conclusion

Any attempt to get back to the realities of the last Cleopatra must contend with a subject profoundly obscured by the propaganda of her enemies and the instrumentalisation of Cleopatra as the Roman 'other'. In the case of Josephus's testimony, I suggest that – despite his noble purpose, the exoneration of the Jews under Roman rule – he has not served truth well in the case of Cleopatra. There is no good evidence for Cleopatra as persecutor of the Jews. Indeed, Josephus gives us glimpses of another Cleopatra, offering refuge to members of the Jewish aristocracy among the Hasmoneans, as they sought survival away from Herod. Cleopatra may have learned Hebrew or Aramaic; among her supporters, someone thought it worthy of record that the queen held conversations, in person,

[177] Heinen, 'Onomastisches zu Eiras', 181: 'Die Frage, ob Eiras, die Zofe Kleopatras, eine Judin gewesen ist, läßt sich anhand der uns zur Verfügung stehenden Quellen nicht entscheiden.'

[178] The suggestion of Eiras's Jewish origins is noted, for example, in the authoritative collection *Women and Society in Greek and Roman Egypt: A Sourcebook*, ed. Jane Rowlandson (Cambridge, 1998), 41, in which Eiras represents the only case-study of a (possibly) Jewish woman in the Ptolemaic era.

[179] The known names of Cleopatra's administrators reveal little of their identity and may well have included individual Jews: most of the administrators have Greek names though a number also have Egyptian theophoric names, cf. Roller, *Cleopatra*, 107–8; for a list of administrators from the reign of Cleopatra VII, see Ricketts, 'The Administration', 137–49. The name of the scribe (*grammateus*) who posted the royal *prostagma* protecting the shipping of wheat (*BGU* VIII.1730, 27 Oct. 50 BCE; see above p. 37), Onias (Ὀνίας) of the Herakleopolite nome, points to his Jewish identity; cf. Ilan, *Lexicon*, 671–2, s.v. '*Honi*' no. 5, 'Jewishness is indicated by name' (672).

with 'Hebrews'. And perhaps among those very few who stayed loyal to Cleopatra at the end, the courtier Eiras may have been a Jew.

But what perhaps speaks most powerfully against the negative tradition about Cleopatra and the Jews is our evidence for her patronage and protection of the fundamental Jewish institution of the prayer-house. After Cleopatra, we have no more decrees of asylum, no dedications of prayer-houses to Roman emperors; this phenomenon simply disappears with the Roman conquest of Egypt. When Philo the Jew from Alexandria despaired at the destruction of his city's Jewish prayer-houses, he insisted that nothing like this had ever happened under Ptolemaic rule.[180] Philo does not hold back in a fight; but, despite the world of Augustan propaganda around him, he never condemns Cleopatra or her Ptolemaic predecessors. His is a voice from within ancient Alexandria, from a man born in the decade after Actium. Philo's voice has the ring of authenticity and it deserves our attention.

[180] Philo, *Embassy to Gaius* 138.

Transactions of the RHS 27 (2017), pp. 65–86 © Royal Historical Society 2017
doi:10.1017/S0080440117000044

THE MAKING OF CHRONICLES AND THE MAKING OF ENGLAND: THE ANGLO-SAXON CHRONICLES AFTER ALFRED

Prothero Lecture

By Pauline Stafford

READ JULY 2016

ABSTRACT. Between *c.* 900 and the mid-twelfth century, a series of Old English vernacular chronicles were produced, growing out of the text produced at the court of King Alfred. These chronicles are collectively known as 'the Anglo-Saxon Chronicle'. They have long been accorded fundamental status in the English national story. No others have shaped our view of the origins of England between the fifth and eleventh centuries to the same extent. They provide between them the only continuous narrative of this period. They are the story that has made England. This paper deals with the relationship between that story, these texts and England: how they have been read and edited – made – in the context of the English national story since the sixteenth century; but also their relationship to, the part they may have played in, the original making of the English kingdom. The focus is on developments during the tenth and eleventh centuries, when a political unit more or less equivalent to the England we now know emerged. It is argued that these texts were the ideological possession and expression of the southern English elite, especially of bishops and archbishops, at this critical period of kingdom-making. Special attention is given to their possible role in the incorporation of Northumbria into that kingdom. These chronicles were made by scribes a millennium ago, and to some extent have been reworked by modern editors from the sixteenth century on. They are daunting in their complexity. The differences between them are as important as the common ground they share. Understanding the making of these foundational texts has its own light to shed on the making of England.

In the early 1950s, the *English Historical Documents* series was launched. Its aim was to 'make generally accessible . . . fundamental sources of English history'. The first two volumes opened with the same text – *The* Anglo-Saxon Chronicle. In the eyes of the editors, this text merited 'pride of place'. In their view, 'English narrative history is so dominated by this compilation that other writers . . . are mainly of interest as providing a commentary on it.'[1] It was 'the most important source for the political

---

[1] *English Historical Documents*, I, ed. D. Whitelock (1955), and II, ed. D. C. Douglas and G. Greenaway (1953), quotations from II, iii and 97.

history of the period'.[2] This text – or rather the series of chronicles which somewhat misleadingly go under this heading – provide between them the only continuous narrative of the Anglo-Saxon period; though continuous is an overstatement given their fragmentary coverage. They have long been accorded fundamental status in the English national story; no other texts have shaped our view of the origins of England between the fifth and eleventh centuries to the same extent. They are in that sense the story that has made England.

The subject of this paper is the relationship between these texts, and that making: how they have been seen and edited – made – in an English context since the sixteenth century; but also their relationship to, the part they may have played in, the original making of the English kingdom. Its focus is on the tenth and eleventh centuries, centuries during which these chronicles first grew and developed, centuries when a political unit more or less equivalent to the England we now know emerged. The making of these foundational texts has its own light to shed on the making of that kingdom.

What are the Anglo-Saxon Chronicles? Seven survive, though there were once more. They all originate in a chronicle produced at the court of Alfred, king of the West Saxons, towards the end of the ninth century.[3] From that text, a series of chronicles grew in the course of the tenth, eleventh and early twelfth centuries. Like Alfred's, they are anonymous – no one ever claims authorship; they are annalistic – material is entered under years not grouped into thematic books or chapters; and like Alfred's chronicle, they are in the vernacular – unusually for this date they are written in Old English not the more normal Latin. They all grew in some way out of Alfred's chronicle, continuing and developing it.

Combining them, we can piece together a story of English history from the arrival of Julius Caesar – but especially from the arrival of people we now call Anglo-Saxons – through to the early twelfth century, and especially to the conquest of England by the Normans in 1066. But that story is decidedly patchy. None of them, including Alfred's, tells anything like a complete or continuous tale. There are remarkable gaps in their coverage: social – all of them, and not merely Alfred's, are king-centred; and chronological – runs of years are blank, including for the tenth century, a century so important in the making of England as we now know it. All of them share some common material with others. But for

---

[2] *The Anglo-Saxon Chronicle: A Revised Translation*, ed. D. Whitelock, D. C. Douglas and S. Tucker (1961), xi. This volume brought together the English Historical Document translations.

[3] Anton Scharer, 'The Writing of History at King Alfred's Court', *Early Medieval Europe*, 5 (1996), 177–89.

the tenth and eleventh centuries, no two surviving chronicles tell exactly the same tale.

People have turned to these chronicles from the twelfth century onwards in pursuit of the story of the English kingdom, often in contexts of national definition. Interest in them has usually been part of a much wider interest in things Anglo-Saxon, where Anglo-Saxon times, the period which preceded the (French) Norman Conquest, have a special originary status: the first, the original, if not the true English. Interest in them tracks periods of national sentiment, of concern for the national past, from reactions to the traumas of 1066 onwards. It has often had official backing.

The Norman Conquest of 1066 produced a flowering of English history writing, in Latin.[4] Authors in search of the English past, of the story of the English, of English kings, turned to the eighth-century *Ecclesiastical History* by Bede, but also to these vernacular chronicles. They were their major sources.

Study of them revived in the later sixteenth and early seventeenth centuries. In the sixteenth century, the preservation of manuscripts of texts like these was explicitly and officially sanctioned. Elizabeth's privy council recorded the queen's 'care and zeale . . . for the conservation of such auncient recordes and monuments' seen as relevant to 'both . . . the state of ecclesiastical and civile government'.[5] Elizabeth's archbishop of Canterbury, Matthew Parker, was to be allowed to peruse such manuscripts, with a promise to restore them safely to their owners. The size of the Parker collection in Cambridge suggests that, like many borrowers of books, the archbishop was not always assiduous at returning them. The names often given to two of these texts, the 'Laud' and 'Parker' chronicles, are witness to this interest, and its politics.[6] Queen Elizabeth's chief minister, Robert Cecil, owned the chronicle which passed later to Archbishop Laud. The circle surrounding Archbishop Parker was especially active in their collection, transcription and study. The hand

[4] Richard Southern, 'Aspects of the European Tradition of Historical Writing: 4. The Sense of the Past', *Transactions of the Royal Historical Society* (*TRHS*), fifth series, 23 (1973), 243–63; James Campbell, 'Some Twelfth-Century Views of the Anglo-Saxon Past', *Peritia*, 3 (1984), 209–28; A. Williams, *The English and the Norman Conquest* (Woodbridge, 1995), especially 155–86.

[5] C. E. Wright, 'The Dispersal of the Monastic Libraries and the Beginnings of Anglo-Saxon Studies', *Transactions of the Cambridge Bibliographical Society*, 1 (1949–53), 208–37, at 212–13; *Correspondence of Matthew Parker D.D., Archbishop of Canterbury*, ed. John Bruce and Thomas Thomason Perowne (Cambridge, 1853), 327–8; see also R. I. Page, *Matthew Parker and his Books* (Kalamazoo, MI, 1993), 2.

[6] Indispensable guide is Angelika Lutz, 'The Study of the Anglo-Saxon Chronicle in the Seventeenth Century and the Establishment of Old English Studies in the Universities', in *The Recovery of Old English. Anglo-Saxon Studies in the Sixteenth and Seventeenth Centuries*, ed. Timothy Graham (Kalamazoo, MI, 2000), 1–82.

of Parker's secretary, Joscelyn, can – literally – be seen in several of these chronicles.[7] Early modern readers blithely made annotations and additions, treating the manuscripts in ways which would give their modern keepers nightmares.

These vernacular chronicles were not, of course, the only, or even the main, manuscripts targeted by Elizabeth's privy council. And interest in them, in the sixteenth century or later, was far from purely political.[8] It would be wrong to exclude disinterested scholarship, or the role of the English antiquarian. By the end of the seventeenth century, their study was located within the English universities, where the first printed editions were produced.

But disinterested scholarship, like antiquarian enthusiasm, has its own contexts. The seventeenth-century shift to a more scholarly locus of study was in part politically motivated and driven.[9] The library of Sir Robert Cotton contained most of these chronicles by the early decades of that century. Cotton's library, situated opposite the houses of parliament, was identified by the Stuart kings as a generator of seditious argument. It was closed from from 1629 to 1631. The first university posts in Anglo-Saxon studies were founded at least in part in reaction to such royalist absolutism. One of the first published products of those posts was an edition of Bede's *Ecclesiastical History of the Gens Anglorum*, of the English people, to which was added one of the vernacular chronicles.

The nineteenth century saw a flourishing of national feeling and medievalism. Translation now made these chronicles available to a wider public, though they were never as popular as tales of King Arthur. The sense of a 'national' chronicle became explicit in some nineteenth-century editions, like that of Charles Plummer at the end of the century.[10] Already for James Ingram in 1823, the Saxon Chronicle was an all-important source of *facts* on England: on '*our* commerce, *our* naval and military glory, *our* liberty and *our* religion'. It contrasted with the 'puerile' 'legendary tales' 'magical delusions' and 'miraculous exploits', which characterised

---

[7] On Joscelyn's work, Page, *Matthew Parker and his Books*; and T. Graham, 'The Beginnings of Old English Studies: Evidence from the Manuscripts of Matthew Parker', in *Back to the Manuscripts: Papers from the Symposium 'The Integrated Approach to Manuscript Studies: A New Horizon' Held at the Eighth Meeting of the Japan Society for Medieval English Studies, Tokyo, December, 1992*, ed. Shuji Sato (Tokyo, 1997), 29–50.

[8] T. Graham, 'Anglo-Saxon Studies: Sixteenth to Eighteenth Centuries', in *A Companion to Anglo-Saxon Literature*, ed. P. Pulsiano and E. Treharne (Oxford, 2001), 415–33, at 422.

[9] As argued by Lutz, 'The Study'.

[10] *Two of the Saxon Chronicles Parallel, with Supplementary Extracts from the Others. A Revised Text, Edited, with Introduction, Notes, Appendices and Glossary* by C. Plummer, on the basis of an edition by J. Earle (Oxford, 1889) (the edition normally used is that of 1892/9), at e.g. II, civ – at n. 3 specifically contrasting it with the Latin *Gesta Northanhymbrorum*.

the native British or Norman French chronicles. The Saxon Chronicle was especially fitted to the 'sober sense of Englishmen'.[11]

The judgement that this was somehow a 'national chronicle' attracted official backing and funding. The *British Historical Monuments*, edited in 1848 by the Keeper of the Records of the Tower of London, Henry Petrie, was one such national project.[12] It was a hugely costly and ultimately abortive attempt to answer the great German historical enterprise, the *Monumenta Germaniae Historica* (Monuments of German History). The first and only volume included the Anglo-Saxon Chronicle.[13] It was also among the first commissioned volumes of Britain's more successful response to the German Monumenta, the Rolls Series. That was launched in 1857 under the auspices of the recently created Public Record Office and with parliamentary backing. It was 'an important national object . . . calculated to fill up the chasms existing in the printed material of English [*sic*] history'.[14] The Rolls Series was to fill that gap – using treasury money. As Charles Plummer later ruefully put it 'Mr Thorpe [who edited these chronicles for the series] had behind him the resources of the English government.'[15]

The context of national feeling and pride is less immediately obvious by the twentieth century. It may simply be coincidence that both excellent modern translations – by Garmonsway and Whitelock – appeared in the early 1950s, in the decade following the Second World War, though it is a coincidence worthy of remark. Since the twelfth century, when writers of history turned to them in the aftermath of 1066, there has been a broadly national, and a loosely political context for the reception of these chronicles.

The Old English vernacular in which they were written has always been one of the special qualifications of these chronicles as 'English stories'. The twelfth-century historian William of Malmesbury saw them as 'barbaric writings': a broken tale in the language of the fatherland. He would 'season [them] with Roman salt', in other words write a Latin history.[16]

---

[11] *The Saxon Chronicle with an English Translation and Notes, Critical and Explanatory. To Which Are Added Chronological, Topographical, and Glossarial Indices, a Short Grammar of the Anglo-Saxon Language, etc.* by J. Ingram (1823), ii–v. His gendered vocabulary would repay analysis.

[12] On nineteenth-century government-backed editions, see D. M. Knowles, 'Great Historical Enterprises, IV. The Rolls Series', *TRHS*, fifth series, 11 (1961), 137–59.

[13] *Monumenta historica Britannica, or, Materials for the History of Britain from the Earliest Period*, ed. H. Petrie and J. Sharpe (London, published by command of Her Majesty, 1848).

[14] General Preface to Rolls Series, cf. Knowles, 'The Rolls Series', 141–2.

[15] Plummer, *Two of the Saxon Chronicles*, II, cxxxvi, commenting on B. Thorpe, *The Anglo-Saxon Chronicle, According to the Several Original Authorities*, published by the authority of the lords commissioners of Her Majesty's treasury, under the direction of the Master of the Rolls (2 vols., 1861).

[16] William of Malmesbury, *Gesta Regum Anglorum*, ed. and trans. R. A. B. Mynors, R. M. Thomson and M. Winterbottom, I (Oxford, 1998), 14.

But for most later seekers of England's past, and even perhaps for William himself,[17] that 'barbaric' tongue has always been part of their attraction. In the sixteenth century, the context for their study was ecclesiastical and political debate about an 'English' church: its beliefs, and its practices, including its use of the vernacular. The vernacular texts of pre-1066 England had special legitimising status. For Ingram in 1823, they were 'a faithful depository of our national idiom'.[18]

But already by the sixteenth century, Old English was a barrier to access. It was the language of the fatherland to some twelfth-century authors, but it was incomprehensible to sixteenth- or seventeenth-century readers. The first editions in the seventeenth century translated these chronicles into Latin, the language of scholars and gentleman-antiquarians.[19] When interest in them revived in the nineteenth century, the first translations into modern English were made. The most influential was that of Ingram. But the first English translation was made by a woman, Anna Gurney, published in 1819, for private circulation.[20] It comes as no surprise to find a woman aware that Latin, as much as Old English, excluded most potential readers.

Many scholarly editions still provided no translation, including what was for long the best – that produced by Charles Plummer at the end of the century. The last thirty years have seen the most important of all the editions, with each single surviving chronicle published in full and separately, again without translation.[21] Consequently, most modern readers, even most non-specialist scholars, still use the two translated versions from the 1950s: that of G. N. Garmonsway, translating

---

[17] R. Thomson, 'William of Malmesbury's Diatribe against the Normans', in *The Long Twelfth-Century View of the Anglo-Saxon Past*, ed. M. Brett and D. A. Woodman (Farnham, 2015), 113–21, for tensions in Malmesbury.

[18] *The Saxon Chronicle with an English Translation*, iii.

[19] First edition was Abraham Whelock, *Historiae Ecclesiasticae gentis Anglorum Libri V* (Cambridge 1643), to which the *Chronologia Saxonica* – essentially an edition of Chronicle G – was appended. The second appeared in 1692 in Oxford, *Chronicon Saxonicum, seu Annales rerum in Anglia præcipue gestarum, a Christo nato ad annum usque 1154 deducti, ac jam demum Latinitate donate . . . accedunt regulæ ad investigandas nominum locorum origines; et nominum locorum ac virorum in chronico memoratorum explicatio. Opera et studio E. Gibson.*

[20] *A Literal Translation of the Saxon Chronicle*, by Miss Anna Gurney, for private circulation (Norwich, 1819). See G. C. Boase, 'Gurney, Anna (1795–1857)', rev. John D. Haigh, *Oxford Dictionary of National Biography*, Oxford University Press, 2004 (http://0-www.oxforddnb.com.wam.leeds.ac.uk/view/article/11759, accessed 1 July 2016).

[21] Under the general editorship of David Dumville and Simon Keynes, published as *The Anglo-Saxon Chronicle, A Collaborative Edition* (Cambridge, 1983–). *MS A*, ed. Janet Bately (1986); *MS B*, ed. Simon Taylor (1983); *MS C*, ed. Katherine O'Brien O'Keeffe (2001); *MS D*, ed. George Cubbin (1996); *MS E*, ed. Susan Irvine (2004); *MS F*, ed. Peter Baker (2000). Chronicle G edited separately, Angelika Lutz, *Die Version G der angelsächsischen Chronik* (Munich, 1981).

Plummer,[22] and the influential *English Historical Documents* translation, by Dorothy Whitelock. The language barrier has had long-lasting scholarly repercussions. Departments of English not Departments of History have been the home to most specialist study of these chronicles. The vernacular Old English enhanced the legitimising 'Englishness' of these chronicles; but it has excluded as well as included.

The title of this paper, and its introduction, stressed chronicles in the plural. Yet this tale of study, edition and reception has often slipped into *The* Anglo-Saxon Chronicle, in the singular. This is no oversight. That slippage is in the titles of the editions themselves. It indicates a common way of referring to these plural chronicles as if they were in some ways one, and the tendency to treat and *publish* them as if they were one, or at least ways of treating and publishing which emphasise their common ground. In the sixteenth century, Joscelyn happily supplied bits missing from one chronicle with excerpts from another. Thorpe's Rolls Series edition published six side by side, but titled his book *The Anglo-Saxon Chronicle*, and prioritised the common material in his translation.[23] Dorothy Whitelock's *English Historical Documents* translation, justifiably the most influential modern edition, forefronts the commonalities in its page layout, and its title is 'The Anglo-Saxon Chronicle'. There is a long and venerable history of discussing, and publishing, *The* Saxon, or Anglo-Saxon, Chronicle.

The habits of editors may seem the arcane concern of the modern Casaubon, ivory-tower navel gazing. It is what these chronicles tell us, surely, which matters, the facts they contain which are of interest. Almost all editors have been fully aware of the differences between individual chronicles.[24] They are constrained by the harsh facts of publishing economics. Plummer recognised four major chronicles, but was able to print only two in full – hence his rueful comment on the luxury of Thorpe's government funding.[25]

But editors make assumptions, overtly or not, about the text they are presenting. Many editors have adopted approaches or titles which enshrine a view of a single historical project, a view consistent with, if not encouraged by, the idea of an English 'national chronicle'. The tendency now is to call them all by letters A, B, C, D, E, F, G, a practice followed here, to avoid confusion. Names are, however, rarely neutral. Such letters

---

[22] *The Anglo-Saxon Chronicle*, translated G. N. Garmonsway (1953).

[23] Joscelyn e.g. replaced a lost section of D, *MS D*, ed. Cubbin, x, added bits to B from A, *MS B*, ed. Taylor, xiii, and to C from D, *MS C*, ed. O'Brien O'Keeffe, xvii–xviii. Thorpe's translation is, as he puts it 'formed from those of the original which, coinciding in matter, are susceptible to collation; all deviations [an interesting choice of word] from which are placed beneath the line', Thorpe, *The Anglo-Saxon Chronicle*, I, xv.

[24] Plummer, *Two of the Saxon Chronicles*, II, xxiii.

[25] *Ibid.*, cxxxvi

follow the practice which denotes manuscripts of a single text. They encourage the notion that we are dealing with precisely that. There is much that is common between these chronicles. It is easy to see why they have so often been treated as one. That common ground is part of their own story. But that common ground, including their shared vernacular language, have to be questions not givens; things we seek to explain, not unexamined assumptions.

Editors also make decisions about what readers want and need. Dorothy Whitelock's express intention was to make available a text of use to historians.[26] 'Textual variants' were not germane to this; a layout in columns would have 'obscured what a lot is common to all or most versions'. But the sort of text 'useful to historians' involves its own assumptions. Like many in the Humanities, early medievalists are increasingly concerned with the readers and reception of texts, at the time they were produced and later. Increasingly, it is the 'versions' and 'variants' that interest us, because it is there that authors, scribes, readers, patrons, contexts, reveal themselves.[27] Attention to editions also reminds us that what we are reading is not always what original authors wrote or audiences read. In the tenth and eleventh centuries, and later, these chronicles were produced – continued – and read – as separate texts. It is difficult to read those separate texts in most editions.

Attention to editions is thus not a marginal question.[28] From the sixteenth century onwards, editions and transcripts have played a major part in the way we conceive of these chronicles, and the way we read them. Their editors and transcribers have in important ways *made* these chronicles – or remade them. Most modern readers never read them as their tenth- and eleventh-century producers made them, or as their tenth- and eleventh-century audiences received them.

Late twentieth-century scholars have redirected attention to those contemporary audiences and meanings, and to the function of these chronicles in tenth- and eleventh-century Englishness.[29] For Janet

---

[26] *Anglo-Saxon Chronicle*, ed. Whitelock, Douglas and Tucker, xi; *English Historical Documents*, ed. Whitelock, I, 135.

[27] See e.g. Walter Pohl, 'Memory, Identity and Power in Lombard Italy', in *The Uses of the Past in the Early Middle Ages*, ed. Yitzhak Hen and Matthew Innes (Cambridge, 2000), 9–28, especially 11–12; M. De Jong, R. McKitterick, W. Pohl and I. Wood, 'Introduction', in *Texts and Identities in the Early Middle Ages*, ed. R. Corradini, R. Meens and C. Pössel (Vienna, 2006); on problems of editions, R. Corradini, 'Die Annales Fuldenses – Identitätskonstruktionen im ostfränkischen Raum am Ende der Karolingerzeit', in *ibid.*, 121–36.

[28] On the *Monumenta Germaniae Historica*, Corradini, 'Die Annales Fuldenses'; David Townsend, 'Alcuin's Willibrord, Wilhelm Levison and the MGH', in *The Politics of Editing Medieval Texts*, ed. Roberta Frank (New York, 1993), 107–30; Alan Frantzen, 'The Living and the Dead: Responses to Papers on the Politics of Editing Medieval Texts', in *ibid.*, 159–81.

[29] Janet Thormann, 'The *Anglo-Saxon Chronicle* Poems and the making of the English Nation', in *Anglo-Saxonism and the Construction of Social Identity*, ed. A. J. Frantzen and

Thormann, the Anglo-Saxon chronicle (still singular) was where the 'English nation was imagined'.[30] They are seen to reveal, construct and enshrine English identity.[31] In these chronicles, as Sarah Foot puts it, 'a collective history was available for those who could read it'.[32] These new approaches signal important new thinking, though they also sharpen the questions. What was available, when and for whom? In whose minds, where and when, was England being imagined?

These chronicles were made, grew and evolved, in a period now seen as critical in the making of the kingdom of England. That making meant the disappearance of old, independent kingdoms in Northumbria, Mercia, East Anglia and Wessex. It centred on the expansion of the West Saxon dynasty's control. That coincidence prompts a new question. How – if at all – was the making and evolution of these chronicles related to these developments and their politics, even implicated in them?

Answering these questions is fraught with difficulty. These chronicles are anonymous, annalistic, vernacular and discontinuous. There is no explicit information about who wrote them, or when or where. Thanks to the busy collecting of people like Robert Cotton, thanks even more to that great library wrecker, Henry VIII, we are often unsure where some of them were at the *end* of the Middle Ages, let alone where they had been made. They survive largely in fair copies made towards the end of their long evolution; only occasionally can hand-writing be used to date or place the stages of their evolution. Behind the surviving undatable, anonymous, unplaceable texts lie earlier stages, collations, continuations; the smooth fair copies hide these, too. The problems of these chronicles – and I have merely scratched the surface – help explain why they have been so little studied as separate texts, perhaps why so many people have quietly taken refuge in *The* Anglo-Saxon Chronicle. Yet understanding the nature of these chronicles is essential to understanding their contemporary makers and readers.

First, chronicles like this are more sophisticated than we sometimes allow.[33] Annalistic chronicles, recording events under years, are often

---

J. D. Niles (Gainesville, FA, 1997), 60–85; T. Bredehoft, *Textual Histories: Readings in the Anglo-Saxon Chronicle* (Toronto, Buffalo and London, 2001).

[30] Thormann, 'The *Anglo-Saxon Chronicle* Poems', 62–3.

[31] Sarah Foot, 'The Making of *Angelcynn*: English Identity before the Norman Conquest', *TRHS*, sixth series, 6 (1996), 25–49; *eadem*, 'The Historiography of the Anglo-Saxon "Nation-State"', in *Power and the Nation in European History*, ed. L. Scales and O. Zimmer (Cambridge, 2005), 125–42.

[32] Foot, 'The Historiography', 132.

[33] Literary scholars have been at the forefront of exposing their apparent naivety as 'artful', thus Jacqueline Stodnick, 'Second-Rate Stories? Changing Approaches to the *Anglo-Saxon Chronicle*', *Literary Compass*, 3/6 (2006), 1254–65, at 1254–5; Alice Jorgensen, 'Introduction: Reading the Anglo-Saxon Chronicle', in *Reading the Anglo-Saxon Chronicle: Language, Literature, History*, ed. A. Jorgensen (Turnhout, 2010), 1–28, at 27.

judged as primitive in comparison with full-blown thematic histories.[34] But annalistic chronicles have advantages. They are open-ended, they can be added to; these are stories that can grow. As they grow, they can change; the ending of any story affects how the rest is read. Their stories can grow by continuation, annotation and through collation. Chronicles like these could be merged together to tell augmented – and different – tales. In the tenth and eleventh centuries, all these things happened. These chronicles combined newer annals – contemporary history – and older ones, in constantly evolving stories.

Second, they are anonymous, but that does not mean they had no authors and creators. They look merely mechanical, resulting from the combining of existing material. They appear to be added to year by year, naïve, unvarnished – mines of unmediated information produced by myopic scribes without perspective or interpretation – people for whom a marvellous eruption of adders in Sussex was on a par with the deaths of kings.[35] Ironically, this can encourage us to read them as just the simple truth, not 'authored' in the sense we would now accept.

But year-by-year arrangement need not mean year-by-year writing; these chronicles are full of indications of re-writing, of additions, of the shaping of hindsight. Even when material is copied, small changes can reveal the scribes and their views. The merging of two sources may not generate any new 'facts' over and above what was in each. But the merging is a fact in itself, and the story which results is new – another 'fact', raising new questions: who wanted it, why and why at that moment?

In sum, these chronicles are complicated: complicated in the sense of difficult – hard to study, unforgiving; complicated in the sense of complex, their own histories more intricate than appears at first glance. They and their histories are facts in themselves, and facts that may have relevance to the English story. The problem is identifying where, when and in connection with whom they were made, continued and merged. The current state of scholarship allows for some answers, with more or less certainty.

Alfred's original chronicle was produced at court, in the circle of those surrounding the king. In the early tenth century, two chronicles continued where Alfred's had left off: one from the perspective of the court of his son and successor in Wessex, Edward the Elder, what we now call Chronicle A; the other very likely from that of the court of Alfred's daughter, Æthelflæd, who became ruler of Mercia, perhaps especially from the perspective of

---

[34] Paul Hayward, *The Winchcombe and Coventry Chronicles: Hitherto Unnoticed Witnesses to the Work of John of Worcester* (Tempe, AZ, 2010), Intro., especially 18–28.

[35] E.g. Cecily Clark, 'The Narrative Mode of "The Anglo-Saxon Chronicle"', in *England before the Conquest. Studies in Primary Sources Presented to Dorothy Whitelock*, ed. Peter Clemoes and Kathleen Hughes (Cambridge, 1971), 215–35, at 220–1.

that Mercian court in the aftermath of her death.[36] At some point in the tenth century, these two were merged into a new, now lost, chronicle, BC the ancestor of Chronicles B and C.[37]

During the tenth century, bishops and archbishops come into the frame. Chronicle A was in the hands of the bishop of Winchester by its end. He probably took it with him when he was appointed to Canterbury in 1006, but not before a copy of it had been made, which was then kept at Winchester, the surviving G.[38] About this same time, another archbishop, Wulfstan II of York, was annotating a different vernacular chronicle – the one which lies behind our Chronicle D.[39]

There were one or more lost chronicles in the West Country, perhaps at Worcester, a see which was often attached to the archbishopric of York from the 970s onwards.[40] And York or Worcester are likely homes for the so-called 'Northern Recension', arguably the most important lost chronicle of them all, the *only* vernacular chronicle which made radical changes to Alfred's original. This was a text with a huge progeny, including the vernacular chronicles D and E and some of the great twelfth-century Latin histories of England. It has been connected to an archbishop of

[36] P. Stafford, '"The Annals of Æthelflæd": Annals, History and Politics in Early Tenth-Century England', in *Myth, Rulership, Church and Charters. Essays in Honour of Nicholas Brooks*, ed. Julia Barrow and Andrew Wareham (Aldershot, 2008), 101–16.

[37] This is the lost BC, identified by Plummer, *Two of the Saxon Chronicles*, II, lxxxviii–lxxxix, discussed in *MS C*, ed. O'Brien O'Keeffe, lvii–lxii. The last common annal in B and C is for 977; for an updating *c.* 977 see P. Conner, *The Anglo-Saxon Chronicle 10: The Abingdon Chronicle AD 956–1066* (Woodbridge, 1996), xxxix and n. 80, lxx. One of the last entries in BC was a long, and thus unusual, obit on Archbishop Oscytel – bishop of Dorchester, archbishop of York, and relative of Archbishops Oda and Oswald.

[38] On A's development *c.* 1000 AD: David Dumville, *Wessex and England, from Alfred to Edgar* (Woodbridge, 1992), especially 56–62; *MS A*, ed. Bately, xxxvii–viii; Patrick Wormald, *Making of English Law: King Alfred to the Twelfth Century*, I: *Legislation and its Limits* (Oxford, 1999), 172–81. Chronicle A was at Canterbury by the end of the eleventh century, but the evidence of the state of its episcopal lists and their relationship to those of Chronicle G suggests no further work on it at Winchester after *c.* 1001; the G lists were updated 1001x1012/13, those in A were not.

[39] On Wulfstan and the evolving D: K. Jost, 'Wulfstan und die Angelsächsische Chronik', *Anglia*, 47 (1923), 105–23; Stephanie Hollis, 'The Protection of God and the King: Wulfstan's Legislation on Widows', in *Wulfstan, Archbishop of York*, ed. Matthew Townend (Turnhout, 2004), 443–60, especially at 450; Sara M. Pons-Sanz, 'A Paw in Every Pie: Wulfstan and the Anglo-Saxon Chronicle Again', *Leeds Studies in English*, new series, 38 (2007), 31–52. Wulfstan tended to annotate MSS in his possession, sometimes arguably to signal ownership: N. Ker, 'The Handwriting of Archbishop Wulfstan', in *England before the Conquest*, ed. Clemoes and Hughes, 315–31; T. Heslop, 'Art and the Man: Archbishop Wulfstan and the York Gospel Book', in *Wulfstan*, ed. Townend, 279–308, at 282–4 and 308.

[40] M. Lapidge, 'Byrhtferth and Oswald', in *St Oswald of Worcester. Life and Influence*, ed. N. Brooks and C. Cubitt (1996), 64–83, at 73–8; C. Hart, 'The Early Section of the *Worcester Chronicle*', *Journal of Medieval History*, 9 (1983), 251–315.

York/Worcester, before 1023, probably in the second half of the tenth century.[41]

The archiepiscopal context continues. Chronicling activity linked Canterbury and Abingdon in the 1040s, when an abbot of Abingdon was made assistant archbishop, then moved back to Abingdon to die.[42] In the mid-century, a new chronicle was collated, and the York archbishop is again in the picture: Chronicle D was evolving.[43] After 1066, Canterbury was a hive of vernacular chronicling – as David Dumville long ago showed.[44] Almost every vernacular chronicle we now have passed through, or was somehow connected to, Canterbury in the later eleventh century. Chronicle E was developing, in dialogue with Chronicle D; Chronicle A was being augmented; Chronicle B was having additions made to its ending and beginning. The first bilingual Latin and Old English Chronicle – F – was made there around the year 1100.

Bishops and archbishops are prominent in this story. But there are laymen too. Ealdorman Æthelweard, a great noble and local ruler, the uncle of a king, had a chronicle *c.* 1000 AD.[45] So too, perhaps, did Earl Leofric, another great noble and local ruler of Mercia, *c.* 1050.[46]

Two vernacular chronicles were still being added to as late as the mid-twelfth century. Chronicle E, as we now have it, was at Peterborough, probably arriving there when a Canterbury prior was appointed abbot.[47] The final form of D was somewhere in north Britain; it should be remembered that the York archdiocese extended as far as southern

---

[41] D. Whitelock, *The Peterborough Chronicle. The Bodleian Manuscript Laud Misc. 636*, Early English Manuscripts in Facsimile, vol. 4 (Copenhagen, 1954), Introduction; D. Dumville, 'Textual Archaeology and Northumbrian History Subsequent to Bede', in *Coinage in Ninth-Century Northumbria*, ed. D. M. Metcalf, BAR, vol. 180 (Oxford, 1987), 43–55, at 48–9.

[42] *MS C*, ed. O'Brien O'Keeffe, xc–xci; D. Dumville, 'Some Aspects of Annalistic Writing at Canterbury in the Eleventh and Early Twelfth Centuries', *Peritia*, 2 (1983), 23–57, especially 28–9.

[43] P. Wormald, *How Do We Know So Much About Anglo-Saxon Deerhurst?*, Deerhurst lecture 1991 (Friends of Deerhurst Church, 1993); P. Stafford, 'Archbishop Ealdred and the D Chronicle', in *Normandy and its Neighbours, 900–1250. Essays for David Bates*, ed. D. Crouch and K. Thompson (Turnhout, 2011), 135–56.

[44] Dumville, 'Some Aspects of Annalistic Writing'.

[45] *The Chronicle of Æthelweard*, ed. A. Campbell (Edinburgh and London, 1962); S. Ashley, 'The Lay Intellectual in Anglo-Saxon England: Ealdorman Æthelweard, and the Politics of History', in *Lay Intellectuals in the Carolingian World*, ed. P. Wormald and J. L. Nelson (Cambridge, 2007), 218–45; M. Gretsch, 'Historiography and Literary Patronage in Late Anglo-Saxon England: The Evidence of Æthelweard's *Chronicon*', *Anglo-Saxon England*, 41 (2013), 205–48.

[46] S. Baxter, 'MS C of the Anglo-Saxon Chronicle and the Politics of Mid-Eleventh-Century England', *English Historical Review*, 122 (2007), 1189–227.

[47] Whitelock, *The Peterborough Chronicle*, Introduction; *MS E*, ed. Irvine, xiii, xc–ci; *eadem*, 'The Production of the Peterborough Chronicle', in *Reading the Anglo-Saxon Chronicle*, ed. Jorgensen, 49–66; Malasree Home, *The Peterborough Version of the Anglo-Saxon Chronicle: Rewriting Post-Conquest History* (Woodbridge, 2015), 1–5.

Scotland. D's last entry is an annal which has been claimed as our earliest example of lowland Scots.[48]

There is thus not one Anglo-Saxon Chronicle, but many. These snapshots of them and their development are often debatable, more or less clear, more or less identifiable, like faded pictures in an old family album. But they are a family without doubt. Resemblances are marked: all in Old English; each beginning with Alfred's chronicle; each continuing his annalistic genre, none of which should be taken for granted. They are a family too in the sense that at various points different ones were in contact, copied from each other, answering each other, in dialogue with each other.

To that extent, editors have been justified in seeing a common historical project. The snapshots suggest that the owners of that project were the court elite, or rather the southern court elite, at least until their destruction in the aftermath of the Norman Conquest. Bishops, archbishops and great nobles were all members of that elite. Two people, or two series of people, stand out: the archbishops, of Canterbury and of York, or, as the latter often were at this date, of York/Worcester. The vernacular chronicles in the tenth and eleventh centuries appear as in some sense the possession, if not expression, of that southern court elite, particularly of its episcopal, but especially archiepiscopal, members. But their shared historiographical project was not a continuous, centrally planned one. It produced different chronicles, made and continued at different times, read by different people; there are significant chronological gaps. To that extent, the editions can mislead and mask. We need to recognise both the common ground and the difference.

A '*southern*' elite which included archbishops of York is surely oxymoronic. What definition of 'southern' includes England north of the Humber? Closer scrutiny of archbishops of York and their chronicles will resolve that oxymoron. It will also give insight into the role of vernacular chronicling in the making of England.

The York archbishopric was prestigious. Its earlier holders had played a prominent role in the politics of the independent Northumbrian kingdom. Prior to the tenth century, archbishops of York had apparently been Northumbrian by origin. During the tenth century, southern kings conquered Northumbria, and began to appoint the northern archbishops. From the 950s onwards, York archbishops hailed consistently from south of the Trent, and appear to have been deliberately chosen for that reason.[49]

---

[48]Stafford, 'Archbishop Ealdred and the D Chronicle'. On the possibly lowland Scots annal, *MS D*, ed. Cubbin, cli.

[49]D. Whitelock, 'Dealings of the Kings of England with Northumbria in the Tenth and Eleventh Centuries', in *The Anglo-Saxons. Studies in Some Aspects of their History and Culture*

The York archbishopric was prestigious, but by the tenth century probably impoverished. From the 950s, it was usually held alongside a rich southern see; first Dorchester-on-Thames, but increasingly the wealthy Worcester. This was an answer to York's poverty, but also to the problem – from a southern king's point of view – of its potential independence. Archbishops now had a substantial stake south of the Humber and Trent. The new situation of the York archbishops is flagged by a new pattern. They begin to appear regularly at the southern king's court. Before the 950s, their appearance there was infrequent, and worthy of remark. From then on, it becomes commonplace.[50] From the 950s, archbishops of York were, in most respects and in almost all cases, members of the southern elite. The changes here are an index of the attempts of southern kings to control the north, attempts of which the archbishops were agents.

Archbishops of York were owners, or patrons, of vernacular chronicles. There is every reason to link that significant new chronicle which made changes to Alfred's original to the York archbishops. It is usually known as the 'Northern Recension'; it might be more accurate to name it 'the chronicle of the Archbishops of York'. Its shape and content repay detailed attention.

The so-called 'Northern Recension' was the only pre-Norman Conquest vernacular chronicle to make significant additions within the original Alfredian chronicle, and the only one to change it substantially.[51] This was done by the typical annalistic practice of collating Alfred's chronicle with other material. The makers of the 'Northern Recension' added almost all the datable information in Bede's *Ecclesiastical History*, together with material from northern sources – the so-called 'York Annals', Northumbrian king lists and Northumbrian bishops' lists. Alfred's chronicle became more northern as a result. Most of the additions came from Northumbrian sources. Bede could be classified as such; writing from his Tyneside monastery, with a geographical bias north of the Humber.

It would, however, be just as true to say that Alfred's chronicle became more broadly 'English' as a result.[52] Bede was a historian of the *gens Anglorum*, of the 'Angles' more broadly conceived than the Northumbrian peoples. Northern material was added into Alfred's story, but more 'Southumbrian' material was added in, too. The narrative was widened;

Presented to Bruce Dickins, ed. P. Clemoes (1959), 70–88; D. Rollason, *Northumbria 500–1100. Creation and Destruction of a Kingdom* (Cambridge, 2003), 202–8, 228–30.

[50] See witness lists of southern royal charters in S. Keynes, *An Atlas of Attestations in Anglo-Saxon Charters c. 670–1066*, www.kemble.asnc.cam.ac.uk/node/31.

[51] Both E and F have additional material, largely in Latin, added into Alfred's chronicle almost certainly post-1066, mostly derived from a Norman set of annals, see *MS E*, ed. Irvine, lxxxviii–xc, and *MS F*, ed. Baker, l–liv.

[52] 'Nationalization', thus Bredehoft, *Textual Histories*, 67–71.

and a theme already present in Alfred's chronicle was underlined – of a people wider than any of the seventh- or eighth-century Anglo-Saxon kingdoms – a people united by their Christian faith.

Alfred's story also became more episcopal, or rather archiepiscopal.[53] Bede's material increased this coverage, as did the 'York Annals', which were probably archiepiscopal in origin.[54]

There was thus much addition to Alfred's tale, until this new chronicle reached the ninth century. Here, it followed Alfred's.[55] This may indicate failure of other sources, though the faithfulness to Alfred's chronicle is noteworthy. The result, however, is the same. The story which this new chronicle told still led to Alfred's dynasty. The additions were to the years before 800; the ninth century remained Alfred's, as in his own chronicle. The expanded, more geographically inclusive, more archiepiscopal tale still culminated in the military successes of Alfred's dynasty, as they had been told at his court. In that crucial sense, this expanded story still legitimised that dynasty, Alfred in particular, and, of course, his successors.

This lost 'Northern Recension' contains few new facts. Almost every entry, every piece of information in it could be found from the sources its makers used. It is now lost, and can only be recovered through painstaking comparison of the progeny it spawned, of the surviving chronicles which used it and grew out of it. But it repays that effort.[56] This was without doubt the most important and far-reaching development within the vernacular chronicling tradition after Alfred; and it is somehow linked to the archbishops of York. We can place chronicles of this type in the hands of southern-appointed archbishops. We can see at least one of them reading it, and annotating it: Wulfstan II *c.* 1020, adding comment, for example, on one of his pet subjects, the protection of widows. It is linked therefore to key players in the politics of tenth- and eleventh-century England; the archbishops of York, members of the southern elite who had been entrusted with the task of bringing Northumbria more firmly under southern control. It was linked to them in the century which saw

[53] E.g. Chronicle E s.a. 625 and 721 extending coverage of Archbishop John – using both Bede and, probably, northern episcopal lists for e.g. precise lengths and dates of his episcopate.

[54] J. Story, *Carolingian Connections: Anglo-Saxon England and Carolingian Francia c. 750–870* (Aldershot, 2003), ch. 4, especially 116–33; *eadem*, 'After Bede: Continuing the *Ecclesiastical History*', in *Early Medieval Studies in Memory of Patrick Wormald*, ed. S. Baxter, C. Karkov, J. L. Nelson and D. Pelteret (Farnham, 2009), 165–84; Peter Hunter Blair, 'Some Observations on the *Historia Regum* Attributed to Symeon of Durham', in *Celt and Saxon: Studies in the Early British Border*, ed. N. K. Chadwick (Cambridge, 1963), 63–118, remains important.

[55] It was at this point that the 'York Annals' apparently petered out, though there were at least fragmentary Northumbrian annals for the ninth century.

[56] On the importance and defensibility of seeking out such lost texts, David Dumville, 'Editing Old English Texts for Historians and Other Trouble Makers', in *The Editing of Old English*, ed. D. Scragg and P. Szarmach (Woodbridge, 1994), 45–52, at 48.

the military advance of southern rule over Northumbria, and the last independent kings in the north ousted. These archbishops were involved in the making of England. Was the making of this chronicle somehow implicated in that?

The 'Northern Recension' incorporated Northumbria into a wider English story. It could be characterised as the historiographical equivalent of the southern kings' conquest of the north. We could see its making as a brutal act, a parallel or even aid to military conquest: made to be sent north with these archbishops; arriving in their baggage train; southern vernacular history thrust down Northumbrian throats, history as control. This is too crude a reading, which begs questions about both audience and makers.

A milder version of this reading might have it created to keep the archbishops loyal, to control *them*: made for them to take north, as salutary bedtime reading in the cold northern fastnesses; a reminder of the Christian past which linked the kingdom either side of the Humber; a reminder of the triumphs of the southern dynasty the archbishops represented. These were certainly among the messages the story carried. But evidence suggests that it was most likely made *for* the archbishops, at their own behest. It certainly continued to be connected to the archbishops, throughout the early and mid-eleventh century. Its makers, the lost scribes who compiled it, reveal themselves as Northumbrian, the sort of men who would have been in the archbishop's entourage.

Its audience is elusive. Was it aimed at Northumbrian elites, Northumbrian clerics? Perhaps, though there is little evidence that it circulated widely in the north, and a Latin historical compilation – available by the end of the tenth century – was more influential north of the Humber.[57] One audience we know it reached was the archbishops themselves. Should we see this chronicle, and its successors, as reactions of the archbishops to their own new situation, taking this vernacular history with them? Was its function to tell their own – southern elite – story to themselves, fulfilling a major role of history, consolatory and reinforcing? These southern archbishops chose to have a vernacular chronicle, to continue it, and to have northern Latin sources translated into its annalistic and Old English vernacular format. Genre, language, the very making of this chronicle, and the additions to it; none of these should be taken for granted. Was a chronicle in the vernacular

---

[57] Probably known at Durham, A. J. Piper, 'The Historical Interests of the Monks of Durham', in *Symeon of Durham, Historian of Durham and the North*, ed. D. Rollason (Stamford, 1998), 301–32, at 312, 321 and n 107. On the Latin compilation, M. Lapidge, 'Byrhtferth of Ramsey and the Early Sections of the *Historia Regum* Attributed to Symeon of Durham', *Anglo-Saxon England*, 10 (1981), 97–122; Hunter Blair, 'Some Observations on the *Historia Regum*. For its twelfth-century significance, John Taylor, *Medieval Historical Writing in Yorkshire* (York, 1961), 4–6.

as much a political statement as an indication of intended audience? Were this chronicle and its continuations expressions of the archbishops' self-inclusion within the ideology of southern rule, centred on Alfred's dynasty?

One other audience is clear, the makers of the original 'Northern Recension' themselves. It was not necessarily produced at York, or even in the north; tenth-century archbishops had links with Dorchester, Ramsey and Worcester, any of which is a possible site. But the making of this chronicle was certainly in the hands of Northumbrians. They revealed themselves unconsciously as they copied and translated; especially when they contrasted 'us' with the 'Southumbrians'.[58] The tone of these vernacular chronicles is usually impersonal; their makers rarely show themselves. But these scribes did. Northern voices are difficult to hear in tenth- and eleventh-century England. These are precious testimonies.[59]

The scribes' self-revelation is a first reaction to the history they were creating and reading, a first reception. And it is far from simply separatist. They reveal themselves as English, or rather Christian English, at the important point of origin when Christianity first arrived, the belief and peace sent to 'us' by Pope Gregory.[60] Here, the scribes were receiving the message of a Christian people, with which they identified. But they also reveal themselves as Northumbrian, significantly, at another point of origin, when they expanded on the arrival of the English people, of *Angelcyn*. They acknowledged that 'our' royal kin were from the same origin as 'that of the Southumbrians'.[61]

These were the makers of this chronicle, the collators of its sources. It was their decisions, conscious, or half-conscious, which nudged what was a wider English story into a more Northumbrian direction; occasionally into a direction which celebrated Northumbrian triumph over Wessex;[62] everywhere into a story which assembled as much as they could of Northumbrian detail.[63] Making a story which made a wider England may,

---

[58] Whitelock, *The Peterborough Chronicle*, 28; Plummer, *Two of the Saxon Chronicles*, II, lxx–lxxi.

[59] The manuscripts from which the 'Northern Recension' can be reconstructed are all later. Without the scribes' autograph, we cannot see what dialect of Old English they were using. Chronicle D was the result of collation with other chronicles, whose language could have affected it. In the later manuscripts, there are some few signs of northern English usage: *MS D*, ed. Cubbin, at e.g. lxxxix; S. M. Pons-Sanz, 'Norse-Derived Vocabulary in the Anglo-Saxon Chronicle', in *Reading the Anglo-Saxon Chronicle*, ed. Jorgensen, 275–304. In general, the language of D is Late West Saxon, *MS D*, ed. Cubbin, lxxxiv–cli.

[60] Chronicle D and Chronicle E s.a. 785.

[61] Chronicle E s.a. 449. The sense of 'us-ness' which recognition of a common past could fuel and feed is discussed by W. Eggert and B. Pätzold, *Wir-Gefühl und regnum Saxonum bei frühmittelalterlichen Geschichtsschreibern* (Berlin, 1984).

[62] E.g. Chronicle E s.a 626, Edwin leading an expedition against the West Saxons and killing five kings.

[63] E.g. Chronicle E s.a. 603, adding extra detail on the Battle of *Degsastane*.

paradoxically, have prompted a sharper awareness of Northumbrian-ness among its actual creators. The reception of history is not straightforward. On one level, this text constructed south-facing loyalty; at another, it may have been capable of enhancing Northumbrian identity.

The chronicle created for a York archbishop carried many messages, including unity and dynastic legitimacy. It expanded the notion of a kingdom united by Christianity. It also had a lot about archbishops. It increased coverage of their role in Christianisation, and of the significance of York archbishops in Northumbria. Archbishops were members of the southern elite, and bishops in the growing English kingdom; *that* is the historical narrative we now prioritise. But they were also bishops, episcopal, with a strong sense of the duties of their position; and, at York and through this chronicle, a strong sense of the long history and prestige of their see. Later tenth- and eleventh-century archbishops of York were among the most confident and visible members of the episcopate. The chronicle created and extended for them reflects that. Did reading and re-reading it contribute to that self-confidence?

By the eleventh century if not before, the vernacular chronicles often stand at a clear if not critical distance from the actions of kings. The complex identities of the patrons for whom they were produced, of the scribes who worked in their entourages, help explain this.

The chronicle made for the southern-appointed York archbishops responded to the making of an England built on southern hegemony, and to the role of York archbishops in that. Other chronicles and continuations responded to other political conjunctures, developed other messages.

In the early tenth century, continuations of Alfred's chronicle were produced in Wessex and Mercia. Their context was the pressing succession question: who could claim Alfred's inheritance, the new kingdom of *Angelcyn*: his son, ruler of Wessex, or daughter, queen in Mercia? The resulting Mercian chronicle contained the most sustained, and unusual, treatment of a woman in the vernacular chronicling tradition. It is a reminder not to ignore Mercia in the making of the English kingdom.

The constantly evolving narratives and messages merit further exploration. The beginning of the eleventh century saw defeat by Danish conquerors, a defeat which included the murder of a Canterbury archbishop. Several chronicles included a very critical account of this. The military triumphs of Alfred and his children were now read alongside that same dynasty's defeat, its exile and return. It was such a chronicle that Archbishop Ealdred of York had, the man who crowned William the Conqueror in 1066.

These chronicles should be read for the contemporary arguments they enshrine and express. An impassioned tone of debate and division sharpens in the eleventh-century chronicles. The dialogue between them, already there in the early tenth century, is now more overt.[64] Some begin to express, even invoke, a sense of Englishness and an England separate from its kings.[65] They are our best guide to elite political argument in the last decades before the Norman Conquest.

Chronicles and chronicling activity after 1066 reacted to Conquest. At Canterbury, the maker of Chronicle F made a Latin translation and attempted to incorporate the Normans into the story. Somewhere in the north, Chronicle D was increasingly engaged with Scottish affairs. Scotland was home to many Anglo-Saxon noble exiles. The continuators of D, by turns bitter and fatalistic, reactivated the dynastic messages of the vernacular tradition, especially à propos the Scottish Queen Margaret, the woman whose daughter would marry a new Norman king, but above all, the woman who carried Alfred's bloodline beyond 1066.[66] D's last solitary annal from the 1130s may, or may not, be in lowland Scots. But its subject was a remote, yet direct, descendant of King Alfred.[67]

The Saxon, or Anglo-Saxon, chronicles have long been seen as the story of England, as 'our national chronicle'. Their unusual vernacular language, their place in a pre-1066, pre-Norman, originary England, marked them out for this role. Editors have often prioritised the common ground, the unity among them. It is necessary also to embrace their diversity, to stress the range of texts produced and available in the course of these centuries and to bring back their scribes, readers and patrons. There were many chronicles, and as many stories, to be read in the tenth and eleventh centuries. These chronicles are sources of fact on the early English past, but their making, their overall shape and content, their continuations are also facts in themselves.

Many were loosely speaking 'court' chronicles. Not 'official', transmitting a centrally crafted royal line;[68] not 'propaganda' in the modern sense, it is unclear how far they spoke and circulated beyond a narrow elite; not 'court' or 'official' in the sense that continuations

[64] On Earl Godwine and his actions, differing lines in different chronicles have long been recognised, e.g. F. Barlow, *Edward the Confessor* (1970), xxii.

[65] P. Stafford, 'The Anglo-Saxon Chronicles, Identity and the Making of England', *Haskins Society Journal*, 19 (2008 for 2007), 28–50, at 32–6.

[66] P. Stafford, 'Noting Relations and Tracking Relationships in English Vernacular Chronicles, Late Ninth to Early Twelfth Century', in *The Medieval Chronicle X*, ed. I. Afanasyev, J. Dresvina and E. Kooper (Leiden and Boston, MA, 2015), 23–48.

[67] Williams , *The English*, 95. Further discussed in my forthcoming 'Fathers and Daughters: The Case of Æthelred II', in *Writing, Kingship, and Power in Anglo-Saxon England*, ed. Rory Naismith and David A. Woodman (Cambridge, 2017).

[68] N. Brooks, 'Why is the *Anglo-Saxon Chronicle* about Kings?', *Anglo-Saxon England*, 39 (2010), 43–70; and *idem*, '"Anglo-Saxon Chronicle(s)" or "Old English Royal Annals"?', in *Gender and Historiography. Studies in the Earlier Middle Ages in Honour of Pauline Stafford*, ed. J. L. Nelson, S. Reynolds and S. M. Johns (2012), 35–48, takes a different line.

of the Royal Frankish annals were. The gaps in their coverage point to an attitude to history writing which was more spasmodic and reactive. Understanding these chronicles will mean minding all the gaps, chronological, geographical and social, returning constantly to the questions of who wanted history in the tenth and eleventh centuries, and precisely where and when. Yet many if not all were 'court' in the sense that the court was a frame, and a framer of minds.

They are connected to men prominent and active at the southern court, particularly to its episcopal and archiepiscopal members. It is *their* need for history, recent and remote; *their* use of history; *their* reading and reception of it we are largely seeing in these chronicles – albeit a need, use, reading and reception filtered through the scribe/authors who made these texts. These chronicles were – to a greater or lesser extent – the possession of a political elite, and thus expressions of its ideological viewpoint, but also of its tensions, concerns and internal arguments. This should make us wary of using them as simple context for understanding other evidence, the bare, unadorned, unconstructed 'truth'. They should be read alongside other evidence, as deeply engaged witnesses to contemporary politics.

Chronicles connected to bishops were not apolitical. In European perspective, early England stands out for the control of kings over episcopal appointments, for the rarity of familial links between great aristocrats and bishops.[69] English bishops were king's men to a remarkable degree. But they were also bishops, admonishers of kings, guardians of notions of just rule, heirs to their own traditions. How far did history reading and writing in tenth- and eleventh-century England reflect that? There are many questions here. How much of these chronicles' complex development might be explained by taking account of changes and movements of bishops, of pluralism and of the diverse personnel of episcopal households? Was chronicle writing sometimes prompted by royal consecrations, episcopally managed; the making of a new king a moment of reflection, counsel and critique, with history as its vehicle? It was certainly affected by the long-standing Christian views of history, as the story of God's dealings with men, of the punishment of sin and of the role of foreign conquest in that – all strongly reflected in eleventh-century annals. We should read with an awareness that their patrons and audiences had complex identities, which affected both their making and their reception.

These chronicles carried messages of unity and dynastic legitimacy – but also of a Christian people, its history *and its episcopal leaders*. Tim Reuter

---

[69]Julia Barrow, *The Clergy in the Medieval World. Secular Clerics, their Families and Careers in North-Western Europe, c. 800–c. 1200* (Cambridge, 2015), at 139–46.

characterised eleventh-century Europe as a Europe of bishops.[70] These bishops and archbishops – and these chronicles – would place England firmly within that.

'*The* Anglo-Saxon Chronicle' – monolithic monument of English national history – needs to be reconceived as multiple and fluid. But only to some extent. What also emerges is the strength of a tradition, and the continuing importance and meanings of a core narrative which that tradition enshrined. Alfred's story remained central. No vernacular chronicle rewrote its crucial ninth-century section, which led directly to Alfred and his successors. To the end, these chronicles retained the potential Alfred's chronicle wrote into them: to be both dynastic and the story of a people united by their Christianity, to legitimise, but also critique, the one through the other.

All history writing has context. The intellectual context of my re-reading of the vernacular chronicles is a Europe-wide re-reading of early medieval history and its sources, acutely sensitive to contemporary agendas and reception, alert to the way editions have remade texts. That is, itself, part of wider scholarly attention to authorship and to narrative and its workings.

These chronicles have always been read politically. They have often been edited in that context. We read them politically whether we recognise that fact or not. *The* Anglo-Saxon Chronicle, vernacular, factual, sober, covering the centuries before Norman Conquest, was an ideal text of English national identity. Are plural chronicles texts for an age of devolution? Not if we are searching for separatist tales, or local stories. These chronicles are neither, though reading one of them provoked an expression of northern pride if not resistance in Northumbrian scribes. We might fruitfully read these chronicles for the 'us' they occasionally reveal, and construct. These are, however, still the stories that made England, directly implicated in and revealing of that process. Their making and remaking is a reminder of the forces that were driving the political developments that made the English kingdom; most notably the southern elite's investment in that project, the strong pressures towards unity which were deeply rooted in that elite's ideology, especially that of its clerical members.

Plural chronicles may, however, be texts for an age of national self-examination: revealing an England not made easily, and far from inevitable; reminding us of the continuing significance of Mercia, the recalcitrance of Northumbria, of political divisions and tensions smoothed over in an annalistic genre with its surface tale of simple facts. It was as a

---

[70] T. Reuter, 'Ein Europa der Bischöfe. Das Zeitalter Burchards von Worms', in *Bischof Burchard von Worms 1000–1025*, ed. W. Hartmann, Quellen und Abhandlungen zur mittelrheinischen Kirchengeschichte, 100 (Mainz, 2000), 1–28.

historian of women that I became acutely aware of the constructedness and partiality of these 'national' chronicles: so few women mentioned, their occasional presence all the more remarkable and demanding attention. Paradoxically, plural, elite chronicles may be texts for a democratic age, increasingly alert to how limited the voices we hear from the past usually are.

The quest for these chronicles is a hazardous one, doomed to only partial fulfilment. We will never be able to answer all the questions they pose. Even asking them demands painstaking, detailed work and the help of many other disciplines – palaeography, manuscript study, language scholarship. The final message of these chronicles should be respect for our craft: skilled, self-aware, increasingly inter-disciplinary. Research does not come cheap; our modern political masters could learn from their nineteenth-century predecessors. These chronicles are worth the investment.

Transactions of the RHS 27 (2017), pp. 87–121 © Royal Historical Society 2017
doi:10.1017/S0080440117000056

GLOBAL CLIMATES, THE 1257 MEGA-ERUPTION OF SAMALAS VOLCANO, INDONESIA, AND THE ENGLISH FOOD CRISIS OF 1258*

By Bruce M. S. Campbell

READ 6 MAY 2016

ABSTRACT. In 1258, as baronial opposition to Henry III erupted and the government became locked in constitutional conflict, the country found itself in the grip of a serious food crisis. To blame was a run of bad weather and failed harvests. Thousands of famished famine refugees flocked to London in quest of food and charity, where many of them perished and were buried in mass graves. The multiple burials recently discovered and excavated in the cemetery of the hospital of St Mary Spital highlight the plight of the poor at this time of political turmoil. Was their fate part of a global catastrophe precipitated by the VEI7 explosion of Samalas Volcano, Indonesia, the previous year or was powerful solar forcing of global climates responsible for the unusually unstable weather? The answer depends in large measure upon establishing the precise chronology of how the crisis unfolded, drawing upon the surviving documentary record of prices and harvests, the comments of contemporary chroniclers and a range of high-resolution palaeo-climatic proxies. Reexamination of this episode illustrates the potential of environmental history to shed fresh light on familiar historical events and its capacity to place them in a global environmental context.

In December 2014, Justin Welby, archbishop of Canterbury, made national headlines when he expressed his concern at the growing resort in Britain to charitably run food banks which he took to be symptomatic of the mounting hunger crisis facing many of the country's poorest families.[1] He confessed that he was unsurprised by the hunger omnipresent in the desperately poor countries of sub-Saharan Africa but shocked to find it in as developed and rich a country as Britain. This is because hunger in modern Britain arises not from any deficiency of food availability but from the lack by some people of the financial means of obtaining it.

---

* This paper is dedicated to Christine Beavon. Christopher Whittick provided invaluable assistance with the Latin chronicles, Richard Cassidy alerted me to relevant entries in the close and patent rolls, Francis Ludlow advised on the 1252 drought and, with Mike Baillie, contributed dendrochronological data.

[1] *The Mail on Sunday*, 6 Dec. 2014, www.dailymail.co.uk/news/article-2863693/I-seen-hunger-stalks-country-shocks-Africa-Stop-wasting-food-feed-poor-says-ARCHBISHOP-CANTERBURY.html, and www.archbishopofcanterbury.org/articles.php/5459/archbishop-of-canterbury-on-hunger-in-britain, accessed 31 Aug. 2016.

Apart from the homeless and the heavily indebted, those most likely to be in this predicament are people on low incomes with poor job security and, especially, unemployed people experiencing delays or reductions in welfare payments.[2] That is what makes this a hunger crisis and not a food crisis, for, historically, food crises have entailed a failure of both food availability and food entitlements, as commonly manifest in a sharp inflation of food prices.[3] Susceptibility to periodic food crises was and remains the lot of most societies at relatively low levels of economic development, including Britain prior to its industrial revolution and the onset of modern economic growth. In the most extreme cases, food scarcities have escalated into famines when starvation and starvation-related diseases elevated deaths above births.[4] Precipitating factors typically included weather-induced harvest failure, diseases of crops and livestock, war and the dislocation of trade.

Prices can be used to track England's own slow and belated escape from serious national food crises. The single longest and most robust price series is for wheat, since it was the most commercialised and universally traded foodstuff. Although wheat scarcely featured in the bare-bones basket of consumables upon which the poorest agricultural, artisanal and labouring households typically subsisted, its price powerfully influenced those of other grains and therefore may be taken as broadly representative of the costs of satisfying basic subsistence.[5] As a general rule, years when wheat prices were high were years when the living standards of the poor were under most pressure. Purchase prices of wheat are recorded in the Exchequer Pipe Rolls from the mid-1160s, sale prices in the Winchester Pipe Rolls from 1209 and then in a growing number of manorial accounts from the 1230s.[6] This information becomes virtually continuous from

---

[2] www.trusselltrust.org/news-and-blog/latest-stats/, accessed 31 Aug. 2016; All-Party Parliamentary Group (APPG) on Hunger, *Feeding Britain: A Strategy for Zero Hunger in England, Wales, Scotland and Northern Ireland* (2014), https://feedingbritain.files. wordpress.com/2015/02/food-poverty-feeding-britain-final-2.pdf, accessed 31 Aug. 2016.

[3] A. K. Sen, *Poverty and Famines: An Essay on Entitlement and Deprivation* (Oxford, 1981), 39–44, 154–66; C. Ó Gráda, *Famine: A Short History* (Princeton and Oxford, 2009), 159–94.

[4] Ó Gráda, *Famine*, 4–5; B. M. S. Campbell, 'Four Famines and a Pestilence: Harvest, Price, and Wage Variations in England, Thirteenth to Nineteenth Centuries', in *Agrarhistoria på många sätt; 28 studier om manniskan och jorden. Festskrift till Janken Myrdal på hans 60-årsdag*, ed. B. Liljewall, I. A. Flygare, U. Lange, L. Ljunggren and J. Söderberg (Stockholm, 2009), 23–56.

[5] S. N. Broadberry, B. M. S. Campbell, A. Klein, B. van Leeuwen and M. Overton, *British Economic Growth 1270–1870* (Cambridge, 2015), 333–9; B. M. S. Campbell and C. Ó Gráda, 'Harvest Shortfalls, Grain Prices, and Famines in Pre-industrial England', *Journal of Economic History*, 71 (2009), 864.

[6] D. L. Farmer, 'Prices and Wages', in *The Agrarian History of England and Wales*, II, ed. Hallam, 779–91. The Froyle and other early accounts are discussed in *Manorial Records of*

1241, thereby providing an annual record of the price of this staple foodstuff spanning seven centuries.[7]

Since prices reflect money supply as well as market conditions, Figure 1 expresses the price of wheat as a percentage of the twenty-five-year moving average.[8] Price variations within two standard deviations of the mean were common, those in excess of that represent an extreme that only occasionally occurred. These were the crisis years when prices were inflated by 51 per cent or more. Rises of this magnitude were experienced on at least thirty-two occasions between 1200 and 1900 and in the five worst of these years – 1203, 1316–17, 1370 and 1439 – prices were more than double the average. More challenging still for consumers were back-to-back years of high prices, of which, following the double back-to-back crisis of 1202–4, there were seven: 1295–6, 1316–17, 1438–9, 1556–7, 1596–7, 1697–98 and 1709–10.[9] These include several of the most notorious food crises on English historical record, of which none was worse than the Great Northern European Famine of 1316–17 when prices more than doubled for two consecutive years, the daily and annual real wage rates of male agricultural and building labourers sank to their respective historical nadirs, and there was heavy excess mortality.[10] Real wage rates were also hit hard during the late Elizabethan crisis of 1596–7, although the associated price inflation was less pronounced and the demographic penalty was less punitive.[11]

It was the 1596–7 crisis that galvanised government into enacting a national Poor Law which thereafter guaranteed the basic food entitlement

Cuxham, Oxfordshire, circa 1200–1359, ed. P. D. A. Harvey, Oxfordshire Record Society 50 (1976), 21–5.

[7] G. Clark, *English Prices and Wages 1209–1914*, Global Price and Income History Group (2009). Currently, no other European country has a wheat-price series that extends over so long a period.

[8] Broadberry *et al.*, *Economic Growth*, 189–92.

[9] B. M. S. Campbell, *The Great Transition: Climate, Disease and Society in the Late-Medieval World* (Cambridge 2016), 45n; Campbell, 'Four Famines', 1–3.

[10] W. C. Jordan, *The Great Famine: Northern Europe in the Early Fourteenth Century* (Princeton, 1996); B. M. S. Campbell, 'Nature as Historical Protagonist: Environment and Society in Pre-industrial England', *Economic History Review*, 63 (2010), 285–93; G. Clark, 'The Long March of History: Farm Wages, Population, and Economic Growth, England 1209–1869', *Economic History Review*, 60 (2007), 130–4; J. H. Munro, 'The Phelps Brown and Hopkins "Basket of Consumables" Commodity Price Series and Craftsmen's Wage Series, 1264–1700: Revised by John H. Munro' (Toronto, no date), www.economics.utoronto.ca/munro5/ResearchData.html, accessed 5 Apr. 2011; J. Humphries and J. Weisdorf, 'Unreal Wages? A New Empirical Foundation for the Study of Living Standards and Economic Growth, 1260–1860', University of Oxford, Discussion Papers in Economic and Social History, Number 147 (2016), 50–3.

[11] Campbell, 'Nature', 294–5; Campbell, 'Four Famines', 25–9, 36–42, 44–5, 66–7; R. M. Smith, 'Dearth and Local Political Responses: 1280–1325 and 1580–1596/7 Compared', in *Peasants and Lords in the Medieval English Economy: Essays in Honour of Bruce M. S. Campbell*, ed. M. Kowaleski, J. Langdon and P. R. Schofield (Turnhout, 2015), 377–401.

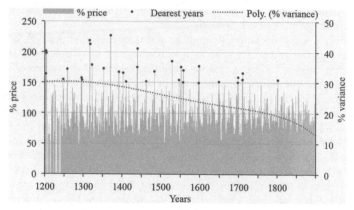

Years when wheat prices were 50% or more above average
(brackets indicate back-to-back high-price years):

Year	% price	Year	% price	Year	% price	Year	% price
1202	164	1322	179	1483	169	1697	151
1203))	201	1352	173	1528	186	1698)	159
1204	198	1370	227	1546	155	1709	155
1247	155	1391	167	1551	176	1710)	166
1258	172	1402	166	1556)	151	1801	155
1295)	158	1410	152	1557	170		
1296	154	1438	176	1596)	150		
1316)	219	1439)	206	1597	178		
1317	213	1462	152	1648	152		

Figure 1 Seven centuries of English wheat prices, 1200–1900 (annual wheat price as a percentage of the twenty-five-year moving average)
Sources and notes: Wheat prices 1209–1914 from G. Clark, *English Prices and Wages 1209–1914*, Global Price and Income History Group (2009), www.iisg.nl/hpw/data.php#united, accessed 15 Aug. 2015, extended and interpolated from 1166–1265 with prices from D. L. Farmer, 'Prices and Wages', in *The Agrarian History of England and Wales*, II: *1042–1350*, ed. H. E. Hallam (Cambridge, 1988), 787–9, and additional prices for 1237–62 from manorial accounts of Froyle, Hampshire: British Library Additional Charters 17,459–78, 13,338–9; Hampshire Record Office, Winchester, 123M88W/1. The trendline of the % variance is the 5th polynomial.

of many of those most vulnerable to scarcity.[12] Once the Poor Law was in place, the incidence of serious food crises appears to have abated and levels of price inflation moderated. There were only six seriously dear years after 1601, compared with twenty-six before, and in none of them did prices rise by more than two-thirds (Figure 1). On this measure of hardship, 1801 was the last significant national food crisis, when a bad harvest coincided with a national military emergency at a time of rapid demographic and economic change.[13] No subsequent scarcity has been as severe, not least because shortfalls in domestic agricultural output have increasingly been made good by significant food imports.[14]

Over the course of these seven centuries from 1200 to 1900, the variance of these annual wheat-price variations subsided from a peak of over 30 per cent during the worst years of the thirteenth and fourteenth centuries to less than 13 per cent at the close of the nineteenth century (Figure 1). That decline first becomes apparent towards the end of the fourteenth century, as shrinking population and monetary deflation together initially took the pressure off prices, but thereafter became a firmly established trend which grew in momentum from the end of the eighteenth century. Driving this trend were the growing effectiveness of market arbitrage, improved institutional responses to scarcity and high prices, provision of a welfare safety net to protect the purchasing power of the poor, higher agricultural productivity and, eventually, the internationalisation of food supplies.[15]

During the centuries prior to the Poor Law high-price years occurred with such frequency that most people will have experienced at least one during their lives. The longest interval between two such dear years was the sequence of forty-five years between 1483 and 1528, whereas until then food crises had occurred at intervals of between five and thirty years. Scarcity, in fact, was commonplace and, since England was poor, underdeveloped and heavily dependent upon the current year's harvest, this must always have been the case.

Among the many crisis years of dear food identified by Figure 1, there is nothing ostensibly about that of 1258 to invite closer inspection: other crises were longer, more acute and greater in their demographic impact. Nevertheless, it merits attention as the earliest food crisis upon which significant historical light can be shed, from recorded prices and harvests, the comments of contemporary chroniclers, excavated skeletal

---

[12] P. Slack, *Poverty and Policy in Tudor and Stuart England* (1988); P. Slack, *The English Poor Law, 1531–1782* (Basingstoke, 1990).

[13] Campbell, 'Four Famines', 45, 48–9.

[14] Broadberry *et al.*, *Economic Growth*, 289.

[15] Campbell and Ó Gráda, 'Harvest Shortfalls', 878–81.

remains and an array of palaeo-climatic proxies, especially precisely dated dendrochronologies.[16] It also occurred at a critical juncture, as the established momentum of demographic and economic expansion began to falter and male daily real wage rates and GDP per head both began to trend down.[17] This meant that it was the augury of worse to come, in 1295–6 and particularly 1316–17.[18] Strikingly, it accompanied, and was overshadowed by, a famous political crisis between Henry III and his barons at a formative stage in the evolution of parliamentary institutions.[19] And most intriguingly of all, it coincided with global fallout from the mega-eruption of Samalas Volcano, Indonesia, the previous year, about which sensational claims have been made.[20]

Since 1999, when Richard Stothers first drew attention to a massive mystery eruption in *c.* 1258, scientific interest in what has now been identified as the Samalas eruption has been high.[21] Comparison is made with the Volcanic Explosivity Index (VEI) 6.9 mega-eruption of Mount Tambora on the neighbouring Indonesian island of Sumbawa on 10 April 1815 and the poor weather and inferior harvests during the following

---

[16] See below, pp. 94–112.

[17] Campbell, *Great Transition*, 136, 160–2, 167, 253.

[18] P. R. Schofield, 'Dearth, Debt and the Local Land Market in a Late Thirteenth-Century Village Community', *Agricultural History Review*, 45 (1997), 1–17; M. Bailey, 'Peasant Welfare in England, 1290–1348', *Economic History Review*, 51 (1998), 223–51; Campbell, 'Four Famines', 42–4; Campbell, *Great Transition*, 191–6.

[19] R. F. Treharne, *The Baronial Plan of Reform, 1258–1263* (Manchester, 1971); S. T. Ambler, 'Simon de Montfort and King Henry III: The First Revolution in English History, 1258–1265', *History Compass*, 11 (2013), 1076–87.

[20] Museum of London Archaeology (MOLA), 'Cataclysmic Volcano Wreaked Havoc on Medieval Britain' (6 Aug. 2012), www.mola.org.uk/blog/cataclysmic-volcano-wreaked-havoc-medieval-britain; 'London's Volcanic Winter', *Current Archaeology*, 270 (Sept. 2012), www.archaeology.co.uk/articles/features/londons-volcanic-winter.htm.

[21] R. B. Stothers, 'Volcanic Dry Fogs, Climate Cooling, and Plague Pandemics in Europe and the Middle East', *Climatic Change*, 42 (1999), 713–23; R. B. Stothers, 'Climatic and Demographic Consequences of the Massive Volcanic Eruption of 1258', *Climatic Change*, 45 (2000), 361–74; C. Oppenheimer, *Eruptions that Shook the World* (Cambridge, 2011), 261–7; A. Witze, 'Thirteenth-Century Volcano Mystery May Be Solved', *Science News*, 182 (14 July 2012), 12, www.sciencenews.org/index.php/issue/id/64122/view/generic/id/341497/title/ 13th_century_volcano_mystery_may_be_solved; F. Lavigne, J.-P. Degeai, J.-C. Komorowski, S. Guillet, V. Robert, P. Lahitte, C. Oppenheimer, M. Stoffel, C. M. Vidal Surono, I. Pratomo, P. Wassmer, I. Hajdas, D. S. Hadmoko and E. de Belizal, 'Source of the Great AD 1257 Mystery Eruption Unveiled, Samalas Volcano, Rinjani Volcanic Complex, Indonesia', *Proceedings of the National Academy of Sciences*, 110 (2013), 16742–7; M. Stoffel, M. Khodri, C. Corona, S. Guillet, V. Poulain, S. Bekki, J. Guiot, B. H. Luckman, C. Oppenheimer, N. Lebas, M. Beniston and V. Masson-Delmotte, 'Estimates of Volcanic-Induced Cooling in the Northern Hemisphere over the Past 1,500 Years', *Nature Geoscience*, 8 (2015), 784–8.

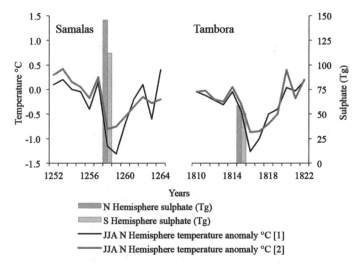

Figure 2 Comparison of the sulphate signatures and temperature impacts of the Indonesian mega-eruptions of Samalas in 1257/8 and Tambora on 10 April 1815
Sources and notes: JJA = June, July, August. Greenland (northern hemisphere) and Antarctic (southern hemisphere) sulphate deposits from C. Gao, A. Robock and C. Ammann, 'Volcanic Forcing of Climate over the Past 1500 Years: An Improved Ice Core-Based Index for Climate Models', *Journal of Geophysical Research: Atmospheres*, 113 (D2311) (2008), data: '1500 Year Ice Core-Based Stratospheric Volcanic Sulfate Data', IGBP PAGES/World Data Center for Paleoclimatology Data Contribution Series # 2009-098, NOAA/NCDC Paleoclimatology Program, Boulder CO, USA. Alternative temperature reconstructions from M. Stoffel, M. Khodri, C. Corona, S. Guillet, V. Poulain, S. Bekki, J. Guiot, B. H. Luckman, C. Oppenheimer, N. Lebas, M. Beniston and V. Masson-Delmotte, 'Estimates of Volcanic-Induced Cooling in the Northern Hemisphere over the Past 1,500 Years', *Nature Geoscience*, 8 (2015), Supplementary information S12.

'year without a summer' for which it was responsible (Figure 2).[22] It is presumed that the Samalas eruption likely had similarly serious human consequences on a global scale. In fact, for scientists interested in volcanic

[22] J. D. Post, *The Last Great Subsistence Crisis in the Western World* (Baltimore and London, 1977); J. Z. de Boer and D. T. Sanders, *Volcanoes in Human History: The Far-Reaching Effects of Major Eruptions* (Princeton and Oxford, 2002), 138–55; C. Oppenheimer, 'Climatic, Environmental and Human Consequences of the Largest Known Historic Eruption: Tambora Volcano (Indonesia) 1815', *Progress in Physical Geography*, 27 (2003), 230–59.

forcing of global climates, the 1257/8 mega-eruption stands out as potentially one of the most dramatic events of the entire Holocene.[23] The possibility that this catastrophic eruption triggered the abnormal weather that ruined harvests and precipitated the serious food crisis in England, thereby heightening latent political tensions, provides a story almost too compelling to resist telling. Whether this presumed historical chain of events fits the available evidence is another matter.

I The chronology of the crisis: prices, harvests and oak growth

Direct evidence of the harvest shortfalls responsible for the food crisis of 1258 comes from recorded grain prices, principally wheat, and the harvest receipts of demesne producers. The prime extant sources for both are the celebrated Winchester Pipe Rolls, the manorial accounts of Froyle in north-east Hampshire (a property of St Mary's nunnery, Winchester) and a scatter of other early accounts.[24] The Froyle accounts are crucial to establishing what happened to prices (Table 1) and harvests (Table 2) from the 1240s through to the early 1260s because they alone provide almost uninterrupted annual coverage of this period. Harvest information is lacking solely for 1245, 1247, 1254 and 1261 (Table 2). Paul Harvey has deciphered the dating of these rolls, which are obscurely dated by year of abbess, and the chronologies of prices and harvests obtained from them correlate exactly with those obtained from the securely dated neighbouring estates of the bishops of Winchester (Figures 3 and 4A).[25]

The Winchester Pipe Rolls are far more voluminous, extending to enrolled accounts for upwards of three dozen manors in any given year. The bishops' estates were spread across southern England, from Buckinghamshire to Somerset, but with a strong focus on Hampshire.[26] Relevant harvest information for all manors on the estate has been extracted by J. Z. Titow.[27] Unfortunately, the Pipe Rolls are less than continuous during the critical decades of the 1240s, 1250s and 1260s. In particular, there is no harvest information for 1250, 1255, 1258–61 – disappointingly – and 1263 (Table 2). The Froyle accounts are therefore

---

[23]C. Gao, A. Robock and C. Ammann, 'Volcanic Forcing of Climate over the Past 1500 Years: An Improved Ice Core-Based Index for Climate Models', *Journal of Geophysical Research: Atmospheres*, 113 (D2311) (2008); J. L. Brooke, *Climate Change and the Course of Global History: A Rough Journey* (Cambridge, 2014), 371, 382–3. Holocene = the period of *c.* 11,500 years since the last ice age.

[24]R. Britnell, 'The Winchester Pipe Rolls and their Historians', in *The Winchester Pipe Rolls and Medieval English Society*, ed. Richard Britnell (Woodbridge, 2003), 1–13; *Records of Cuxham*, 16–29.

[25]*Records of Cuxham*, 22n; Tables 1 and 2.

[26]For a map of the estates see the preface to *Winchester Pipe Rolls*.

[27]Hampshire Record Office, Winchester (HRO), 97097 Titow Research Papers 97M97/B.

Table 1 *Southern English wheat prices 1241–69*

	Indexed wheat price (100 = mean 1252–4):			
Years	(A) Southern England	(B) Froyle, Hants.	A and B interpolated	Interpolated de-trended
1240				
1241		87	*78*	75
1242		129	*116*	112
1243		87	*78*	73
1244		110	*99*	93
1245	61	70	66	59
1246	85		*96*	88
1247	158	206	182	173
1248	150		*165*	155
1249	82	82	82	71
1250		130	*123*	112
1251	84	105	95	82
1252	86	84	85	72
1253	131	135	133	119
1254	83	81	82	67
1255	76		*69*	59
1256		125	*137*	121
1257	180	138	159	142
1258	204	225	215	197
1259		138	*121*	102
1260	109	189	149	129
1261	114	115	114	93
1262	123		123	101
1263	106		106	84
1264	102		102	79
1265	114		114	90
1266	110		110	85
1267	125		125	99
1268	97		97	70
1269	131		131	104

Sources: Southern England: G. Clark, *English Prices and Wages 1209–1914*, Global Price and Income History Group (2009); Froyle, Hants.: British Library Additional Charters 17,459–78, 13,338–9; Hampshire Record Office, Winchester, 123M88W/1.

Table 2 *Quantities harvested on the Winchester estates and the manor of Froyle, Hampshire, 1240–69*

		Harvested quantity (quarters):			
	Winchester estate (mean per demesne):	Manor of Froyle, Hants:			
Years	Wheat	Wheat	Winter and spring barley	Oats	Legumes
1240		267.75	48.25	269.19	1.63
1241		[a]228.88	58.50	185.63	1.50
1242		244.50	69.00	307.88	13.00
1243		257.00	78.38	338.63	13.63
1244	109.03	303.63	110.00	385.13	5.25
1245	99.03				
1246	83.63	362.31	122.88	364.00	2.50
1247	87.56				
1248	108.89	321.25	112.00	254.00	9.88
1249		249.00	132.75	432.00	8.63
1250		242.88	132.00	334.00	12.13
1251	110.04	307.50	110.50	285.88	11.13
1252	97.36	385.50	107.63	323.25	12.38
1253	100.88	335.00	184.25	351.75	12.00
1254	103.58				
1255		292.38	115.00	370.88	13.00
1256	80.08	146.88	91.13	252.25	12.00
1257	79.28	239.38	83.06	271.38	10.50
1258		337.63	[b]117.75	290.25	9.00
1259		[a]252.38	75.63	262.25	16.75
1260		303.88	123.63	244.88	3.13
1261					
1262	99.04	187.50	69.13	229.38	8.13
1263					
1264	83.40				
1265	97.04				
1266					
1267	79.15				
1268	88.09				
1269	[c]80.68				

Sources and notes:
[a]Includes small quantities of rye and maslin.
[b]Includes 28 quarters of dredge.
[c]3 demesnes only (37 in all other years).
Winchester estates: Hampshire Record Office, Winchester (HRO), 97097 Titow Research Papers 97M97/B. Froyle, Hants.: British Library Additional Charters 17,459–78, 13,338–9; HRO 123M88W/1.

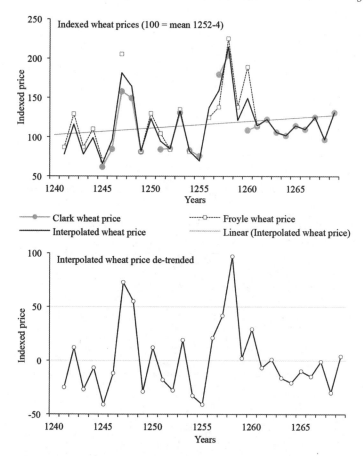

Figure 3 Indexed southern English wheat prices, 1241–69 (100 = mean 1252–4)
Source: See Table 1.

invaluable for plugging these gaps, with 1261, 1263 and 1266 the only years lacking harvest information from either source (Table 2).

For the sale price of grain, there is no more abundant source of information during the thirteenth century than the Winchester Pipe Rolls, hence David Farmer drew extensively on this source for his reconstructed wheat-price series.[28] Farmer's price data have in turn been re-analysed by

[28] Farmer, 'Prices and Wages', 779–89; University of Saskatchewan Archives, 'The Papers of David Farmer', MG 145 (hereafter 'Farmer Papers'), vols. 14–16.

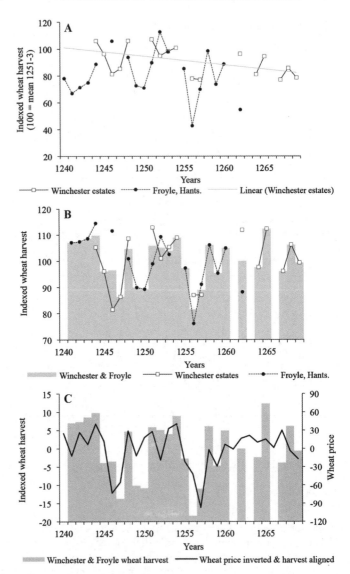

Figure 4 Wheat harvests on the Winchester estates and the manor of Froyle, Hampshire, 1240–69

Sources and notes: (A) Absolute quantities harvested from Table 1; (B) Winchester harvests de-trended, Froyle harvests as % of previous 7 years and combined index of harvests; (C) Combined index of Winchester and Froyle harvests and de-trended wheat price from Table 2, inverted and moved back 1 year.

Gregory Clark and augmented with additional information from other sources to provide the master grain-price series running from 1209 to 1914 hosted on the Global Prices and Incomes website.[29] These are the prices tabulated in Table 1 and plotted in Figure 3A for the years 1240–69. Note the steady annual inflation rate of 1.7 per cent across this thirty-year period stoked by the expanding money supply. Annual price variations were, however, largely the result of fluctuations in harvest output, with prices in year x typically reflecting the harvest in year x-1. Although they do not measure output directly, prices have the great merit of reflecting supply conditions over an area far more extensive than a single manor. This means that wheat prices recorded in the Froyle accounts can be used to fill many of the gaps in Clark's master wheat-price series (Table 1 and Figure 3A). On the evidence of the wheat-price series interpolated from this raw information, prices were low in 1254 and 1255, rose steeply in 1256, rose again in 1257 and then soared in 1258 – the year of the national food crisis – before falling back in 1259. The next year, 1260, brought a rebound before prices finally subsided and stabilised.

Stripping out the effects of inflation brings these annual price fluctuations into sharper focus (Figure 3B). This identifies 1247 and 1248 as conspicuously high-price years, when prices were inflated by over 50 per cent, with the implication that harvests had been poor in 1246 and 1247. A run of otherwise low-price years followed, to which 1253 was the sole exception, culminating in 1254 and 1255 when, presumably because of bumper harvests, prices were 33 per cent and 41 per cent below trend. In 1256, 1257 and 1258, prices then rose progressively, until they were almost double their normal level. At the peak of this inflationary spike in June and July 1258, chroniclers reported that wheat was selling at 15 shillings a quarter in London and 20 shillings in Northampton.[30] This compares with an average sale price of a little over 3 shillings in 1254–5.[31] Prices fell back sharply in 1259, as the supply situation briefly improved, but then rose again with the return of grain shortage in 1260 to 29 per cent above trend. This was the last of five consecutive years when prices were consistently above normal. The price evidence implies that there were significant harvest shortfalls in 1255, 1256 and 1257, an adequate harvest in 1258 and then a final poor harvest in 1259. The food crisis of 1258 was therefore the product of a back-to-back supply-side failure during the previous two years.

[29] Clark, *Prices and Wages*, drawing upon 'Farmer Papers'.

[30] *The Chronicle of Bury St Edmunds 1212–1301*, ed. and trans. A. Gransden (1964), 22; D. J. Keene, 'Crisis Management in London's Food Supply, 1250–1500', in *Commercial Activity, Markets and Entrepreneurs in the Middle Ages: Essays in Honour of Richard Britnell*, ed. B. Dodds and C. D. Liddy (Woodbridge, 2011), 52.

[31] Farmer, 'Prices and Wages', 789.

Corroboration of this price chronology is provided by recorded harvested volumes on the thirty-seven demesnes of the Winchester estate and that at Froyle, as tabulated in Table 2 and plotted in Figure 4A. Note that on the Winchester estates annual variations were superimposed upon a downward output trend, as the bishops scaled down direct management on their demesnes from its peak in the 1230s.[32] Figure 4B therefore re-plots the same information de-trended. On the St Mary Abbey demesne at Froyle, in contrast, output rose steadily to a peak in the early 1250s, before contracting. In Figure 4B, therefore, this output information is re-plotted as a percentage of the mean of the previous seven years. Interpolation between these two de-trended series then gives a single indexed output series for the entire period 1240–69 with gaps only in 1261, 1263 and 1266 (Figures 4B and C).

On the Winchester estates, but not at Froyle, the poor harvests of 1246 and 1247 that preceded the high prices of 1247 and 1248 stand out clearly. The same applies to the dismal harvests of 1256 and 1257 responsible for the high prices of 1257 and 1258. In 1256 and 1257, wheat harvests on the Winchester estates were 22–3 per cent below the average of 1251–4, while at Froyle the harvest of 1256 was less than half that of 1250–3 and the 1257 harvest fell short by 25 per cent. These were very substantial shortfalls and, at Froyle, were compounded by oats harvests deficient by 22 per cent and 16 per cent, which must have hit the budgets and diets of the poor hard, since oats were a staple component of the bare-bones basket of consumables.[33] Thus far, the price and harvest information accord well. Prices imply that the 1258 harvest was not particularly defective, and that was certainly the case at Froyle although there is unfortunately no corresponding information for the Winchester estates. The one exception is Highclere, for which harvest information for 1258 and 1259 does survive, and in neither year was there a shortfall.[34] Complete Pipe Rolls are missing for 1258–61 but in 1262, when the next Pipe Roll survives, output of wheat across the estate was back to normal and the crisis had evidently passed.

The available price and harvest information from southern England thus concur in identifying the 1256 and 1257 harvests as a major back-to-back failure, responsible for the acute scarcity and massively inflated food prices of 1258. This was the second and more serious of two back-to-back harvest shortfalls to have occurred within the space of a dozen years. Not until the early 1260s did grain output and prices return

[32] J. Z. Titow, 'Land and Population on the Bishop of Winchester's Estates 1209–1350' (Ph.D. thesis, University of Cambridge, 1962), 15, 21–2, 50; B. M. S. Campbell, 'A Unique Estate and a Unique Source', in *Winchester Pipe Rolls*, 27.

[33] Broadberry *et al.*, *Economic Growth*, 333.

[34] The National Archives, PRO SC6/1141/22.

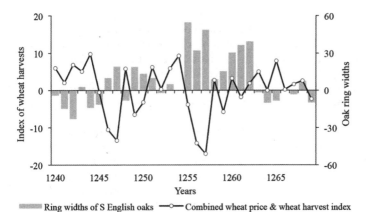

Figure 5 Combined price and harvest index of wheat harvests and the ring widths of southern English oaks, 1240–69
Sources and notes: Wheat-harvest and wheat-price index from Figure 4C; data on Oxford oak ring widths and southern English ring widths supplied by M. G. L. Baillie.

to their pre-crisis levels. The close fit between harvests and prices is readily apparent from Figure 4C, where wheat prices in year *x* + *1* have been inverted and moved back a year to align with the harvest information in year *x*. Combining these two time series maximises use of the available information and yields the index of wheat harvests plotted in Figure 5. The significant double shortfall of 1246–7 emerges clearly but is eclipsed by the greater reduction that evidently began in 1255 but was at its most pronounced in 1256–7. The 1259 harvest was also indifferent and it was not until 1262 and 1263 that output was restored to its former level.

Since the growing conditions that favoured oaks were more or less the opposite of those that suited grain (oaks thriving on cool and wet, and grain on hot and dry, summers), for comparison the ring widths of southern English oaks are also plotted in Figure 5.[35] The correlation between the two series is a strongly negative -0.59. Oaks put on wider than average growth rings in 1246 and 1247, which implies that the poor harvests of these two years were due to cool and wet summer (i.e. June, July and August) weather. Oaks then put on far wider rings in 1255–7 – some of the widest, in fact, on record – which indicates that abnormal weather conditions prevailed at that time, boosting oak growth but devastating

[35] Campbell, 'Nature', 297–301.

grain crops. This wide-ring phenomenon also shows up in a master chronology of British Isles oaks and an oak chronology for northern France.[36] The following year proved to be as unexceptional for oaks as it was for grain, but from 1259 to 1262 oak growth increased again, at a time when grain was yielding indifferently, possibly due to the growth stimulus induced by additional diffuse radiation caused by lingering stratospheric volcanic aerosol clouds from the 1257 mega-eruption.[37] This sustained wide-ring episode then ended abruptly in 1263.

Taken together, the index of wheat harvests and chronology of oak ring widths indicate a major eight-year growth anomaly from 1255 to 1262, divided into two phases pivoting on 1258. The first, from 1255 to 1257, was the most pronounced and led to the food crisis of 1258. The second, following the 1257 mega-eruption, was more muted and lasted from 1259 to 1262. This bears out Derek Keene's observation that 'the poor harvest of 1255 [sic] and even that of 1257 may have arisen from a "normal" pattern of bad weather and the successive atmospheric events of 1258–60 from a single eruption in 1257'.[38]

II The chronology of the crisis: chronicles and climate reconstructions

Contemporary chroniclers had a good deal to say about the weather and abundance or otherwise of harvests during these years, and their qualitative observations can be matched against reconstructions of spring and early summer (March to July) precipitation (Figure 6A) and summer (June, July, August) temperatures (Figure 6B) derived from the precisely dated growth rings of trees.[39] Further amplification of this picture is provided by (i) an annually resolved multi-proxy reconstruction of the North Atlantic Oscillation, which determined pressure gradients and thereby drove winter circulation patterns over Europe, and (ii)

---

[36] British Isles oak dendro-chronology provided by M. G. L. Baillie. In northern France, the widest oak growth rings occurred in 1256 (data supplied by Francis Ludlow).

[37] A. Robock, 'Cooling Following Large Volcanic Eruptions Corrected for the Effect of Diffuse Radiation on Tree Rings', *Geophysical Research Letters*, 32 (2005), 4 pp.

[38] Keene, 'Crisis Management', 55.

[39] R. J. S. Wilson, D. Miles, N. J. Loader, T. M. Melvin, L. Cunningham, R. J. Cooper and K. R. Briffa, 'A Millennial Long March–July Precipitation Reconstruction for Southern-Central England', *Climate Dynamics*, 40 (2012), 997–1017, www.ncdc.noaa.gov/paleo/study/12907, accessed 19 Aug. 2016; R. J. Cooper, T. M. Melvin, I. Tyers, R. J. S. Wilson and K. R. Briffa, 'A Tree-Ring Reconstruction of East Anglian (UK) Hydroclimate Variability over the Last Millennium', *Climate Dynamics*, 40 (2013), 1019–39, www.ncdc.noaa.gov/paleo/study/12896, accessed 19 Aug. 2016; J. Luterbacher, J. P. Werner, J. E. Smerdon, L. Fernández-Donado, F. J. González-Rouco, D. Barriopedro, F. C. Ljungqvist, U. Büntgen, E. Zorita, S. Wagner and J. Esper, 'European Summer Temperatures since Roman Times', *Environmental Research Letters*, 11 (2016), 024001, www.ncdc.noaa.gov/paleo/study/19600, accessed 19 Aug. 2016.

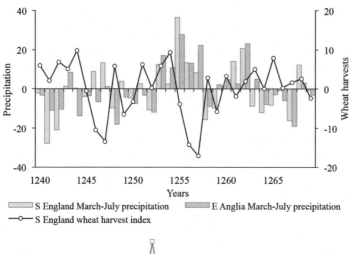

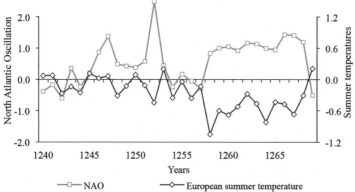

Figure 6 Index of wheat harvests in southern England, March–July precipitation in southern England and East Anglia, the North Atlantic Oscillation and European summer (June, July, August) temperatures, 1240–69

Sources and notes: Index of wheat harvests from Figure 5. March–July precipitation in southern England and East Anglia from R. J. S. Wilson, D. Miles, N. J. Loader, T. M. Melvin, L. Cunningham, R. J. Cooper and K. R. Briffa, 'A Millennial Long March–July Precipitation Reconstruction for Southern-Central England', *Climate Dynamics*, 40 (2012), 997–1017, www.ncdc.noaa.gov/paleo/study/12907, accessed 19 Aug. 2016; and R. J. Cooper, T. M. Melvin, I. Tyers, R. J. S. Wilson and K. R. Briffa, 'A Tree-Ring Reconstruction of East Anglian (UK) Hydroclimate Variability over the Last Millennium', *Climate Dynamics*, 40 (2013), 1019–39, www.ncdc.noaa.gov/paleo/study/12896, accessed 19 Aug. 2016. North Atlantic Oscillation from P. Ortega, F. Lehner, D. Swingedouw,

a tree-ring-based annual reconstruction of summer (June/July/August) wetness/dryness across the Old World.[40] Matching these reconstructions against the comments of contemporary chroniclers is especially revealing, for the latter shed light on the timing of meteorological events and their effects on agricultural activities and give information about weather conditions during the winter months when trees were dormant.

The thirteenth century has been described as 'the golden age of the monastic historians' and the available chronicle information is particularly rich for the eventful 1250s.[41] Care nevertheless needs to be exercised in distinguishing between first-hand observations and those reported at second hand and not always in the year in which they occurred. Dating can therefore be a problem. Of contemporary chroniclers, Matthew Paris, a monk at the Benedictine Abbey of St Alban's in Hertfordshire, twenty-five miles to the north of London, made a particular point of commenting upon weather conditions and unusual environmental events either during the course of the year or in his annual summary of each year's more notable events.[42] For example, over the

---

[40] P. Ortega, F. Lehner, D. Swingedouw, V. Masson-Delmotte, C. C. Raible, M. Casado and P. Yiou, 'A Model-Tested North Atlantic Oscillation Reconstruction for the Past Millennium', *Nature*, 523 (2015), 71–4, www.ncdc.noaa.gov/paleo/study/18935, accessed 31 July 2016; E. R. Cook, R. Seager, Y. Kushnir, K. R. Briffa, U. Büntgen, D. Frank, P. J. Krusic, W. Tegel, G. Van Der Schrier, L. Andreu-Hayles, M. Baillie, C. Baittinger, N. Bleicher, N. Bonde, D. Brown, M. Carrer, R. Cooper, K. Čufar, C. Dittmar, J. Esper, C. Griggs, B. Gunnarson, B. Günther, E. Gutierrez, K. Haneca, S. Helama, F. Herzig, K. U. Heussner, J. Hofmann, P. Janda, R. Kontic, N. Köse, T. Kyncl, T. Levanič, H. Linderholm, S. Manning, T. M. Melvin, D. Miles, B. Neuwirth, K. Nicolussi, P. Nola, M. Panayotov, I. Popa, A. Rothe, K. Seftigen, A. Seim, H. Svarva, M. Svoboda, T. Thun, M. Timonen, R. Touchan, V. Trotsiuk, V. Trouet, F. Walder, T. Ważny, R. Wilson and C. Zang, 'Old World Megadroughts and Pluvials during the Common Era', *Science Advances*, 1 (2015), e1500561.

[41] W. Lewis Jones, 'Latin Chroniclers from the Eleventh to the Thirteenth Centuries', in *Cambridge History of English Literature*, I: *From the Beginnings to the Cycles of Romance*, ed. Sir A. W. Ward and A. R. Waller (Cambridge, 1907), 178. For a compendium of contemporary comments on the weather, see C. E. Britton, *A Meteorological Chronology to A.D. 1450*, Meteorological Office Geophysical Memoirs 70 (1937).

[42] Matthew Paris's year ran from Christmas to Christmas.

V. Masson-Delmotte, C. C. Raible, M. Casado and P. Yiou, 'A Model-Tested North Atlantic Oscillation Reconstruction for the Past Millennium', *Nature*, 523 (2015), 71–4, www.ncdc.noaa.gov/paleo/study/18935, accessed 31 July 2016. European summer temperatures from J. Luterbacher, J. P. Werner, J. E. Smerdon, L. Fernández-Donado, F. J. González-Rouco, D. Barriopedro, F. C. Ljungqvist, U. Büntgen, E. Zorita, S. Wagner and J. Esper, 'European Summer Temperatures since Roman Times', *Environmental Research Letters*, 11 (2016), 024001, www.ncdc.noaa.gov/paleo/study/19600, accessed 19 Aug. 2016.

course of 1251 he reports on serious sea flooding in Friesland, a terrible storm on St Dunstan's Day (19 May) at Windsor and St Alban's, extensive coastal flooding in England in September and then sums up the year as 'stormy, turbulent, and awful, with lightning' but also 'productive of corn and fruit in sufficiency, even to abundance', a verdict that is corroborated by the index of wheat harvests (Figure 6A).[43] Unfortunately, his unusually informative record of weather conditions ends prematurely with his death in 1259, at the very point when climatic fallout from the 1257 eruption of Samalas Volcano is an issue.

The sea flooding and turbulent weather of 1251 were precursors of worse to come the following year when, according to a recent multi-proxy reconstruction at annual resolution, the North Atlantic Oscillation was more strongly positive than at any time in the previous 200 years (Figure 6B). This accounts for the powerful south-westerly gales which Matthew Paris described 'blowing with a dreadful roaring and with fierce violence' at the start of the year. These gave way in March to four months of 'intolerable heat and drought' unrelieved by 'any fall of rain or dew' that lasted until well into July. The Tewkesbury and Welsh annalists comment on the same phenomenon.[44] These contemporary descriptions are consistent with the below average rainfall registered by the tree-ring-based indexes of precipitation in southern England and East Anglia (Figure 6A) and corresponding reconstruction of drought conditions prevailing that summer right across Europe from Iberia and Ireland in the west to Romania in the east.[45] The upshot in England was an indifferent wheat harvest (Figure 6) and poor barley and oats harvests, which, on the testimony of the Dunstable annalist, gave rise the following year to 'a dearth of corn in England'.[46] When rain finally came in September, it was incessant and was accompanied by a 'deadly disease amongst the cattle', which had gorged themselves on the sudden flush of

---

[43] *Matthew Paris's English History: From the Year 1235 to 1273*, trans. and ed. J. A. Giles (vols. II and III, s.l., 1853 and 1854), II, 446, 465–7; *Matthai Parisiensis, Monachi Sancti Albani, Chronica Majora*, ed. H. R. Luard (vols. IV and V, 1872 and 1880) (hereafter *Chronica Majora*), V, 240, 258, 263–4, 265–6. Paris makes no mention of the severe start to winter 1251 reported in Ireland by the Annals of Lough Ce: Britton, *Meteorological Chronology*, 99.

[44] *Annales Monastici*, ed. H. R. Luard (5 vols., 1864–9), I, 147 (Annals of Tewkesbury, 1252): 'In the same year drought prevailed for four months, causing the grass to disappear.' *Brut y Tywysogion or The Chronicle of the Princes of Wales*, trans. and ed. J. W. ab Ithel (1860), 337: 'the heat of the sun was so great that all the earth became so dry therefrom, that no fruit grew on the trees or (crops in) the fields and neither fish of the sea nor of the river was obtained'.

[45] Cook *et al.*, 'Old World Megadroughts', map for 1252.

[46] *Annales monastici*, I, 189 (Annals of Dunstable, 1253): 'in many places a quarter of wheat sold for 8 shillings, and more; but at Dunstable for 5 shillings'. On the Winchester estates, the harvest of barley, oats and dredge was down by 10 per cent: calculated from HRO 97097 Titow Research Papers 97M97/B.

grass growth.[47] Matthew Paris summed up the year as 'one of trouble to the whole of mankind' and in the palaeo-environmental record it stands out as a year of climate extremes right across the northern hemisphere. There is a clear implication that climate forcing of some sort was very strong at this time.

The next two years brought a significant amelioration of these conditions. The North Atlantic Oscillation weakened, spring and summer precipitation over southern England and a broad swathe of Europe returned to slightly above normal and the English wheat harvest was average or better (Figure 6A). Matthew Paris notes more heavy rain in 1253 and some serious river and sea flooding but not enough to prevent the year from delivering such an 'abundance of corn and fruit, that the price of a measure of corn fell to thirty pence'.[48] Partly because the North Atlantic Oscillation had turned negative and anti-cyclonic conditions had set in, the winter of 1253–4 was long and hard and 1254 brought very unsettled weather, such that 'from Ascension-day (25 May) till that of All Saints (1 November), scarcely two or three days passed undisturbed by some commotion of the elements'.[49] Yet, notwithstanding these unsettled conditions, Matthew Paris reported that 'this year throughout was abundantly productive in fruit and corn, so that the price of a measure of corn fell to two shillings; and in like proportion oats, and all other kinds of corn and pulse fell in price, to the benefit of the poor'.[50] Prices remained low until well into the following year, making 1254 and 1255 two cheap years in a row and possibly lulling producers and consumers into a false sense of security (Figures 3A and 6A).

According to tree-ring-based climate reconstructions, the spring and early summer of 1255 proved to be exceptionally wet across southern England and East Anglia (Figure 6A), and June, July and August then brought heavy rain to Ireland, England and much of France.[51] Matthew Paris, in contrast, while confirming the general wetness of February and early March, dwells upon the persistent dry northerly winds that prevailed from the middle of March to the beginning of June, which dried up the atmosphere and lent it a citron-like hue.[52] Timely rain then rescued the

---

[47] *Paris's English History*, II, 514–15; *Chronica Majora*, V, 321. *Brut y Tywysogion*, 337, stresses the extensive and destructive flooding that occurred that autumn in Wales.

[48] *Paris's English History*, III, 60; *Chronica Majora*, V, 420.

[49] *Paris's English History*, III, 96; *Chronica Majora*, V, 465.

[50] *Paris's English History*, III, 110–11; *Chronica Majora*, V, 483. Towards the end of the year, a deadly murrain of horses struck in both England and France: *The Flowers of History, especially such as Relate to the Affairs of Britain. From the Beginning of the World to the Year 1307. Collected by Matthew of Westminster*, II: *From A.D. 1066 to A.D. 1307*, trans. C. D. Yonge (1853), 340.

[51] Cook *et al.*, 'Old World Megadroughts', map for 1255.

[52] *Paris's English History*, III, 115, 120; *Chronica Majora*, V, 488, 495.

situation and produced a good harvest.[53] Provisions therefore continued cheap, although at Froyle, possibly because of the summer rain, less wheat was harvested than in previous years (Figure 4). In contrast, growing conditions proved ideal for southern English oaks, which put on some of the widest growth rings on record (Figure 5).

Rainfall then remained well above average for the next two years. Oaks continued to grow vigorously in 1256 and 1257 (Figure 5), precipitation levels across southern England and East Anglia as reconstructed remained elevated (Figure 6A), and in 1256 much of Europe experienced another unusually wet summer.[54] In June, following a succession of storms, the River Ouse burst its banks and swept away houses at Bedford and the year ended with torrential rain and serious flooding in the north of England, where houses, mills and seven bridges were destroyed.[55] Matthew Paris leaves no doubt that in 1256 the weather had taken a turn for the worse. He reports that 'from the day of the Assumption of the Blessed Virgin [15 August] to the anniversary of her Purification [2 February], the rain ceased not to fall daily in deluges, which rendered the roads impassable and the fields barren'.[56] His observation that by 'the end of harvest the corn was rotted in the ear' is borne out by a slump in the amounts of wheat harvested on the Winchester estates and at Froyle and a sharp rise in the prices of staple foodstuffs (Figures 3 and 4B).[57] This would prove to be the first of two consecutive bad harvests.

The following winter was mild but overcast without a single frosty or fine day and the ensuing year 'beyond measure stormy and rainy'.[58] The continuing inclement weather hit the winter-sown crops especially hard:

> from the first day of February up to . . . the beginning of May the air was disturbed by storms of wind and rain, which rendered England like a muddy marsh. The furrows bore the appearance of ditches; the ditches were like marshes; and the rivers seemed to be arms of the sea. Thus a period of three months rendered the earth barren and fruitless, so that many farmers sowed fresh seed in their land.[59]

It is therefore no surprise that 1257 delivered another deficient wheat harvest (Figure 4B), but this was then compounded by renewed heavy

[53] *Paris's English History*, III, 121, 155–6; *Chronica Majora*, V, 496, 536–7.

[54] Cook *et al.*, 'Old World Megadroughts', map for 1256.

[55] *Paris's English History*, III, 175, 212; *Chronica Majora*, V, 561, 607.

[56] *Paris's English History*, III, 207; *Chronica Majora*, V, 600.

[57] *Paris's English History*, III, 207; *Chronica Majora*, V, 600. In April the following year, Matthew Paris reports that Earl Richard of Cornwall, while waiting to take ship at Yarmouth, had to pay over the odds for essential provisions: 'a measure of wheat was sold for fifteen shillings, and the same quantity of oats for six shillings; fowls and ducks were very scarce and extremely dear; and beef and mutton were sold at any price that the venders chose to fix', *Paris's English History*, III, 228–9; *Chronica Majora*, V, 628; *Chronicle of Bury St Edmunds*, 21.

[58] *Paris's English History*, III, 207, 255–6; *Chronica Majora*, V, 600, 660–1.

[59] *Paris's English History*, III, 230–1; *Chronica Majora*, V, 630.

rain at harvest time, which threatened as well the yields of spring-sown oats and barley.[60] East Anglian chroniclers John of Oxnead and John de Taxter both mention that heavy rain in mid-July flooded land, bore away bridges, houses and mills, rendered roads impassable, ruined the hay meadows and destroyed crops.[61] Fear of a second harvest failure prompted fasting, prayer and religious processions but these pious acts proved incapable of converting scarcity into abundance.[62] The upshot was that 'whatever had been sown in winter, had budded in spring, and grown ripe in summer, was stifled and destroyed by the autumnal inundations'.[63]

By autumn 1257, the damage had been done, the grain harvest had fallen seriously short for two years in succession and the next year, 1258, bar large-scale food imports, an escalating national food crisis was unavoidable. Grain already scarce and dear had become scarcer and dearer. By the year's close, wheat had risen sharply in price to 10 shillings a quarter, fruit was scarce, 'land lay uncultivated' and 'great numbers of people' were dying from 'starvation'.[64] This, of course, had been the year when, sometime in late spring or summer (and certainly no earlier than May), the Samalas Volcano erupted in Indonesia but as far as the English wheat harvest was concerned, the disaster had already been set in train by the floods and inundations of the previous winter.[65] The one hint that by the end of the year England may have been experiencing fallout from a major stratospheric sulphate injection is Matthew Paris's mention that chronic breathing difficulties were troubling numbers of people.[66] Climate reconstructions nevertheless demonstrate that there was a lag of approximately a year before the eruption's main forcing effects were felt (Figure 2). These show up in a sudden drop in European summer temperatures and marked strengthening of the North Atlantic Oscillation in 1258 (Figure 6B). As Matthew Paris cryptically observed,

---

[60]Spring-sown barley, oats and dredge on the Winchester estates fared unevenly, with output down by at least 10 per cent on over a third of the bishop's demesnes: calculated from HRO 97097 Titow Research Papers 97M97/B.

[61] *Rerum Britannicarum medii aevi scriptores* or *Chronicles and memorials of Great Britain and Ireland during the Middle Ages*, XIII: *Chronica Johannis de Oxnedes*, ed. Sir H. Ellis (1859), 212; *Chronicle of Bury St Edmunds*, 22.

[62] *Paris's English History*, III, 242, 255–6; *Chronica Majora*, V, 644–5, 661.

[63] *Paris's English History*, III, 255–6; *Chronica Majora*, V, 661.

[64] *Paris's English History*, III, 255–6; *Chronica Majora*, V, 661.

[65]Lavigne *et al.*, 'AD 1257 Mystery Eruption'. A dark total lunar eclipse reported at Genoa on 12 Nov. 1258 bears testimony to the continuing suspension of volcanic aerosols in the atmosphere and implies that the eruption had occurred sometime during the previous eighteen months: S. Guillet, C. Corona, M. Stoffel, M. Khodri, F. Lavigne, P. Ortega, N. Eckert, P. Dkengne Sielenou, V. Daux, O. Churakova, N. Davi, J.-L. Edouard, Y. Zhang, B. H. Luckman, V. S. Myglan, J. Guiot, M. Beniston, V. Masson-Delmotte and C. Oppenheimer, 'Climate Response to the Samalas Volcanic Eruption in 1257 Revealed by Proxy Records', *Nature Geoscience*, 10 (2) (2017), Supplementary information S4.

[66] *Paris's English History*, III, 255–6; *Chronica Majora*, V, 661.

'this year throughout was very dissimilar to all previous ones, bringing disease and death, and heavy storms of wind and rain'.[67] The unusual weather and atmospheric conditions provided the context rather than the cause of both the food crisis and the political row between Henry III and his barons which separately now came to a head.

III The chronology of the crisis: the crisis breaks

Details of the human tragedy that began in 1257 and then became greatly magnified over the course of the following year are given in most of the English chronicles. John de Taxter, the Bury St Edmund's annalist, makes the key point that 'there was a great shortage of everything *because of the floods of the previous year* [emphasis added]'.[68] After two deficient harvests, the inflated price of staple foodstuffs provoked considerable comment, with wheat, which as recently as 1254 had sold for as little as 2 shillings, costing at its peak as much as 15–20 shillings a quarter.[69] Unable to afford grain, those on the lowest incomes desperately made shift with such alternative foodstuffs as 'horsemeat, the bark of trees and even more unpleasant things'.[70] The Tewkesbury and London chroniclers plus Matthew Paris, Matthew of Westminster and John de Taxter all concur that it was the poor who bore the brunt of the crisis and succumbed in greatest numbers to starvation and famine-related diseases.[71] To add to their misery, after an unusually mild start to the winter, from February a bitter northerly wind 'blew without intermission, a continued frost prevailed, accompanied by snow and such unendurable cold, that it bound up the face of the earth, sorely afflicted the poor, suspended all cultivation, and killed . . . the ewes and lambs'.[72] Harsh weather continued through to June and then in July was followed by heavy rain, which, by delaying and damaging the next harvest, both heightened and prolonged the food crisis, prompting further religious processions and prayers for deliverance from the persistent bad weather and accompanying state of famine.[73] To contemporaries, it must have looked as if harvests were about to fail for the third consecutive year.

[67] *Paris's English History*, III, 312; *Chronica Majora*, V, 728.

[68] *Chronicle of Bury St Edmunds*, 22.

[69] *Ibid.*; Keene, 'Crisis Management', 51–2.

[70] *Chronicle of Bury St Edmunds*, 22.

[71] *Close Rolls of the Reign of Henry III Preserved in the Public Record Office*, III: *A.D. 1256–1259* (1932), 212: on 16 Apr. 1258, orders were sent to the sheriffs of Lincolnshire, Norfolk, Suffolk and Essex to bury paupers without the need for a coroner's inquest. The next month, report was made that many vagrants were dying due to famine: *Annales Monastici*, I, 441–2 (Annals of Burton, 1258).

[72] *Paris's English History*, III, 266; *Chronica Majora*, V, 674.

[73] *Paris's English History*, III, 299–300; *Chronica Majora*, V, 710–11. Matthew Paris and Matthew of Westminster both report that torrential rain in late June caused the River

For those bereft of material support, confronted by destitution and driven by hunger, London, with the greatest concentrations of wealth and charitable institutions in the realm, was a magnet, especially once it became known that in March the city had taken delivery of fifty shiploads of relief food supplies from Germany.[74] The city, however, lacked the welfare and financial resources necessary to cope with the influx of famine refugees.[75] As the Chronicles of the Mayors and Sheriffs of London reported, 'the people from the villages resorted to the City for food; and there, upon the famine waxing still greater, many thousand persons perished'.[76] By May 1258, when the crisis was approaching its peak, Matthew Paris put the number of dead at 15,000 and later the Tewkesbury annalist cites a death toll of 20,000, a majority of them, presumably, non-Londoners.[77] The metropolis, in effect, was drawing to itself the excess mortality of its hungry hinterland. The scenes which there resulted were harrowing and anticipated those in 1943 in Bengal which inspired Amartya Sen's analysis of famine as an entitlements failure, whereby those who starved and died had in one way or another forfeited their economic entitlement to food.[78] Matthew Paris describes how the bodies of those who perished 'were found in all directions, swollen and livid through hunger, lying by fives and sixes in pigsties, on dunghills, and in the muddy streets, their bodies woefully and mortally wasted'.[79] The city authorities gathered up their corpses and gave them Christian burial, often in mass graves dug for the purpose, in the city's cemeteries.

The graveyard of the hospital of St Mary Spital, located on the northeast outskirts of the city, was one such repository. Here, a major excavation by Museum of London Archaeology, directed between November 1988 and August 2001 by Christopher Thomas, revealed what are very likely some of these 1258 mass graves. Of 10,516 skeletons excavated, over half

Severn to burst its banks, resulting in devastating flooding from Shrewsbury to Bristol: *Paris's English History*, III, 283–4; *Chronica Majora*, V, 693–4; *Flowers of History*, II, 357.

[74] *Paris's English History*, III, 265–6; *Chronica Majora*, V, 673.

[75] For the proactive response of the Florentine authorities to the food crises of 1329–30 and 1347–8, see K. L. Jansen, 'Giovanni Villani on Food Shortages and Famine in Central Italy (1329–30, 1347–48)', in *Medieval Italy: Texts in Translation*, ed. K. L. Jansen, J. Drell and F. Andrews (Philadelphia, 2009), 20–3.

[76] 'Chronicles of the Mayors and Sheriffs: 1257–8', in *Chronicles of the Mayors and Sheriffs of London 1188–1274*, ed. H. T. Riley (1863), 31–42, British History Online: www.british-history.ac.uk/no-series/london-mayors-sheriffs/1188–1274/pp31–42, accessed 20 Aug. 2016.

[77] *Paris's English History*, III, 283–4; *Chronica Majora*, V, 693–4; *Annales Monastici*, I, 166 (Annals of Tewkesbury, 1258).

[78] Bengal Famine of 1943 – A Photographic History – Part 2, www.oldindianphotos.in/2009/12/bengal-famine-of-1943-part-2.html, accessed 6 Sept. 2016; Sen, *Poverty and Famines*, 52–85; Ó Gráda, *Famine*, 45–8.

[79] *Paris's English History*, III, 280, 291; *Chronica Majora*, V, 690.

of those carbon[14]-dated to the thirteenth century were interred in mass graves of eight or more individuals. The earliest of these mass graves, dug before *c.* 1250, typically contained eight to twenty bodies. Subsequent graves, dug after a short interval and sometimes inter-cutting the earlier pits, were larger and contained from twenty to forty bodies in stacked layers. Both sets of pits have been dated to *c.* 1235–55 and together they contained *c.* 2,300 of the skeletons that were analysed. The earlier mass burials have been attributed to the drought-induced dearth of 1252/3, although the subsistence crisis of 1247–8 seems a more likely cause, and the later and larger number of burials to the more serious food crisis of 1257–8, as is consistent with the description provided by Matthew Paris.[80]

The age and sex profiles of those interred in these mass graves, compared with those given more individual (i.e. attritional) burials, reveal much about the demographically selective nature of this crisis (Figure 7). The nature and location of St Mary Spital as an institution meant that even at the best of times its graveyard was the repository of those who were socially marginalised and economically disadvantaged and whose health, stature and life expectancy were diminished by poor nutrition, hard physical toil and unhealthy living and working environments.[81] At normal times, two-thirds of those whose skeletons can be allocated an age were younger than thirty-five at death and more than a third were younger than twenty-five, with females accounting for 43 per cent of adults whose bodies can be sexed. During the crisis years that gave rise to the mass burials, the bias towards younger adults became more pronounced, with the proportion younger than twenty-five rising from 36 per cent to 42 per cent and of those younger than thirty-five from 66 per cent to 70 per cent. Among adults, the proportion of females also rose, to half, reflecting the fact that single women were economically more deprived and vulnerable than almost any other demographic group other than orphaned children.[82] Some of the individuals buried in these mass graves may have expired while seeking succour from the hospital; most, however, as Matthew Paris, describes, had suffered forlorn deaths in the back lanes and alleys of the city.[83] Parentless, landless, jobless, single and/or female, they lacked the family support and economic resources required to survive

---

[80] B. Connell, A. G. Jones, R. Redfern and D. Walker, *A Bioarchaeological Study of Medieval Burials on the Site of St Mary Spital: Excavations at Spitalfields Market, London E1, 1991–2007* (2012), 229; *Paris's English History*, III, 280; *Chronica Majora*, V, 690, 701–2.

[81] Connell *et al.*, *Bioarchaeological Study*, 36, 38, 271–2.

[82] J. M. Bennett, 'Women and Poverty: Girls on their Own in England before 1348', in *Peasants and Lords in the Medieval English Economy*, ed. Kowaleski, Langdon and Schofield, 299–323.

[83] *Paris's English History*, III, 280; *Chronica Majora*, V, 690.

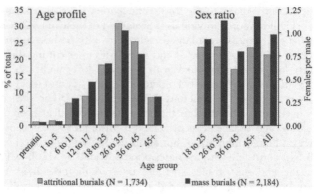

	Attritional burials:	Mass burials:
Age at death:		
Younger than 18	17.6%	22.9%
Younger than 25	35.8%	41.5%
Younger than 35	66.4%	70.1%
Females as % total burials	43.2%	49.6%

Figure 7 Age and sex profiles of those buried at St Mary Spital, London, 1200–1400

Sources and notes: B. Connell, A. G. Jones, R. Redfern and D. Walker, *A Bioarchaeological Study of Medieval Burials on the Site of St Mary Spital: Excavations at Spitalfields Market, London E1, 1991–2007* (2012), 31–2.

the food crisis and as such exemplify the socially and demographically selective nature of all famine mortality.[84]

IV A global catastrophe?

Was a tropical mega-eruption ultimately responsible for the food crisis in England? In 2011, Keene speculated that 'the crisis of 1258 appears to have arisen from a worldwide climatic disaster, caused by the effects of an immense volcanic explosion', and on 6 August 2012, the Museum of London Archaeologists responsible for the St Mary Spital excavation issued a press release claiming that a 'cataclysmic volcano wreaked havoc on medieval Britain', a claim taken up and repeated in the press.[85] At the time, there was intense scientific interest in the identity of a mystery eruption responsible for 'the largest sulfur signature of any eruption

[84] Ó Gráda, *Famine*, 98–102, 178–84, 190–3.
[85] Keene, 'Crisis Management', 54; MOLA, 'Cataclysmic Volcano'.

in the Holocene' in both the Greenland and Antarctic ice cores and dated to *c.* 1258.[86] Given that sulphate was deposited at both poles (Figure 9), an equatorial source was suspected, probably somewhere in the Pacific Ring of Fire.[87] It took until 2013, however, before a French-led international team was convincingly able to demonstrate that the culprit was Samalas Volcano, Indonesia, a mere 170 kilometres west of Tambora.[88] Frank Lavigne and his team estimate that the eruption had a VEI of at least 7. Such was its explosive force that its eruption column reached an altitude of up to 43 kilometres and at least 40 cubic kilometres (dense-rock equivalent) of tephra were ejected. Crucially, the glass geochemistry of the associated pumice deposits closely matches that found in both the Greenland and Antarctic ice cores and provisionally dated to 1258/9 CE. Radiocarbon dates of tree trunks carbonised by the eruption are also consistent with a mid-thirteenth-century date of *c.* 1257. Further confirmation that the eruption occurred sometime between May 1257 and November 1258 is provided by the dark total lunar eclipse reported at Genoa on 12 November 1258, with the balance of palaeo-environmental evidence favouring 1257 over 1258.[89] Of course, once the volcano exploded some weeks and probably months will then have elapsed before fallout from it began to affect the weather almost 60° of latitude to the north and 12,600 kilometres to the north-west over England.

The analogue mega-eruption for which good scientific observations are available is that of Mount Pinatubo in the Philippines on 15 June 1991.[90] It was smaller, with a VEI of 6.1, and released 18 megatonnes of sulphur dioxide into the upper atmosphere. Within twenty-two days, its volcanic dust cloud had encircled the globe and spectacular solar, lunar and other optical effects resulted. In due course, the screening out of solar radiation lowered global temperatures by 0.5° centigrade. The implication is that a similar dust veil must have been created following the VEI7 Samalas eruption in May, June or July 1257 with corresponding optical and climatic effects. Some scientists, most notably Michael E. Mann, impressed by the unparalleled size of the polar sulphate deposits, have inferred that subsequent forcing of global climates must have been on an almost

[86]Brooke, *Climate Change*, 382; C. Oppenheimer, 'Ice Core and Palaeoclimatic Evidence for the Timing and Nature of the Great Mid-Thirteenth Century Volcanic Eruption', *International Journal Climatology*, 23 (2003), 417–26; Oppenheimer, *Eruptions*, 261.

[87]De Boer and Sanders, *Volcanoes*, 13, 256.

[88]Witze, 'Volcano Mystery'; Lavigne *et al.*, 'AD 1257 Mystery Eruption'.

[89]Guillet *et al.*, 'Climatic Impacts', Supplementary information S4.

[90]Oppenheimer, *Eruptions*, 54–66.

unparalleled scale, resulting in climate cooling of about 2° centigrade.[91] This, however, is at variance with tree-ring-based reconstructions of the eruption's temperature effects, which imply that the volume of sulphate ejected by the eruption was disproportionate to its more modest climate impact.[92]

Most recently, a sub-set of the Lavigne team, led by Markus Stoffel, has demonstrated that maximum cooling of global temperatures typically occurs in the first and second years following an eruption, with the precise scale of that impact depending upon the season of the eruption, the injection height of the sulphate plume, the mass of sulphur dioxide (SO_2) released and the size of the ejected aerosol particles. Taking these factors into account, they argue that although the Samalas eruption was a major climatic event, with optical effects visible around the world soon afterwards and significant physical effects then felt in 1258 and 1259 and for sometime thereafter, the eruptions of Ilopango (El Salvador) in c. 535, Kuwae (Vanuatu) in c. 1453, Huaynaputina (Peru) on 19 February 1600, Mount Parker (Philippines) in c. 1641, Laki (Iceland) in June 1783 and Tambora (Indonesia) on 10 April 1815 all had greater negative forcing effects upon global temperatures.[93] Yet, although the Samalas eruption's impact on climate was smaller than once thought, it nonetheless was globally significant. It had an immediate negative effect upon temperate tree growth across Eurasia, European summer temperatures and the El Niño Southern Oscillation, and a positive effect upon the North Atlantic Oscillation (Figures 6 and 8). Six years after the eruption northern hemisphere temperatures had still not fully recovered.

Chronologically, however, the eruption occurred too late to account for the bad weather that ruined the southern English grain harvests in both 1256 and 1257 (Figure 8). Instead, by depressing temperatures and greatly delaying the harvest in 1258, it compounded and prolonged the hardship arising from the earlier back-to-back shortfall.[94] It was the sting in the tail of a food crisis which had arisen from other causes. In that respect,

[91] M. E. Mann, J. D. Fuentes and S. Rutherford, 'Underestimation of Volcanic Cooling in Tree-Ring Based Reconstructions of Hemispheric Temperatures', *Nature Geoscience*, 5 (2012), 202–5.

[92] K. J. Anchukaitis, P. Breitenmoser, K. R. Briffa, A. Buchwal, U. Büntgen, E. R. Cook, R. D. D'Arrigo, J. Esper, M. N. Evans, D. Frank, H. Grudd, B. E. Gunnarson, M. K. Hughes, A. V. Kirdyanov, C. Körner, P. J. Krusic, B. Luckman, T. M. Melvin, M. W. Salzer, A. V. Shashkin, C. Timmreck, E. A. Vaganov and R. J. S. Wilson, 'Tree Rings and Volcanic Cooling', *Nature Geoscience*, 5 (2012), 836: 'Reconstructing simulated temperatures in the same manner as Mann and colleagues, but using a well-tested tree-ring growth model and realistic parameters provides no support for their hypothesis.'

[93] Stoffel *et al.*, 'Volcanic-Induced Cooling', Supplementary, Table S4.

[94] *Paris's English History*, III, 312; *Chronica Majora*, V, 728; Britton, *Meteorological Chronology*, 108.

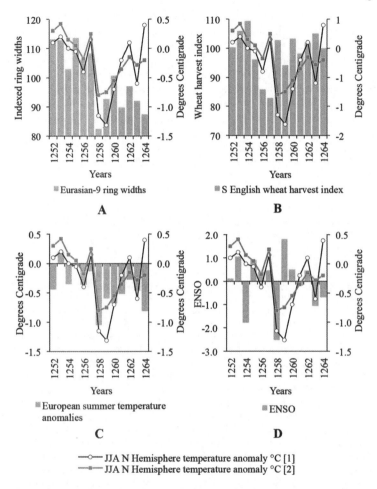

Figure 8 The 1257 Samalas eruption and reconstructed northern hemisphere temperatures, 1252–64, and (A) ring widths of Eurasian trees, (B) southern English wheat harvests, (C) European summer temperatures and (D) the El Niño Southern Oscillation.

Sources and notes: JJA = June, July, August. Northern hemisphere temperatures: M. Stoffel, M. Khodri, C. Corona, S. Guillet, V. Poulain, S. Bekki, J. Guiot, B. H. Luckman, C. Oppenheimer, N. Lebas, M. Beniston and V. Masson-Delmotte, 'Estimates of Volcanic-Induced Cooling in the Northern Hemisphere over the Past 1,500 Years', *Nature Geoscience*, 8 (2015), Supplementary, Table S12. (A) Eurasian-9 ring widths: Alpine conifers (U. Büntgen, W. Tegel, K. Nicolussi, M. McCormick, D. Frank, V. Trouet, J. O. Kaplan, F. Herzig, K.-U. Heussner, H. Wanner, J. Luterbacher

the population was doubly unlucky. It could, however, have been worse. Had volcanic forcing caused harvests to fail for the third year running, the situation in 1259 would have been perilous in the extreme. Instead, ongoing distortion of normal weather patterns meant that agricultural producers were hampered in their efforts to restore output to pre-1255 levels. Scarcity and high prices returned in 1260, leading to bans on the shipping of grain from the ports of East Anglia and the south-east, except to London, and in June causing the eyre to be prorogued until after the harvest.[95] Not until 1261 did wheat prices settle back at a level close to normal (Figure 3A), signalling that the food crisis was effectively at an end. As the Oseney Abbey annalist laconically reported, 'the fruits of

[95] *Calendar of the Patent Rolls Preserved in the Public Record Office: Henry III 1258–66* (1910), 73; *Close Rolls*, IV: *A.D. 1259–1261* (1934), 52, 172.

---

and J. Esper, '2500 Years of European Climate Variability and Human Susceptibility', *Science*, 331 (2011), 578–83, data: 'Central Europe 2500 Year Tree Ring Summer Climate Reconstructions', IGBP PAGES/World Data Center for Paleoclimatology, Data Contribution Series Number: 2011–026, NOAA/NCDC Paleoclimatology Program, Boulder CO, USA; European oaks, Fennoscandian pines, Polar Urals pines, Aegean oaks, pines and juniper, Siberian larch (data supplied by M. G. L. Baillie); Tien Shan juniper (data supplied by Jan Esper); Qinghai juniper (B. Yang, C. Qin, J. Wang, M. He, T. M. Melvin, T. J. Osborn and K. R. Briffa, 'A 3,500-Year Tree-Ring Record of Annual Precipitation on the North-Eastern Tibetan Plateau', *Proceedings of the National Academy of Sciences*, 111 (2014), 2903–8); Mongolian larch (G. C. Jacoby, R. D. D'Arrigo, B. Buckley and N. Pederson, 'Mongolia (*Larix Sibirica*): Solongotyn Davaa (Tarvagatay Pass)' (no date), NOAA Paleoclimatology Tree Ring Data Sets, http://hurricane.ncdc.noaa.gov/pls/paleo/ftpsearch.treering, accessed 18 Dec. 2010). (B) Southern English wheat-harvest index: Figure 5. (C) European summer temperatures: J. Luterbacher, J. P. Werner, J. E. Smerdon, L. Fernández-Donado, F. J. González-Rouco, D. Barriopedro, F. C. Ljungqvist, U. Büntgen, E. Zorita, S. Wagner and J. Esper, 'European Summer Temperatures since Roman Times', *Environmental Research Letters*, 11 (2016), 024001, www.ncdc.noaa.gov/paleo/study/19600, accessed 19 Aug. 2016. (D) El Niño Southern Oscillation: J. Li, S.-P. Xie, E. R. Cook, G. Huang, R. D'Arrigo, F. Liu, J. Ma and X.-T. Zheng, 'Interdecadal Modulation of El Niño Amplitude during the Past Millennium', *Nature Climate Change*, 1 (2011), 114–18, data: '1,100 Year El Niño/Southern Oscillation (ENSO) Index Reconstruction', IGBP PAGES/World Data Center for Paleoclimatology, Data Contribution Series Number 2011–064, NOAA/NCDC Paleoclimatology Program, Boulder CO, USA.

the earth ended the famine which had prevailed in England for the last several years'.[96] It had been a crisis of almost Biblical duration.

If eruption of the Samalas Volcano in spring or early summer of 1257 was not responsible for the initial harvest failures that precipitated the food crisis, what was? Or was the unseasonably wet weather that began in late 1255 and extended through 1256 and 1257 merely a random occurrence? In fact, the run of unusual weather had begun even earlier, with the wet weather that boosted oak growth and depressed grain yields in 1246–7 (Figure 6) and, more particularly, the 'intolerable heat and drought' of spring and early summer 1252, of which Matthew Paris and the Tewkesbury and Welsh chroniclers make such explicit report. Significantly, these twin setbacks occurred at the culmination of an exceptional period of 200 years of sustained high solar irradiance, which peaked in the late 1240s at levels unparalleled since the opening of the fourth century CE and not since equalled (Figure 9). Evidently, the problematic weather experienced by England in the late 1240s and early 1250s coincided with strong solar forcing of the global climate system. At that time, La Niña conditions predominated in the Pacific, the Pacific-west of the Americas was in the grip of mega-drought, the Asian monsoon was at near maximum strength and the North Atlantic Oscillation was strongly positive.[97] It was as these extreme conditions eased abruptly in the mid-1250s that the unstable and unseasonable weather set in over Europe and England that is chronicled by Matthew Paris and his contemporaries, documented by recorded wheat prices and harvests and enshrined in the growth rings of oak trees (Figures 3–5).

Dramatic explosion of the Samalas Volcano occurred in the immediate aftermath of this strong solar-generated global climate perturbation, and that VEI7 eruption's spectacular sulphate signature has diverted scientific attention from the climatic context within which it occurred and caused other potentially important climatic developments to be overlooked. The power of the countervailing solar forcing is one reason why negative volcanic forcing of global and hemispherical temperatures was not greater, in contrast to the eruptions of Kuwae in the 1450s and Tambora in 1815 whose effects were probably amplified by their concurrence, respectively, with the Spörer and Dalton solar minima (Figure 9).[98] In fact, Samalas erupted just after output of solar irradiance

---

[96] *Annales monastici*, IV (Annals of Oseney), 127. And in spring 1261, the baronial council observed that the kingdom had been impoverished by 'evil years': *Documents of the Baronial Movement of Reform and Rebellion, 1258–1267 Selected by R. E. (i.e. R. F.) Treharne*, ed. I. J. Sanders (Oxford, 1973), 221.

[97] Campbell, *Great Transition*, 38–58.

[98] S. Wagner and E. Zorita, 'The Influence of Volcanic, Solar and CO_2 Forcing on the Temperatures in the Dalton Minimum (1790–1830): A Model Study', *Climate Dynamics*, 25 (2005), 205–18.

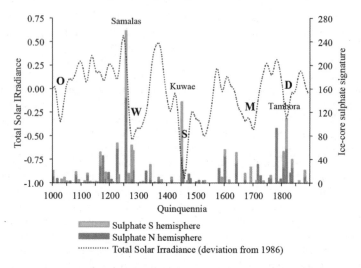

Figure 9 Total solar irradiance and volcanic sulphate deposits in the Greenland (northern hemisphere) and Antarctic (southern hemisphere) ice cores, 1000–1899 CE

Sources and notes: O = Oort solar minimum; W = Wolf solar minimum; S = Spörer solar minimum; M = Maunder solar minimum; D = Dalton solar minimum Total solar irradiance (watts per square metre) expressed as the deviation from the PMOD composite during the solar cycle minimum of the year 1986 CE (1365.57W/m²): F. Steinhilber, J. Beer and C. Fröhlich, 'Total Solar Irradiance during the Holocene', *Geophysical Research Letters*, 36 (2009), L19704, data: Steinhilber *et al.*, 'Holocene Total Solar Irradiance Reconstruction', IGBP PAGES/World Data Center for Paleoclimatology, Data Contribution Series Number 2009-133, NOAA/NCDC Paleoclimatology Program, Boulder CO, USA, www.ncdc.noaa.gov/paleo/study/8744, accessed 25 Aug. 2016. Northern hemisphere and southern hemisphere sulphate deposits from from C. Gao, A. Robock and C. Ammann, 'Volcanic Forcing of Climate over the Past 1500 Years: An Improved Ice Core-Based Index for Climate Models', *Journal of Geophysical Research: Atmospheres*, 113 (D2311) (2008).

began to decline and it was this double development which shaped the weather patterns that first created and then prolonged the 1258 English food crisis and transformed it from a three-year to a seven-year phenomenon.[99] For those caught up in the unfolding scenario, this was no ordinary run of bad weather, for unbeknown to them the effects of the

[99]Keene, 'Crisis Management', 55.

climate perturbation were felt around the globe. Confronted by powerful environmental forces far beyond their comprehension, they prayed for divine intervention to halt the rain and save the harvest.

V Hunger and high politics in spring/summer 1258

Meanwhile, a quite different and wholly independent set of forces was brewing up a political storm in England. In spring and summer of 1258, as the food crisis came to a head and the weather turned first cold and then wet, the tragedy engulfing the poor provided the context for eruption of the long-impending power struggle between Henry III and his magnates. At issue were dissatisfaction with the king's personal rule, favouritism towards his half-brothers, the Poitevins, and the cost of his misguided enterprise at the initiative of the pope to secure the kingdom of Sicily to his younger son, Edmund Crouchback.[100] Open political conflict between the king and his barons ignited in March when Pope Alexander IV's envoy delivered a fresh ultimatum respecting the financial and military obligations entered into by the king respecting the crown of Sicily. This placed Henry in dire financial difficulty from which only the grant of an aid by his magnates could rescue him. Given the immiserated state of the country, with food scarce and prices rising steeply (Figure 10), the timing of this request could hardly have been less propitious. At the end of April, the barons responded and presented their own demands to the king, who had little choice but to acquiesce. In early May, as the food crisis grew steadily worse and with little respite in the bitter weather, Henry III granted significant political concessions and in return the barons reluctantly agreed to expedite the grant of an aid. On 10 and 11 June, parliament, meeting in Oxford, ratified the reforms, which required the king to rule with a council of twenty-four appointed in part by the barons. Henry's personal rule was ended and the hated Poitevins were expelled. Finally, on 23 July, the City of London – swamped with starving famine refugees and with heavy rain making a grim situation worse – signed up to the agreed political reforms.[101]

In one important respect, the unfolding political crisis helped relieve the food crisis. In March 1258, to ease mounting pressure on his beleaguered half-brother, Henry III, and relieve the provisioning situation in the capital, Richard of Cornwall, newly elected king of the Germans, sent fifty shiploads of food aid to London. As Matthew Paris recorded, 'any three counties of England united had not produced so much corn as was brought by these vessels; but...although it in some slight degree mitigated the effects of the famine, which was general

---

[100] Treharne, *Baronial Plan*, 1–63, 64–81.
[101] *Ibid.*, 64–81; D. A. Carpenter, *The Reign of Henry III* (1996), 183–98.

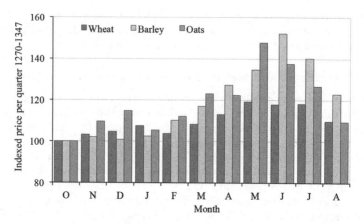

Figure 10 Mean monthly prices of wheat, barley and oats, 1270–1347
Sources and notes: Calculated from N. Poynder, 'England Monthly
Grain Prices, 1270–1955' (no date), Global Price and Income History
Group, http://gpih.ucdavis.edu, accessed 12 Dec. 2015. 100 = mean
September/October price of each grain.

throughout England, it did not entirely do away with them'.[102] In
fact, the arrival of food aid proved double-edged, since it attracted
further migration by famine-stricken refugees to London and thereby
magnified the problems of public order, health and disposal of the
dead faced by the metropolis. Overwhelmed by these challenges and
distracted by fast-moving political events, London's own administration
proved impotent and neglected even to enforce the assize of bread,
as would normally have been the case at a time of soaring grain
prices.[103]

Conceivably, reluctance to tax a famine-stricken countryside may have
stoked baronial resistance to the king's frantic requests for an aid to
help buy off the papacy. Certainly, those attending parliament in Oxford
in early June, when food prices very likely reached their absolute peak
(Figure 10), can have had no illusions about the scarcity and costs of
provisions. Moreover, Oxford, with parliament sitting and many great
men and their retinues in attendance, must also have been inundated
by a flood of hungry vagrants. Yet, although the hardship endured by
many of the common people will have been plain for all to see, the
government, locked in constitutional conflict, was in no position to relieve

[102] *Paris's English History*, III, 265–6; *Chronica Majora*, V, 673–4.
[103] Keene, 'Crisis Management', 56.

the food crisis even if it had been inclined so to do.[104] The unfolding political drama claimed everyone's attention, with chroniclers, including Matthew Paris, increasingly devoting far more space to it than either the adverse weather or the desperate plight of the poor. Eventually, as the food crisis eased, interest in it appears to have lapsed altogether with the result that there is a significant falling off in the amount and quality of annalistic information about the weather, harvests and prices. Concern and compassion for those facing starvation had evidently worn thin. In contrast, the baronial reform movement escalated into civil war and many dramatic reversals of fortune ensued before Simon de Montfort and the baronial cause that he led were routed at the Battle of Evesham on 4 August 1265. That reform movement, its flawed leader and his eventual defeat have fascinated historians ever since, to the neglect, until recently, of the concurrent food crisis and the exceptional environmental events responsible for the precipitating harvest failures.[105] This is unfortunate, for climate change, extreme weather, food crises, hunger and the plight of the poor are subjects no less worthy of scholarly attention.[106] After all, they are issues that still confront us today.[107]

---

[104] For the limited relief measures subsequently adopted by late medieval English governments and administrations, see B. Sharp, 'Royal Paternalism and the Moral Economy in the Reign of Edward II: The Response to the Great Famine', *Economic History Review*, 66 (2013), 628–47; Keene, 'Crisis Management'.

[105] Treharne, *Baronial Plan*, 412–39; R. F. Treharne, *Simon de Montfort and Baronial Reform: Thirteenth-Century Essays*, ed. E. B. Fryde (1986); D. A. Carpenter, *The Battles of Lewes and Evesham 1264/65* (Keele, 1987); Carpenter, *Henry III*; J. R. Maddicott, *Simon de Montfort* (Cambridge, 1996); J. Sadler, *The Second Barons' War: Simon de Montfort and the Battles of Lewes and Evesham* (Philadelphia, 2008); A. Jobson, *The First English Revolution: Simon de Montfort, Henry III and the Barons' War* (2012); R. Brooks, *Lewes and Evesham 1264–65: Simon de Montfort and the Barons' War* (2015); J. Maddicott, 'Who Was Simon de Montfort, Earl of Leicester?', *Transactions of the Royal Historical Society*, 26 (2016), 43–58; Keene, 'Crisis Management'; Connell *et al.*, *Bioarchaeological Study*; R. C. Hoffmann, *An Environmental History of Medieval Europe* (Cambridge, 2014).

[106] Campbell, 'Nature'.

[107] APPG, *Feeding Britain*; House of Commons, Environment, Food and Rural Affairs Committee, *Oral Evidence: Winter Floods 2015–16*, HC 666, 11 Jan. 2016, http://data. parliament.uk/writtenevidence/committeeevidence.svc/evidencedocument/environment-food-and-rural-affairs-committee/winter-floods-201516/oral/26721.html, accessed 6 Sept. 2016; Intergovernmental Panel on Climate Change, *Climate Change 2014: Synthesis Report (Contribution of Working Groups I, II and III to the Fifth Assessment Report of the Intergovernmental Panel on Climate Change)*, ed. R. K. Pachauri and L. A. Meyer (Geneva, 2014).

Transactions of the RHS 27 (2017), pp. 123–152 © Royal Historical Society 2017
doi:10.1017/S0080440117000068

OLD WORDS AND THE NEW WORLD: LIBERAL EDUCATION AND THE FRANCISCANS IN NEW SPAIN, 1536–1601*

The Whitfield Prize Winner

By Aysha Pollnitz

ABSTRACT. The Colegio de Santa Cruz de Tlatelolco, established in 1536, liberally educated the sons of Nahua (Aztec) leaders in New Spain. Its Franciscan pedagogues, including Bernardino de Sahagún (*c.* 1499–1590), Andrés de Olmos (1491–1571) and Juan Bautista (*c.* 1555–1606/13), worked with indigenous students and alumni to collect, edit and circulate Nahuatl *huehuetlahtolli*, or 'speech of the ancients'. This paper examines the largest collection of these orations printed in pre-modern Mexico, the *Huehuetlahtolli* [1601] edited by Juan Bautista and indigenous intellectuals from the college. It argues that the Tlatelolcans adapted Nahuatl 'old words' for the New World of colonial society. They ornamented the speeches with rhetorical techniques derived from Santa Cruz's Erasmian curriculum. They interpolated biblical sentences, particularly from Proverbs and Sirach, to enhance the evangelising potential of the discourses. Finally, they drew on Erasmus's theory of speech, as expressed in his pedagogical and spiritual writings, to explicate Nahuatl *los difrasismos* concerning eloquence and good counsel. Contextualising the *Huehuetlahtolli* [1601] in Santa Cruz's Erasmian schoolroom reveals the contours of its argument for vernacular evangelisation, the liberal education of indigenous youth and for the elegance of the Nahuatl tongue.

On 6 January 1536, the feast of the epiphany was marked by a solemn procession in Mexico City. It began with a sermon at the convent of San Francisco near Tenochtitlan, the fallen Aztec capital.[1] Then friars processed behind the viceroy, Antonio de Mendoza (*c.* 1490–1552), the former president of the second Audiencia of Mexico and the second bishop of Santo Domingo, Sebastián Ramírez de Fuenleal (*c.* 1490–1547)

* The author thanks Rice University, the John Carter Brown Library and Grinnell College for their generous support. She is grateful to the *Transactions*'s editor and anonymous reviewers for their perspicacious counsel. She thanks members of the Sixteenth-Century Historical Society, the Harvard Early Modern Workshop, fellows of the John Carter Brown Library, the Rice Medieval and Early Modern Workshop, Andrew Laird, David Armitage and Susan Kellogg for their sage advice on earlier versions of this article.

[1] Gerónimo de Mendieta, *Historia eclesiástica Indiana*, ed. Joaquín García Icazbalceta (Mexico, 1870) IV:15, 414–18; Pedro de Gante to Charles V, 31 Oct. 1532 in *Cartas de Indias* (Madrid, 1877), 52.

and the Franciscan bishop of Mexico, Juan de Zumárraga (1468–1548). They walked two miles north to the Convent of Santiago, Tlatelolco where they inaugurated the Colegio Imperial de Santa Cruz. There, indigenous students would study Latin grammar, rhetoric, philosophy, logic and (some hoped) theology. Prior to the conquest, the site at Tlatelolco had been a *calmecac*, a traditional school where Nahua elites had learned to speak well, to govern and to hear suits. Now, liberal education at the college would lay the path towards an epiphany for New World gentiles.[2]

Santa Cruz was immediately, if not durably, an academic success. Its alumni became native governors and allies in the spiritual conquest of New Spain. Erudite trilingual students, whom the friars called *gramaticos* or *ladinos*, also helped the Franciscans to create texts that described pre-contact Nahua language and culture. Pride of place in their endeavours went to the collection of *huehuetlahtolli*, 'speech of the ancients', or *palabras antiguas*, *historia antigua* or *dichos de viejos* in Spanish.[3] These speeches were Nahuatl orations including: prayers to the gods, counsel to officeholders and moral exhortations to children. The 'ancients' spoke in highly figurative language, larded with *los difrasismos*, couplets of juxtaposed synonyms or syntactically linked words that formed metaphors. Not only did *los difrasismos* elevate the discourse stylistically but it enriched it conceptually, one of the reasons that *huehuetlahtolli* are central to scholarly attempts to explicate Nahuatl thought.[4] The largest collection of 'speech of the ancients' is contained in Book VI of the *Florentine Codex*.[5] On the Spanish title-page, the Tlatelolcan missionary and teacher, fray Bernardino de Sahagún (1499–1590), described the speeches as 'the Rhetoric, and moral philosophy, and theology of Mexican people'

---

[2] Mendieta, *Historia*, IV:15, 414–18; *Informe de la provincia de Santo Evangelio, al visitador Lic. Juan de Ovando*, in *Códice Franciscano, siglo XVI*, ed. Joaquín García Icazbalceta (Mexico, 1941), 62–5; Juan Bautista Pomar, *Relación de Tezcoco (siglo XVI)*, ed. Joaquín García Icazbalceta (Mexico, 1975), 28.

[3] Andrés de Olmos, *Arte para de la lengua Mexicana [1547]*, ed. Ascensión Hernández de León-Portilla and Miguel León-Portilla (Mexico, 2002), 177; Alonso Molina, *Aqui comiença vn vocabulario enla lengua Castellana y Mexicana* (Mexico: Juan Pablos, 1555), fo. 151r, and (Mexico: Antonio de Spinosa, 1571), fo. 157r. See *The Art of Nahuatl Speech: The Bancroft Dialogues*, ed. Frances Karttunen and James Lockhart (Los Angeles, 1997), 8 n. 11.

[4] Mercedes Montes de Oca Vega, *Los difrasismos en el Náhuatl de los siglos XVI y XVII* (Mexico, 2013), 13, 21–8, 38–41; Thelma D. Sullivan, 'The Rhetorical Orations, or Huehuetlatolli, Collected by Sahagún', in *Sixteenth-Century Mexico: The Work of Sahagún*, ed. Munro S. Edmonson (Albuquerque, 1974), 79–109; Ángel María Garibay Kintana, *Historia de la literature Náhuatl* (2 vols., Mexico, 1953), I, 65–7; but see M. José García Quintana, 'Los huehuetlahtolli en el *Códice Florentino*', in *Fray Bernardino de Sahagún y su tiempo*, ed. Jesús Paniagua Pérez and María Isabel Viforcos Marinas (Leon, 2000), 553–71.

[5] Bernardino de Sahagún, *Florentine Codex: General History of the Things of New Spain*, ed. Charles E. Dibble and Arthur J. O. Anderson (13 vols., Santa Fe, 1950–82), I, 54. In subsequent footnotes, Sahagún is credited with authorship of Spanish prologues and glosses but treated as an editor of Nahuatl *huehuetlahtolli*.

and as pertaining to both 'the foundations of their language' and 'the moral virtues'.[6] According to the *Codex*, *huehuetlahtolli* were traditional instruments of native education, a topic that held considerable interest for the denizens of the Colegio de Santa Cruz.

Rather than considering the *Florentine Codex*, this article focuses on a less frequently discussed collection of *Huehuetlahtolli* [1601] printed in Mexico by fray Juan Bautista (1555–*c*. 1613), the guardian of the convent at Tlatelolco. This octavo, printed in a plain style on ninety-five leaves of inexpensive paper, contains twenty-nine Nahuatl speeches and eight Spanish *pláticas*. They were predominantly speeches to youths, with a few exhortations to rulers. Bautista claimed to have received a number of Nahuatl and Spanish orations from fray Andrés de Olmos (1480?– 1568), a missionary who had arrived in New Spain with Zumárraga in 1528.[7] The published text constitutes the second largest collection of Nahuatl oratory to survive and the only such anthology printed in Mexico.[8] While it was not reprinted, Spanish versions of the orations were circulated widely. The *Huehuetlahtolli* shares certain features with the *Florentine Codex*: topics of discourse, the use of certain metaphors, and an emphasis on humble conduct, obedience to higher powers and self-discipline. As such, studies of the *huehuetlahtolli* have mined them for evidence of pre-contact Nahuatl language, culture and cosmo-vision.[9]

---

[6] 'de la Rethorica y philosophia moral, y theologia: de la gente mexicana . . . tocantes a los primores de su lengua y . . . a las virtudes morales': Sahagún, *Florentine Codex*, VII, unpaginated front matter.

[7] *Huehuetlahtolli*, ed. Juan Bautista (Tlatelolco: [Melchior Ocharte? Cornelio Adrián César? Diego López Dávalos?], [1601]), sigs. L5r, N3v–N4r. The two surviving copies of the text (John Carter Brown Library, Providence RI, B601 .J91h and B601 .J91h c.2) are missing their title-page and several leaves from the first quire. On possible reconstructions for the title-page, see Juan Pascoe, *Cornelio Adrián César: impresor holandés en México, 1597–1633* (Santa Rosa, 2016), 262–71. In subsequent footnotes, Bautista is credited with authorship of the Spanish prologue but treated as an editor of Nahuatl *huehuetlahtolli*.

[8] The speeches in Sahagún's *Florentine Codex* and *Primeros memoriales* remained in manuscript. Following the royal prohibition of the *General History* in April 1577, the friar's papers were confiscated. Some documents, possibly including the *Primeros memoriales*, were sent to Madrid. The illustrated Nahuatl and Spanish version of the *General History*, known as the *Florentine Codex*, was protected by Fray Rodrigo de Sequera, the Franciscan's general commissary in New Spain. Sequera took the *Codex* to Spain in 1580 and it arrived in Florence prior to 1588: Lluís Nicolau d'Olwer, *Fray Bernardino de Sahagún, 1499–1590*, trans. Mauricio J. Mixco (Salt Lake City, 1977), 72–7. Also in manuscript was the short collection of conversations and brief speeches from late sixteenth- or seventeenth-century Texcoco, associated with Horacio Carochi: *The Bancroft Dialogues*, ed. Karttunen and Lockhart, 2–10.

[9] For example: Ángel María Garibay Kintana, 'Huehuetlatolli, documento A: nota introductoria', *Tlalocan*, I (1943), 31–80; Josefina García Quintana, 'El huehuetlatolli – antigua palabra – como fuente para la historia sociocultural de los nahuas', *Estudios de Cultura Náhuatl*, 12 (1976), 61–71; Sullivan, 'The Rhetorical Orations, or Huehuetlatolli', 79– 109; Miguel León-Portilla, *The Aztec Image of Self and Society: An Introduction to Nahua Culture*, ed. J. Jorge Klor de Alva (Salt Lake City, 1992); Georges Baudot, *Utopia and History in Mexico*:

Nevertheless, the *Huehuetlahtolli* contains more loan words and Christian doctrine than the *Codex*. Some recent scholarship has identified its colonial context and evangelising purpose.[10]

This paper develops this research in a novel direction by considering the significance of the Colegio de Santa Cruz and its humanist orientation on the generation of the *Huehuetlahtolli*. The collection of speeches was probably created for the instruction of Franciscan novices, who were learning to preach in Nahuatl, and indigenous students. School use would explain the inexpensive print and low rate of surviving copies. The first section examines the way that Santa Cruz missionaries used the orations in their classicised arguments about the civility of the *indios*. The second section investigates the humanistic source of this impulse by surveying the ideological leanings of the friars, the curriculum of Santa Cruz and the intellectual activities of its students and alumni. It identifies the persistent influence of Erasmus of Rotterdam (1466–1536), whose writings continued to be used at Tlatelolco despite their placement on papal and Spanish indices. As the final section shows, the friars and students who created the *Huehuetlahtolli* drew on the style and content of Erasmian 'good letters', or *bonae litterae*. Indeed, by contextualising the Nahuatl orations in Erasmus's pedagogical and spiritual writings, it is possible to see that the printed text was more than a collection of evangelising *pláticas*. The *Huehuetlahtolli* also made a powerful argument for the moral and political value of good speech, and for the spiritual benefits of Nahuatl-language evangelisation in the New World.

I The cultural encounter between old words in the New World

Historians are increasingly cognisant that the encounter between European, Amerindian and African cultures shaped the institutions, laws and religion of New Spain. The texts created in this colonial environment were almost inevitably hybrid.[11] Sophisticated studies by new philologists of Nahuatl translations of European texts and Nahuatl compositions in various European genres have opened a new vista on New Spain. Of particular importance for this study is the research that has shown

---

The First Chronicles of Mexican Civilisation (1520–1569), trans. Bernard R. Ortiz de Montellano and Thelma Ortiz de Montellano (Niwot, CO, 1995).

[10] Mónica Ruiz Bañuls, *El huehuetlatolli como discurso sincrético en el proceso evangelisador novohispano del siglo XVI* (Rome, 2009).

[11] Peter Burke, *Cultural Hybridity* (Cambridge, 2009), 22–3; Serge Gruzinski, *The Mestizo Mind: The Intellectual Dynamics of Colonisation and Globalisation*, trans. Deke Dusinberre (New York, 2002); Diana Magaloni Kerpel, *Los colores del Nuevo Mundo: artistas, materiales y la creación del Códice Florentino* (Mexico, 2014); Gauvin Alexander Bailey, *Art of Colonial Latin America* (2005).

that Christianity was transformed by Nahuatl translation.[12] Until very recently, however, scholars have tended to treat *huehuetlahtolli* as immune from European influence. These repositories of authentic 'linguistic information' were deemed to reveal the 'political and religious speech used in the most diverse situations of daily life in the Mexica culture' and shed light on 'the pre-Hispanic Indian mind and thought'.[13] This study, however, asks whether and how the *Huehuetlahtolli* was inflected by its colonial context. It takes its point of departure from scholars' frequent descriptions of the Nahuatl speech of the ancients as analogous to Greek and Roman discourse, as it was revived by humanists in the sixteenth century.[14] It contends that these modern comparisons derive from the way that the *huehuetlahtolli* was framed by humanists associated with the Colegio de Santa Cruz.

This is not an attempt to suggest that Europeans invented the *huehuetlahtolli*. Both pictorial codices and Nahuatl morphology show that eloquence played an important role in pre-contact Mesoamerica. Images in pre-Columbian and early contact codices depict rulers, priests and parents with the attribute of speech scrolls.[15] The Nahuatl terms for ruler (*tlatoani*, 'speaker') and ambassador (*tlatocatitlantli*, 'messenger of the speaker') derive from the verb *(i)htoa* ('to speak').[16] Nahua political, religious and familial culture evidently had recourse to a repository of past speech acts, which they described to the Franciscans as *huehuetlahtolli*. Nevertheless, the surviving *pláticas* were recorded in alphabetised form after the arrival of Europeans; Franciscans and Jesuits, including Andrés de Olmos, Bernardino de Sahagún, Juan Bautista and, later, Horacio Carochi (1586–1666), initiated the process. Liberally educated Tlatelolcans did not concoct the 'speech of the ancients, but they certainly inflected the form in which we have received it.

[12] See the research of Louise M. Burkhart, Mark Z. Christensen, Rebecca Horn, Frances Karttunen, James Lockhart, Stafford Poole, Barry D. Sell, Susan Schroeder, John Frederick Schwaller, David Tavárez, Camilla Townsend and Stephanie Wood, among others.

[13] Baudot, *Utopia and History in Mexico*, 223; and Sullivan, 'The Rhetorical Orations, or Huehuetlatolli', 79. See similarly León-Portilla, *Aztec Image of Self and Society*, 76; Garibay Kintana, 'Huehuetlatolli, documento A' 31; García Quintana, 'El huehuetlatolli – antigua palabra', 61–71.

[14] Miguel León-Portilla, 'Huehuehtlahtolli: antigua palabra: la retórica Náhuatl', in *La palabra florida: la tradición retórica indígena y nova hispana*, ed. Helena Beristáin and Gerardo Ramírez Vidal (Mexico, 2004), 23–40, at 39; Walter D. Mignolo, *The Darker Side of the Renaissance: Literacy, Territoriality, and Colonisation* (Ann Arbor, 1995), 143.

[15] Elisabeth Hill Boone, *Stories in Red and Black: Pictorial Histories of the Aztecs and Mixtecs* (Austin, 2000), 46, 57–8; Joyce Marcus, *Mesoamerican Writing Systems: Propaganda, Myth, and History in Four Ancient Civilisations* (Princeton, 1992), 48.

[16] Molina, *Vocabulario* (1571), fos. 4v, 120r, 140v, 141r; Susan Kellogg, *Law and the Transformation of Aztec Culture, 1500–1700* (Norman, OK, 1995), 221, 227; Thelma D. Sullivan, 'Nahuatl Proverbs, Conundrums, and Metaphors, Collected by Sahagún', *Estudios de Cultura Náhuatl*, 4 (1963), 93–178, at 150–1.

Indeed, Franciscans teaching at Santa Cruz initiated descriptions of the *huehuetlahtolli* as analogous to classical rhetoric. In his Spanish prologue to Book VI of the *Florentine Codex*, Sahagún argued that, like the Greeks and Romans, and the modern Europeans who imitated them, the Nahua elected 'wise, virtuous and forceful Rhetoricians', who knew the *huehuetlahtolli*, to be 'high priests, lords, leaders, and captains, no matter how humble their estate. These [orators] ruled the states, led the armies, and presided in the temples.'[17] Missionaries claimed that pre-contact Nahua intellectuals had taught the *huehuetlahtolli* much as Renaissance humanists taught Virgil or Cicero. In a letter to the Jesuit José de Acosta (1540–1600), fray Juan de Tovar (1543–1623) argued that Nahuatl orators and priests trained 'the principal youths, who were to be their successors', using 'continual repetition' of the speech of the ancients until they 'remain in their memories, without any discrepant words'.[18] In the prologue to the *Huehuetlahtolli*, fray Juan Bautista claimed that the study of ancient speech inculcated 'the precepts of natural law' and 'the virtues of Prudence, Justice, Fortitude, and Temperance' in Nahuatl youth, much as liberal education (allegedly) did in Europe.[19] Book III of the *Florentine Codex* located this instruction in the *calmecac*, a place dedicated to 'the teaching of good letters (*qualli tlahtolli*)'. *Qualli tlahtolli* was a Nahuatl cognate of the Latin phrase, *bonae litterae*, that Erasmus had popularised to describe classical literature and scripture.[20]

Many educated Europeans saw the New World through a classical lens.[21] When they compared classical Latin or Greek pedagogy to Mexican education, the missionaries were emphasising the wit and civility of the *indios* and the value of their mission. In the 1530s, Ramírez de Fuenleal, the president of the second Audiencia, the body responsible for the administration of justice in Mexico, responded to Dominican attempts

---

[17] Sahagún, *Florentine Codex*, I, 65, and see 165.

[18] 'sus oradores y poetas, había cada día ejercicio dello [en los colegios] de los mozos principales que habían de ser sucesores a estos, y con la continua repetición se les quedaba en la memoria, sin discrepar palabra': Juan de Tovar in *Don Fray Juan de Zumárraga: Primer Obispo y Arzobispo de Mexico*, ed. Joaquín García Icazbalceta, 2nd edn, ed. Rafael Aguayo Spencer and Antonio Castro Leal (4 vols., Mexico, 1988), IV, 92–3. See also *The Bancroft Dialogues*, ed. Karttunen and Lockhart, 153.

[19] 'todas las reglas y colores de la Rethorica' and 'podra dezir ... delos preceptos de la ley natural ... conciernen a las Virtudes de la Prudencia y Iusticia, y Fortaleza y Temperança': *Huehuetlahtolli*, ed. Bautista, fo. 92r–v.

[20] 'cenca vel nemachtiloia in qualli tlahtolli': *Florentine Codex*, ed. Sahagún, III, 67 (quotation), and VII, 93, 99, 105, 113. Cf. Erasmus, *Collected Works of Erasmus*, V: *Letters 594–841*, ed. R. A. B. Mynors, trans. D. F. S. Thomson (Toronto, 1979), 411. Works in this series will be referred to hereafter as *CWE*.

[21] Anthony Pagden, *The Fall of Natural Man: The American Indian and the Origins of Comparative Ethnology* (Cambridge, 1982); David A. Lupher, *Romans in a New World: Classical Models in Sixteenth-Century Spanish America* (Ann Arbor, 2003); Sabine MacCormack, *On the Wings of Time: Rome, the Incas, Spain, and Peru* (Princeton, 2007).

to disparage the *indios'* intellectual and moral capacities by turning to the Franciscans.[22] He asked Andrés de Olmos and Bernardino de Sahagún to compile accounts of indigenous language and customs. Between 1533 and 1539, Olmos alternated between teaching Latin at Santa Cruz and meeting native *principales* in Tenochtitlan, Texcoco and Tlaxala to collect evidence of their political culture. A manuscript associated with Olmos described him seeking out 'the accounts of the elders, and of those who were priests and fathers in the time of their infidelity'.[23] With the assistance of indigenous collaborators, Olmos transcribed and translated the speeches. He turned at least one *plática* into an appendix to his *Arte de la lengua Mexicana* [1547], a Nahuatl–Spanish grammar.[24] It offered a version of indigenous culture that was well fashioned to please (or at least, to avoid frightening) fellow-missionaries.

In 1601, Juan Bautista asserted that Olmos's Spanish translation of Nahuatl speeches were reliable. 'Nothing was added, and nothing of substance was taken away', he insisted. Olmos and his collaborators had exchanged 'sense for sense, not word for word', as Cicero and Erasmus had advised.[25] Even a cursory comparison between the Spanish and Nahuatl versions of Olmos's speech reveals the translation to be a loose summary. As with other humanist translations, moreover, the object was not verisimilitude but an elegant argument.[26] In this case, translations were intended to support the Franciscan mission.

---

[22] Sahagún, *Florentine Codex*, I, 53–6; José María Kobayashi, *La educación como conquista: empresa franciscana en México* (Mexico, 1986), 231–4. For an example of such criticism, see Jeronimo Lopez, letter to Charles V, 1541, in *Colección de documentos para la historia de México* (Mexico, 1866), II, 148–50.

[23] 'por dicho de los señores y principales á quien se enseñaba la ley y criaban en los templos para que la deprendiesen': [Anon. poss. Olmos], 'Historia de los mexicanos por sus pinturas', in *Teogonia e historia de los Mexicanos: tres opúsculos del siglo XVI*, ed. Ángel María Garibay Kintana (Mexico, 1965), 23.

[24] The speech survives in the following manuscripts of the *Arte de la lengua Mexicana*: Library of Congress, Washington, DC, Miscellaneous Manuscript Collection, box 183 (old number L.A. Misc. 11I-48-C, 4) Ac. 8 (1898); Bibliothèque nationale, Paris, Fonds espagnol, 259, Trichet du Fresne, Colbert (1665); Biblioteca Nacional de Madrid, MS 10081/Reservado 165. See John F. Schwaller, 'Small Collections of Nahuatl Manuscripts in the United States', *Estudios de cultura Náhuatl*, 25 (1995), 377–416, at 414–15; Andrés de Olmos, *Arte de la lengua Mexicana* [1547], ed. Miguel Léon-Portilla (Madrid, 1993), xxxviii; Judith M. Maxwell and Craig A. Hanson, *Of the Manners of Speaking that the Old Ones Had: The Metaphors of Andrés de Olmos in the TULAL Manuscript* (Salt Lake City, 1992), 10–11; Ruiz Bañuls, *El huehuetlatolli*, 239–43; 'Exhortación de un padre a su hijo. Texto recogido por Andrés de Olmos', ed. Josefina García Quintana, *Estudios de cultura Náhuatl*, 11 (1974), 137–82.

[25] 'na sin añadir, ni q[ui]tar cosa q[ue] fuesse de substa[n]cia: saca[n]do sentido de sentido, y no palabra de palabra': *Huehuetlahtolli*, ed. Bautista, fo. 77r. Cf. Cicero, *De optimo genere oratorum*, IV.13–V.15, and Erasmus, *Capita argumentorum contra morosos quosdam ac indoctos*, in *Opera omnia*, ed. Jean le Clerc (Leiden: Van der Aa, 1706), VI. sig. **v. See also ***r.

[26] See Paul Botley, *Latin Translation in the Renaissance: The Theory and Practice of Leonardo Bruni, Giannozzo Manetti and Desiderius Erasmus* (Cambridge, 2004); Erika Rummel, *Erasmus'*

Olmos circulated selected Spanish orations to carefully chosen allies. In the wake of the 1550 Valladolid debate with Juan Ginés de Sepúlveda (*c.* 1490–1573), Olmos sent eight *pláticas* to Bartolomé de las Casas (*c.* 1484–1566), Dominican and bishop of Chiapas. Las Casas incorporated them in the second part of his *Apologética historia* (written *c.* 1556–9, printed 1909). The *Apologética* vindicated the intellectual, moral and spiritual capacities of the *indios* against Sepúlveda's assertion that 'in prudence, wisdom, every virtue, and humanity' indigenous people were 'inferior to the Spaniards...almost as monkeys are to men'.[27] Las Casas retorted that the *indios* lived in a different but comparable manner to the gentiles. He used Olmos's *huehuetlahtolli* to show that the Mexica's discourse was sophisticated, even though they lacked an alphabetic script, and that their pedagogy rivalled the ancient Athenians and Romans. Indeed, Nahuatl speech could not be heard 'without great advantage to most of us who call ourselves Christian'. The Nahua, 'who have never read [Greek or Roman] philosophy', nevertheless adhered more 'closely to the rules of Aristotle' than supposedly civilised nations.[28]

Other early modern defenders of the *indios* also used Olmos's speeches in translation. In 1585, for instance, the royal judge, Alonso de Zorita (1514–85), incorporated several in his *Relación* to Philip II. Zorita's renderings were similar to Las Casas's speeches but more compressed. Like Las Casas, Zorita used them to evidence the Mexica's pre-contact prudence in 'government and judicature, and in keeping the laws and doing justice and in raising their children'. The *indios*, he argued, were called 'barbarous' on account of their former idolatry and different customs, rather than their lack of elegant speech or civility. They owed much of their contemporary corruption to the rapaciousness of their conquerors.[29]

Annotations on the New Testament: From Philologist to Theologian (Toronto, 1986); *Cultural Translation in Early Modern Europe*, ed. Peter Burke and R. Po-chia Hsia (Cambridge, 2007).

[27] 'qui prudentia, ingenio, virtute omni ac humanitate tam longe superantur ab Hispanis...denique quam simiae prope dixerim ab hominibus': Juan Ginés de Sepúlveda, *Democrates alter, sive de justis belli causis apud Indos*, ed. Marcelino Menéndez y Pelayo [1892] (Alicante, 2006), paragraph no. 304, access via URI: www.cervantesvirtual.com/nd/ark:/59851/bmccv4wo. Cf. Aristotle, *Politics*, 1254b15–1255a2. Regarding Indians and apes, see Pagden, *Fall of Natural Man*, 117.

[28] 'sino muy grande ventaja muchos de los que nos llamamos christianos...Parece, pues, tanto...y más de propincuo a las reglas del Philósopho, éstas, que nunca leyeron su philosophía, que otras muchas naciones en la crianza delos hijos haberse allegado': Bartolomé de las Casas, *Apologética historia sumaria*, III, in *Obras completas*, ed. Vidal Abril Castelló *et al.* (14 vols., Madrid, 1988–98), VIII, 1393–4 (quotation), 1398–1407 (speeches).

[29] 'aquellas gentes tenian en su gobierno y Judicatura y en guarder sus leies y hazer justiçia y en criar sus hijos': Alonso de Zorita, *Relación de la Nueva España: Relación de algunas de las muchas cosas notables que hay en la Nueva España y de su conquista y pacificación y de la conversión de los naturales de ella*, ed. Wiebke Ahrndt, Ethelia Ruiz Medrano and José Mariano Leyva (Mexico, 1999), 152–5, 209–18, 228–31 (quotation).

Zorita had probably acquired the Spanish speeches from a draft of fray Gerónimo de Mendieta's (1525–1604) *Historia eclesiástica indiana* (*c.* 1595). In addition to praising the Nahua's eloquence, Mendieta hazarded that their capacity to assimilate the liberal arts derived from their pre-contact pedagogy.[30] Either Mendieta or, more probably, Bautista shared eight Spanish *huehuetlahtolli* with fray Juan de Torquemada (*c.* 1557–1624), who printed expanded versions in his *Monarquía Indiana* (1615). Torquemada augmented the *pláticas* with scriptural references so that the ancient *indios* seemed to anticipate the words of the ancient Israelites. Their concern for 'good education and teaching of the youths' was Aristotelean and Platonic. The *indios* were clearly 'rational and political and living the lives of [civilised] men' and ripe for conversion.[31] In the late seventeenth century, Augustín de Vetancurt (1620–1700) took up the refrain, arguing that the speeches proved that the *indios* had 'put into practice honest customs in the education of their children' prior to European contact.[32]

The tradition of using Olmos's *huehuetlahtolli* as classical artefacts in the defence of the *indios* spread to accounts of the Americas printed in Europe. Fray Diego Valadés's *Rhetorica Christiana* (1579) described the glyphs that accompanied the 'speech of the ancients' as approaching letters for fixity and sophistication. In his oft-translated *De natura Noui Orbis* (1589), the Jesuit, Juan de Acosta, distinguished the 'barbarous' Chichimeca from the Mexica, who used 'the speeches that the orators and ancient rhetoricians made'.[33] Subsequently, Joannes de Laet's and Samuel Purchas's seventeenth-century compendiums of travel literature reiterated Acosta's claims for Dutch, French and English readers.[34] These works did not include the speeches gathered by Olmos but they certainly referred to the *huehuetlahtolli* to propagate the mendicants' account of Mexican civility.

---

[30] Mendieta, *Historia*, II.20–2, 112–20.

[31] 'la buena educación y doctrina de los niños . . . para hacerlos racionales y políticos y que viviesen la vida de hombres que tenían': Juan de Torquemada, *Monarquía indiana: de los veinte y un libros rituales y monarquía indiana, con el origen y guerras de los indios occidentales, de sus poblazones, descubrimiento, conquista, conversión y otras cosas maravillosas de la mesma tierra*, ed. Miguel León-Portilla (7 vols., Mexico, 1975–83), IV (13:16), 261 (quotation), 260–70 (speeches).

[32] 'aprenderan a poner en ejecución las costumbres honestas en la crianza de sus hijos': Augustín de Vetancurt, *Teatro mexicano: descripción breve de los sucessos exemplares, historicos, politicos, militares, y religiosos del nuevo mundo occidental de las Indias* (Mexico: Maria de Benavides, [1697–8]), I, 85.

[33] Diego Valadés, *Rhetorica Christiana* (Perugia: Petrus Jacobus Petrutius, 1579), 93; 'parlamentos que hacían los oradores y retóricos antiguos': Juan de Acosta, *Historia natural y moral de las Indias* (Seville: Juan de Léon, 1590), 408.

[34] Joannes de Laet, *Nieuwe wereldt ofte beschrijvinghe van West-Indien* (Leiden: Isaack Elzevier, 1625), and quickly thereafter in Latin and French; Samuel Purchas, *His Pilgrimage. Or Relations of the World and the Religions Obserued in All Ages and Places* (William Stansby for Henrie Fetherstone, 1625), and thereafter.

There was, as Thelma Sullivan argued, 'a striking similarity' between humanist rhetoric and 'the method used by the Aztecs, and this similarity could not have escaped the friars'.[35] Rather than merely noticing this similarity, however, the mendicants amplified it in their translation and use of the *Huehuetlahtolli*. As we will see, moreover, the Tlatelolcan editors actually reshaped the style and arguments of the Nahuatl orations to enhance their neo-classical qualities. Franciscans did not invent the 'speech of the ancients' but they certainly initiated its transformation and dissemination in order to defend the *indios'* capacities and their mission.

II Liberal education and the Colegio de Santa Cruz, Tlatelolco

The propagators of the *Huehuetlahtolli* had close ties to Tlatelolco. Sahagún and Olmos were among the first Latin masters at the Colegio de Santa Cruz and Bautista and Torquemada were guardians of the Convent de Santiago.[36] The college was managed for much of its history by indigenous alumni, but it lost vice-regal support in 1564 and was returned to Franciscan oversight in 1570. At any time, in its prime, it was liberally educating between 60 and 100 sons of *caciques*, a term used by the Spanish for indigenous leaders.[37] This much is well established. The debt that the college's intellectual culture owed to Erasmus of Rotterdam is less frequently recognised. Erasmians were persecuted in Spain after 1543 and in Mexico in the 1570s, particularly.[38] There is evidence to suggest, however, that the humanist's pedagogical influence endured at Tlatelolco. In addition to furnishing the *ladinos* with a grammatical and rhetorical

---

[35] Sullivan, 'The Rhetorical Orations, or Huehuetlahtolli', 83.

[36] Sahagún, *Florentine Codex*, I, 82; Mendieta, *Historia*, IV.15, 414–18; Torquemada, *Monarquía Indiana*, V (15:43), 174–9; Louise Burkhart, *Holy Wednesday: A Nahua Drama from Early Colonial Mexico* (Philadelphia, 1996), 55–65, 68–9; Robert Ricard, *The Spiritual Conquest of Mexico*, trans. Lesley Bryd Simpson (Berkeley, 1966), 218–24; Lino Gómez Canedo, *La educación de los marginados durante la época colonial: Escuelas y colegios para indios y mestizos en la Nueva España* (Mexico, 1982), 131–215; Kobayashi, *La educación como conquista*, 214–16.

[37] *Códice de Tlatelolco* in *Códice Mendieta: documentos Franciscanos siglos XVI y XVII*, ed. Joaquín García Icazbalceta (2 vols., Mexico, 1892), II, 241–9; Andrew Laird, 'Teaching of Latin to the Native Nobility in Mexico in the Mid-1500s: Contexts, Methods, and Results', in *Learning Latin and Greek from Antiquity to the Present*, ed. Elisabeth P. Archibald, William Brockliss and Jonathan Gnoza (Cambridge, 2015), 118–35; SilverMoon, 'The Imperial College of Tlatelolco and the Emergence of a New Nahua Intellectual Elite in New Spain (1500–1760)' (Ph.D., Duke University, 2007).

[38] Marcel Bataillon, *Erasmo y España: estudios sobre la historia espiritual del siglo XVI*, trans. Antonio Alatorre (2 vols., Mexico, 1950), II, 311–55, 435–54; Martin Austin Nesvig, *Ideology and Inquisition: The World of the Censors in Early Mexico* (New Haven, 2009), and *idem*, 'The Epistemological Politics of Vernacular Scripture in Sixteenth-Century Mexico', *The Americas*, 70 (2013), 165–201.

tool kit, Erasmus's works may have informed their intellectual activities, including their work on the *Huehuetlahtolli*.

The initial impulse for founding the Colegio de Santa Cruz may have been the creation of an indigenous clergy.[39] Yet well before 1555, when the first church council of New Spain determined against native or mestizo ordination, the purpose of the school had broadened.[40] The Tlatelolcans' enthusiasm for Erasmus's spiritual and pedagogical writings contributed to the process. In sixteenth-century Europe, Erasmus's jibes at the friars' expense had not gone unnoticed. Spanish Franciscans joined with other mendicant orders in submitting a list of Erasmus's errors in biblical scholarship and theology to the convenors of the Valladolid Assembly in 1527.[41] Nevertheless, within the observant friars in Spain, many were drawn to aspects of Erasmus's work. Franciscans at the University of Alcalá, founded by the observant friar and archbishop of Toledo, Francisco Jiménez de Cisneros (1436–1517), used Erasmus's pedagogical works to hone their Latin. Some Alcalán Franciscans, including Fray Francisco de los Ángeles Quiñones (1482–1540), engaged critically with Erasmus's New Testament scholarship.[42] A number of Franciscans associated with the *alumbrados*, mysticism and the *devotio moderna* drew on Erasmus's spiritual writings for their Christocentricity, criticisms of superstition, praise of apostolic simplicity and calls for ecclesiastical reform. Indeed, contemporaries often conflated Erasmianism with these other strands of spiritualism in sixteenth-century Spain.[43]

The first twelve Franciscans who travelled to New Spain in 1524 were observant friars who practised apostolic poverty and contemplative piety. They were instructed by Quiñones, who became commissary general of the order in 1523.[44] Once the Franciscans began their New World missions, Erasmus's Christocentric and scriptural account of faith proved

[39] Rodrigo de Albornoz to Charles V, 15 Dec. 1525, in *Colección de documentos para la historia de México: versión actualizada*, ed. Joaquín García Icazbalceta, on www.cervantesvirtual.com; Toribio de Benavente Motolinia, *History of the Indians of New Spain*, ed. Francis Borgia Steck (Washington, DC, 1951), 297.

[40] *Don fray Juan de Zumárraga*, ed. Icazbalceta, III, 204; Andrew Laird, 'Latin in Cuauhtémoc's Shadow: Humanism and the Politics of Language in Mexico after the Conquest', in *Latinity and Alterity in the Early Modern World*, ed. Yasmin Annabel Haskell and Juanita Feros Ruys (Tempe, AZ, 2010), 169–99, 274–6.

[41] For example, Erasmus, *CWE*, XXVII: *Praise of Folly*, ed. A. H. T. Levi (Toronto, 1986), 131–5, and *CWE*, XL: *Colloquies*, ed. Craig R. Thompson (Toronto, 1997), 763–95. On the Franciscan response, see Lu Ann Homza, 'Erasmus as Hero, or Heretic? Spanish Humanism and the Valladolid Assembly of 1527', *Renaissance Quarterly*, 50 (1997), 78–118, at 82–4.

[42] Bataillon, *Erasmo y España*, I, 1–59, 181, 326, 368, 405–7; Massimo Firpo, *Juan de Valdés and the Italian Reformation*, trans. Richard Bates (Farnham, 2015), 6–25.

[43] Bataillon, *Erasmo y España*, I, 190, 206–21, 368–424; José C. Nieto, 'Luther's Ghost and Erasmus' Masks in Spain', *Bibliothèque d'Humanisme et Renaissance*, 39 (1977), 33–49.

[44] Bataillon, *Erasmo y España*, II, 445–6; Steven Turley, *Franciscan Spirituality and Mission in New Spain, 1524–1599: Conflict beneath the Sycamore Tree (Luke 19:1–10)* (Farnham, 2014), 24–49.

useful for tackling indigenous idolatry. In New Spain, moreover, his support for vernacular preaching and scripture sounded like practical solutions to the challenges of evangelisation rather than the germs of Lutheranism. Juan de Zumárraga, the Franciscan, first bishop of Mexico and co-founder of Santa Cruz drew on Erasmus's *Paraclesis* (1516) and *Enchiridion* (1501) to make these arguments in his *Doctrina breue* (1544) for catechising the *indios*.[45] He excerpted Erasmus's defence of turning scripture 'into all the languages of the world, not only that it might be read by the *Indios*, but also that all other barbarous nations may read and know' it too.[46] Zumárraga owned at least fourteen of Erasmus's works, including his *Paraphrases on Luke* and *On the Apostolic Letters*.[47] The bishop used Erasmus's writings to emphasise the spiritual and civic benefits that elite laymen in the Americas could derive from studying classical texts and scripture. Rather than churning out candidates for ordination, Erasmus's *bonae litterae* could prepare noble Nahuatl youths to be faithful magistrates in the localities, champions of the gospel and moral *exempla* in New Spain.

Santa Cruz's commitment to vernacular scripture and the liberal education of indigenous students survived Zumárraga. Indeed, their interest in Erasmus persisted, despite the placement of all his writings on the Tridentine Index of 1559, fourteen of them on the Spanish Index of 1559, the prohibitions and expurgations listed in Gaspar de Quiroga's Indices of 1583 and 1584 and the blanket ban in 1612. In 1571, Pedro Moya de Contreras (*c.* 1528–91), the first inquisitor general and third archbishop of Mexico, ordered a general purge of prohibited books in his diocese. Bibles, Erasmus's works (predominantly the *Adagia*) and Zumárraga's Erasmian *Doctrina* dominated the haul from convents and clerics.[48] New evidence, however, from books in the convent library at Tlateloco shows that the Franciscans managed to save some editions of Erasmus. The front matter of their copies of Erasmus's *Life of Origen* and Erasmus's edition of Hilary's (d. 367?) *Lucubrationes*, were expurgated, since they were 'full of heresies and impiety'. Yet the convent retained the texts themselves, even after 1612. Not only did the Tlatelolco's copy

[45] Bataillon, *Erasmo y España*, I, 131–2, II, 445–51; Andrew Laird, 'Classical Letters and Millenarian Madness in Post-Conquest Mexico: The *Ectasis* of Fray Cristóbal Cabrera', *International Journal of the Classical Tradition*, 23 (2016), 1–31.

[46] 'estuviessen traduzidas en todas las lenguas de todos los del mundo para que no solamente las leyessen los Indios: pero aun otras naciones barbaras: leer y conocer': Juan de Zumárraga, *Doctrina breue muy p[ro]uechosa delas cosas q[ue] p[er]tenecen ala fe catholica y a n[uest]ra cristiandad en estilo llano p[ar]a comu[n] intelige[n]cia* (Mexico: Juan Cromberger, 1544), sigs. Kviir, Kviiir (quotation). Cf. Erasmus, *Paraclesis* (Basel: J. Froben, 1519), 7–8.

[47] *Zumárraga and his Family: Letters to Viscaya*, ed. Richard Greenleaf (Washington, DC, 1979), 122–6.

[48] *Libros y libreros en el siglo XVI*, ed. Francisco Fernández de Castillo, 2nd edn (Mexico, 1982), 473–95; Henry Kamen, *The Spanish Inquisition: A Historical Revision* (New Haven, 2014), 126, 132–3; Nesvig, *Ideology and Inquisition*, 5, 119–22, 145–7, 151, 233, 235.

of Erasmus's edition of Arnobius's commentary on the Psalms survive unmolested but Erasmus's prefatory material was annotated approvingly by a sixteenth-century clerical reader.[49] This pattern suggests they may have retained other works, too. By sticking with Erasmus, the Tlatelolcan Franciscans do not seem to have been trying to be obstreperous. Their attitude to the deliberately subversive Erasmian, fray Alonso de Cabello (*c.* 1555–83), who used Erasmus's writings to criticise the rules of his order, is suggestive. The convent assumed responsibility for Cabello's house arrest while he was under Inquisitorial investigation in 1576 and 1577, yet he seems to have had access to Erasmus's works in his cell.[50] Tlatelolcan friars could see the danger posed by Cabello's sermons but they did not necessarily blame his source texts.

The college adopted and probably kept using Erasmus's grammatical and rhetorical works because they were fit for purpose. Material from the northern humanist's *Libellus de octo orationis partium constructione* (1513), *Formulae colloquiorum familiarium* (1518), *De conscribendis epistolis* (1522) and *De copia* (1512) filled fray Maturino Gilberti's *Grammatica* (1559), the first Latin grammar printed in New Spain. Gilberti and his publisher were confident that they could sell textbooks in Mexico by openly declaring that 'the works of Erasmus demonstrate no small degree of learning'.[51] Treatises by Erasmus's pedagogical ally, Juan Luis Vives, were also popular. Indeed, demand for his *Exercitationes linguae latinae* (1539) was sufficient that Francisco Cervantes de Salazar (*c.* 1514–*c.* 1575), the first professor of rhetoric at the Real y Pontificia Universidad de México, produced a Mexican edition in 1554. He supplemented it with three Latin dialogues about the New World, the second of which described and commended the Colegio de Santa Cruz.[52] Cross-referencing 1571 and 1574 inventories of Santa Cruz, surviving items from the library at Tlatelolco and indigenous students' compositions confirms that Erasmus's prescriptions guided Nahua students through *Aesop's Fables*, Cato's *Disticha*

---

[49] 'que heresib[us] & impietate erat plena': annotation on the verso of the frontispiece, Hilary, *Lucubrationes*, ed. Desiderius Erasmus (Basel: J. Froben, 1535), Sutro Library, San Francisco, Vault, BT25 .H54 1535; Origen, *Opera, quae quidem extant omnia*, ed. Desiderius Erasmus (Basel: Froben, 1557), Sutro Library, San Francisco, Vault, BT25 .O74 L3 1557; Arnobius, *Commentarij, pr[i]iuxta ac eruditi in omnes psalmos sermone Latino*, ed. Desiderius Erasmus (Basel: Hieronymus Froben and Nicolaus Episcopius, 1537), Sutro Library, San Francisco, Vault, B650 .A763 I56 1537.

[50] Martin A. Nesvig, *Forgotten Franciscans: Writings from an Inquisitional Theorist, a Heretic, and an Inquisitional Deputy* (University Park, PA, 2011), 7–8, 22, 56, 56–8, and *idem*, 'The Epistemological Politics', 192–4.

[51] Maturino Gilberti, *Grammatica Maturini: Tractatus omnium fere qu[a]e Grammatices studiosis tradi solent*, ed. Rosa Lucas González (2 vols., Zamora, 2003), I, 21–3, 63, 310–11, II, 530 (quotation), 598–717; Nesvig, *Ideology and Inquisition*, 122–3.

[52] Francisco Cervantes de Salazar, *Commentaria in Ludovici Vives exercitationes linguae latinae* (Mexico: Juan Pablos, 1554).

and works by Virgil and Cicero.[53] Given the many copies of Erasmus's *Adagia* owned by friars and convents before 1574 (and possibly after), it seems likely that the *ladinos* extracted commonplaces from them to enliven their Latin compositions.[54] Next, Erasmus recommended that students read the Proverbs of Solomon and Ecclesiasticus. The 1577 debates about the Nahuatl translations of both these texts, which climaxed in the prohibition of fray Luis Rodríguez's indigenous version of Proverbs, suggests that the *colegiales* did just that.[55] Erasmus proposed that one of the most important exercises for enhancing students' speech and their capacity to explicate rich concepts was translation between tongues and across genres.[56] Tlatelolco's *ladinos* performed this exercise by translating Christocentric devotional works that encouraged personal piety and the preeminence of the spirit over the flesh. Scripture and Erasmus's spiritual writings almost certainly featured but the Franciscans prudently advertised their students' familiarity with less controversial texts. In 1570, for instance, Mendieta presented Juan de Ovanda (1515–75), president of the Council of the Indies, with a Nahuatl rendering of Thomas à Kempis's *De imitatione Christi* (1424–7). This classic of the *devotio moderna* was often associated with Erasmus's *Enchiridion militis Christiani* (1501), but spared its infamy.[57]

Under this Erasmian regime, the students' progress in grammar and rhetoric impressed their teachers and confounded detractors.[58] In October 1584, for instance, Alonso Ponce (fl. 1584–92), the proposed Franciscan commissary general for the New World and an opponent of teaching indigenous boys grammar, visited the college. The students greeted him with Latin orations in which they protested their inability, as *indios*, to speak good Spanish. Tlatelolco's annotated copy of the *Institutio oratoria* (8.6.54–5) suggests that Quintilian's lesson on irony had not been

---

[53] *Códice Mendieta*, II, 255–6, 259–61; *Aesop in Mexico: die Fabeln des Aesop in Aztekischer sprache*, ed. G. Kutscher, G. Brotherston and G. Vollmer (Berlin, 1987); Laird, 'Teaching of Latin to the Native Nobility in Mexico in the Mid-1500s', 127 n. 37.

[54] *Libros y libreros*, ed. Fernández del Castillo, 476, 485–7, 493–5.

[55] Nesvig, *Ideology and Inquisition*, 153–7; David Tavárez, 'A Banned Sixteenth-Century Biblical Text in Nahuatl: The Proverbs of Solomon', *Ethnohistory*, 60 (2013), 759–62. Cf. Erasmus, *CWE*, XXXIX: *Colloquies* (Toronto, 1997), 184, and *idem*, *Education of a Christian Prince*, trans. N. M. Cheshire and M. J. Heath, ed. Lisa Jardine (Cambridge, 1997), 61.

[56] Erasmus, *CWE*, XXIV: *De copia, De ratione studii*, ed. Craig R. Thompson (Toronto, 1978), 306.

[57] David Tavárez, 'Nahua Intellectuals, Franciscan Scholars, and the *devotio moderna* in Colonial Mexico', *The Americas*, 70 (2013), 203–35, at 203–5, 210–11; Bataillon, *Erasmo y España*, I, 57, 240–51.

[58] Julián Garcés, 'Humanism and the Humanity of the Peoples of the New World: *De habilitate et capacitate gentium* (1537)', ed. and trans. Andrew Laird, *Studi umanistici Piceni*, 34 (2014), 183–226; Ignacio Osorio Romero, *Le enseñaza del latín a los indios* (Mexico, 1990), 26–8.

lost on the *ladinos*.[59] Erasmus's curriculum was producing results in the New World. The *gramaticos* learned 'to instruct others in the schools of their towns . . . to translate from Spanish or Latin ecclesiastical matters, [and] to serve as interpreters for the Audiencias'. They prepared to serve as 'judges and governors, and to [undertake] other duties in the republic'.[60] Finally, Erasmus taught boys how to translate devotional works, sermons and scripture, an activity that Tlatelolcan friars lobbied (in vain) to continue when they resumed responsibility for Santa Cruz in the 1570s.[61]

The Franciscans praised their former students for their intellectual and literary contributions to evangelisation and the *huehuetlahtolli*. Sahagún identified Martín Jacobita of Tlatelolco, Alonso Vergerano and Pedro de San Buenaventura of Cuautitlán for their contributions to Book VI of the *Florentine Codex*. In particular, these *trilinguales* 'amended, explained, and expanded' the orations.[62] Juan Bautista similarly praised Santa Cruz's *ladinos*. Hernando de Ribas (d. 1597) had 'written and translated over 30 quires of paper on diverse things for [Bautista]'. Don Juan Berardo (d. 1594) and Don Francisco Baptista de Contreras served as native governors, writers and translators. Diego Adriano of Tlatelolco had 'learned to compose and to set type for the printing press in any language'.[63] Estevan Bravo of Texcoco wrote in Latin, Spanish and Nahuatl and was notable for *copia*, a rhetorical virtue in all three tongues. Pedro de Gante (d. 1605), native of Tlatelolco, had taught at Santa Cruz and translated the lives of saints for Bautista. Finally, Agustin de la Fuente, college master during Bautista's guardianship, had 'gone over everything that [Bautista had] printed here'. He had also learned to compose sermons and composite type in order to correct missionary texts.[64] The *ladinos*' Erasmian education had made them textual editors,

[59] Quintilian, *Oratoriarum institutionum libri 12* (Paris: Nicolaus Savetier, 1527), Sutro Library, San Francisco, Vault, PA6649 .A2 1527; Antonio de Ciudad Real, *Tratado curioso y docto de las grandezas de la Nueva España*, ed. Josefina García Quintana and Victor M. Castillo Farreras (2 vols., Mexico, 1976), I, 16–17.

[60] 'los indios que salen deste colegio de enseñar á otros en las escuelas de sus pueblos . . . y interpretar en ella las cosas eclesiásticas que se vuelven de latín ó romance, y asimismo sirven de intérpretes en las Audiencias . . . se suelen encomendar los oficios de jueces y gobernadores y otros cargos de república': *Códice Mendieta*, I, 178.

[61] Torquemada, *Monarquía Indiana*, V (15:43), 175; Sahagún, *Florentine Codex*, I, 83; Motolinia, *History of the Indians of New Spain*, 38; *Códice Mendieta*, I, 72–3; Burkhart, *Holy Wednesday*, 65–73; Gómez Canedo, *La educación de los marginados*, 180–8; Nesvig, 'The Epistemological Politics'; Tavárez, 'Nahua Intellectuals'.

[62] Sahagún, *Florentine Codex*, I, 44, 54–5.

[63] 'el qual me escriuio, y traduxo de cosas diuersas mas de treynta manos de papel' and 'aprendio acomponer, y componia en la Emprenta en qualquier lengua': Juan Bautista, 'Prologo', *A Iesu Christo S.N. ofrece este sermonario en lengua Mexicana* (Mexico: Diego Lopez Davalos, 1606), sig. *VIIv.

[64] 'passado todo quanto he impresso hasta aqui': Bautista, 'Prologo', *Sermonario*, sigs. **Ir (quotation),*VIIIr–**Ir.

translators and persuasive speakers, and prepared several to serve as Christian governors in New Spain.

The *gramaticos*' liberal educations may have encouraged them to collaborate on the *Huehuetlahtolli*. Don Antonio Valeriano of de Azcapotzalco (1526?–1605) was 'the principal and wisest' of Sahagún's collaborators on the *Florentine Codex* and praised by Bautista for 'speaking Latin *ex tempore* with so much propriety and elegance that he seemed another Cicero or Quintilian'.[65] After completing his studies at Santa Cruz, Valeriano remained at the college, first as a Latin *lector* and then as the *rector*. He translated Cato's *Disticha* into Nahuatl for the students, assisted Alonso Molina with the *Vocabulario en lengua castellana y Mexicana* (1555, 1571) and collaborated with Juan de Gaona on a set of Erasmian *Colloquios de la paz y tranquilidad christiana en lengua Mexicana* (1582). Valeriano was an editor of the *Florentine Codex* and contributed to Sahagún's *Los coloquios de los doce*, and *Primeros memoriales*. He provided Spanish glosses for Bautista's 1606 collection of Nahuatl sermons. It seems likely that he also worked on the *Huehuetlahtolli*.[66] What motivated his intellectual activities?

Valeriano was probably aware that his liberal education facilitated his success in colonial government. After serving on the *cabildo* of Azcapotzalco, he married Doña Isabel de Alvarado, the daughter of the first judge-governor of Tenochtitlan. Valeriano was elected to that office himself in 1573. Don Antonio was not humbly born but the indigenous chronicler, Fernando Alvarado Tezozmoc, also associated his status as a *tlatoani*, or ruler, with his wisdom – he was a *tlamatini* or 'one who knows things'.[67] Valeriano served the Spanish empire but he was not a craven puppet. In February 1561, he petitioned Philip II on behalf of Azcapotzalco for exemptions from labour and tribute, the restitution of lands, the translation of their city's status from town to city (*oppidum* to *civitas*) and permission to establish a traditional market (*tiyanquiliztli*). These were typical *cacique* demands but Valeriano expressed them in good Latin and warranted his appeal by referring to Acapotzalco's 'antiquity and nobility'. He added a more unusual request, too, a licence to establish

---

[65] 'hablaua ex tempore . . . con tanta propriedad, y elegancia, que parecia un Ciceron, o Quintiliano': Bautista, 'Prologo', *Sermonario*, sig. *VIIIr–v; Sahagún, *Florentine Codex*, I, 54–5.

[66] Cervantes de Salazar, *Commentaria in Ludovici Vives*, fo. 276r; Bautista, 'Prologo', *Sermonario*, sig. *VIIIr–v; Sahagún, *Florentine Codex*, I, 83–4, and *idem*, *Coloquios y doctrina cristiana: con que los doce frailes de San Francisco, enviados por el papa Adriano VI y por el emperador Carlos V, convirtieron a los indios de la Nueva España*, ed. Miguel León-Portilla (Mexico, 1986), 75; Torquemada, *Monarquía Indiana*, V (15:43), 176–7; Burkhart, *Holy Wednesday*, 66, 68–70, 73; Gómez Canedo, *La educación de los marginados*, 166.

[67] Fernando Alvarado Tezozomoc, *Crónica mexicáyotl*, ed. Adrián León (Mexico, 1975), 176; María Castañeda de la Paz, 'Historia de una casa real: origen y ocaso del linaje gobernante en México-Tenochtitlan', *Nuevo Mundo Mundos Nuevos* (2011), http://nuevomundo.revues.org/60624; William F. Connell, *After Moctezuma: Indigenous Politics and Self-Government in Mexico City, 1524–1730* (Norman, OK, 2011), 55, 60.

a 'house of the muses' for teaching '[Latin] grammar and Spanish'. 'These [tongues]', Valeriano explained, 'may be taught conveniently by some of us [Nahua], who have professed Latin frequently, and as well as the Spanish.'[68] The letter was suitably unctuous but it also asserted its author's intellectual and cultural parity. As governor of Tenochtitlan, Valeriano continued to fight with his pen. In 1575, he roused a crowd of several thousand *indios* to protest at Spanish interference in the Convent de Santiago's jurisdiction over the nuns of Santa Clara. In 1578, he complained to Philip II again, this time about the ignorance of the secular clergy. 'Most of them have no languages, the rest know [too] little, and they do not preach to the indigenous', he fumed.[69] Like Erasmus and the Tlatelolcan friars, he insisted on the effectiveness of evangelisation in the vernacular.

Valeriano's instruction at Santa Cruz had rendered him a sincere Christian, loyal to the friars, and ready to participate in imperial government. By urging him to write in Nahuatl and for the Nahua, however, his teachers had fostered his native cultural knowledge and affinities. As Valeriano told Philip II, he had learned to be both 'cacique y gobernado'.[70] In Erasmus's account of the responsibilities of rulers to advance the spiritual welfare of their subjects, moreover, Don Antonio may have found a model for reconciling his dual identities. He could use his trilingual rhetorical skills and his knowledge of the normative power that the past possessed for Europeans and Nahuas to advocate for the religious and moral education of the *indios*. Alumni like Valeriano may have collaborated with Bautista on the *Huehuetlahtolli* for the same reason that they defended Santa Cruz; the institution and its ancient texts offered indigenous boys opportunities for advancement, devotion and the preservation of Nahuatl culture in the new (colonial) world.

By the 1590s, the college needed support from alumni like Valeriano. It had been struggling for more than fifteen years. Sahagún lamented

[68]'antiquitate et nobilitate', 'iudicamus nos etiam musarum domo donari debere... at certe grammatica cum lingua Hispana quae commodius praelegi possunt a quibusdam nostri qui sermonem Latinum perinde ac Hispani saepe sunt professi': Alcaldes and regidores of Azcapotzalco to Philip II, 10 Feb. 1561, in *La nobleza indígena del centro de México despues de la conquista*, ed. Emma Pérez-Rocha and Rafael Tena (Mexico, 2000), 218, 222; Andrew Laird, 'Nahuas and Caesars: Classical Learning and Bilingualism in Post-Conquest Mexico; An Inventory of Latin Writings by Authors of the Native Nobility', *Classical Philology*, 109 (2014), 150–69, 157–60. On native governors, see Peter Villella, *Indigenous Elites and Creole Identity in Colonial Mexico, 1500–1800* (Cambridge, 2016), 37–9, 85–6.

[69]'Porque los más dellos no eran lenguas, y algunos que lo eran sabían poco y no predicaban a los naturales': Don Antonio Valeriano, letter to Philip II, 1578, in Miguel León-Portilla, 'Una carta inédita de don Antonio Valeriano, 1578', *Estudios de cultura Náhuatl*, 49 (2015), 199–207. For Valeriano's attempts to protect the convent, see Archivo General de Indias, Seville, Mexico 283, fos. 20v, 30v–36r.

[70]Valeriano, letter to Philip II, in León-Portilla, 'Una carta inédita', 206.

that it had lost its income-generating estates to the mismanagement of the Spanish majordomo, Diego Ruiz, and its good order to 'the negligence... of the rector', the counsellors and friars. The greatest blow, however, was the plague of 1576, which killed many of the college's pupils.[71] In this weakened state, Santa Cruz faced Archbishop Moya de Contreras's renewed criticisms of the Franciscan's educational mission, especially the Latin instruction of the *indios*. Indeed, by Sahagún's death in 1590, Santa Cruz's humanist curriculum had atrophied.[72] When Bautista became the guardian of the convent in 1597, he involved alumni like Valeriano in his Nahuatl-language print campaign to revive the college's fortune. It was time, he argued, to reassert the importance of 'raising young people in the fear and love of Our Lord'. 'Consider', he wrote, 'on the one hand the lack of education, respect or regard, and the barbarity of speech, and the little policy of the native youth of these times, and, on the other, the careful education, civility, respect, courtesy, and good diction and elegant speech of the ancient natives.'[73] The text in which Bautista announced his campaign for vernacular education was the *Huehuetlahtolli*. The *gramaticos* brought their native knowledge of the 'speech of the ancient' Nahuas and their Erasmian study of the speech of the ancient Israelites, Greeks and Romans to bear on the project.

III Tlatelolco and the creation of the *Huehuetlahtolli*

Georges Baudot argued influentially that when fray Juan Bautista discovered Andrés de Olmos's collection of Nahuatl orations, he deemed them a 'gift from God' and printed them expeditiously.[74] In fact, the last six Nahuatl speeches in Bautista's *Huehuetlahtolli*, one of which is addressed 'to those who go to school or learn doctrine with the Religious in the Monasteries', indicate that Bautista initiated more

---

[71] Sahagún, *Florentine Codex*, I, 82–4, 92; *Códice de Tlatelolco* in *Códice Mendieta*, II, 250–1.

[72] Mendieta, *Historia*, IV:15, 418; Torquemada, *Monarquía Indiana*, V (15:43), 176–7; Pilar Gonzalbo Aizpuru, *Educación y colonisación en la Nueva España, 1521–1821* (Mexico, 2001), 120–7; SilverMoon, 'The Imperial College of Tlatelolco', 93–8; Burkhart, *Holy Wednesday*, 62–5; Kobayashi, *La educación como conquista*, 250–71; Gómez Canedo, *La educación de los marginados*, 188–95.

[73] 'criar a los niños enel temor y amor de nuestro Señor' and 'Considerando pues yo . . . por una parte la poca criança, respecto y miramiento, barbaridad enel hablar, y poca policia de los Indios moçuelos deste tiempo, y por otra parte la mucha criança, urbanidad, respecto, cortesia, buen termino y elegancia enel hablar de los Indios viejos': Bautista, 'Prologue', in *Huehuetlahtolli*, sigs p*6v, *7v.

[74] Baudot, *Utopia and History in Mexico*, 229–34; and Miguel León-Portilla, 'Estudio introductorio', *Huehuetlahtolli: Testimonios de la antigua palabra*, trans. Librado Silva Galeana, ed. Miguel León-Portilla (Mexico, 1988), 14–19, which influenced Louise Burkhart, *The Slippery Earth: Nahua-Christian Moral Dialogue in Sixteenth-Century Mexico* (Tucson, 1989), 102–4, 173–4, 179, despite this study's broader and ground-breaking argument for the mutual contamination of Nahua religion and Christianity.

extensive augmentation and *inventio*. With a circle of *ladinos*, he adapted the 'old words' for their colonial, Christian context.[75] Scholars have begun to recognise the syncretic style and evangelising purpose of the printed *Huehuetlahtolli*.[76] By contextualising the collection in the Erasmian pedagogy of Santa Cruz, however, we glean a sharper sense of the rhetorical tools that Olmos, Bautista and the *ladinos* collaborators used to enhance the force of the orations for novices and indigenous readers. We are also better able to discern the contours of the theory of speech that animates the printed collection.

Andrés de Olmos gathered only eight of the twenty-nine speeches printed in 1601 but his 1547 *Arte de la lengua Mexicana* showed Bautista how *huehuetlahtolli* could extend the rhetorical lessons of Nahuatl–Spanish grammars and vocabularies for evangelising purposes. Olmos attached a speech, 'Of a father to his son', and the son's reply, to his *Arte*, and Bautista printed them with only slight modifications. The friar asked his indigenous collaborators to substitute the name of God *verdadero* for traditional Nahuatl deities in the *huehuetlahtolli*.[77] The result is that the father and son of the speeches venerate a single, personalised deity, 'Our Lord', *Totecuyo* and *Ipalnemohuani*, 'Giver of Life' or 'by whom one lives', an epithet for God favoured by mid-century Franciscans.[78] Further, Olmos and his collaborators inserted passages that taught readers and auditors how to worship the Christian deity. 'When you pass before the venerable image of Our Lord, or his loved ones, or of the cross, (*cruz*)', the father counselled, 'you should bow before Him or bend the knee and much more if you go before the venerated body of Our Lord Jesus Christ (*Iesu Christi*), that is before the Holy Sacrament (*isanto sacramento*)'.[79] Olmos understood the potential of *huehuetlahtolli* to lure new Christians back to old, idolatrous ways.[80] By cleansing the Nahua antiquities of idolatry and

---

[75] 'In nonotzaloca immomachtia teupan, in quenin huel quimotlayecoltilizque Dios', *Huehuetlahtolli*, ed. Bautista, fos. 54r, 60r (quotation), 67r, 69v, 71r, 73r. Sahagún also noted the evangelising potential of the *huehuetlahtolli*: *Adiciones, apéndice a la postilla y ejercicio cotidiano*, ed. Arthur J. O. Anderson and Miguel León-Portilla (Mexico, 1993), 105.

[76] Ruiz Bañuls, *El huehuetlahtolli*, 127.

[77] Zorita, *Relación de la Nueva España*, ed. Ahrndt *et al.*, 209; 'Exhortación', ed. García Quintana, 137–82; *Huehuetlahtolli*, ed. Bautista, fos. 1r–14r (Nahuatl), fos. 77v–82r (Spanish).

[78] See Susanne Klaus, *Uprooted Christianity: The Preaching of the Christian Doctrine in Mexico, Based on Franciscan Sermons of the Sixteenth Century Written in Nahuatl* (Bonn, 1999), 144.

[79] 'Ihuan in canin ixpantiquisaz in ixiptlatzin in Totecuiyo, ahnozo in itlazohuan, ahnozo cruz, huel ticmahuiztiliz: ixpan timopachoz ahnozo timotlancuacoloz. Auh intla huel yehualt in Totecuiyo Iesu Christi in inacayotzin, isanto sacramento, ixpan tiquisaz, tlapanahuia': 'Exhortación', ed. García Quintana, 152. With minor variations in *Huehuetlahtolli*, ed. Bautista, fo. 2r–v.

[80] See Andrés de Olmos, *Tratado de hechicerías y sortilegios* [1553], ed. Georges Baudot (Mexico, 1990), 89.

enhancing their evangelising content, he showed the friars how to deploy the orations as weapons for spiritual conquest.

The friars and collaborating *gramaticos* also made accommodations in the *Huehuetlahtolli* to explain Christianity to Nahua readers and auditors. For instance, the father of the first speech explained to his son that, 'God is your very mother, your father. [He] strives greatly to take good care of you.'[81] While sixteenth-century *spirituali* occasionally compared God to a nursing mother, it is unlikely that the dual-sex deity of this *difrasismo* is of European origin.[82] Traditional Nahuatl prayers, spoken during childbirth, frequently invoked a divine pair, 'Our Mother, Our Father, the two lord and two lady' who had power over human generation.[83] One might assume that the editors had simply missed this reference to the old gods when they Christianised the speech but they knew it was there. They cleansed the Spanish-language version of its feminine aspect, leaving a conventional sentiment '[God] raised you to help you, for he is your Father.'[84] This suggests that indigenous *gramaticos* had retained, or even added, the 'mother, father' couplet to explicate the life-giving power of the Christian God for Nahua students. Olmos and his collaborators may have made the 'speech of the ancients' sound Christian, but the *inventio* of the native linguists also made Christianity sound more like Nahuatl.[85]

Mónica Ruiz Bañuls has shown that Olmos, Bautista and their collaborators increased the evangelising potential of the *huehuetlahtolli* by interpolating biblical proverbs into the texts. They drew especially heavily on the Books of Proverbs and Sirach (or Ecclesiasticus), which Erasmus had prescribed for future rulers and which the *gramaticos* studied at Santa Cruz. The Vulgate places that they wove into the speeches described the duties of piety and filial obedience, the dangers of lust, intoxication

---

[81]'Ca yehualt Dios, huel monantzin, motatzin; icenca, tlapanahuia': 'Exhortación', ed. García Quintana, 152; with minor variations in *Huehuetlahtolli*, ed. Bautista, fo. IV.

[82]In her *Meditations on the Song of Songs*, for instance, Teresa of Avila (1515–82) followed Ramon Llull and compared the human soul to a baby and God to a 'mother who loves her baby, nourishes it, and attends to it': Teresa of Avila, *Obras completas de Santa Teresa*, ed. Efrén de la Madre de Dios and Otger Steggink (Madrid, 1986), 452. Nevertheless, this metaphor was far from orthodox during the Catholic Reformation. Indeed, fray Luis de Léon left Teresa's *Meditation* out of his 1588 edition of her works. Vernacular interpretations of the *Song of Songs* had been proscribed by the Council of Trent and Luis had been imprisoned from 1572 to 1575, partly for circulating a Spanish version himself: *Proceso inquisitorial de Fray Luis de León*, ed. Ángel Alcalá (Valladolid, 1991), 221, 376–8.

[83]'in ome tecutli, in ome ci[hualt]': *Florentine Codex*, ed. Sahagún, VII, 175. See Richard Haly, 'Bare Bones: Rethinking Mesoamerican Divinity', *History of Religions*, 31 (1992), 269–304, at 278.

[84]'[Dios] te crio, que te ayude pues es tu Padre': *Huehuetlahtolli*, ed. Bautista, fo. 77v.

[85]See, similarly, Mark Z. Christensen, *Nahua and Maya Catholicisms: Texts and Religion in Colonial Central Mexico and Yucatan* (Stanford, 2013); Burkhart, *The Slippery Earth*, 184–94.

and gluttony, the need for self-discipline, the duties of officeholders and the inevitability of death.[86] Strikingly, moreover, the *gramaticos* shaped the Nahuatl text to imitate the Vulgate Latin stylistically. Proverbs 4:1–4, for instance, begins with an exhortation:

> Listen, my sons, to the instruction of your father and pay attention, so that you might learn prudence. I offer you good precepts; do not forsake my rules . . . [4, My father] said to me 'Let your heart cling to my words and keep my precepts and you will live.'[87]

In Latin, Proverbs 4:4 reads *suscipiat verba mea . . . custodi praecepta mea*, a syntactical pattern of jussive subjunctive + plural neuter + first person possessive, then the same with an imperative verb, then a future indicative, *et vives*, to soften the command into a conditional. The Nahuatl oration 'Of the mother to her daughter' in the *Huehuetlahtolli* concluded with a very similar admonition:

> If you do this, what I have spoken of, what I have instructed you, then truly you will live well, with people's favour, alongside the people. So I fulfil my duty . . . Because you will never fall into error if you follow [this advice], if you listen, if you take it into your stomach, if you swallow it down your throat.[88]

In Nahuatl, the final phrase reads *oticcuic intla moxillan, intla motozcatlan oticmopachilhui*. It is a plaited pattern of preterit verb + conditional conjunction + possessed noun that mimics the syntax of the Vulgate proverb while incorporating a traditional Nahuatl couplet, 'into your stomach, down your throat'. The effect is to merge the prophetic tone and account of moral causation contained in the 'speech of the ancient' Israelites with the elevated tone and vivid, corporal imagery of traditional *difrasismo*. To the well-trained humanist, writing was 'most learned and eloquent' when it was sprinkled 'freely with adages'.[89] By seasoning their *huehuetlahtolli* with Vulgate passages, the Tlatelolcans enhanced their evangelising potential and demonstrated the stylistic complementarity of Latin and Nahuatl. They also got away with printing some Old Testament proverbs in the vernacular.

The friars and *ladinos* did not merely integrate Vulgate passages. Rather, they adopted Erasmus's advice that an orator might vary proverbs

---

[86] Ruiz Bañuls, *El huehuetlahtolli*, 166–85. She notes that biblical proverbs also occur in Book VI of the *Florentine Codex*.

[87] 'audite filii disciplinam patris et attendite ut sciatis prudentiam/ donum bonum tribuam vobis legem meam ne derelinquatis . . . atque dicebat suscipiat verba mea cor tuum custodi praecepta mea et vives': Vulgate, Proverbs 4:1–4.

[88] 'Yntla yuh ticchihuazin inic onimitznonotz, inic onimitzizcali, yc nelli huel tinemiz in tepaltzinco, in tenahuactzinco. Yc mohuicpa ninoquixtia in nihuehue in nilama, in nitlacazcaltiani, in nitlacahuapahuani. Inic ahtle nahualoca yez in quemmanian intla otican, intla oticcac, intla oticcuic, intla moxillan, intla motozcatlan oticmopachilhui': *Huehuetlahtolli*, ed. Bautista, fo. 20v. See, similarly, *Florentine Codex*, ed. Sahagún, VII, 79, 105, 113.

[89] Erasmus, *Adages of Erasmus*, ed. William Watson Barker (Toronto, 2001), 11.

syntactically or substitute their diction in order to explicate their meanings and ornament speech. For instance, the father of Sirach 4.7 urged his son: 'Address yourself courteously to the congregation of the poor, and humble your soul before the elders of the church, and bow your head before the great men.'[90] When the editors of the *Huehuetlahtolli* interpolated this passage into the first speech of the father to the son they used the future tense in place of the imperative and maintained the ascending tricolon of identities that gave Sirach 4.7 its force. Nevertheless, they inverted the order of the original set, rendering it as, 'You will greet them . . . the nobles . . . the *padres* . . . but also . . . the humble.'[91] The effect was to emphasise the courtesy due to impoverished people, an appropriate sentiment for a Franciscan text.

Within this inverted tricolon structure, moreover, the Tlatelolcans made further elaborations. They took their strategies for copiousness from Erasmus's *Familiarium colloquiorum formulae* (1522), as it was relayed in the Mexican *Grammatica Maturini*. Erasmus began his instructions by telling schoolboys to greet others and by identifying the circumstances in which a salutation was appropriate: 'It is a mark of politeness (*urbanitas*) to greet those who meet us, or those we meet . . . likewise [to greet] those carrying out some work.'[92] The friars and *ladinos* followed their main verbal clause of instruction, 'You will greet them', with congruent details, 'anywhere they are going about their doings or simply where you will encounter them.'[93] Where Erasmus had used an active present participle + ablative construction (*operis . . . agentes*) for 'going about . . . work', the Tlatelolcans derived an equivalent with a possessed deverbalised noun + stative verb (*itlachihul[huan] . . . cate*) for 'going about their business'. They showed Nahuatl's capacity to match the plenty and dignity of Latin, a desirable achievement among vernacular tongues in the renaissance, not least because it demonstrated the cultural and political sophistication of its speakers.[94]

Next, the Tlatelolcans ornamented the passage by synthesising elements of Nahuatl and European rhetoric. They inserted pairs of synonyms (*los difrasismos*) for the three sorts of people requiring salutation (the nobility, clergy and indigent) and used the particle '*in*' to connect them

---

[90]'Congregatione pauperum affabilem te facito, et presbytero humilia animam tuam, et magnato humilia caput tuum': Vulgate, Ecclesiasticus 4.7; Erasmus, *Adages*, 19–20.

[91]'Yhuan tiquintlahpaloz . . . in pipiltin . . . in padreme[h] . . . auh . . . in ycnotlacatl': 'Exhortación', ed. García Quintana, 152–4; *Huehuetlahtolli*, ed. Bautista, fo. 2v.

[92]'Urbanitatis est salutare obuios, qui nos adeu[n]t, aut quos adimus . . . ite[m] operis aliquid agentes . . . ': Erasmus, *Familiarum colloquiorum opus* (Basel: Froben, [1522] 1538), sig. A3r; *Grammatica Maturini*, ed. Lucas González, II, 598.

[93]'Yhuan tiquintlapaloz in itlachihualhuan in campa cate in ahnozo cana': 'Exhortación', ed. García Quintana, 152; with slight variations in *Huehuetlahtolli*, ed. Bautista, fo. 2v.

[94]Peter Burke, *Languages and Communities in Early Modern Europe* (Cambridge, 2004), 61–88.

syntactically and subordinate them to the main clause of the tricolon. Olmos's team explained that the 'nobles' were also 'rulers and those standing over the people' (*in tlatoque yhaun in tepan ihcanime*). To the category of *padres*, Bautista's team added 'religious leaders and prelates' (*in teoyotica teyacanque in tepachohuanime*). The meek, the largest class of persons, was distinguished by the new sentence particle, *auh*. It included 'the old man, the old woman', whose decrepitude (rather than wisdom) was suggested by mock reverential suffixes (*in huehuentzin in ilamatzin*), along with 'the humble and the lowly, the unhappy and the joyless'.[95] *Los difrasismos* are the most important figure of Nahuatl rhetoric yet Erasmus also described synonyms as the 'first and simplest form' of *copia*. He followed Quintilian in encouraging schoolboys to 'collect a vast supply of words like this' so that they could deploy them in their speaking and writing.[96] By enhancing the Nahuatl *plática*, the editors displayed their own storehouses of *los difrasismos*. By putting them in print, the Tlatelolcans provided clerical and indigenous readers with sets of paired entries to start building their own rhetorical reed chests. With the *Huehuetlahtolli*, the *ladinos* used their knowledge of Latin grammar and rhetoric to demonstrate the powerful techniques of Nahuatl discourse for a colonial audience.

In explaining why eloquent Nahuatl was morally, politically and religiously valuable, the friars and *gramaticos* also drew on Erasmus's account of the nature and function of good speech. It is striking, for instance, that despite the Tlatelolcans' frequent recourse to Proverbs and Sirach in the *Huehuetlahtolli*, they avoided the (many) Old Testament adages that associated ready speech with moral degeneracy. 'Listen, children, to the doctrine of the tongue', the speaker of Sirach 23 warns in a representative passage, 'He who guards it shall not perish by his lips; he will not be led into sin by the most wretched deeds.'[97] In contrast, in the *Huehuetlahtolli* the father urges his son to address others 'by means of most elegant speech (*huel qualli tlahtotica*). You will not go about as if you are voiceless.'[98] Moreover, when the editors of the *Huehuetlahtolli* did draw on Sirach's prescriptions (5:13–17, 32:10–13), they adapted the proverbs to emphasise the benefits that accrued to civil speakers. For example, a father tells his son to be modest in the company of social superiors:

---

[95] 'yhuan in ycnotlacatl, in nentlacatl, in ahmo ahuiya, in ahmo paqui': 'Exhortación', ed. García Quintana, 152–4; with the variation described in *Huehuetlahtolli*, ed. Bautista, fo. 2v.

[96] Erasmus, *CWE*, XXIV, 307; Quintilian, *Institutio oratoria*, 10.1.6–7.

[97] 'doctrinam oris audite filii et qui custodierit illam non periet in labiis suis nec scandalisabitur in operibus nequissimis': Vulgate, Ecclesiasticus 23:7. See similarly *Ecclesiasticus*, 9:13, 19:4–17, 20:4–5, 28:13–26, and *Proverbs*, 11:13, 12:23, 14:23, 15:21, 28:20.

[98] 'huel qualli tlahtoltica. Ahmo yuquin tinontli yc tinemiz': 'Exhortación', ed. García Quintana, 154; *Huehuetlahtolli*, ed. Bautista, fo. 2v.

If it is not your place to hold forth, you will not speak, you will not give orders, you will refrain [from talking]. If it is not your place to speak, and yet you are questioned, then you will speak prudently (*zan melahuac*), you will never tell lies, you will not disparage anyone. You will prepare your words very carefully (*huel ticnehmachiliz*) so that you do not answer like an idiot or like a braggart. When you do speak, when you answer, if you hang your words out swiftly, you will be honoured.[99]

Erasmus had evoked the same Vulgate authorities in a different order in his colloquy, *Lesson on Manners* (1522), for boys at a feast:

> Your speech should not be foolish or hasty. Do not let your mind wander but pay attention to what is said. If a response is needed, make it concisely and prudently (*paucis, ac prudenter*) . . . Avoid loquaciousness, indeed you should not speak unless you are questioned . . . Don't disparage anybody, or make assumptions. Don't boast about your things, or belittle another's . . . Don't slander anyone . . . You should not let your tongue wag idly. So it is, that without prejudice, you will win praise and make friends.[100]

Erasmus anticipated and possibly guided the *ladinos* in specifying the social circumstances that called for restraint and in concluding the Vulgate admonitions with a clause emphasising that good speech brought honour to the orator and strengthened civil bonds.

Indeed, *qualli tlahtolli*, the *ladinos*' phrase for 'good speech', was an exact Nahuatl cognate for Erasmus's preferred term, *bonae litterae*.[101] To qualify as 'good', Erasmus argued that speech had to emerge from the careful study of classical texts and scripture, imitate ancient usage (though not slavishly) and enhance the moral probity and religious devotion of orator and auditor. In an early epistle, Erasmus contended that good speech or letters 'were not conferred, like worldly honours, upon the idle and undeserving. They did not distract one from practising virtue but themselves conferred it . . . without them we could not even be human.'[102] To be human meant to be drawn from the caves of the savages and into society, as Cicero had argued in *De Inventione*. For Erasmus, eloquence and virtue encouraged civility, concord and piety. As such, Erasmus argued

[99] 'in tlacamomo tlahtohuayan, ahmo tehuan titlahtoz ahmo tinahuatiz, zan timocahuaz. Auh intla no tehuatl motlahtohuayan, ahnozo titlatlaniloz, zan melahuac inic titlahtoz, ahtle tiquiztlacaihtoz, ayac ticchicoihtoz, huel ticnehmachiliz immotlahtol inic titlananquiliz, ahmo yuhquin tixolopitli, ahmo no yuhquin timopohuani inic titlahtol inic titlananquiliz, zan tecpilhuetziz immotlahtol, yc timahuizoloz': *Huehuetlahtolli*, ed. Bautista, fos. 6v–7r.

[100] 'Ne sis inepte loquax, aut praeceps. Ne uagetur animus interim, sed sis attentus quid ille dicat. Si quid erit respondendum, id facito paucis, ac prudenter . . . Arride loquentibus: ipse ne quid loquaris, nisi rogatus . . . Ne cui obtrectato: ne cui temet ante ponito: ne tua iactato: ne aliena despicito . . . Ne sis lingua futili. Ita fiet, ut sine inuidia laudem inuenias, & amicos pares': Erasmus, *Familiarum colloquiorum opus*, sigs. C8v, D1r–v.

[101] The Nahuatl introductions to familial speeches in book six of the *Florentine Codex*, ed. Sahagún, VII, 93, 99, 113, also describe the discourse they announce as 'qualli in tlatolli', or 'good in speech'.

[102] Erasmus, *CWE*, I: *Letters 1 to 141 (1484 to 1500)*, trans. R. A. B. Mynors and D. F. S. Thomson, ed. Wallace K. Ferguson (Toronto, 1974), no. 61, 127. See Jacques Chomarat, *Grammaire et rhétorique chez Érasme* (2 vols., Paris, 1981), I, 231–63.

that governors had a particular responsibility to speak well and champion scripture.[103] God's word was the most powerful way to cultivate virtue, peace and the Christian faith. While Erasmus's account of personal piety owed much to the *devotio moderna* tradition, his emphasis on language as central to the human capacity to understand and embrace Christ and to order moral and political life accordingly was distinctive.

The *Huehuetlahtolli* drew on Erasmus's argument to elucidate good Nahuatl discourse. *Tlahtolli* was *qualli* when it encouraged moral probity and civility. In one speech, a Nahua mother instructed her daughter that if she wished 'to live very well' (*yc nelli huel tinemiz*) and be of good reputation, she would follow maternal guidance and the precepts of 'the good song, the good words' (*in qualli cuicatl, qualli tlahtolli*). The mother confirmed that she, herself, was transmitting these precepts in her advice. She took on the identity of 'a male elder, a female elder, and a pedagogue, a tutor' when she addressed good words to her daughter.[104] In another discourse, a father instructed his son to imitate ancient usage: 'May you speak [those words] that the ancient man, the ancient woman spoke.'[105] Like humanist Latin, moreover, ancient usage in Nahuatl *qualli tlahtolli* had a particular grammar, diction and syntax. We overhear a different Nahuatl father tell his son: 'Don't you forget those good letters (*qualli tlahtolli*), when conversing. If [words] are not spoken correctly by you, then you will practice extensively, then you will correct them according to those [words] that the ancients speak.'[106] Yet ancient usage was also intimately connected to virtuous conduct. As another father exhorted his just-married son, 'Let your words be good (*qualli immotlahtol*), let them be pure (*yectli*) because you must respect them, you must honour them.'[107] The creators of the *Huehuetlahtolli* employed traditional couplet metaphors for wise counsel, 'a lip, a mouth', for repositories of ancient wisdom, 'the black, the red', and for the value of good advice, which was like 'the jade, the turquoise'.[108] The Tlatelolcans drew on Erasmus's

[103] Erasmus, *CWE*, LXVI: *Handbook of the Christian Soldier*, trans. Charles Fantazzi, ed. John O'Malley (Toronto, 1977), 40–7, and *CWE*, XXVI: *The Right Way of Speaking Latin and Greek*, trans. Maurice Pope, ed. J. K. Sowards (Toronto, 1985), 369. Cf. Cicero, *De Inventione*, I.ii, 2–3.

[104] 'in nihuehue, in nilama, in nitlacazcaltiani, in nitlacahuapahuani': *Huehuetlahtolli*, ed. Bautista, fo. 20v.

[105] 'ma tiquihto tlein quihtohua in huehue, in ilama': *Huehuetlahtolli*, ed. Bautista, fo. 23v.

[106] 'ahmo ticteilcahualtiz in tleyn qualli tlahtolli inic nenonotzalo. Auh intlacamo melahuac quitohua in tehuatl huel timoyeyecoz intla tiquintlahpatiliz in aquique huehueyntin tlahtozque': *Huehuetlahtolli*, ed. Bautista, fo. 6v.

[107] 'ma qualli immotlahtol, auh ma yectli inic xiquimonixtili, inic xiquimonmahuiztili': *Huehuetlahtolli*, ed. Bautista, fo. 28r.

[108] 'in cententli, in cencamatl': *Huehuetlahtolli*, ed. Bautista, fos. 15r–v, 22r, 32v, 39r, 41r–v, 49r, 64r; 'in tilli, in tlapalli', fos. 38r, 39v; 'in chalchihuitl, in teoxihuitl', fos. 8v, 9r, 23v, 27r, 33v, 56v, 61v among others. See, similarly *Florentine Codex*, ed. Sahagún, VII, 248.

defence of the *bonae litterae* to unpack these metaphors for novices and convent-educated indigenous students. They argued that Nahuatl 'good speech' demonstrated individual virtue, encouraged moral probity in others and tightened the bonds of family.

The *Huehuetlahtolli* also echoed Erasmus's insistence that rulers should speak well, 'so that [they] are always educating [their people], instructing them' with their words.[109] In one of the political orations in the collection, a Nahua nobleman reminds a new ruler that the virtue and piety of the city depended on his discourse:

> You are [God's] substitute, you are his representative . . . You serve as [God's] interpreter here, you pronounce his words, you speak for him. The divine word (*in ihiyotzin, in tlahtoltzin*) of Our Lord does not depart, does not falter, [but rather] it flourishes, it shimmers, it goes honourably, it goes nobly.[110]

A prince's speech, then, needed to be more than *qualli*. In Book VI of the *Florentine Codex*, Sahagún had glossed the couplet that the Tlatelolcans used in this passage, 'ihijo, itlatol' or 'ihijotzin, itlatoltzin' in the reverential, as literally 'his breath or spirit[,] or his word'. He emphasised that the metaphor traditionally referred to the speech of rulers (*tlatoque, principales*) but was now employed by Christian preachers.[111] On their arrival in the Mexico valley, the Franciscans had been struck by 'his breath, his word', a phrase so pleasingly redolent of 2 Timothy 3:16–17, 'All scripture is divinely inspired [or breathed] and useful for teaching', and 2 Peter 1:21, 'Inspired [or breathed into] by the Holy Spirit, the holy men were speaking of God.' They swiftly coopted *ihiyotzin, tlahtoltzin* to refer to the Christian message.[112] In this passage of the *Huehuetlahtolli*, Bautista and the *ladinos* connected the traditional and missionary meanings of the metaphor – the ruler's speech is also divine speech – to allude to Proverb 16:10, 'Divination comes from the lips of the king.'

It seems unlikely that the *Huehuetlahtolli* was openly proposing that *tlatoque* should be preachers without ordination. Its authors may have been encouraging noble Nahua to consider a path tacitly reopened by

[109] 'ca ye titlacazcaltia, ca ye titlacahuapahua': *Huehuetlahtolli*, ed. Bautista, fo. 37r. A noble woman receives similar advice, fo. 44r. Cf. Erasmus, *Education of a Christian Prince*, 99.

[110] 'in tipatca, in tixiptla, in tixtelolo, in ticamachal . . . ca ticnahuatlatalhuiya, tictlatenquixtilia, tictlahtolquixtilia. In ahnen yauh, in ahnen huetzi, in xotlatiuh, in pepetzcatiuh, in tleyotiuh, in mahuizzotiuh, in ihiyotzin, in tlahtoltzin Totecuiyo': *Huehuetlahtolli*, ed. Bautista, fo. 35r.

[111] 'su resuello o esp[irit]u o su palabra': Sahagún, *Florentine Codex*, VII, 246.

[112] For example, Sahagún, *Coloquios y doctrina cristiana*, ed. León-Portilla, 103–4, 116–17, 146–7, 154–5; *Vida y milagros del bien auenturado Sanct Antonio de Padua*, ed. Juan Bautista and Agustín de la Fuentes (Mexico: Diego Lopez Davalos, 1605), sigs. A4r, C3v. Use of the phrase in context in Bartolomé de Alva, *A Guide to Confession Large and Small in the Mexican Language, 1634*, ed. Barry D. Sell and John Frederick Schwaller, with Lu Ann Homza (Norman, OK, 1999), 93, 117, 155, shows a range of possible valences, including 'preaching' or 'holy teaching', 'the Mass' and 'the Gospel'.

the Third Provincial Council (1585) and the example of noble Texcocan, Antonio del Rincón (1555–1601).[113] Alternatively, they may have been thinking of temporal *caciques y gobernadors* like themselves. Erasmus had described the prince's religious duties to Charles V in the dedicatory letter to his *Paraphrase on Matthew*. Charles had been 'anointed and consecrated expressly' to 'propagate the religion of the gospel'. He was not 'a teacher of the gospel' in the manner of a bishop, but he was 'its champion' (*propugnator*).[114] As Don Antonio Valeriano's letters to Philip II showed, Tlatelolcan *caciques* considered advocating for indigenous liberal education, Nahuatl preaching and evangelisation as pertaining to their civil office. In fact, another speech in the *Huehuetlahtolli* depicted the *tlatoque* of Texcoco, championing Christianity to their people:

> You [the people] should pay close attention, you should give yourself completely to Our Lord, God. Perhaps you [singular] have heard it already, you have received it (*oticonili, oticcuili*), a lip, a mouth, the divine word (*in ihiyotzin, in tlahtoltzin*). You [plural] should engrave it on your hearts (*xocommoyollotican*), let it fill you, let it make you drunk (*ma amechihuinti ma amechxocomicti*).[115]

The rulers' advice was woven from Vulgate places, the threads of which were revealed by the abrupt shift between the second person singular (*oticonili, oticcuili*) of Job 22:22 'you [singular] shall receive instructions from His mouth' and the second person plural (*xocommoyollotican*) of Deuteronomy 11:18 'Receive these words of mine in your [plural] hearts and minds.'[116] The final *difrasismo* of the passage (*ma amechihuinti ma amechxocomicti*) evokes, more poetically, Peter's sermon at Pentecost (Acts 2:1–22). Peter explained that the diverse people before him, speaking in tongues, were not 'full with wine' but 'filled with the Holy Spirit'. It had come over them 'like a sudden gust of wind (*spiritus*)'. The Lord had 'poured from [His] Spirit onto all flesh' and they were drunk with it. Despite their varied natural languages, the crowd before him understood each other perfectly; they spoke to one another in God's word.[117] Tlatelolcan *gramaticos*, like Valeriano, were keenly aware of the

[113] Kelly McDonough, 'Indigenous Intellectuals in Early Colonial Mexico: The Case of Antonio del Rincón, Nahua Grammarian and Priest', *Colonial Latin American Review*, 20 (2011), 145–65, 150–1; Stafford Poole, 'Church Law on the Ordination of Indians and Castas in New Spain', *Hispanic American Historical Review*, 61 (1981), 637–50.

[114] Erasmus, *CWE*, XLV: *Paraphrase on Matthew*, trans. Dean Simpson, ed. Robert D. Sider (Toronto, 2008), 5–6, cf. Erasmus, *Education of a Christian Prince*, 99, 202.

[115] 'Xicmocemittili, xicmocenmacatzinco in Totecuiyo, Dios. Azo cententli, cencamatl, oticanili, oticcuili in ihiyotzin, in tlahtoltzin. Xocommoyollotican, ma amechihuinti ma amechxocomicti': *Huehuetlahtolli*, ed. Bautista, fo. 49r.

[116] 'pone sermones eius in corde tuo': Vulgate, Job 22:22; 'ponite haec verba mea in cordibus et in animus vestris': Vulgate, Deuteronomy 11:18.

[117] 'musto pleni sunt isti', 'repleti sunt omnes Spiritu Sancto', 'tamquam advenientis spiritus vehementis', 'effundam de Spiritu meo super omnem carnem': Vulgate, Acts 2:13, 2:4, 2:2, 2:17.

challenges that multi-lingual New Spain posed for Christianity. They had observed imperial and papal reversals on language education, vernacular preaching and scripture.[118] The *Huehuetlahtolli* made an argument in Nahuatl for the importance of religious education in native tongues and the liberal education of an indigenous elite for evangelisation. When the Mexica were filled by *ihiyotzin, tlahtoltzin*, they could participate fully in the spiritual discourse of New Spain.

In the *Huehuetlahtolli*, moreover, divine speech provided a pattern for good human speech in its political, social and familial manifestations. As Erasmus had explained in his *Adagia* and *Paraphrase on John*, good speech 'carries the heart of the speaker by an invisible energy into the heart of the hearer'. Thanks to God's first and foremost creation, the word, 'there is no other thing more effective for stirring up every movement of our heart than speech'.[119] The editors of the *Huehuetlahtolli* drew on two cultures of 'old words' – traditional Nahua practices of counsel and rhetorical techniques, and the resources of the Vulgate and of Erasmian humanism – to model the affective and instructive power of good vernacular speech in the New World.

The *Huehuetlahtolli* did not arrest single-handedly the college's decline in the seventeenth century but its argument did not go unheard. We have seen that the Spanish translations of Olmos's speeches circulated widely to defend the capacities of the *indios*. Fuller engagement with the argument of the Nahuatl orations came in the Enlightenment, when creole patriots and indigenous intellectuals campaigned for the revival of the Colegio de Santa Cruz and the creation of similar institutions.[120] In particular, the Jesuit Francisco Javier Clavijero (1731–87) responded to Bourbon reforms, secularisation and the deprecations of Mexico by certain Europeans in his *Historia Antigua de Mexico* (1780). Clavijero included two of the *Huehuetlahtolli*, the father's speech to his son and the mother's exhortation to her daughter, in his *Historia* in order 'to confound the arrogance of those who believed that the empire of reason belonged only to Europe'.[121] While the Jesuit drew on the Spanish versions of the orations, there is every reason to think that he knew the Nahuatl *Huehuetahtolli*. Clavijero had studied the language extensively, taught in indigenous schools and researched colonial Nahuatl texts in Mexico's convent libraries. He identified Olmos as a collector of antiquities, Bautista as an accomplished

[118] Nesvig, 'The Epistemological Politics'.

[119] Erasmus, *CWE*, XLVI: *Paraphrase on John*, ed. Jane Phillips (Toronto, 1991), 16.

[120] Mónica Díaz, 'The Education of Natives, Creole Clerics, and the Mexican Enlightenment', *Colonial Latin American Review*, 24 (2015), 60–83.

[121] 'a confundir el orgulloso desprecio de los que creen limitado a las regions europeas el imperio de la razón': Francisco Javier Clavijero, *Historia Antigua de Mexico*, trans. J. Joaquín de Mora, ed. Luis Gonzalez Obregon (2 vols., Mexico, 1917), I, 335 (quotation), 338–434 (speeches).

writer of evangelical Nahuatl texts and named the Tlatelolcan *ladinos* as examples of the indigenous facility for higher learning.[122] Through their good speech in Nahuatl, Clavijero argued, the Mexicans 'engraved their instructions on their children's hearts'. Further, the 'great copiousness of the words that shape the flow of the Mexican language' made it well suited to communicate abstract ethical concepts and Christian doctrine.[123] Clavijero invoked the *Huehuetlahtolli*'s account of Nahuatl *qualli tlahtolli* to defend indigenous liberal education and vernacular Christianity in Mexico.

IV Conclusion

Contextualising the *Huehuetlahtolli* in the activities of the Colegio de Santa Cruz sheds light on the significance of old words in the New World. The college's missionaries initiated the collection of Mexican antiquities and the classical framing of the 'speech of the ancients'. Its liberally educated alumni incorporated the speech of the ancient Mesoamerican and Mediterranean worlds in the *Huehuetlahtolli*. The Tlatelolcans' facility with two rhetorical traditions and two treasuries of 'old words' reveals the rigour of the cultural and linguistic encounter at Santa Cruz. Considerable powers of *inventio* were necessary to adapt a Nahuatl literary genre using biblical proverbs and humanist rhetorical techniques. To this extent, the literary achievement of the *Huehuetlahtolli* certainly equals and exceeds the Latin epistles and Nahuatl translations of European texts for which the collegians are often praised.

Both Nahua culture and Erasmian education had encouraged the editors of the *Huehuetlahtolli* to associate elegant, ancient speech with civil conduct. Language was the tool through which humans could be persuaded towards virtue and in which they could perform their familial and civic duties. While the *Florentine Codex* collected evidence of Nahuatl *qualli tlahtolli*, the *Huehuetlahtolli* used the 'old words' to make an argument in the New World. Contextualising the Nahuatl speeches in Erasmus's theory of speech, which shaped the pedagogy and spiritual culture of Santa Cruz throughout the sixteenth century, helps to reveal its contours. It was critical for evangelisation, the Tlatelolcans posited, that indigenous leaders learned to preach or at least champion the divine word (*ihiyotzin*, *tlahtoltzin*), a capacity that depended on their recourse to liberal education. In step with the claims of the friars, the *Huehuetlahtolli* also posited that for the *indios* to embrace the divine spirit fully, 'to be drunk with it', they needed to taste it in their native tongue. With the editors' integration

---

[122] *Ibid.*, I, 410 477, II, 359, 391, 428, 430.
[123] 'Tales eran las instrucciones que los mexicanos inculcaban en el ánimo de sus hijos' and 'la excesiva cantidad de estas voces que forman el caudal de la lengua mexicana': Clavijero, *Historia*, I, 341, and II, 314, respectively.

of translated Vulgate proverbs, the *Huehuetlahtolli* showed the potential of Nahuatl scripture. After its printing, the Colegio de Santa Cruz fell on hard times but the collegians' argument for the evangelising capacities and political sophistication of Nahuatl continued to find auditors in the Enlightenment.

Santa Cruz's *gramaticos* did more than use 'old words' to spread the new word of the Gospels. They demonstrated the capacity of Nahuatl to incorporate the techniques and texts of the *bonae litterae*. In the context of the renaissance view of languages, this was an important display of the commensurability of Latin and Nahuatl. The Tlatelolcans used their liberal education to show that their vernacular was, indeed, a 'most elegant' form of speech by American *and* European standards. Like the engraved image of the Mexica in Diego Valadés's *Rhetorica Christiana*, the *Huehuetlahtolli* established that the Nahua could wear the classical toga of ancient Rome with aplomb.[124] There was no reason, the *Huehuetlahtolli* argued, that the Nahua should 'go about as if they were voiceless' in New Spain.[125]

---

[124] Valadés, *Rhetorica Christiana*, 111.
[125] 'huel qualli tlahtoltica. Ahmo yuquin tinontli yc tinemiz': 'Exhortación', ed. García Quintana, 154; *Huehuetlahtolli*, ed. Bautista, fo. 2v.

Transactions of the RHS 27 (2017), pp. 153–173 © Royal Historical Society 2017
doi:10.1017/S008044011700007X

MIGRATION FROM WITHIN AND WITHOUT: IN THE FOOTSTEPS OF EASTERN CHRISTIANS IN THE EARLY MODERN WORLD*

By John-Paul A. Ghobrial

READ 5 FEBRUARY 2016

ABSTRACT. From Lebanese politicians in Argentina to Iraqi immigrants in Sweden, Middle Eastern Christians can be found today scattered across the entire world. Too often, however, this global migration has been seen purely as a modern development, one arising from contemporary political and religious tensions in the Middle East. In fact, this type of mobility had earlier manifestations in the early modern period. From the sixteenth century onwards, Christians from the Ottoman Empire set out for distant worlds and foreign lands, travelling as far as Europe, India, Russia and even the Americas and leaving traces of themselves in countless European and Middle Eastern archives, chanceries and libraries. This paper lays out a framework for understanding movement in the early modern world in a way that pays as much attention to how migrants understood their own travels as to contemporary European ideas about Eastern Christian mobility. Focusing on the intersection of two traditions of sources, I explore here how European and Eastern Christian perspectives about migration drew from one another, reinforcing and feeding on each other in powerful, mutually constitutive ways. In doing so, this paper seeks to make a contribution to our understanding of the everyday experience of circulation and mobility in the early modern world.

Let me begin with three signatures that do not belong. The signature in Figure 1 comes from the will and testament of a man described in Spanish as 'Manuel de Elías the Greek (*de nacion griego*)'. Originally from Aleppo,

* I am grateful to Professor Peter Mandler and the RHS Council for its kind invitation to speak and to the members of the Society in attendance for their helpful questions and comments. I have preserved here the original tone of the lecture. This paper is dedicated to Jack Tannous with whom I spent a happy year discussing the issues in this paper, among other things, while on research leave in 2016–17 as a Visiting Fellow at the Institute for Advanced Study at the University of Konstanz. I am grateful to Professor Rudolf Schlögl, Fred Girod and all the staff and Fellows at the Kulturwissenschaftliches Kolleg for making my stay such a stimulating and memorable one. The paper draws on research conducted for the project *Stories of Survival: Recovering the Connected Histories of Eastern Christianity in the Early Modern World*, which is supported by funding from a European Research Council Starting Grant under the European Union's Horizon 2020 research and innovation programme (grant agreement no. 638578).

Figure 1 (Colour online) Manuel de Elías, or 'Abd al-Masīḥ Ilyās, Cádiz 1679. Reproduced with permission from the Archivo Histórico Provincial de Cádiz, Cádiz, Spain.

Manuel had travelled to Iberia at some point, where he started a new life for himself in Cádiz. At any rate, he had been in Spain long enough to marry, have children and accumulate a sizeable array of possessions. In February 1679, presumably during the last days of his life and after so many years spent away from home, Manuel still decided to sign his will in the language of his parents. When faced with this document, anyone who reads Arabic might be forgiven for imagining that Manuel actually had forgotten how to write his name in Arabic: the ligatures joining the Arabic letters seem malformed and, at the very least, he could not remember where to place the diacritics.[1]

The second signature is that of Athanasius Safar, a bishop from Mardin in today's south-eastern Turkey. In the 1680s, Athanasius began to cultivate links with the Catholic church, which culminated in his visiting Rome and then Spain in 1689 where he secured permission to travel to the New World to collect alms. As he and his servant boarded a ship bound for Mexico, Athanasius signed a document at the Casa de Contratación, or Board of Trade, which is presented here in Figure 2. What are we to make of the pronounced right-to-left smudge to the left of his signature? He may well have started instinctively to sign his name in Arabic only to

---

[1] In other words, there are simply too many unnecessary dots in this man's signature, rendering him as 'And al-Masīḥ Ilyāsh instead of 'Abd al-Masīḥ Ilyās. The document is preserved today in the Archivo Histórico Provincial de Cádiz among the notarial protocols for Cádiz, PROT, 18 Feb. 1679, t. 1150, fos. 39–42. 'Manuel' must be the name taken by 'Abd al-Masīḥ in Spain, and the reference to his being 'Greek' almost certainly a sign that he was a member of the Orthodox church in his native Aleppo.

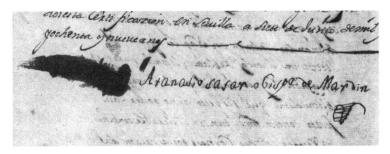

Figure 2 Athanasius Safar, bishop of Mardin, Seville 1689. Reproduced with permission from the Archivo General de Indias, Seville, Spain.

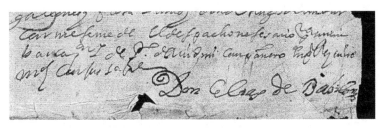

Figure 3 Don Elías de Babilonia, Seville 1675. Reproduced with permission from the Archivo General de Indias, Seville, Spain.

suddenly stop, blot out the signature and rewrite it again – this time in the Latin alphabet as 'Atanasio Safar, bishop of Mardin'.[2]

Perhaps my favourite signature is that in Figure 3 belonging to Ilyās ibn Ḥanna al-Mawsilī, or Elías de Babilonia, a priest from Mosul who travelled across Europe and as far as Peru in the late seventeenth century. Note, here, the fantastic curl in the first letter of 'Don', a testament to the great concentration with which Elias signed his name in the Latin script. And yet, in this instance, he seems to have made a crucial miscalculation: he ran out of space at the end of the line. The reason for this is not surprising: for a man accustomed to signing his name from right to left in Arabic, even the simple act of signing in the Latin script risked becoming

[2] Documents related to Athanasius Safar and his servant, described here only as Juan José, are in the Archivo General de Indias (AGI) in Seville in Contratación, 5451, no. 37; on his experiences in the New World, see AGI, Mexico 312, 'Memorial sobre Don Athanasio Safar, 1691'. See also Bernard Heyberger, *Les chrétiens du Proche-Orient au temps de la Réforme catholique (Syrie, Liban, Palestine, XVIIᵉ–XVIIIᵉ siècle)* (Rome, 2014), 217.

a moment of cognitive dissonance in the everyday life of an individual living in a new society.[3]

If we are persuaded by what some historians have been telling us for decades about the importance of small details, then we might imagine that these signatures offer clues into the everyday experience of circulation and mobility in the early modern world.[4] Indeed, we could develop at least three different interpretations of migration as reflected here in these signatures. There is Manuel de Elías who in the last days of his life was persuaded (by nostalgia?) to sign his name in Arabic as 'Abd al-Masīh Ilyās even though he may have forgotten how to do so properly; Athanasius Safar whose hand seemed instinctively to sign in Arabic, only for his mind immediately to correct this impulse a moment later; and finally Elias of Babylon whose determined curls in the first letter of his signature appear contrived, perhaps even artificial, on the page.

Of course, there are countless ways of interpreting these signatures (assuming we accept that they can even be interpreted). I begin in this way, therefore, not out of some amateur fascination with graphology or psychoanalysis, but rather because this paper is about how we make sense of the diverse historical record that survives about Eastern Christians and their experiences of life in early modern Europe. Fortunately, we need not rely only on signatures because there exist today a wide variety of sources, documents and witnesses to this type of movement by Ottoman Christians. For when we cast our eyes across the horizons of early modern Europe, we find Christian subjects of the sultan lurking in all sorts of places: urban centres and port cities, to be sure, but also small towns and villages further afield. Drawing on their unique linguistic skills, some of these individuals created new lives for themselves as copyists, translators and librarians, leaving marginalia, colophons and autobiographical notes scattered across the manuscripts they encountered. Still others struggled to eke out a living for themselves as itinerant alms-collectors, merchants and purveyors of luxuries and marvels. In a few cases, a considerable amount of evidence can be drawn together to tell the story of the life of a single person. But more often than not, these wayfarers left nothing behind apart from a thin paper trail in the archives of the countries

---

[3] This example of Elias's signature comes from AGI, Contratación, 5440, no. 2, r. 135. More generally, see John-Paul A. Ghobrial, 'The Secret Life of Elias of Babylon and the Uses of Global Microhistory', *Past and Present*, 222 (2014), 51–93, especially 92 for another example of his signature.

[4] See, for one example, Carlo Ginzburg, 'Clues: Roots of an Evidential Paradigm', in *Clues, Myths, and the Historical Method* (Baltimore, 1990), 96–125; Carlo Ginzburg and Carlo Poni, 'The Name and the Game: Unequal Exchange and the Historiographical Marketplace', in *Microhistory and the Lost Peoples of Europe*, ed. Edward Muir and Guido Ruggiero (Baltimore and London, 1991), 1–10; and, most recently, Ginzburg's reflections in *Threads and Traces: True False Fictive* (Berkeley, 2012).

through which they walked. Or even less: in the case of a man from Mount Lebanon who travelled through Germany in 1727, all that remains today are a few vague printed news reports and some of his personal effects – a pair of slippers and the gown that he left behind for the cabinet of curiosities of his host, the duke of Saxe-Gotha – which can still be visited today in the Schlossmuseum of the Friedenstein Castle in Gotha.

Signatures, scraps of paper, slippers: all like shiny objects to a magpie. Yet one might reasonably wonder whether it is even possible to construct a wider history of early modern circulation based on such trinkets? Perhaps we would feel that we were standing on firmer ground if we focused our attention instead on the growing collection of first-hand narratives that have become the subject of sustained interest by specialists working in oriental and Eastern Christian studies. Consider, for example, a couplet of poetry that appears in a letter written in May 1642 by one Niqūlāwus ibn Butrus, a copyist from Aleppo who was persuaded to come to Europe by Christian Ravius, a German orientalist who had been travelling in the Ottoman Empire. Soon after his arrival in England, Niqūlāwus was disappointed by the scheming ways of his new patron. In a remarkable set of his letters recently given new life by Hilary Kilpatrick and Gerald Toomer, this was how Niqūlāwus summed up his experiences in a letter to a friend:

> A slave who has left your service kisses the ground [before you],
> victim now of wrongs which have no like –
> detention, captivity, living under guard are his lot,
> separation from children and wife, and ceaseless anxiety.[5]

So much for everyday life in the Republic of Letters. But if we consider the context of this letter, then we must ask ourselves whether in fact first-hand narratives such as these are any more useful as sources than the signatures with which I opened this paper. The letter was in fact written to the Dutch orientalist, Jacob Golius, who Niqūlāwus hoped would be able to help him secure a new patron, a new job, a new life. It comes as no surprise then that the strategy adopted in his letter recalls those of others in need, for example letters requesting poor relief or petitions submitted to municipal authorities. We struggle to hear the perspectives of dislocated souls, cast adrift in the early modern world, whose voices have been drowned out by their poignant attempts to endear themselves to their host societies. Put simply, working with the very sources that appear to give us the most direct access to this category of migrants can sometimes feel like falling down a rabbit hole.

---

[5] Hilary Kilpatrick and Gerald J. Toomer, 'Niqūlāwus al-Ḥalabī (*c*. 1611–*c*. 1661): A Greek Orthodox Syrian Copyist and his Letters to Pococke and Golius', *Lias: Journal of Early Modern Intellectual Culture and its Sources*, 43 (2016), 16.

In recent years, the movement of people has become a subject of particular interest among early modern historians. In part, this is a reflection of contemporary developments and the politics of migration flows today, but it is also the expression of a genuine sense among historians that movement really mattered when it comes to making sense of the key transformations of the early modern period. From an 'alternative history of the Reformation' that focuses on religious exiles to the growing body of work by social and economic historians interested in migration, diasporas and trade networks, movement is on the historical agenda today in a real and substantive way.[6] Even so, we still have a long way to go in terms of developing a critical approach to the study of movement, circulation and migration. One particular issue concerns me here, what we might think of as a problem of perspective. When historians write about migration, what they often seem to be referring to is physical movement, that is, the purposeful movement of individuals, families or entire communities from one geographic place to another. In most cases, this work has focused on certain forms of movement that, on the surface at least, appear to be permanent, unidirectional and intentional. And yet, migration probably looks much different in retrospect than it did to contemporaries. It is only when studied from afar that the day-to-day itinerary of a seasonal worker, for example, adopts for itself the trappings of a clear pattern or structure of labour. As a subject of historical study, therefore, movement seems to lose any lingering sense of ambiguity with the passage of time. When placed under the historian's microscope, a particular pattern of movement may become a victim to our own overriding interests in issues of causation, agency and even intentionality. The risk here is that in making movement a subject of historical analysis in this way, we will view the movement of individuals as little more than blips moving across a radar screen. In this context, we may feel more confident than we should about our ability to explain movement and its meaning in the lives of the people we study. Unlike anthropologists or sociologists, when we study movement, we are at the mercy of the distorting mirror of time.

One way to address this challenge is to think more about how we incorporate contemporary ideas about movement into our own analysis of it. Individuals did not travel across maps, but rather over land, through fields, on rivers, onto ships and off of them and into and out of gates and

---

[6] The examples are many, but see, for example, Nicholas Terpstra, *Religious Refugees in the Early Modern World: An Alternative History of the Reformation* (Cambridge, 2015); Peter Burke, *Exiles and Expatriates in the History of Knowledge, 1500–2000* (Waltham, MA, 2017); *Religion and Trade: Cross-Cultural Exchanges in World History, 1000–1900*, ed. Francesca Trivellato, Leor Halevi and Catia Antunes (Oxford, 2014); and Sanjay Subrahmanyam, *Three Ways to Be Alien: Travails and Encounters in the Early Modern World* (Waltham, MA, 2011).

walls that carried them into diverse towns, cities and societies. While doing so, they travelled through different contexts – often straddling multiple contexts simultaneously – and these contexts helped them to explain, represent and make sense of their movement as much to themselves as to the worlds around them. For this reason, we must explore movement and migration from within and from without. This paper is intended as an experiment in how we might study movement in this way with reference to the case of Christians under Ottoman rule and their circulation in early modern Europe. In the case of Eastern Christians, I argue, we have to pay as much attention to how they themselves understood their circulation in Europe as to how this experience of migration was imagined by the European societies they encountered.

This paper considers two contemporary ideas about movement and how they intersected with each other. On the one hand, there was a European tradition, rooted in the anxieties and suspicions of state bureaucrats, doctrinally obsessed clerics and theologians and officials entrusted with poor relief. Such people worried unceasingly about Eastern Christians in Europe. The testament to this comes in European sources, archives and even literature, where the stereotype of the wandering Eastern Christian – usually fleeing Muslim persecution – had crystallised by this period into a stock character. 'Princes of Lebanon', 'knights of Jerusalem', 'priests of Babylon': all language coming straight from the documents and witnesses to how Europeans imagined Eastern Christians in their midst. But alongside this, there was a second story of movement that was reflected in Eastern Christian sources. Based on correspondence, first-person narratives, travelogues and manuscript colophons, this tradition offers us a glimpse of how Eastern Christians understood their own circulation in the early modern world.

These two contemporary perspectives about migration intersected with each other: they drew from one another, reinforcing and feeding on each other in powerful, mutually constitutive ways. Of course, neither of these perspectives were more 'true', 'genuine' or 'real', but rather they informed one another in a reciprocal manner with Eastern Christians increasingly representing their movement in Europe in ways that satisfied the expectations of Europeans. In as much as we seek to access the experience of Eastern Christians, we can do so only by setting our sights squarely on the interaction between these two traditions. In what follows, I will begin by presenting some aspects of European ideas of Eastern Christian migration. Next, I will give a sense of the phenomenon as viewed from within the Eastern Christian tradition with a particular focus on the Arabic- and Syriac-speaking churches of the Ottoman world.[7]

---

[7] I have adopted the nomenclature of 'Eastern Christians' to refer here mainly to the array of Christian communities living under Ottoman rule, although these communities lacked a

As this paper is intended for a general audience, I will not be able to address here specific, philological questions raised by the sources although I have engaged with these problems elsewhere in my research. In the last section, I will briefly explore some aspects of what life was like for Eastern Christians in early modern Europe. These concluding remarks are intended only to signal some avenues for further research. Although I do not have the space here to treat the subject adequately, I do at least want to end this paper by suggesting some ways in which we might begin to hear the voices of these people through the white noise of the historical record.

I Migration viewed from without

Was there really a 'phenomenon' of Eastern Christian circulation to Europe in the early modern period – that is, a pattern of migration perceived by contemporaries as something more than a mere handful of exceptional cases of individual movement? To be sure, the late nineteenth and early twentieth centuries witnessed important changes in the movement of people from the Middle East to Europe, Asia and the Americas, all of which we understand better today thanks to several important works by such scholars as William Clarence-Smith, Andrew Arsan and Akram Khater.[8] These works have brought to life in vivid ways the practices, motivations and strategies that carried Ottoman Christians and Muslims to new lives and careers in places as different from each other as New York, Manila, Brazil and West Africa. Where an older generation of scholarship saw such migration as a reaction to the sectarian tensions of the late Ottoman Empire, these recent approaches have emphasised instead how these migrants were in fact drawn towards new opportunities in the worlds around them. There is even a new journal, *Mashriq & Mahjar*, dedicated exclusively to the study of migration in the Middle East, a testament to the energy and interest of modernists working in this field.

In light of such work, however, we must be careful not to project such migration flows uncritically back to the early modern period, a period

single term to refer to what were, it must be said, a set of communities with a complicated relationship to each other. But for one perspective on the use of the term 'Eastern Christianity', which I find compelling, see Françoise Micheau, 'Eastern Christianities (Eleventh to the Fourteenth Century): Copts, Melkites, Nestorians and Jacobites', in *The Cambridge History of Eastern Christianity*, ed. Michael Angold (Cambridge, 2006), 373–403.

[8] See, for example, William Clarence-Smith, 'Lebanese and other Middle Eastern Migrants in the Philippines', in *Population Movement beyond the Middle East: Migration, Diaspora, and Network*, ed. Akira Usuki et al. (Osaka, 2005), 115–43; Andrew Arsan, *Interlopers of Empire: The Lebanese Diaspora in Colonial French West Africa* (2014); and Akram Khater, *Inventing Home: Emigration, Gender and the Making of a Lebanese Middle Class, 1861–1921* (Berkeley, 2001). These are just a few examples from a rich and growing literature.

when both the scale and structure of migration was rather different. Unlike modern historians, early modernists do not have anything approaching the requisite sources needed to speak in a meaningful way about the actual size of the phenomenon. Even so, it is useful at least to try to consider just how many people we are actually talking about. To give an idea, consider one estimate based on some of the finest work on the subject written by Bernard Heyberger. In a detailed study of the Vatican archives, Heyberger identified no fewer than 178 Eastern Christians in Rome whose presence was noted by the authorities of the Propaganda Fide during the period of 1690 to 1779.[9] This estimate is especially revealing if we consider that it is based only on a single archive, and that it includes only those individuals who addressed themselves specifically to Catholic officials in Rome. A full survey would require a more extensive study of other types of evidence, for example European correspondence, diplomatic and financial archives, registers of poor relief, and even the catalogues and accounts of oriental manuscript libraries in Europe, all of which would suggest we could easily build upon Heyberger's initial research to arrive at a more general estimate of numbers of Eastern Christians across Europe. Be that as it may, there is still little to suggest that the movement of Eastern Christians approaches anything like the sort of mass migration that scholars have identified for other groups of religious refugees in this period. Even if we were being generous, we might hazard an estimate of, say, only 1,000 or 2,000 separate individuals that can be identified in specific documents over the course of the sixteenth to the eighteenth centuries. For all that a quantitative history of circulation promises to offer, the truth is that we simply do not know how many Eastern Christians migrated to early modern Europe, at least not yet.

We must look for other barometers to assess the significance of Eastern Christians, and their movements, in the eyes of Europeans. Law provides one such measure. Consider, for example, the anxieties of Spanish imperial officials who clearly worried that Eastern Christians roamed wildly across the early modern world. This is at least the impression given by the *Book of the Laws of the Indies*, a four-volume codification of Spanish laws related to the Indies printed in Madrid in 1681. Among the regulations laying out everything from the proper administration of jails to the bureaucratic permissions required by pearl-divers, we find a curious law in book 1, chapter 21, sandwiched between several laws on 'questores y limosnas', or alms-collectors. Migration to the New World was strictly regulated by Spanish officials, and the Atlantic crossing

[9] The estimate is from Bernard Heyberger, 'Chrétiens orientaux dans l'Europe catholique (XVIIe–XVIIIe siècles)', in *Hommes de l'entre-deux: parcours individuels et portraits de groupes sur la frontière de la Méditerranée (XVIe–XXe siècle)*, ed. Bernard Heyberger and Chantal Verdeil (Paris, 2009), 63.

required an individual to have obtained a special licence to travel. Even so, this bureaucratic regime, imposing as it was, could not prevent a trickle of people without papers across the Atlantic. And in the *Laws of the Indies*, among the undesirables who were explicitly not to be permitted to travel to the Americas, special mention was made in fact of a specific category of Ottoman subjects, namely 'Greeks, Armenians' and 'monks of Mount Sinai'.[10]

The law had been issued in 1634 by Philip IV, and the logic behind it is interesting. As it explained, Christian subjects of the sultan had in the past managed to obtain licences to travel to the New World for the purpose of collecting alms ('para pedir limosnas en nuestros Reynos'), ostensibly for the holy sites in Jerusalem but also for the protection of their communities from Muslim persecution in the Ottoman Empire. The law expressed a concern about the 'ill-treatment (malos modos)' of Christians by Muslims in the Ottoman Empire. There was also a risk that money collected by such wayfarers might ultimately be confiscated by the Ottoman authorities upon their return to the Ottoman Empire. In this way, alms given by faithful Christians could potentially end up in the hands of the Ottoman sultan. In hopes of putting an end to these problems, Philip IV ordered that 'such licences are not to be given to Greeks, Armenians, or monks of Sinai, of whatever quality they may be, or under any other pretended titles'. To the viceroys of Peru and New Spain, he instructed 'if any such people are known to be present in your domains, they are to be apprehended' and sent back to Spain. While the law may reflect competition between Eastern Christian and local, probably Franciscan, attempts to monopolise the collection of alms, it is nonetheless an important testament to the growing circulation and presence of Eastern Christians in the New World.[11]

That this was more than imperial paranoia is suggested from the intensity of efforts carried out by those entrusted with the task of monitoring the movements of such people in everyday life. In 1694, for example, among the survivors who made it safely to land after a shipwreck near Buenos Aires, there was a Greek man who called himself Joseph Georgirenes and claimed to be the archbishop of Samos. In his company were two priests – one English, one Portuguese – two servants from Naples, and two African slaves. This motley crew found themselves at the mercy of local, suspicious bureaucrats, setting off a flurry of paperwork between imperial officials anxious to figure out who this man was, how

---

[10] For the full text of the law, see *Recopilación de Leyes de los Reynos de las Indias* (Madrid, 1681), book 1, chapter 21, law 10.

[11] For a comparison, consider Spanish approaches to gypsies in Richard Pym, *The Gypsies of Early Modern Spain, 1425–1783* (2007). I am grateful to Cecilia Tarruell for her advice on the wider context in which this law was issued.

he got there and what was his story. The result was an inquiry that lasted over a decade and involved dozens of interviews with people who had encountered Georgirenes in South America. The case book runs today to some 500 folios, and the archbishop of Samos would also be tried by the Inquisition.[12]

Such anxieties were not only the reflection of bureaucratic concerns within the Spanish empire, but rather they were rooted more generally in the religious and confessional divides that tore Europe apart in this period. The Reformation unleashed a renewed interest in Eastern Christianity, not least because the practices and beliefs of the Eastern churches could prove useful and instrumental in polemics between Protestants and Catholics.[13] The consequence was that where some officials spurned the wayward circulation of Eastern Christians, others were more interested in interrogating them about the practices and beliefs of their communities. This was the case for one itinerant Chaldean priest in Paris who we know only as 'Dom Hissa' ('Isa?) who celebrated mass in 1673 in the chapel of Saint-Germain-en-Laye. Afterwards, he gave his hosts a Syriac manuscript of the liturgy, which was subsequently translated into French and published as a testament to the conformity of the ancient Eastern churches with Roman practices.[14] The importance of the confessional context here cannot be understated: time and time again, Catholic concerns about the movement of Eastern Christians are directly connected to the worry that if left to their own devices, they might cross over into Protestant countries and convert. That this was certainly plausible is clear from the handful of cases of Eastern Christians who did exactly this. Already in 1643, one Josephus Adjutus, originally from Mosul, had publicly declared his renunciation of the Catholic church, which resonated with the occasional presence of Eastern clergy in Protestant

[12] See John Penrose Barron, *From Samos to Soho: The Unorthodox Life of Joseph Georgirenes, a Greek Archbishop* (Oxford, 2017), and my comments in the epilogue 'The New World (1682–c. 1700)' on 219–23. I am now preparing a fuller study of Georgirenes's experiences in the New World. In the meantime, let me express my appreciation here to Professor Caroline Barron for her support for my research into this final stage of his adventures.

[13] See, for example, Heyberger, *Les chrétiens du Proche-Orient au temps de la Réforme catholique*; Alastair Hamilton, 'Eastern Languages and Western Scholarship', in *Rome Reborn: The Vatican Library and Renaissance Culture*, ed. Anthony Grafton (Washington and New Haven, 1993), 225–50; and Frédéric Gabriel, 'Les témoins orientaux d'une querelle latine: orthodoxie et professions de foi dans *La perpétuité de la foi*', in Marie-Hélène Blanchet and Frédéric Gabriel, *L'union à l'épreuve du formulaire: professions de foi entre Églises d'Orient et d'Occident (XIIIᵉ – XVIIIᵉ siècle)* (Leuven, 2016), 373–89.

[14] *La Sainte Messe des caldéens et des maronites du Mont-Liban: mise en françois, suivant le souhait de plusieurs personnes pieuses, & par l'ordre exprès de la Reyne, lors que sa Majesté voulut bien entendre celle que Dom Hissa Prestre Caldéen, celebra en Langue Syriaque, & avec les ceremonies qui sont propres aux chrestiens de son pays, dans la chapelle du vieux chasteau de S. Germain en Laye, le vingt-deuxieme iour du mois d'avril de l'an 1673* (Paris, 1678).

centres of learning.[15] There was also the example of more notable figures like Cyril Lukaris, the patriarch of Constantinople who had allegedly flirted with Calvinism in the 1630s.[16]

Looking beyond law and religion, popular literature also offers an indicator of the importance of the figure of the Eastern Christian in the European imagination. News reports and travel literature, for example, were full of stories of Eastern Christians who had travelled to Europe, often in search of a safe haven far away from their Muslim neighbours in the Ottoman Empire. The *Histoire du Prince Junès* is typical in this respect.[17] It tells the story of a Christian notable, the Maronite prince Junès, who had earned the scorn of the local Muslim governor. Hoping for a more peaceful life, his brother, Yusuf, travelled to France where, the author claimed, he had secured a patron in none other than Louis XIV himself. Such tales circulated across a wide variety of scribal and print media from travel literature to missionary correspondence and even in private letters. They were so effective in constructing an ideal type of the Christian vagabond from the East that we even have evidence of a few cases where European charlatans impersonated Eastern Christians in an attempt to secure posts or collect alms. In the early twentieth century, some scholars continued to debate whether Carolus Dadichi – a man who would occupy several posts including interpreter for oriental languages in Britain – was really from Aleppo, as he claimed, or rather if he was a fraud from the south of France.[18]

By a later period, these whispered stories of Ottoman Christians in Europe's midst accumulated one on top of another, crystallising into the stock character of the wandering Eastern Christian. The nineteenth century, for example, witnessed the emergence of a vibrant tradition of

---

[15] See Burchard Brentjes, 'Josephus Adjutus, der Chaldäer zu Wittenberg', *Wissenschaftliche Zeitschrift der Martin-Luther-Universität Halle-Wittenberg*, 26, 4 (1977), 131–8; the essays collected in *Anglicanism and Orthodoxy 300 Years after the 'Greek College' in Oxford*, ed. Peter Doll (Oxford, 2005); Barron, *From Samos to Soho*; John-Paul A. Ghobrial, 'The Life and Hard Times of Solomon Negri: An Arabic Teacher in Early Modern Europe', in *The Teaching and Learning of Arabic in Early Modern Europe*, ed. Jan Loop, Alastair Hamilton and Charles Burnett (Leiden, 2017), 90–111. I am grateful to David Taylor for first drawing my attention to Josephus Adjutus's writings.

[16] See, for example, George A. Chatziantoniou, *Protestant Patriarch: The Life of Cyril Lucaris, 1572–1638, Patriarch of Constantinople* (1961).

[17] The story was published as part of Jean de La Roque, *Voyage de Syrie et du Mont-Liban ... avec un abregé de la vie de monsieur de Chasteuil et l'Histoire du prince Junès, Maronite* (Paris, 1722).

[18] Christian Friedrich Seybold, 'Der gelehrte Syrer Carolus Dadichi (S 1734 in London), Nachfolger Salomo Negri's (S 1729)', *Zeitschrift der Deutschen Morgenländischen Gesellschaft*, 64 (1910), 591–601; Wolfram Suchier, *C.R. Dadichi oder wie sich deutsche Orientalisten von einem Schwindler düpieren liessen, ein Kapitel aus der deutschen Gelehrtenrepublik der ersten Hälfte des 18. Jahrhunderts* (Halle, 1919). For the most recent and productive study of Dadichi, see Wolfgang Hage, 'Carolus Dadichi in Marburg (1718): Bittgesuch eines rum-orthodoxen Studenten im Universitäts-Archiv', *Oriens Christianus*, 95 (2011), 16–28.

fictional writing based around such characters. J. F. Coakley has described how from the 1840s, British publishers released a series of novels about Assyrian Christians and their adventures in the world. Likewise, the short stories of the nineteenth-century Peruvian novelist Ricardo Palma included the tales of a prince of Lebanon ('el prícipe del Líbano') who lived in Lima in the eighteenth century. Similarly, in a collection of fantastic tales, the fanciful writer Manuel Mujica Láinez described a sorcerer called the 'archbishop of Samos' who found himself imprisoned in a jail in seventeenth-century Buenos Aires. The prisoner uses Eastern magic to transform himself into an owl that travels great distances to torment the servants who have abandoned him to his fate. Such works presented truth in the guise of storytelling.[19]

Perhaps the most salient characteristic of this stereotype of the Eastern Christian was the idea that he (rarely she) was fleeing persecution and, more often than not, forced conversion to Islam. These claims reflected details that were drawn directly from the very letters of recommendation that Eastern Christians brought with them to Europe. This was the case, for example, in 1727 when Solomon Negri, a Damascene in London, died and left behind a trunk full of old correspondence. When his friends sifted through the papers, they found certificates and letters of recommendation from the head of the Franciscans in Jerusalem explaining how 'Solomon Negri in or about the month of April 1688 being under fear of being forced to turn Turk and renounce Christianity fled from Damascus and went to Rome [and] from thence to France and proceeded to Holland and afterwards to England.'[20] In fact, this story conflicts with another story that Negri had told some friends during his life, namely that he had been dispatched to Europe by the Jesuits in Damascus who admired his scholarly talents. Although a great deal of work remains to be done on the subject of conversion in the Ottoman world, we have learned enough from Ottoman historians to know to be suspicious about such claims that seem a world away from Ottoman realities. Nonetheless, the theme of persecution by Muslims found a sympathetic audience among Europeans, and for this reason it crops up again and again in the language used to describe donations given to Eastern Christians. In Mexico in 1682, for example, a donation given to Elias of Babylon was recorded as being made 'to relieve the 20,000 Christians living under the cruel oppression of the Muslim barbarians'.[21] This is perhaps one of the clearest examples

---

[19] See, for example, J. F. Coakley, 'Assyrian Tales in English Fiction, 1849–1967', *Journal of Assyrian Academic Studies*, 23 (2009), 18–25; Ricardo Palma, *Tradiciones peruanas* (Lima, 1883); Manuel Mujica Láinez, *Misteriosa Buenos Aires* (Buenos Aires, 1950).

[20] Ghobrial, 'The Life and Hard Times of Solomon Negri', 317.

[21] See the record dated 18 July 1682 in Alberto María Carreño, *Efemérides de la Real y Pontificia Universidad de México según sus libros de claustros* (Mexico City, 1963), I, 298.

of how European discourses about Eastern Christian migration had the potential to shape the actual practices and strategies used by specific Eastern Christians who presented their own life-stories in such a way as to conform with European expectations. This was a sort of wishful thinking on the part of Europeans, which Eastern Christians accommodated and used in order to achieve their own goals.

II Migration viewed from within

What does this sort of circulation look like from within, that is, from the perspective of the people who were actually in motion? Unlike the migrations of the late nineteenth century, the movement of Ottoman Christians to early modern Europe did not always involve an active decision to leave the Ottoman Empire in search of a particular type of economic opportunity. Instead, movement to Europe in this period unfolded outwards from localised, internal practices of circulation within the Ottoman Empire. Indeed, we should be careful not to over-exaggerate the importance of Europe as a destination within a much wider landscape of sites scattered across the Ottoman world and indeed beyond its frontiers. That this connectedness within Eastern Christianity has been forgotten owes something to the ways in which the field of Eastern Christian Studies has developed historically. First, scholars have tended to restrict themselves to local and nationally oriented studies of particular Eastern Christian communities such as the Copts of Egypt, the Maronites of Lebanon or the Chaldeans of Iraq. Such an approach risks ignoring the interactions that took place between specific communities within Eastern Christianity. Moreover, this approach over-emphasises the doctrinal differences that separated particular Eastern Christian churches from each other – Christological and theological debates that go back to late antiquity – while ignoring the fact that many of these communities shared a common vernacular in the language of Arabic (e.g. the Maronites, Melkites and Orthodox of Lebanon and Syria; the Copts of Egypt; and the West and East Syrians of Iraq) and, for some, the historical and liturgical use of Syriac (e.g. the Maronites, West Syrians and East Syrians).[22]

Seen in this way, Eastern Christianity looks too much like a world of islands, a Christian archipelago isolated in a sea of Islam. Instead, it is more accurate to imagine a Christian population spread across a wide geography but connected linguistically by the use of Arabic, Greek and Syriac and, socially, through intermarriage, the shared use of religious spaces, and popular devotional practices, and imaginatively through a

---

[22] For an ecumenical approach from within the Christian Arabic tradition, see Gérard Troupeau, 'Le livre de l'unanimité de la foi de Ali Ibn Dawud al-Arfadi', *Parole de l'Orient*, 5 (1969), 197–219, which describes a work first written in the fourteenth century but copied several times in the seventeenth.

set of shared traditions, stories and literatures. Nor did the boundaries of Eastern Christianity stop at the frontiers of the Ottoman Empire. To take one example, the church of the East – referred to, incorrectly, as the 'Nestorian' church by Europeans in the period – had its origins in the Christian community established beyond the boundaries of the Roman Empire in Persia.[23] The church had played an important role in the spread of Christianity, having sent its own missionaries to Central Asia and China in the seventh century. Not only was the memory of these missions still alive in the seventeenth century, but evidence from sermons reveals that the church of the East might have imagined itself to be in direct competition with the Catholic church for the 'hearts and minds' of Indian communities.[24] By the late eighteenth century, the result would be renewed interests in closer relations with India on the part of patriarchs based in Aleppo and Mosul. Like Europeans in this period, therefore, some Eastern Christian churches saw the world as a theatre for missionary outreach.

The literary production of Eastern Christianity bears witness to this worldview. We know, for example, that the Christians of Mosul would gather together in the evening to hear tales about India from merchants and pilgrims who had travelled there.[25] If we look across other sources – local chronicles, ecclesiastical histories, even sermons – they all speak to the intricate ways in which the experience of Eastern Christianity 'at home' was intimately bound up with the fortunes and misfortunes of Eastern Christians abroad, and vice versa. Not surprisingly, therefore, the global horizons of Eastern Christianity made for a world in which of two priests who left Baghdad together in 1668, one would end up spending a decade in Peru trying to 'convert the barbarians', as Elias of Babylon had put it, while another, Simon of Ada, would spend the last thirty years of his life in Pondicherry. We only know that the latter even existed because his death was reported in Jesuit correspondence in August 1720 after the poor man reportedly fell down a flight of stairs and died.[26]

[23] Dietmar W. Winkler and Wilhelm Baum, *The Church of the East: A Concise History* (2003); Sebastian Brock, 'The "Nestorian" Church: A Lamentable Misnomer', *Bulletin of the John Rylands Library*, 78 (1996), 23–35.

[24] See, for example, R. Y. Ebied and M. J. L. Young, 'An Arabic Treatise on the History of the Nestorians', *Parole de l'Orient*, 3 (1972), 375–98. More recently, this has been the subject of a considerable and excellent series of studies by Professor István Perczel, which promises to transform our understanding of relations between the Eastern churches and south India, for example his 'Some New Documents on the Struggle of the Saint Thomas Christians to Maintain the Chaldaean Rite and Jurisdiction', in Peter Bruns and Heinz Otto Luthe, *Orientalia Christiana: Festschrift für Hubert Kaufhold zum 70. Geburtstag* (Wiesbaden, 2013), 415–36.

[25] Justin Perkins, *A Residence of Eight Years in Persia, among the Nestorian Christians* (Andover, 1843), 415–16.

[26] Édouard René Hambye, 'Le métropolite chaldéen Simon d'Ada et ses aventures en Inde', *Parole de l'Orient*, 6–7 (1975–6), 493–513.

In terms of practices of movement and the genres used to document such practices, migration to Europe developed outwards from localised forms of internal movement in the Ottoman Empire. Two revealing examples relate to the act of pilgrimage to Jerusalem and the act of alms-collecting. The pilgrimage account represents an important genre for documenting movement in the Eastern Christian tradition. It is striking, therefore, that nearly every account of travel to Europe by an Eastern Christian begins with the expression of a desire to travel to Jerusalem. As in the Christian West, the act of pilgrimage to Jerusalem was part of a wider landscape of sacred destinations that included local shrines, tombs and holy sites. A fourteenth-century copy of a guide to pilgrimage included some seventy sites to visit in the Holy Land.[27] Christians who had travelled there were marked out by the appellation *maqdīsī*, which was used much like the term *ḥajjī* for Muslims who had travelled to Mecca. An Ottoman report on tax collected from pilgrims to Jerusalem in 1582 reflects the overwhelming presence of Eastern Christians: of some 1,359 pilgrims recorded by the authorities, the lion's share – over 1,000 of them – were Christian subjects of the sultan.[28] Yet as a practice, pilgrimage was not simply a form of internal movement within the Ottoman Empire. Rather, it was necessarily an outward-looking practice, which also gazed towards sites in the Mediterranean world like the tombs of Lazarus, Mary and Martha in Cyprus as well as to pilgrimage sites further afield in Europe. Rome may have been of particular importance given its grand churches, descriptions of which feature in several Arabic accounts written by Eastern Christians in this period. But among those communities that professed loyalty to Rome, such as the Maronites, pilgrimage also extended to Catholic sites of devotion and piety such as the Madonna di Montenero in Livorno, described in one account written by a Maronite who visited there in 1709.[29]

A second, important expression of local practices of movement related to alms-collecting. Like the pilgrimage narrative, alms-collecting left behind a particular type of source in the form of notebooks and cashbooks carried by alms-collectors. We know something of the way alms-collecting was carried out in this period from a description of the practice in Mount Athos written in the 1670s.[30] Every year, a handful of monks were chosen to raise funds. They travelled together, normally in groups of two or three,

---

[27] Gérard Troupeau, 'Un ancien guide arabe des lieux saints', *Parole de l'Orient*, 21 (1996), 47–56.

[28] Oded Peri, *Christianity under Islam in Jerusalem: The Question of the Holy Sites in Early Ottoman Times* (Leiden, 2001), 166.

[29] *D'Alep à Paris: Les pérégrinations d'un jeune Syrien au temps de Louis XIV*, ed. Bernard Heyberger, Jérôme Lentin and Paul Fahmé-Thiéry (Paris, 2015), 223.

[30] Joseph Georgirenes, *A Description of the Present State of Samos, Nicaria, Patmos, and Mount Athos* (1678), 99–101.

and they were dispatched to a particular region where they were expected to work for a period of a few years. They were sent off by their leaders and given permission to celebrate mass and hear confessions: any funds collected in this way were to be handed back to the institution. Armed with letters of recommendation, these collectors travelled ostensibly to visit members of their own community living abroad but their missions quickly expanded also to include a search for European patrons and donors. In Heyberger's aforementioned study of the Propaganda Fide, alms-collecting was identified as the main reason invoked for their presence in Europe by a third of the Eastern Christians under study. Be that as it may, we should not assume that alms-collecting was a type of movement that invariably led to Europe. In the same period that alms-collectors like Elias of Babylon set their sights on the Catholic world, Macarius ibn al-Zaʿīm, the Orthodox patriarch of Antioch, travelled in 1656 – and again, a decade later – to Moscow in hopes of raising funds from the tsar.[31] In this way, Eastern Christian movement across the early modern world stretched from the Americas in the west to Russia and India in the east.

By the nineteenth century, it appears that alms-collecting had become institutionalised, so to speak, almost as a form of 'seasonal' work carried out by particular communities of Christians in the Ottoman Empire. For a later period, Andrew MacDonald has described brilliantly the global movement of the so-called 'thieves of the cross', a network of alms-collectors who all came from the village of Jīlū in today's south-eastern Turkey.[32] As MacDonald describes it, the men of Jīlū set out across the world in search of alms. The fact that their movements were reported in detail in local newspapers enabled MacDonald to recover a sense of practices that may go back to earlier patterns of alms-collecting that are less easily identified in early modern sources. At any rate, scholars in several fields have increasingly acknowledged the importance of a thriving, global industry of alms-collectors in this period, one in which Eastern Christians appear to be just one of several groups operating.[33] Historians of migration in the early modern period need to think more about the significance of such forms of seasonal, temporary or back-and-forth migration, which may in fact represent a more common type of movement in the early modern world than we have appreciated. Not all migrants were exiles.

[31] On exchanges between Syria and Eastern Europe more generally, see Constantin A. Panchenko, *Arab Orthodox Christians under the Ottomans: 1516–1831*, trans. Brittany Pheiffer Noble and Samuel Noble (Jordainville, NY, 2016).

[32] Andrew MacDonald, 'The Thieves of the Cross: Assyrian Charity Collectors and World History, 1860s–1940s', *Past and Present*, 229 (2015), 161–200.

[33] Compare, for example, to Matthias B. Lehmann, *Emissaries from the Holy Land: The Sephardic Diaspora and the Practice of Pan-Judaism in the Eighteenth Century* (Stanford, 2014).

Interestingly, when we do have evidence of what we might think of as deliberate movement to Europe by Eastern Christians, the Eastern Christian sources tend to tell a rather different story from those that crop up in European archives. I have written elsewhere, for example, about how Eastern Christians were lured to Europe by Europeans they encountered in the Ottoman Empire.[34] Evidence from Arabic sources also suggests that some Eastern Christians did seek to escape persecution in the Ottoman Empire, importantly not from Muslims but rather from their own Christian brothers and sisters. Ottoman Christian communities sometimes experienced divisions when it came, for example, to disagreement over the appointment of bishops or the succession of patriarchs. The possibility of schism was reinforced in the seventeenth century by the extension of Catholic missions into the Ottoman Empire, which contributed to the development of internal rivalries within Eastern Christian communities between pro-Catholic factions and those less persuaded by the missionaries in their midst. These disputes could turn violent, and it was not uncommon for one group of Christians to call on the support of a local Ottoman (Muslim) official to help rid them of their Christian enemies. This was the fate of a priest and schoolteacher in Mosul named Khiḍr bin Hormizd as he described it in his journal (about which, see below). In 1719, the Vatican sent an agent to Mosul in search of Arabic and Syriac manuscripts, and Khiḍr hosted the agent and helped him obtain manuscripts. Rumours began to circulate about his 'Catholic' sympathies, which were of particular concern because Khiḍr was also the tutor to the patriarch's own nephews. When news circulated that Khiḍr might be elevated to the rank of archbishop, he became the target of violent attacks from lay members of his community. The tension lasted for over a year before Khiḍr finally decided to travel to Rome with the help of the Capuchins in Aleppo. Because the letters of recommendation that Khiḍr carried with him have not survived, we cannot know what stories Khiḍr carried with him from the Capuchins. At any rate, his example is a telling reminder of how far from reality were European tropes about the Eastern Christian refugee escaping Islam in the Ottoman Empire.

III Stories of migration

What, if anything, therefore can we know about the actual experience of the types of people whose signatures opened this paper? I have already suggested that European expectations conditioned and shaped the production of Arabic sources in particularly significant ways. In addition, we face a certain asymmetry in the sources in as much as the general paucity of first-hand narratives by Eastern Christians makes it difficult to

---

[34] Ghobrial, 'The Life and Hard Times of Solomon Negri', 315.

say anything in a general way about the lives of these individuals. Even so, we can benefit from a handful of sources that were written by Eastern Christians explicitly for an Eastern Christian audience. These include not only first-hand accounts of travel but also journals or diaries and a small, but growing collection of correspondence, which has become the focus of recent attention by a community of scholars working today in Arabic and Syriac studies. Drawing on such sources, I want to end this paper by attempting to give at least a sense of a few aspects of life for Ottoman Christians in early modern Europe.

First, there is a distinct sense of simultaneity between East and West that betrays something of how these migrants preserved their ties to the worlds they left behind. Khiḍr of Mosul's journal is a case in point. On the one hand, we find in it moving lamentations in Arabic and Syriac written on the occasion of the death of new friends he had made in Rome, mostly Catholic priests. But at the same time, in one of his entries, we find a testament to the emotional ties that kept Khiḍr remembering home, namely a list of every student he had ever taught in Mosul and a list of all the books he was forced to leave behind when he fled to Rome.[35] (Even today, this makes for especially poignant reading for any scholar or teacher.) In the case of another priest from Mosul named Behnam, who was one of Khiḍr's companions in Rome, parts of his notebook have survived. In it, Behnam kept a detailed record of the names of those individuals whose memory he celebrated at mass each day: many of these names appear to be friends and family from his home in Mosul.[36] Wayfarers they may have been, but even so they continued to inhabit the worlds they had left behind.

This simultaneity in their interior lives was reinforced by the connectedness that they saw in the world around them. While historiography too often emphasises the great cultural and religious distance between Europe and the Ottoman world, scholars like Jocelyne Dakhlia and Wolfgang Kaiser have encouraged us to look for the continuities and practices that linked both sides of the Mediterranean.[37] A single family might stretch across the Mediterranean world, connecting the western and eastern shores of the great sea in personal and intimate ways. Immediately upon his arrival in Marseille, for example, the Maronite Hanna Diyab encountered the brother of a merchant whose family he had known well in Aleppo. Later, he learned that the chief secretary to the archbishop of Paris was the brother of the head of

[35] The journal is held today in the Mingana Collection at the University of Birmingham, Christian Arabic MS 72, fo. 27a for the books, and fos. 28–9 for the students.

[36] Bibliothèque nationale de France, MS Syriaque 279, fo. 66.

[37] Jocelyne Dakhlia and Wolfgang Kaiser, *Les Musulmans dans l'histoire de l'Europe* (2 vols., Paris, 2011–13).

the Franciscans in Jerusalem, a man that Hanna had seen only a few months before his arrival in France.[38] In this way, families, commerce and friendship all underpinned a set of connections that made the arrival to Europe less disorienting than might have otherwise been the case.

When we do find feelings of strangeness or foreignness expressed by individuals in the sources, it tends to come at moments of acute illness or physical discomfort. The fear of travel on the seas, for example, is a recurring theme in these sources. As Elias of Babylon began his journey across the Atlantic to Peru, he wrote that he wished he had someone 'from among his own people' with him.[39] More basic, perhaps, was the daily rhythm of ordinary life: eating, washing and defecation. Hanna Diyab, for example, tells an amusing yet revealing story about an unnerving experience he had in a small inn called 'Le Petit Paris' in the south of France. One day, he went to the innkeeper explaining that he needed to relieve himself, to which the innkeeper responded, 'You can find what you need in your room under your bed.' Returning to his room, Hanna found what he called a 'large pot', presumably a chamber pot. Confused, he returned to the innkeeper who instructed him again to return to his room. It took Hanna a few moments before he finally realised what he was being asked to do, at which point he quickly left the inn and went out to the fields on the outskirts of town to relieve himself. The next day, he discussed the matter with another man from Aleppo who instructed him next time simply to throw the contents of his chamber pot out the window in the evenings. This, it seemed, is what the locals did.[40] An anecdote perhaps, but still an important reminder that for many migrants the experience of foreignness was not only or even primarily expressed in cultural terms but rather it was rooted in the physicality of everyday life.

Amid all of this, there was nonetheless in the Eastern Christian imagination a belief in the possibility for resurrection in exile. We have already seen something of this in the life of Manuel de Elías, the Aleppan in Cádiz whose signature opened this paper. In many ways, Manuel's life resonates with one last story told by Hanna Diyab about a close friendship he developed with a man called Stephen. After arriving in Paris – the circumstances of which are never mentioned – Stephen lived for some time as a beggar, mainly travelling from one saint's festival to another and collecting alms. Before long, though, he had collected enough money to do what one of his friends (another Eastern Christian?) suggested to him, namely to purchase two kettles, a few glasses, and whatever else he needed to make and sell coffee at the fairs. Stephen quickly established a successful trade for himself with a few coffee shops in Paris. His reputation

[38] *D'Alep à Paris*, ed. Heyberger *et al.*, 283.
[39] Ghobrial, 'The Secret Life of Elias of Babylon', 62.
[40] *D'Alep à Paris*, ed. Heyberger *et al.*, 241–2.

spread far and wide, and he even managed to set up one of his agents in Versailles – or so he claimed.[41] It was a tale that told at least of the possibility for permanence and the potential for success to be had by newcomers from the Ottoman Empire. One must wonder what those listening to Hanna's story in Aleppo would have imagined about the world that beckoned to them from across the Mediterranean.

IV Conclusion

Making sense of the movement of Eastern Christians to Europe requires us to start by focusing on localised, internal practices of movement that began in the Ottoman Empire. The idea that Christians under Muslim rule longed to migrate to Europe was clearly a powerful and compelling idea in the early modern period, but it reveals more about how Europeans imagined the Ottoman world than about the reality of everyday life for Ottoman Christians on the move. Amid the cacophony of the sources, the voices of Eastern Christians are sometimes the hardest to hear. In part, this is because we have so little by way of first-hand accounts about their experiences but also, as I have tried to suggest, because of the way in which European expectations of Eastern Christians had an immensely strong influence on the production of sources. European expectations had the effect of inciting certain types of stories from certain types of people. In this way, the documentary record that speaks to the experiences of these migrants is one in which Europeans and Eastern Christians were complicit.

At any rate, the lives of these individuals remind us of the emotional and lived experience of migration and mobility in the early modern Mediterranean. Making sense of these lives requires us to hold them in our hand and examine them closely, in multiple contexts simultaneously, turning them around and around in our hands like a pair of dice so that we can carefully view them from different perspectives. When we do so, we find that the smallest of details – even the signature of a man running out of space – really do matter. They help us recover something of the lost worlds through which these people travelled, and the dreams, motivations and stories that kept them moving onwards.

[41] *Ibid.*, 340–5.

Transactions of the RHS 27 (2017), pp. 175–191 © Royal Historical Society 2017
doi:10.1017/S0080440117000081

REFLECTIONS ON THE POLITICAL THOUGHT OF THE IRISH REVOLUTION*

By Richard Bourke

READ 9 SEPTEMBER 2016

AT THE UNIVERSITY OF TEESSIDE

ABSTRACT. Examining the political thought of the Irish Revolution poses two distinct problems. First, we need to establish how we should date the Revolution for the purposes of intellectual history. There is no doubting that the 1916 Easter Rising was an event in British and Irish politics, but it was also an event in the world of ideas. Any serious consideration of this episode and its aftermath therefore needs to trace its origins to patterns of thought as well as shifts in affairs, and the two processes do not necessarily coincide. The second requirement for understanding the role of political thought in the Revolution is to reconstruct carefully the actual doctrines articulated and deployed. Irish historians have been reluctant to engage in this process of interpretation. Yet a more searching account of political ideas in the period has the potential to change our approach to the Revolution as a whole.

Any general discussion of the political thought of the Irish Revolution requires clarification at the outset of at least two things: first, we have to specify what the 'Irish Revolution' is supposed to cover; and, second, we need to delineate what we mean by 'political thought'.

Let me begin with the concept of revolution. By the time the events which are today described as the Irish Revolution took place, the modern idea of revolution had a long established pedigree going back to 1789.[1] The French case introduced the notion of decisive rupture – of a deliberately radical disruption in the course of history that reconfigured society and politics altogether. Recently, at least one historian has argued that the

---

* My thanks to Ultán Gillen and Roisín Higgins for organising the symposium at which this lecture was delivered, and to the Royal Historical Society for their support.

[1] The classic text on the distinctly revolutionary character of the French Revolution is of course Edmund Burke, *Reflections on the Revolution in France Edmund Burke*, ed. J. C. D. Clark (Stanford, CA, 2001), whose arguments have been variously deployed ever since – by advocates and detractors alike. For further discussion of the general theme, see Hannah Arendt, *On Revolution* (New York, 1963); François Furet, *Penser la révolution française* (Paris, 1978); Reinhart Koselleck, 'Historische Kriterien des neuzeitlichen Revolutionbegriffs', in *idem, Vergangene Zukunft: zur Semantik geschichtlicher Zeiten* (Frankfurt am Main, 1979); John Dunn, 'Revolution', in *Political Innovation and Conceptual Change*, ed. Terence Ball, James Farr and Russell L. Hanson (Cambridge, 1989).

revolutionary characteristics that are standardly ascribed to the French 'deluge' could equally be applied to 1688.[2] Thus, the Glorious Revolution did not amount to a process of pragmatic adaptation, Steve Pincus has argued, challenging standard wisdom from Burke to Macaulay; instead, it involved the violent overthrow of a regime.[3] Yet however one interprets the Glorious Revolution, it is clear that it did not inaugurate the modern tradition of revolution. In subverting a regime, it did not challenge a complete 'order', relegating the annals of previous history to the status of an Ancien Régime.

Similarly, the American Revolution of 1776 never claimed to be a comprehensive annulment of past values. Beginning in 1765, much American protest against parliamentary taxation self-consciously sought to restore a preexisting state of affairs. A decade later, the mood had certainly shifted, and a new agenda had been set. But even then, as insurrection gathered momentum among outraged colonists, there was no absolute denial of all legitimating principles associated with conditions under the empire. A generation of scholars managed to demonstrate that the original upheaval in the colonies drew on venerable political doctrines.[4] Many of these were backward looking in character. In fact, according to one prominent historian, even the putative 'radicalism' of the Revolution was a betrayal of the republican ethos of the American founding.[5] More recently, it has been shown how the struggle over the constitution re-deployed constitutional principles developed over the previous 130 years.[6] The unqualified denial of the validity of an epoch began in France in 1789.

In light of this observation, it is worth noting that at least one commentator has seen fit to argue that the principles guiding the Revolution in Ireland amounted to nothing new. Instead, old ideas were recycled again for use by a new class of rulers.[7] There may be something to this, though surely it is overstated. It seems implausible to deny cultural experimentation, and even intellectual innovation, to the protagonists of the Irish Revolution, including those who fashioned themselves as mere conduits for earlier streams of thought. And besides, the simple fact of a transfer of power to wholly new personnel tells its own story. Who shafts whom, Stalin saw, is a basic question in politics; and the answer

---

[2] Steve Pincus, *1688: The First Modern Revolution* (New Haven, 2009).

[3] *Ibid.*, esp. 3–48.

[4] See, classically, Bernard Bailyn, *The Ideological Origins of the American Revolution* (Cambridge, MA, 1967).

[5] Gordon Wood, *The Radicalism of the American Revolution* (New York, 1992).

[6] Eric Nelson, *The Royalist Revolution: Monarchy and the American Founding* (Cambridge, MA, 2014).

[7] D. G. Boyce, *Nationalism in Ireland* (1982; 3rd edn, 1995), 312.

certainly changed in Ireland in the early twentieth century.[8] The spectacle of public control and political authority suddenly falling to a new cadre of politicians, along with the establishment of new forms of allegiance among the population at large, is clearly indicative of revolutionary change to the organising structure of a society.

So there seems to be little difficulty in depicting the relevant events in Ireland as revolutionary in nature, though what kind of revolution has yet to be determined. Any such effort at specification has to be a fundamentally comparative exercise, though such a perspective is barely to be found in the existing literature. Since the republican tradition in Ireland traces its lineage to the enlightenment, attempts at comparison should begin with the late eighteenth century.[9] Yet it soon becomes clear that although Irish revolutionaries invoked eighteenth-century precedents, the earlier period provided nothing like an exemplary model that the Irish followed. For instance, the Irish Revolution was quite different from the American, even though there have been intelligent bids to equate the two episodes.[10] To begin with, the Americans revolted reluctantly against parliamentary 'tyranny', building militant resistance that won incremental support, whereas the Irish were moved to sever a parliamentary union at the behest of a vanguardist conspiracy. That is not to say that there is nothing to compare – the most interesting overlap is the persistence of British loyalism in both cases, which was more diffuse, although still considerable, in the case of America.[11] Yet it is to say that America cannot be viewed as a precedent.

Equally, the French Revolution was not adopted as a template in Ireland, even if it was invoked by some as an inspiration. The pivotal drama in the Irish case, the rising of 1916, cannot credibly be described as 'Ireland's 1789'.[12] To begin with, the French established some kind of a parliamentary monarchy in 1789, not a republic, or a constitutional democracy. Events in France began with telling divisions within the military, and proceeded by political encroachment on state power. Matters then advanced by a transfer of control over the armed forces. Polarisation in due course led to purges, and annexations, but never to partition; and France throughout remained a major European power. Nonetheless,

---

[8] Stalin adapted the phrase from Lenin's кто кого опередит ('who overtakes whom'). On the Leninist criterion, see Raymond Geuss, *Philosophy and Real Politics* (Princeton, 2008), 23ff.

[9] On the earlier period, see Ultán Gillen, 'Le directoire et le républicanisme Irlandais', in P. Serna, *Républiques sœurs: Le directoire et la révolution atlantique* (Rennes, 2009).

[10] Roy Foster, *Vivid Faces: The Revolutionary Generation in Ireland, 1890–1923* (2014), xvii.

[11] See Leonard W. Labaree, 'The Nature of American Loyalism', *Proceedings of the American Antiquarian Society*, 54 (Apr. 1944), 15–58; Maya Jasanoff, *Liberty's Exiles: American Loyalists in the Revolutionary World* (New York, 2011).

[12] For 1916 as Ireland's 1789, see Foster, *Vivid Faces*, 14.

despite these salient differences, key aspects of the Irish Revolution do stand at least in the 'tradition' of 1789. Yet this very fact underlines its derivative character, thus fundamentally distinguishing it from the spirit of its French precursor. In Ireland, there occurred a definitive break with what went before, but the idea of a breach as such was nothing new: the conception of revolution was not revolutionised. Moreover, the canon of values to which the Irish appealed actually existed in the world, and already had complicated histories to their names. Thus, by 1923 on the island of Ireland there was a new polity and two new regimes, but not an unprecedented style of politics. Finally, even while revolutionaries in Ireland might be placed in a tradition that began in 1789, France's revolutionary experience, including 1848 and 1871, was characterised by the variety of its forms. The idea of a revolutionary tradition has been imaginatively seductive, but in fact each new instalment of revolt in France diverged importantly from 1789, making the notion of an unbroken heritage an ideological fabrication.[13]

The Irish Revolution was therefore in some sense part of a continuity, obliging us to reflect on its various aspects comparatively, while also recognising that it was very much its own thing. Some of the problems involved in anatomising its features are revealed by the difficulty in defining its historical limits. The view that it was brought to an end in 1923 has rarely been disputed, although it has been claimed that it really ended in 1921, succeeded by a movement of counter-revolution lasting until 1936.[14] Of course, 'counter-revolution' has both morally charged and blandly descriptive usages.[15] In descriptive terms, a militant assault on the settled path of a revolution constitutes a *counter*-revolution. It is often a matter of fine judgement what a 'settled' course of development is, and so in practice the difference between a revolution and a counter-blow can be difficult to determine, leaving us wondering, for example, whether Jacobinism was the fulfilment of 1789 or a violent conspiracy against

---

[13] For the seductions of the revolutionary tradition in France, see John Plamenatz, *The Revolutionary Movement in France, 1815–1871* (1952); Albert Soboul, 'Tradition et création dans le mouvement révolutionnaire française au XIXe siècle', *Le mouvement social*, 79 (Apr.–June 1972), 15–31; Patrick H. Hutton, *The Cult of the Revolutionary Tradition: The Blanquists in French Politics, 1864–1893* (Berkeley and Los Angeles, 1981); Christine Piette, 'Réflexions historiques sur les traditions révolutionnaires à Paris au XIXe siècle', *Historical Reflections / Réflexions historiques*, 12 (1985), 403–18.

[14] John Regan, *The Irish Counter-Revolution, 1921–1936: Treatyite Politics and Settlement in Independent Ireland* (Dublin, 1999).

[15] Its normatively inflected meaning is largely indebted to the Marxist philosophy of history: see, classically, Friedrich Engels, *Revolution und Konterrevolution in Deutschland* (1851–1852), in Karl Marx und Friedrich Engels, *Werke* (43 vols., Berlin, 1956–90), VIII, 5–108. For a sociological analysis, see Charles Tilley, 'An Analysis of Counter-Revolution', *History and Theory*, 3 (1963), 30–58.

it.[16] The term is usually burdened with ideological baggage, based on moral intimations of a 'true' revolutionary spirit. Thus, depending on one's taste, anti-treatyites in Ireland can be seen as a betrayal of revolutionary pragmatism, or as a continuation of the Revolution's original purpose. But of course on either reading, the main struggle in Ireland ended in 1923, as revolution and counter-revolution congealed into a settlement.

Unlike the *terminus* of the Revolution in Ireland, its beginnings have been much debated. One of the earliest endeavours to discover its origins appeared at the end of the civil war. W. Alison Phillips's 1923 study, *The Revolution in Ireland*, traced the transformation of Irish politics to 1906.[17] This periodisation may be odd, but it is not completely without any rationale. In February of that year, Henry Campbell-Bannerman led the Liberals to a landslide victory, ending just over a decade of Tory rule. In theory, this spelled the end of committed unionism in power, though in truth the issue of Home Rule was contained until the election of 1910, when John Redmond's Irish Parliamentary Party secured the balance at Westminster. There then followed the Parliament Act the following year, preparing the way for the introduction of Home Rule. Since this is the issue that proved explosively divisive in Irish politics, one might better (even on Phillips's assumptions) date the Revolution from the Liberal alliance with the Irish party, beginning in 1910.

Yet all this is to trace the origins of the crisis to the rhythms of parliamentary politics. For this reason, Alison Phillips's lead has rarely been followed. More plausible as a starting point is 1912. This lends primary significance to the reaction to Asquith's Home Rule bill, which mobilised a determined unionist opposition, led to the assertion of a Protestant general will in Ulster, and the founding of a popular militia in Ireland for the first time in over 130 years. It was these events that convinced Eoin MacNeill, and indeed Patrick Pearse, that 'the north began'.[18] Popular sentiment in the north-east was inflamed, the bargaining power of militancy was publicly demonstrated and constitutional propriety was fatally undermined. Yet still, to fixate on this date is to privilege unionist dissent as the chief driver towards confrontation. For this reason, historians have sometimes preferred to settle on 1858, when James Stephens founded the Irish Republican Brotherhood; or 1879, when organised agitation over land began in earnest; or 1891, when the fall of Parnell shattered Catholic confidence in

---

[16] The former case has been variously articulated, from Burke to Furet; the latter case has most recently been put by Jonathan Israel in *Revolutionary Ideas: An Intellectual History of the French Revolution from The Rights of Man to Robespierre* (Princeton and Oxford, 2014).

[17] W. Alison Phillips, *The Revolution in Ireland, 1906–1923* (Dublin, 1923).

[18] Eoin MacNeill, 'The North Began', *An Claidheamh Soluis*, 1 Nov. 1913.

parliamentarism; or 1916, when the slide toward bloody conflict became irreversible.[19]

Two other moments in time deserve serious consideration. As the examples of Michael Davitt, Roger Casement and Sean MacBride make plain, the Boer War encouraged Irish opposition to imperialism among a generation who lost faith in the righteous pretentions of British rule. Even more decisive, of course, was the Great War itself, without which the Easter Rising, and its results, are inconceivable. Roy Foster correctly identified the formative character of these events as having contributed to the 'radicalization' of politics in Ireland.[20] Yet in general terms, the impact of international developments has been under-emphasised, although Irish awareness of the wider world in the period has been recently demonstrated.[21] Above all, the transformative significance of the First World War needs to be accentuated – a vital context, as Theda Skocpol saw, for the Russian Revolution, just as it was for developments in Ireland.[22]

The War immediately altered popular attitudes to violence, from some perspectives promising a rebirth of noble valour after a Victorian age of enervating peace. 'There are few men in whom the blast of the bugles of war do [*sic*] not arouse the fighting instinct', James Connolly commented in February 1916.[23] As soon as the cause of the War began to look hollow, revivified patriotism was free to pin its hopes on other apparently more elevated causes. For Connolly, of course, the War amounted to 'fratricidal slaughter'.[24] It was a 'war for civilisation' that destroyed the conditions of civilisation. As early as August 1914, the vista of depravity appeared so vast to him that even a vain attempt at socialist revolution by 'force of arms' would have the advantage at least of paralysing the economic vitals of the War.[25] In due course, he lowered his sights: the War might not be stopped in its tracks, but the tradition of resistance could be kept alive by an insurrectionary 'leap in the dark'.[26] In short, given that a

[19] See, respectively, Tom Garvin, *Nationalist Revolutionaries in Ireland, 1858–1928* (Oxford, 1987); D. G. Boyce, *The Revolution in Ireland, 1879–1923* (Basingstoke, 1988); Roy Foster, *Modern Ireland, 1600–1972* (1989; first published 1988), 431ff; Peter Hart, *The I.R.A. at War, 1916–1923* (Oxford, 2003), esp. ch. 1.

[20] Foster, *Modern Ireland*, 456.

[21] Maurice Walsh, *Bitter Freedom: Ireland in a Revolutionary World, 1918–1923* (2015).

[22] Theda Skocpol, *States and Social Revolutions: A Comparative Analysis of France, Russia and China* (Cambridge, 1979).

[23] James Connolly, 'What Is a Free Nation?', *Worker's Republic* (12 Feb. 1916), in *The Revolutionary and Anti-Imperialist Writings of James Connolly, 1893–1916*, ed. Conor McCarthy (Edinburgh, 2016), 247.

[24] James Connolly, 'A Continental Revolution', *Forward* (15 Aug. 1914), in *Writings of Connolly*, 216.

[25] *Ibid.*, 217.

[26] James Connolly, 'Last Testament', in *Writings of Connolly*, 244, 255.

culture of militarism had spread since 1914, opposition was increasingly disposed to make its stand in battle. At the same time, the sense that resistance would be self-defence increased throughout the period: first, the suppression of the Volunteers was fairly widely expected, then the prospect of conscription began to seem an immediate threat long before it was finally unfurled in April 1918. In the United Kingdom, the War not only eroded the pacific protocols of civil life, it also fostered potentially inimical patriotisms. The year 1914, we have to conclude, was a game changer.

For all the possible richness of discussion that debate over the origins of the Irish Revolution is capable of stirring, Easter 1916 must retain its peculiar significance as the moment when Irish nationalism made a military stand, and opinion began to turn against British authority. However, equally clearly, the political ideas that proved influential during the revolutionary tumult pre-date the actual uprising itself. It makes sense to privilege political events in plotting the outlines of the Irish Revolution since affairs were so conspicuously propelled by dramatic deeds. Yet we still need to accept that, fundamentally, the Revolution was an intellectual-political episode, and that its intellectual origins did not begin in 1916. These, according to Pearse, should be traced to 1893. There had been two revolutions in Ireland, he observed in 1914: the second was the founding of the Volunteers – first north, then south – but before that it was the establishment of the Gaelic League that had been transformative.[27] The intellectual history of the Irish Revolution began in the 1890s, he was arguing. Thomas Davis was the 'lineal ancestor' of the League, which rejuvenated the consciousness of nationality.[28] The successful raising of consciousness was a prophecy according to Pearse; it was, indeed, 'more than' a prophecy. It looked forward to the assertion of nationality in arms.[29] There occurred, in other words, a long gestation.[30]

As this last remark implies, W. B. Yeats in broad outline agreed with Pearse. Cultural efflorescence, a new 'stir of thought', seemed to him to have likewise begun in the 1890s. He traced the moment specifically to

[27] Pádraic H. Pearse, 'How Does She Stand II: Robert Emmet and the Ireland of Today' (1914), in *Collected Works of Pádraic H. Pearse: Political Writings and Speeches* (Dublin, Cork and Belfast, 1924), 73.

[28] Pearse, 'The Spiritual Nation' (13 Feb. 1916), in *Political Writings*, 304.

[29] Pearse, 'The Coming Revolution' (Nov. 1913), in *Political Writings*, 91.

[30] On this, see W. B. Yeats, 'The Irish Dramatic Movement' (Nobel Lecture, 15 Dec. 1923), in *idem, Dramatis Personae: Autobiographies* (1936), 177: 'The modern literature of Ireland . . . and indeed all that stir of thought that prepared for the Anglo-Irish war, began when Parnell fell from power in 1891. A disillusioned and embittered Ireland turned from Parliamentary politics; an event was conceived; and the race began, as I think, to be troubled by that event's long gestation.' The motif of a 'long gestation' has been influential in the historiography of the period. See, for example, Patrick Maume, *The Long Gestation: Irish Nationalist Life, 1891–1918* (Dublin, 1999).

1891 when the fate of Parnell disillusioned the public with parliamentary agitation. It was at that moment, Yeats thought, that the war of independence was effectively conceived. Later commentators have rightly challenged Yeats's rigid fatalism, yet they have also tended to misconstrue his point.[31] He never argued that the succession of literary, cultural and intellectual movements after 1891 should be viewed as an 'alternative' to politics, which, as Pearse made plain, they were not. Instead, Yeats viewed the 'stir of thought' as an alternative to parliamentarism: not politics altogether, but parliamentary politics – the cut and thrust of quotidian deliberation and compromise that were coming to be viewed as corrosive of principle.

This observation fits with a more widely felt sentiment in the period – namely, that parliamentary methods were somehow jaded and counterproductive, and that therefore other means of cultivating new values were needed.[32] There was no benefit that parliament could confer on the Irish people, Connolly believed, that could not be 'extorted by the fear of a revolutionary party'.[33] Scepticism about Westminster only grew over the following decade. 'People speak as if the outcry against Parliamentarianism were a novel and unique thing', Tom Kettle observed in 1908.[34] Eight years later in the House of Commons, William O'Brien spoke of an accumulated 'loathing of Parliamentaryism' that underlay the impulse to rebellion.[35] Direct action seemed more effective and authentic. In fact, the view that political struggle was epiphenomenal went back at least to Marx, Kettle had remarked. Yet for him, there were nonetheless limits to this anti-parliamentary rhetoric: cultural development could only fully prosper under conditions of achieved political autonomy, and that required a parliamentary strategy.

So debate about the relationship between culture and politics was pervasive. For some, like Kettle and O'Brien, the parliamentary campaign was a precondition of national self-expression. For Yeats and Pearse, the relationship worked the other way round: consciousness was to be refashioned by intellectual means, creating new opportunities for shaping public life in general. Either way, cultural rebirth was refashioning public consciousness. As Connolly put it as early as 1897, 'Irish Language movements', 'Literary Societies' and 'Commemoration Committees' were 'helping to save from extinction the precious racial and national

---

[31] Foster, *Modern Ireland*, 431–2.

[32] This sentiment had a wider European resonance, culminating in Carl Schmitt, *Die geistesgeschichtliche Lage des heutigen Parlamentarismus* (Munich, 1923).

[33] James Connolly, 'Patriotism and Labour' (Aug. 1897), *Shan Van Vocht*, in *Writings of Connolly*, 29.

[34] Louis François Alphonse Paul-Dubois, *Contemporary Ireland* (Dublin, 1908), ix.

[35] HC Deb. (Hansard), 24 July 1916, vol. 84, col. 1456.

history, language and characteristics of our people'.[36] The danger was that recourse to tradition would trap politics in retrospect. Nonetheless, a forward-looking programme required cultural sustenance too.

The revival of national sensibility was also charted by Erskine Childers. In his 1911 monograph, *The Framework of Home Rule*, he set out the 'various movements' – 'agricultural, industrial, economic, literary, political' – which amounted to proximate demonstrations of Home Rule in operation.[37] Explicitly following Lecky, Childers argued that public spirit was the only viable antidote to sectarianism in Ireland.[38] In practice, this meant fostering national institutions. The principle of nationality was an expression of an irrepressible urge for political freedom, which in Ireland would best be expressed through devolved government. Interestingly, for Childers the 'ideas' of Sinn Fein, if neither its methods nor ultimate objectives, were indices of the same spiritual striving. It was these very ideas, he went on, that 'animate the Industrial Development Associations, the Co-operative movement, the thirst for technical instruction, the Gaelic League, the literary revival, and the work of the only truly Irish organ of government, the Department of Agricultural and Technical Instruction'.[39] Thus, as far as Childers was concerned, since the 1890s there had emerged new movements, new associations, new programmes and new thought, including 'political thought' in a broadly understood sense.

Here we need to pause to consider what we mean by political thought, the second objective of this paper that I signalled at the start. This task is somewhat onerous since the terrain is so thinly populated. With a very few distinguished exceptions, there has been no intellectual history of this period in Ireland, let alone a self-conscious effort to examine its political thought.[40] Sometimes, it is assumed that an intellectual history of political 'troubles' involves dignifying base opportunism with a veneer of idealism; or that the absence of 'great' political thinkers around 1916 implies that no thinking about politics occurred – or at least none that could merit sustained attention. These adverse assumptions are then compounded by the occasional argument that ideology played no decisive role in Ireland at the time. Diarmaid Ferriter has recently argued that there is no evidence of 'sophisticated ideological debate' in Ireland between 1913 and 1923.[41]

---

[36] James Connolly, 'Socialism and Nationalism' (Jan. 1897), *Shan Van Vocht*, in *Writings of Connolly*, 23.

[37] Erskine Childers, *The Framework of Home Rule* (1911), 155.

[38] *Ibid.*, 183.

[39] *Ibid.*, 168.

[40] One exception is Nicholas Mansergh, *Ireland in the Age of Reform and Revolution* (1940). The book was reissued as *The Irish Question, 1840–1921: A Commentary on Anglo-Irish Relations and on Social and Political Forces in Ireland in the Age of Reform and Revolution* (1965).

[41] Diarmaid Ferriter, *A Nation and Not a Rabble: The Irish Revolution, 1913–1923* (2015), 9.

In fact, he seems to argue that reflective discussion came later, rather inverting the actual sequence of events. Given the serious intellectual interventions made by Home Rulers, socialists, feminists, unionists and separatists in the period, it is remarkable to imply that intelligent argument had somehow ceased.

However, it is true that reconstructing the debates is a demanding task. The difficulty is twofold: first, it is necessary to trawl a dismaying array of sources, and second, these have to be placed in their appropriate milieux. The most prominent and successful histories of political thought since the 1960s have for the most part dealt with a canon of classic texts, most of these steeped in extended European and Anglophone traditions, and cast in explicitly philosophical idioms. Revolutionary thought in Ireland in the early twentieth century is altogether less architectonic in style, and media other than the treatise predominate. Journalism in its various forms enjoyed a peculiar importance. The primary object of analysis is perforce less canonical, and rarely addressed exclusively to a political and scholarly elite. Clearly, journalism and the popular tract did not begin in the twentieth century. Their roots lie in the seventeenth and eighteenth centuries. Nonetheless, in Ireland in the period under examination, these are the principal materials with which the historian of ideology has to deal. Understanding them historically requires particular forms of attention. The kind of contextualism that has predominated in the study of political thought is unsurprisingly inadequate to the task. The framing contexts employed by 'Cambridge'-trained historians of ideas have been explicitly intellectual in type: thus, ideas have largely supplied the context for ideas, with (for example) Machiavelli being explained in terms of his use of classical sources, and Locke in terms of Filmer and Pufendorf.[42]

In many ways, this is a product of an understandable division of labour. Everyone accepts that in principle all contexts are potentially relevant to the interpretation of canonical authors. Keith Thomas demonstrated the importance of social context for Thomas Hobbes, and Quentin Skinner originally argued that political context was required to make proper sense of *Leviathan*.[43] Yet, in practice, the Cambridge School has largely focused on intellectual context, even among nineteenth-century specialists (for instance Gareth Stedman Jones, Stefan Collini, John Burrow and Donald

---

[42] The classic texts here are John Dunn, *The Political Thought of John Locke: An Historical Account of the Argument of the 'Two Treatises of Government'* (Cambridge, 1969); J. G. A. Pocock, *The Machiavellian Moment: Florentine Political Thought and the Atlantic Republican Tradition* (Princeton, 1975); Quentin Skinner, *The Foundations of Modern Political Thought* (2 vols., Cambridge, 1978).

[43] Keith Thomas, 'The Social Origins of Hobbes Political Thought', in *Hobbes Studies*, ed. K. C. Brown (Oxford, 1965); Quentin Skinner, 'Conquest and Consent: Hobbes and the Engagement Controversy', in *The Interregnum: The Quest for Settlement, 1646–1660*, ed. G. E. Aylmer (1972).

Winch).[44] We can all agree that this involves a constricted conception of context, although we can also see why a historian might narrowly focus on the intellectual milieu of Locke: the research involved in mastering the sources is laborious. The same limitations hardly apply to studying the political ideas of the Irish Revolution. Intellectual context of course remains important. Indeed, it is remarkable how little work has been done on Pearse's or Connolly's sources. But cultural context has to assume some kind of prominence since so many of the relevant figures were expressly involved in cultural projects. And political context, of course, is indispensable.

While a broad conception of context is therefore essential, so too is careful *analysis* of the various positions proposed. By 'analysis' I mean close attention to how the argument works – its key propositions, its underlying assumptions and its organising principles. It is this that has been strikingly lacking in Irish histories of the period. For instance, given his prominent role in the Rising itself, it is notable how little work has been done on Connolly as an intellectual figure. There has been no real scrutiny of the political ideas of Tom Kettle, and little close examination of the arguments of Childers. Women writers have fared altogether better, not least thanks to work done by Senia Pašeta.[45] By comparison, there has been little sensitive handling of the political works of Pearse. The biographical treatments have been substantially based on psychological speculation, with little careful analysis of his writings.[46] In the same vein, there is much to be done with the elder Plunkett, Casement and Carson, as well as Robert Lynd, Arthur Griffith, Alice Stopford Green and Eoin MacNeill. All too often, some of these figures have been treated as fairly mindless bearers of prejudice rather than as vehicles for concerted thought. This is partly because of an anti-intellectual strain in Irish history writing, but also because relevant doctrines tend to be blamed rather than discussed: blamed, that is, for their consequences, or their 'intrinsic' tendencies.

This outcome is partly a product of the habit of reducing thought to 'attitudes', or inchoate 'emotional' responses. Of course, intellectuals do have attitudes, but their ideas are not simply an extension of them. Hegel experienced moods, and possessed a sensibility, but the *Philosophy of Right* is more than a mere reflection of them. Yet the same is true of George

---

[44] Gareth Stedman Jones, *An End to Poverty? A Historical Debate* (2004); John Burrow, Stefan Collini and Donald Winch, *That Noble Science of Politics: A Study in Nineteenth-Century Intellectual History* (Cambridge, 1983).

[45] Senia Pašeta, *Irish Nationalist Women, 1900–1918* (Cambridge, 2013).

[46] This is conspicuously the case in the standard studies: their authors were so keen to dismantle a then-dominant hagiography that they could not condescend to take their subject's thought at all seriously. See, for instance, Ruth Dudley Edwards, *Patrick Pearse: The Triumph of Failure* (1979).

Russell, D. P. Moran and Louie Bennet.[47] A recurrent problem among Irish historians is well illustrated by Tom Garvin in his innovative study of nationalist revolutionaries in Ireland. Garvin explicitly drew on the political sociologist Barrington Moore and the Czech historian Miroslav Hroch to argue that an insurrectionary spirit was encouraged by social resentment among a rising generation of Catholic nationalists.[48] So the meaning of revolutionary nationalism is reduced to a shared posture, determined by the relative social position of its emissaries. This style of argument is originally indebted to Karl Mannheim who proposed to characterise social philosophies in terms of the backgrounds of their proponents.[49] Locating a figure socially naturally makes good sense if we want to understand where they are coming from. But assuming we know their ideas because we can guess their attitudes is just another way of saying that we do not need to read their work.

In this way, publicists and thinkers become vectors of abstractions instead of actors with intricate intentions: they are made into exemplars of 'revolutionary romanticism', gratuitous 'supremacists' or deluded 'solipsists'.[50] At worst, they become the expression of a 'syndrome'.[51] The net result is that ideology is reconstructed under the influence of social and political theories developed after the fact rather than the opinions of the protagonists actually involved. A recent attempt to return us to the perspectives of the original actors offers a welcome map of revolutionary 'mentalities'.[52] But here again the emphasis is on 'attitudes' rather than ideas, or at least ideas are more often presented than examined. In many ways, this follows quite naturally from the *Annales* style of history, from which the preoccupation with *mentalités* derives.[53] Peter Burke has traced the *Annales* approach to eighteenth- and nineteenth-century precursors: distantly to Voltaire's *Essai sur les moeurs*, but more immediately to Jacob Burkhardt, Jules Michelet and

[47] A. E. [George Russell], 'Nationality and Imperialism', in *Ideals in Ireland*, ed. Lady Gregory (1901); D. P. Moran, *The Philosophy of Irish Ireland* (Dublin, 1905); Louie Bennett, *Ireland and a People's Peace: Paper Read by Miss Louie Bennett at a Joint Meeting of the Irishwomen's International League and the Irish Section of the Union of Democratic Control, Feb. 27, 1918* (Dublin, 1918).

[48] Garvin, *Nationalist Revolutionaries*, 6–8, using arguments indebted to Barrington Moore, *The Social Origins of Dictatorship and Democracy* (Harmondsworth, 1969), and Miroslav Hroch, *Die Vorkämpfer der nationalen Bewegungen bei den kleinen Völkern Europas* (Prague, 1968).

[49] Karl Manheim, *Essays on the Sociology of Knowledge* (1952).

[50] F. S. L. Lyons, *Ireland since the Famine: 1850 to the Present* (1990; first published 1971, revised edn 1973), 330; J. J. Lee, *Modern Ireland: 1912–1985* (Cambridge, 1992; first published 1989), 2–4; Richard English, *Irish Freedom: The History of Nationalism in Ireland* (2006), 274.

[51] Oliver MacDonagh, *States of Mind: A Study of Anglo-Irish Conflict 1780–1980* (1992; first published 1983), 89.

[52] Foster, *Vivid Faces*, xvii–xviii.

[53] My thanks to Colin Jones for discussing this tradition with me.

Fustel de Coulanges.[54] Yet this may amount to lumping all histories of manners and opinions into a single, indiscriminate pile, whereas in fact the characteristic concern of Marc Bloch and Lucien Febvre with 'mémoire collective' or shared 'representations' was meant to identify deep-set, enduring structures of belief – hardly a notable interest among nineteenth-century historians. More importantly, for our purposes, *longue-durée* forms of mental activity are very distinct from revolutionary thought. As Jacques Le Goff has written, 'the historian of mentalities will tend to move towards the ethnologist: both seek to discover the stablest, most immobile level of a society's existence'.[55] By comparison, social and political upheaval is accompanied by *new* attitudes and ideas. The relevant ideas might not be globally innovative, but they are likely to be transformative in context – as indeed, in the case of Ireland, they were.

The reluctance among Irish historians to examine the political theory as well as the background consciousness of the revolutionary generation has meant that ideology in the early twentieth century has been constructed after the fact in accordance with pre-established schemes of interpretation.[56] Cumulatively, this has brought about a situation in which the period has too often been approached in terms of positions that have been manufactured on the basis of ideal doctrines assembled by academics generations later. The most common abstract theory employed by historians is that of 'nationalism', which is assumed to capture the essence of the Revolution in Ireland. However, rather strangely, ideas of nationalism advanced at the time are rarely examined. Instead, ingredients from Hans Kohn, John Plamenatz, Benedict Anderson, Eric Hobsbawm and Ernest Gellner are collected, and projected (somewhat haphazardly) onto opinion in the earlier era.[57] Curiously, however, the doctrine is projected inconsistently, ascribed almost exclusively to the self-styled 'nationalist' party, as if national sentiment were only a property of Irish Catholics, when clearly some kind of national allegiance mobilised Ulster Protestants and determined the actions of the British state.

[54] Peter Burke, *The French Historical Revolution: The Annales School, 1929–2014* (Cambridge, 2014; first published 1990), ch. 1.

[55] Jacques Le Goff, 'Mentalities: A History of Ambiguities', in *Constructing the Past: Essays in Historical Methodology*, ed. Jacques Le Goff and Pierre Nora (Cambridge, 1985), 167.

[56] On the difference between 'political theory' and 'political consciousness', see Eric Nelson, 'What Kind of Book is the *Ideological Origins*?' (forthcoming).

[57] Hans Kohn, *The Idea of Nationalism: A Study in its Origins and Background* (New York, 1944); John Plamenatz, 'Two Types of Nationalism', in *Nationalism: The Nature of an Evolution of an Idea*, ed. Eugene Kamenka (Canberra, 1975); Benedict Anderson, *Imagined Communities: Reflections on the Origin and Spread of Nationalism* (1991); Eric Hobsbawm, *Nations and Nationalism since 1780: Programme, Myth, Reality* (Cambridge, 1990); Ernest Gellner, *Nations and Nationalism* (Ithaca, NY, 1983).

The most popular claim is that nationalism was peculiarly destabilising because it combined political ambition with religious sentiment.[58] However, more recent studies have underlined the range of religious conviction among revolutionary activists, from obsessive piety to anti-clericalism.[59] It is clear that Catholicism will be found among nationalists who are Catholic, but it does not follow that their nationalism will be uniquely 'mystical', or that fanaticism is its inevitable product.

For L. T. Hobhouse writing about Ireland in 1912, nationalism was continuous with liberal principle insofar as it contributed to the 'democratic cause'.[60] Democracy thus understood was devoted to terrestrial improvement, and so was not in any obvious sense religious in nature. The principle of democracy comprised two elements, Hobhouse thought. First, it required the existence of popular consent, and second, it depended on effective representation. Both were absent, he believed, in the case of Ireland in 1912. 'A free government', he contended, 'must be founded on the voluntary adhesion of the mass of the people.'[61] Yet there was no evidence of broad-based support for the Union in Ireland. At the same time, it was structurally impossible for Irish interests to find a hearing at Westminster. By this, he did not mean that Irish MPs had no leverage, which they clearly did, but that the government of Ireland did not reflect Irish preferences. It was this set-up that led to widespread complaints that, despite the Union, Ireland was a colonial dependent on metropolitan power, rather than a free political agent. 'It may have equality of franchise', Hobhouse wrote, 'but its representatives are in a permanent minority.'[62]

Hobhouse's intervention demonstrates two things. First, it shows that debate about nationalism in the period turned on constitutional questions that are not reducible to controversy over 'identity', in contrast to more recent academic analysis.[63] Second, it provides an example of competing

---

[58] English, *Irish Freedom*, 274. The claim derives immediately from Conor Cruise O'Brien. On O'Brien in this context, see Richard Bourke, 'Languages of Conflict and the Northern Ireland Troubles', *Journal of Modern History*, 83 (2011), 544–78. O'Brien's underlying assumption has a longer history, mediated by Raymond Aron, and going back to Alexis de Tocqueville and Edmund Burke. The claim is in any case based on a misreading of both Burke and Tocqueville. See Raymond Aron, 'L'avenir des religions séculières' (1944), *Commentaire*, 8 (1985), 369–83; Alexis de Tocqueville, *The Old Regime and the Revolution* (1856), trans. Alan S. Kahan (2 vols., Chicago, 1998–2001), I, 99–101; Edmund Burke, *Second Letter on a Regicide Peace* (1796), in *The Writings and Speeches of Edmund Burke*, ed. Paul Langford (9 vols., Oxford, 1970–2015), IX, 278.

[59] Foster, *Vivid Faces*, 36.

[60] L. T. Hobhouse, 'Irish Nationalism and Liberal Principle', in *The New Irish Constitution: An Exposition and Some Arguments*, ed. J. H. Morgan (1912), 361.

[61] *Ibid.*, 364.

[62] *Ibid.*, 365.

[63] Typical of the idiom is Anthony D. Smith, *National Identity* (Harmondsworth, 1991).

conceptions of nationalism. There was no single doctrine of nationalism shared by activists at the time, but rather a rich diversity in understandings. To comprehend this diversity, and thus to appreciate the issues that galvanised contemporary actors, we must return to the original sources in the appropriate spirit: that means, in the spirit of historical criticism – not taking professions of faith at face value, but nonetheless aiming to reconstruct them dispassionately. Paul Bew began this task in relation to Redmondism and unionism, and Matthew Kelly has probed the intricacies of Fenianism.[64] Yet still the full complexity of republicanism remains under-explored.

As commonly represented in the historiography, Irish republicanism is interpreted as a doctrine of exclusion. This charge is hardly meaningless, but it has been inadequately understood. A good example of the intricacies can be found in Pearse, with whom I shall conclude.

Pearse presented himself ostentatiously as standing in the tradition of Wolfe Tone. Tone, he believed, preached a philosophy of inclusion, not exclusion. As Pearse put it, Ireland was not populated by two nations, or three, but by a single, inclusive culture, comprising Catholic, Protestant and Dissenter.[65] Naturally, this meant inclusion on republican terms, which for Pearse's opponents could mean nothing but exclusion. Nonetheless, Pearse's principles of inclusion are worthy of exploration in their own right. His programme was addressed to people of 'every rank and class', and of all sections of opinion.[66] Yet not all members of each section were expected to lend their support. Pearse saw himself as a spokesman for a democratic agenda that did not require active popular endorsement. Mass sentiment might be corrupted, leaving a minority to represent preexisting popular rights. Most usually, he commented in 1915, it is 'the few' who fight for what is right, the many for what is wrong. Yet it is the few, he believed, who, ultimately, 'win'.[67]

What licenses the few, then, to act on the majority's behalf? The answer here, though sometimes difficult to grasp, is that it is democratic principle that authorises a minority to act as unelected delegates of the many. As Pearse argued a matter of months before the Easter Rising, the goal of republicanism was to put the people, 'the actual people', 'in effectual ownership and possession of the soil of Ireland'.[68] This did not necessarily entail a wholesale redistribution of wealth, but rather the right of the sovereign nation to dispose of its resources. The same point was articulated

---

[64] Paul Bew, *Ideology and the Irish Question: Ulster Unionism and Irish Nationalism, 1912–1916* (Oxford, 1994); Matthew Kelly, *The Fenian Ideal and Irish Nationalism, 1882–1916* (Woodbridge, 2006).

[65] Pearse, 'Oration on Wolfe Tone' (1913), in *Political Writings*, 59.

[66] Pearse, 'Oration on Robert Emmet' (1914), in *Political Writings*, 73.

[67] Pearse, 'The Separatist Idea' (1 Feb. 1916), in *Political Writings*, 215.

[68] Pearse, 'The Sovereign People' (31 Mar. 1916), in *Political Writings*, 350.

in the Easter Proclamation: 'We declare the right of the people of Ireland to the ownership of Ireland and to the unfettered control of Irish destinies, to be sovereign and indefeasible.'[69] The final determination of property was a national right, even if in practice possessions were to be held in private hands. It is not this determination that resides with the few, but the right to create conditions in which it can be made. So while the exercise of democracy derives from an electorate, the right of self-government might be asserted by a derisively small number.

What then were the origins of this right? In Pearse's view, self-determination is a natural right, prescribed at once by natural law and the law of nations, although access to that right can only be sustained by tradition.[70] That means, on the one hand, that Pearse's argument is contractual. On the other hand, the right of contract is transmitted by tradition. So, primordially a people might contract with itself to govern. For Pearse, this means that a people is not entitled to betray its liberty, 'any more than a contract of perpetual slavery is binding on an individual'.[71] For this reason, he could write that 'the national demand of Ireland is fixed and determinate'.[72] It could not be modified by transitory, popular whim. Yet it could expire from generalised neglect. As soon as the historical memory of nationality disappeared, there would be no basis on which to assert the primordial right of self-government. Consequently, Pearse ascribed nationality to tradition: while the original entitlement to form a democracy was pre-historic, a natural right could only retain its force in history if it was periodically realised in action.

In Ireland, the right to self-government pre-dated the Norman Conquest: 'It will be conceded to me that the Irish who opposed the landing of the English in 1169 were Separatists', Pearse wrote.[73] From that point on, the knowledge of nationality was transmitted historically. Consciousness of the right to self-determination was preserved by exemplary acts of personal sacrifice across the generations. It was in this sense that national tradition had to be treated with reverence: 'Patriotism is like a religious faith', Pearse asserted. Note that it was *like*, but was not in fact, a religious faith.[74] The faith was kept alive through the memory of the dead 'striving' to accomplish some unfinished task. Pearse's political vision was therefore fundamentally secular. His doctrines were, if anything, a threat to Christian orthodoxy. The people, not Christ, is the messiah, he once proclaimed. It is true that the messiah was to be foreshadowed by

[69]Poblacht na hÉireann: Proclamation of the Irish Republic, Easter 1916, para. 3.

[70]For natural law, see Pearse, 'Ghosts' (Christmas 1915), in *Political Writings*, 230.

[71]*Ibid.*, 231.

[72]*Ibid.*, 230.

[73]*Ibid.*, 232.

[74]Pearse, 'Oration on Robert Emmet' (1914), in *Political Writings*, 66.

a Christ-like sacrifice.[75] But once again the very analogy amounts to a Christian heresy.

Sacrifice, we need to understand, was not intended as self-immolation. It was a vivid means of generating consent. Accordingly, the sacrificial stand of Easter Monday was not 'symbolic', but pragmatic, a protest in arms that might, at best, awaken immediate support or, at worst, inspire as an example of public virtue. As with the Romans, Pearse wagered, a show of virtue might generate mass appeal. Minimally, it might garner support for separatist insurrection. It was for this reason that Pearse could view bloodshed as 'a cleansing and a sanctifying thing'.[76] This was not a simple cult of wanton violence. After all, Pearse had been vociferous in his condemnation of Redmondism as 'a peace-holocaust' that spilled the blood of 50,000 Irishmen.[77] War, he believed, was terrible, but slavery was worse. Like Gandhi, Pearse followed a train of English authors from Carlyle to Ruskin in condemning the culture of utility as having inured the people to slavery.[78] The first duty of the Irish democrat was therefore to preach heroism against self-interest as a prelude to the rebirth of national will.[79] Sacrifice for one's country was a renunciation of self-advancement. The hope was that it would successfully transform popular consciousness; it was not an ideology of morbid failure.

The Irish Revolution was a republican revolution: assorted doctrines of republicanism lay at its heart. Any doctrine will appear exclusive to those who reject its principles. Unionism and republicanism were both built on exclusions with a view to advancing inclusion on their own terms. Republican exclusivism is usually opposed by liberal 'pluralism' in both the historical and political literature. Pluralism implies acceptance of the voices of dissent. From the vantage of now-dominant historiographical perspectives, republican orthodoxy occupies a dissenting position, and so a pluralist history is obliged to extend to it the requisite understanding. Understanding, naturally, does not mean approbation. Yet equally, glib repudiation is a refusal to comprehend.

---

[75] *Ibid.*, 69, 71.

[76] Pearse, 'The Coming Revolution' (Nov. 1913), in *Political Writings*, 99.

[77] Pearse, 'Ghosts' (Christmas 1915), in *Political Writings*, 231–2.

[78] See Mahatma Gandhi, *'Hind Swaraj' and Other Writings*, ed. Anthony J. Parel (Cambridge, 1997, 2009), 118, on key texts that guided the author's critique of English civilisation.

[79] Pearse, 'The Murder Machine' (1912), in *Political Writings*, 25.

Transactions of the RHS 27 (2017), pp. 193–209 © Royal Historical Society 2017
doi:10.1017/S0080440117000093

FEMINIST POLITICAL THOUGHT AND ACTIVISM IN REVOLUTIONARY IRELAND, *c.* 1880–1918

By Senia Pašeta

READ 9 SEPTEMBER 2016

AT THE UNIVERSITY OF TEESSIDE

ABSTRACT. Feminist thought and activism was a feature of Irish political life in the late nineteenth and early twentieth centuries. Because the women's suffrage campaign coincided with and was at times influenced by wider debates on the national question, it has often been understood almost entirely in relation to Irish nationalism and unionism, and usually in the specific context of acute political crisis such as the third Home Rule. The Irish suffrage movement should instead be understood both in terms of wider political developments and in particular Irish contexts. This paper surveys aspects of feminist political culture with a particular emphasis on the way that nationalist Irish women articulated and negotiated their involvement in the women's suffrage movement. It argues that the relationship between the two was both more nuanced and dynamic than has been allowed, and that opposition to women's activism should be understood in structural and cultural terms as well as in broadly political ones. The relationship should also be understood in longer historical terms than is usual as it also evolved in the context of broader political and social shifts and campaigns, some of which predated the third Home Rule crisis.

There was no single body of feminist thought in late nineteenth- and early twentieth-century Ireland. Neither should we expect there to have been, given how broad feminism was and how likely Irish women were to be motivated by a range of political ideas well beyond their feminist concerns. For many of the activists at the heart of the Irish Revolution, male and female, this was a period of multi-faceted political and cultural activity. It was, according to the actress and nationalist, Maire Nic Shiubhlaigh, who thrived in Dublin's nationalist *demi-monde*, an era of 'innumerable little clubs and societies, of diverse moments, aimed at the establishment of a new order'.[1] Activists dedicated to one cause alone were a rare species: most were extraordinarily busy and deeply involved in a range of organisations and programmes as well as working, studying and often bringing up families. Feminist activists were no exception as they too

---

[1] Maire Nic Shiubhlaigh, *Splendid Years: Recollections of Maire Nic Shiubhlaigh's Story of the Irish National Theatre as Told to Edward Kenny* (Dublin, 1955), 3.

threw themselves into supporting a variety of political, cultural and social causes.

This paper is primarily concerned with the question of how nationalist women articulated and negotiated their feminist ideas and activism during the revolutionary period, with an emphasis on women's suffrage as a manifestation of feminist political thought and action. While remaining a very under-researched area, a historiographical consensus on the way that feminism and nationalism interacted in revolutionary Ireland emerged in the 1980s and was, until relatively recently, largely unchallenged. Spearheaded by the research of Beth McKillen and Margaret Ward, it set the tone of most subsequent analysis of the relationship between nationalism and feminism.[2] Ward's pioneering research explored the barriers to women's involvement in male and mixed sex nationalist organisation in late nineteenth- and early twentieth-century Ireland. She argued that the 'contradictions' between feminism and nationalism were at times overwhelming for the women involved,[3] and concluded that an overriding 'emotional and ideological identification with nationalism' was an important factor in preventing politically active women from developing a broader form of liberation, and that this identification 'ultimately dissipated their radical potential'.[4]

McKillen addressed related questions, arguing that 'the feminist cause in Ireland' had been deeply damaged by constitutional and, in particular, separatist nationalism before 1916.[5] Her argument was based on three fundamental premises: that male (and female) separatists failed to support suffrage 'because of their belief that women's emancipation had to be deferred until Irish independence was won';[6] that divisions between feminists over prioritising women's suffrage over Irish nationalism weakened the women's movement; and that the Easter Rising, and the Proclamation of Independence which guaranteed equal rights for all Irish citizens, changed this dynamic fundamentally.

Underlying both positions was the idea that 'nationalist groups in Ireland were profoundly conservative on issues relating to gender equality'.[7] Although both Ward and McKillen identified individuals

---

[2] Beth McKillen, 'Irish Feminism and Nationalist Separatism, 1914–23', *Eire-Ireland*, 17 (1982), 52–67; Beth McKillen, 'Irish Feminism and Nationalist Separatism, 1914–23', *Eire-Ireland*, 17 (1982), 74–90; Margaret Ward, *Unmanageable Revolutionaries: Women and Irish Nationalism* (1989).

[3] Ward, *Unmanageable Revolutionaries*, 3.

[4] *Ibid.*, 248.

[5] McKillen, 'Irish Feminism', 74.

[6] *Ibid.*, 62.

[7] Maria Luddy, 'Women and Politics', in *The Field Day Anthology of Irish Women's Writing and Traditions*, ed. Angela Bourke, Andrew Carpenter and Seamus Deane (5 vols., Cork, 1991–2002), V, 71.

and organisations which proved to be exceptions to this premise, this idea nonetheless informed most subsequent analysis of Irish women's involvement in and contribution to feminist and nationalist activism in modern Ireland. This has had a number of historiographical consequences. Our understanding of the dynamics of the Irish suffrage movement itself has been affected, but so too has our understanding of aspects of Irish nationalism in the revolutionary period and beyond. The often dynamic, sometimes fraught and almost always flexible relationship it enjoyed with feminism has been all too often reduced to a series of mutually exclusive positions which inevitably led to quarrels, most of them coinciding with political flashpoints such as the debate over the third Home Rule Bill.

Unsurprisingly, the reality was far more nuanced and depended as much on changing political circumstances as it did on the particular ideological convictions of individual nationalists. Antipathy towards women's activism was neither universal nor perpetual, and it was based on specific experiences and contexts at least as much as it was based on unmitigated prejudice. Attitudes to suffragism must be seen in structural as well as cultural terms. They must also be seen in longer historical terms than is usually the case. The development of women's political activism in Ireland was clearly affected by the national question, but it also evolved in the context of broader political and social shifts and campaigns, some of which predated the third Home Rule crisis.

Irish nationalism and Irish feminism were diverse and complex movements, both of which consisted of a number of political and social agendas and networks of adherents. The borders of each were elastic. While this made cooperation possible, it did not always make it straightforward. When, for example, the fate of both Home Rule and women's suffrage was largely dependent on Irish votes in the House of Commons in 1912, women's suffrage was pushed to the back of the political queue, sometimes aggressively. Yet, while nationalism could and did constrain feminist activism at times, it could also make possible new forms of political expression for women, and it could even strengthen feminist arguments. Constitutional nationalists recognised this implicitly when they frequently linked the national demand with women's suffrage. As one campaigner argued, the 'two analogous movements, like all those making for human freedom, ought, of course, to advance together'.[8] Their ideological and intellectual linking was for many feminist nationalists both logical and irrefutable.

Strikingly, while many of their nationalist colleagues did not always agree, very few of their organisations were institutionally hostile to feminism's most public manifestation, women's suffrage. The exception

---

[8] *Freeman's Journal*, 10 Apr. 1912.

to this general rule was the Irish Parliamentary Party, one of Ireland's longest established nationalist organisations. Though radical in British constitutional terms, the Irish Party represented the more respectable face of Irish nationalism as it was dedicated to the peaceful implementation of Home Rule by constitutional means and, in its later phase, to a parliamentary alliance with the Liberal Party. It had little interest in women members though it did, as the pro-suffrage nationalist MP William Redmond complained bitterly, happily accept their money. Criticising anti-suffragist MPs who spoke in a 'lordly way of women' from the Commons' benches, he accused them in 1911 of, 'metaphorically speaking', going down on their knees and begging help from them during election campaigns.[9]

Such criticism was not unusual in high political circles across the UK where women were similarly blocked from the major public institutions of government, while also asked to give generously to the Liberal and Conservative Parties. But, while all the major political parties in the UK adapted to changing circumstances by accepting female members or, at the very least, by sanctioning women's associations in the late nineteenth and early twentieth centuries, the Irish Party alone refused to do so. This was to cost it dearly, especially during the election campaign of 1918 by which time, as its more perceptive critics argued, franchise reform had become the Party's 'winding sheet'.[10]

As has long been recognised by British political historians, legislative changes, especially the Corrupt Practices Act of 1883, ushered in a new period of women's political engagement in the UK. Women had been active in national and local politics before this time, but their work as canvassers and organisers and in party administration and publicity became more prominent, recognised and indispensable from the 1880s.[11] These shifts were reflected in the extraordinary spread and success of the Primrose League from 1883, and of the Women's Liberal Federation from 1886. Both organisations were active in Ireland and played an important role in politicising Irish women, though their impact and reach has not been studied. The Primrose League in particular developed a lively and influential network, which reached a peak of at least thirty-five branches, some of which boasted many hundreds and even thousands of members.[12] The organisation itself was ruled by an exclusively male Grand Council, but women probably took on most of the responsibilities of the local

---

[9] Parliamentary Franchise (Women) Bill, HC Deb., 11 July 1910, vol. 19, col. 123.

[10] *Irish Independent*, 16 July 1917.

[11] Kathryn Gleadle, *Borderline Citizens: Women, Gender, and Political Culture in Britain, 1815–1867* (Oxford, 2009), 28–42; Jon Lawrence, *Electing our Masters: The Hustings in British Politics from Hogarth to Blair* (Oxford, 2009), 84–5.

[12] Martin Pugh, *The Tories and the People, 1880–1935* (Oxford, 1985), 25–7, 90; Primrose League, Roll of Habitations, MSS Primrose League Adds. 5, Bodleian Library, Oxford.

branches.[13] They canvassed, fund-raised, engaged in propaganda and spoke from public platforms; Primrose League work thus serving as an important apprenticeship for the women who subsequently became involved in new varieties of unionism.

At the same time, women's influence in formal unionist circles expanded. They were excluded from the upper echelons of the Irish Unionist Alliance (IUA) but worked effectively through their network of associated ladies' committees which expanded to twenty-eight branches by 1912.[14] Their influence grew as women became more integral to the unionist machine: by 1900, women could enjoy all the privileges of membership of the IUA 'except election to the General Council or Executive Committee';[15] by 1905, they were sitting on county committees, and the remaining restrictions on their membership were removed from the constitution.[16] The establishment in 1911 of Ireland's largest women's political organisation, the Ulster Women's Unionist Council was, therefore, much more than a reaction to the extraordinary circumstances produced by the third Home Rule crisis. It was the product of the active involvement of women in unionist politics for more than thirty years and, indirectly, it was a reflection of the expansion of women's political activism more generally, especially in the suffrage movement.

There was no equivalent in constitutional nationalist Ireland despite the fact that the majority of the Irish population was Catholic and nationalist, and that nationalist Ireland had a long and successful history of mobilising impressively large swathes of the population. Some nationalist strategists had recognised the potential impact of women's groups. The Irish National League, for example, had vowed to organise ladies' branches in 1889, hoping that nationalist women would 'fight the Primrose Leaguers on their own ground', but nothing seemed to have come of this.[17] This failure to organise women was to have a profound impact on the development of feminism and suffragism, and on constitutional politics more generally.

Why did the Irish Party fail to accommodate women members and so to adapt to what was, by the early twentieth century, a British political norm? It was certainly true, as Diane Urquhart has suggested, that the Irish Party's secure hold on nationalist Ireland meant that it did

---

[13] Philippe Vervaecke, 'The Primrose League and Women's Suffrage, 1883–1918', in Myriam Boussahba-Bravard, *Suffrage outside Suffragism: Women's Vote in Britain, 1880–1914* (New York, 2007), 182–3.

[14] Irish Unionist Alliance, *Notes from Ireland*, no. 9, vol. 21, 1 Sept. 1912, 98.

[15] Public Record Office of Northern Ireland (hereafter PRONI), D989/c/3/62, Irish Unionist Alliance, *Annual Report for 1901* (Dublin, 1902), 26.

[16] PRONI, Irish Unionist Alliance, *Annual Report for 1905–06* (Dublin, 1906), 5, 60.

[17] *Nation*, 5 Oct. 1889.

not need to cultivate women's support.[18] Its dominance of nationalist Ireland was such that there was next to no chance of its failing to secure votes and thus parliamentary seats. The same point could, however, be made about the Unionist Party which could likewise count on the votes of its adherents but did not stand in the way of activist women. One might also look to the condition of the Irish Party itself, especially before the First World War. The idea that the Party was in terminal decline, riven by dissent, haemorrhaging financial and moral support and increasingly out of touch with modern Ireland is a well-established theme.[19] Its failure to incorporate women might be viewed in the same context as its alleged failure to promote young parliamentarians and cultural revivalism. But recent studies by James McConnel and Michael Wheatley have challenged these views, suggesting instead that the Party was in fact functioning well, its members and supporters generally united behind its leader, John Redmond, and willing to follow his lead.[20]

The social context in which the Party organised must also be considered. The Irish Parliamentary Party depended on Catholic votes and Catholic money. Necessarily mindful of its relationship with the church and aware of the potential consequences of challenging it too publicly, it was unlikely to depart from Catholic social teaching about gender roles. There was no agreed Catholic position on a woman's role, let alone on women's suffrage, but the Catholic hierarchy was socially conservative. It was suspicious of progressive ideas about higher education and careers for women and it would remain mistrustful of their forays into political activism well into the twentieth century.[21] It is telling that although the Catholic Women's Suffrage Society was founded in England in 1911, an Irish branch was not formed until 1915.[22] The Irish founders did so in order to combat the notion that 'in a Catholic country' the Protestant dominance of existing suffrage societies 'is enough to make people say that the majority of Irishwomen do not want the vote'.[23] It is equally striking that an explicitly nationalist suffrage organisation was never founded in Ireland. The Catholic Women's Suffrage Society came closest as all of its most prominent members were constitutional nationalists, but the organisation remained strictly non-party. By contrast,

[18] Diane Urquhart, *Women in Ulster Politics, 1890–1940* (Dublin, 2000), 100.
[19] James McConnel, *The Irish Parliamentary Party and the Third Home Rule Crisis* (Dublin, 2013), 14–22; Michael Wheatley, *Nationalism and the Irish Party: Provincial Ireland, 1910–1916* (Oxford, 2005), 3–7.
[20] McConnel, *Irish Parliamentary Party*, 23–7.
[21] Senia Pašeta, 'Another Class? Women and Higher Education in Ireland, 1870–1909', in *Politics, Society and the Middle Class in Modern Ireland*, ed. Fintan Lane (Basingstoke, 2010), 181–90.
[22] *Catholic Suffragist*, vol. 1, no. 3, 15 Mar. 1915.
[23] *Irish Catholic*, 27 Feb. 1915.

branches of the (Anglican) Church League of Women's Suffrage were founded in all of Ireland's major cities and prominent clerics including the bishop of Limerick lined up to support the cause.[24] The Conservative and Unionist Suffrage Association likewise developed a network of branches across the country. It appears that despite being in a clear majority in Ireland, Catholic and nationalist women were the least likely to organise on explicitly confessional or political lines.

There were obvious cultural and structural reasons for this as Catholic Ireland presented fewer opportunities to women for social and political engagement than Protestant Ireland. This was partly because of the emphasis within Protestant denominations on the personal responsibility of individuals to undertake practical and godly work in the world. It was also due to the enormous expansion in Ireland of Catholic orders, especially nuns, whose work in teaching, nursing and other caring positions impeded the development of lay Catholic women's organisations.[25] This in turn limited their opportunity to earn the kind of valuable experience in lobbying, organising and fund-raising that their unionist contemporaries developed through the Primrose League and the Irish Unionist Alliance.

Yet, despite these restrictions, an appetite for political involvement clearly existed among nationalist women. From 1800, they had been involved in fund-raising, negotiating 'political bribes' and turning out to campaign for favoured electoral candidates.[26] Although they could not vote, they could exert a private influence on their enfranchised male relatives, a phenomenon acknowledged by at least some hopeful candidates.[27] Their participation in more public forms of political engagement grew steadily and by the middle of the century, female involvement in Ireland's rich culture of political rioting and disorder in particular had reached new heights.[28] The combination of parliamentary agitation and, sometimes, intense periods of direct political action which characterised the Irish Party from the early 1880s, proved to be especially conducive to women's activism.

Their political engagement reached a peak during the Land War, 1879–82. Although they were excluded from the more formal political work of the Land League, women could become members; some were imprisoned as activists while others became active fund-raisers through their work in ladies' branches of the Prisoners' Aid Society and the Political Prisoners'

[24] *Church League of Women's Suffrage,* June 1913, no. 18.
[25] Maria Luddy, *Women and Philanthropy in Nineteenth-Century Ireland* (Cambridge, 1995), 5.
[26] Theodore Hoppen, *Elections, Politics, and Society in Ireland, 1832–1885* (Oxford, 1984), 406.
[27] *Ibid.*
[28] *Ibid.,* 407.

Sustentation Fund.[29] More striking and innovative was the Ladies' Land League. Founded in 1880, this organisation was, in the words of one early member, 'the first national organisation of Irishwomen' to have been organised for and by women.[30] The establishment of the Ladies' Land League was a radical and risky step. This was well understood by the male leadership of the Land League as it was founded despite the express displeasure of most leading male Land Leaguers, including Charles Stewart Parnell himself.[31] He, John Dillon and Patrick Egan feared that the Land League would 'invite ridicule in appearing to put women forward in places of danger'; leading Land Leaguer, Andrew Kettle, also subsequently admitted that he too had been dubious about the wisdom of exposing women 'to such a rough and tumble business as an agrarian combination'.[32] This is hardly surprising for the Ladies' Land League took women's political activism to a virtually unprecedented level of organisation, public exposure and impact in the United Kingdom. Despite some reservations, the women's League was sanctioned by the male leadership. Its creation signalled a new era in women's politics.

It is difficult to know precisely what the male organisers expected the women to do. The Ladies' League was established in anticipation of the wholesale arrest of the male leadership, but the women's leader, Anna Parnell, complained that the exact nature of the women's work and the context in which they were to undertake it were unclear and that this led to instability from the outset.[33] The evident confusion around the women's remit was destabilising but the women were nonetheless efficient and determined. By July 1881, they had founded 420 branches across Ireland and were providing relief for about 3,000 evicted people.[34] They did the same work as the men they had replaced. Like their male colleagues, they were harassed by police, they were publicly condemned by 'certain church dignitaries', and at least thirteen served prison sentences on account of their work with the Land League.[35] They initiated and oversaw the building of more than 200 huts, which would house evicted tenants, and they took on the publication of *United Ireland* after the arrest of

[29]Janet K. TeBrake, 'Women in Revolt: The Land League Years', *Irish Historical Studies*, 28 (1992), 66–8. See also, for example, *Nation*, 26 Nov. 1881, 24 Dec. 1881, 11 Mar. 1882, 25 Mar. 1882, 10 June 1882 and 12 Aug. 1882.

[30]Jennie Wyse Power, text of a lecture on the Ladies' Land league, Captured Document 193, Bureau of Military History, Dublin, S. 222.

[31]Andrew J. Kettle, *Material for Victory: The Memoirs of Andrew J. Kettle*, ed. Laurence J. Kettle (Dublin, 1958), 48; Michael Davitt, *The Fall of Feudalism in Ireland* (London and New York, 1904), 299.

[32]Davitt, *Fall of Feudalism*, 299; Kettle, *Material for Victory*, 48.

[33]Dana Hearne, 'Introduction' to Anna Parnell, *The Tale of a Great Sham* (Dublin, 1986), 24.

[34]Jane McL. Côté, *Fanny and Anna Parnell: Ireland's Patriot Sisters* (1991), 190.

[35]Jennie Wyse Power, Ladies' Land League lecture.

its entire staff.[36] According to Michael Davitt, the women 'kept the organisation alive' while the leaders of the Land League were incarcerated in Kilmainham.[37]

Their usefulness to the League and its tolerance of the women ended when the Land League changed political course and the women's organisation 'disobeyed' direct instructions from the leadership, attempting instead to direct the policy of the Land League against Charles Stewart Parnell's wishes.[38] A bitter feud developed between the factions before the women finally managed to extricate themselves from the Land League. The result was the complete estrangement of Anna Parnell from the political life of her country, the minimisation of the Ladies' Land League in the national story and an abiding suspicion of 'women politicals'. Margaret Ward has argued that 'the backlash against women's participation in the campaign for tenant rights foreshadowed their exclusion from the task of nation building'.[39] Suspicion of the Ladies' League may indeed help to explain why, as I have argued elsewhere, no nationalist equivalent of the Primrose League was formed in Ireland and why some Irish Party men remained implacably opposed to women's political involvement well into the twentieth century.[40] Having been pioneers in formally mobilising women, the Irish Party swiftly and determinedly retreated when the women veered off course.

The legacy of the Ladies' Land League was, therefore, paradoxical: its radicalism and independence of thought mitigated against women's nationalist organisation, while at the same time, it acted as a vital spur for radical nationalist women. This is not to suggest that the women who were active in the Ladies' Land League were typical or even unequivocally feminist as there is no question that they were exceptionally politically active and unusually visible by any contemporary standards. Nonetheless, their impact was real and it did influence the way that subsequent generations of nationalist men and women regarded women's political activism. Anna Parnell herself believed that the characterisation of the Ladies' League as fanatical and extreme had been deliberately cultivated by Davitt's *Fall of Feudalism*, published in 1904.[41] She maintained that the

---

[36] McL. Côté, *Fanny and Anna Parnell*, 202–3; Jennie Wyse Power, Ladies' Land League lecture.

[37] D. B. Cashman, *The Life of Michael Davitt, Founder of the National Land League* (1882), 233.

[38] Parnell, *Great Sham*, 117–18; McL. Côté, *Fanny and Anna Parnell*, 216.

[39] Margaret Ward, 'The Ladies' Land League and the Irish Land War 1881/82: Defining the Relationship between Women and Nation', in *Gendered Nations: Nationalism and Gender Order in the Long Nineteenth Century*, ed. Ida Bloom, Karen Hageman and Catherine Hall (Oxford, 2000), 229.

[40] Senia Pašeta, *Irish Nationalist Women, 1900–1918* (Cambridge, 2013), 32.

[41] Anna Parnell letter in *Peasant*, 5 Oct. 1907, unpaginated; McL. Côté, *Fanny and Anna Parnell*, 237–8.

women's League had been utterly misrepresented and that women had 'next to no influence in Ireland'.[42]

Parnell *may* have exaggerated somewhat, but she was not alone in her assessment of the threat posed to the nationalist establishment by the women's refusal to follow orders. Hanna Sheehy Skeffington, whose own father and uncle had been imprisoned as Land Leaguers with Parnell, spoke wistfully of 'the glorious days of the Ladies' Land League', in her 1909 condemnation of constitutional nationalist Ireland's refusal to integrate women into the movement.[43] She maintained that the Irish Party had been profoundly weakened when 'the fine enthusiasm, the generous spirit of cooperation revealed by those noble-hearted women' had been 'diverted' and 'repressed'. More presciently, she argued that:

> with the death of the women's organization, there being no effort by a further reorganization to maintain for Ireland the fine reserve forces so called up, either in a new league under new conditions, or (better still) by encouraging women to enter and strengthen the ranks of the male branches, women lost touch with Parliamentarianism and have not since regained it. Since then, as I have already shown, their energies and enthusiasm have been turned to other channels, their force is expended in directions indifferent to or hostile to Parliamentarianism ... but it will be a matter of wonderment to the future historian of Ireland to note the silence imposed on Irishwomen from the early eighties down to the dawn of the twentieth century.[44]

Sheehy Skeffington was uniquely qualified to comment on this. The daughter of an MP, and a staunch nationalist and feminist herself, she experienced first-hand the absolute refusal of the Irish Party to open its doors to women. She led a group of women, which attempted to force its way into the United Irish League (UIL), the Party's constituency organisation, in the early twentieth century. Founded in 1898, the UIL expanded rapidly: by the end of 1909, it had at least 193 branches and more than 24,000 members.[45] Its membership was open to 'all Irish Nationalists alike, without any distinction of class or creed'.[46] It did not spell out its policy on sex, but it is clear that the recruitment of women was not a priority. Some individual women's branches were founded, but they were rarities, especially in Ireland. Press reports suggest that ladies' branches were formed in Westmeath, Belfast and Louth;[47] the Louth organisers predicted that more would follow, but this did not come to pass.[48] The very few ladies' branches that did exist in Ireland were evidently so badly

[42] *Peasant*, 26 Oct. 1910.
[43] Hanna Sheehy Skeffington, 'Women in the National Movement', Sheehy Skeffington papers, National Library of Ireland, MS 22,266.
[44] *Ibid.*
[45] Wheatley, *Nationalism and the Irish Party*, 44–5.
[46] United Irish League, *Objects, Constitution and Rules*, no date.
[47] *Donegal News*, 14 May 1904; *Connacht Tribune*, 26 Feb. 1910; *Westmeath Examiner*, 25 Sept. 1909.
[48] *Anglo-Celt*, 28 Aug. 1909.

organised or impoverished that only two managed to pay their £3 annual subscription to the United Irish League over the entire 1905–18 period.[49] UIL organisers attempted to stimulate both membership and branch formation, but they did not appear to target potential women members.[50] The result was the lack of a women's organisation, which was available to fund-raise, campaign and register potential voters. Some of this work was taken up by the republican Cumman na mBan from 1914, which managed to attract around 19,800 women by early 1919.[51] The Ulster Women's Unionist Council, by contrast, built up an estimated membership of between 115,000 and 200,000 members in the same period.

Strikingly, British branches of the UIL were more responsive to women than their Irish counterparts. Ladies' branches of the British UIL were formed from at least 1906, and some divisions hosted mixed memberships. By 1907, at least thirteen ladies' branches in England and Scotland were active and women had begun to attend annual general meetings of the United Irish League of Great Britain as representatives of their branches.[52] The executive council of the United Irish League of Great Britain urged at its 1918 Convention that more ladies' branches should be formed in order to 'advise the Irish women's vote in the best interests of the Irish cause'.[53] Prominent nationalists including Alice Stopford Green and Sophie Bryant took the lead in the London Ladies' Branch, while Ireland produced no such equivalents and no evidence that the recruitment of women was desirable, let alone a priority.

The partial exception to this rule was the Young Ireland Branch (YIB) of the United Irish League, the most progressive branch of the UIL in Ireland.[54] The YIB's own rules explicitly decreed that potential members should not be disqualified by sex, class or creed,[55] but a number of women members were less than satisfied with the organisation. They were in a difficult positon, however, because they were loath to antagonise their YIB colleagues, let alone the wider Irish Party which, some nationalist feminists believed, might be persuaded to adopt women's suffrage.

Those Irish suffragists who remained loyal to the Irish Party had good reason to be so as a good deal of support for women's suffrage existed among nationalist MPs. Mary Sheehy Kettle argued in 1910 that at

[49] These were a Belfast Ladies' branch in 1905–6 and a county Westmeath branch in 1909–10: Minute Book of the Directory of the United Irish League, 147 and 372, National Library of Ireland, MS 708.

[50] Wheatley, *Nationalism and the Irish Party*, 46.

[51] Cal McCarthy, *Cumann na mBan and the Irish Revolution* (Cork, 2007), 108, 112–13.

[52] United Irish League of Great Britain, *Annual Reports and Reports of Proceedings at Annual Conventions, 1906–1909* (no date).

[53] *Freeman's Journal*, 10 Aug. 1918.

[54] Pašeta, *Irish Nationalist Women*, 68–9.

[55] *Rules of the Young Ireland Branch of the United Irish League* (Dublin, c. 1905), v.

least three-quarters of the Irish Party was sympathetic to the cause.[56] Her husband, a liberal nationalist MP, claimed in the following year that there was 'no substantial opposition' in the Irish Party to women's suffrage.[57] The Irish Women's Franchise League (IWFL), a militant organisation co-founded by Hannah Sheehy Skeffington, declared itself to be 'not dissatisfied' with the attitude of individual Irish Party MPs.[58] Their optimism was well founded. Although Party leader John Redmond remained implacably opposed to women's suffrage, both in principle and for strategic reasons, his fellow-MPs were permitted to vote freely on any suffrage bill and many – including his own brother – had become outspoken supporters of the cause. Philip Snowden claimed in 1912 that the Irish nationalist MPs had 'contributed a larger share of votes in favour of woman suffrage' than any other party except the Labour Party, and the IWFL's own calculations support this claim.[59] The Franchise League and its nationalist allies deliberately developed parallels between suffrage and Irish nationalism, arguing, for example, that 'the principles of self-government and self-reliance which vitalise the nationalist movement are identical with the basic principles of the women's suffrage movement. The spirit of Liberty is one and indivisible.'[60]

The problem remained, however, that while the idea that women's suffrage was intimately linked with Irish nationalism was supported by a large number of MPs, none were prepared to give the two demands equal billing when they were forced to prioritise. Even those who had vocally and strongly supported women's suffrage and had lobbied for change among their fellow-MPs turned their backs on the suffrage movement when it refused to put Home Rule before women's suffrage. When Irish MPs, even those once strongly pro-suffrage, voted under the direction of a whip against a series of franchise bills and amendments in 1912 and 1913, largely to ensure that the Home Rule Bill could pass through the parliament with minimal distraction, some of their feminist supporters abandoned any hope of a meaningful relationship between women's suffrage and the Irish Party. When around seventy suffragists marched on the UIL's Convention in 1912 to protest against this apparent abandonment of the suffrage cause, they were met by violence and hostility, mainly from UIL stewards, and even well-known constitutional nationalist women were

---

[56] *Votes for Women*, 3: 139 (4 Nov. 1910), 67.

[57] *Irish Times*, 18 Oct. 1911.

[58] *Freeman's Journal*, 16 July 1910.

[59] Lists of Irish MPs' attitudes on the woman suffrage question, reprinted from the Sheehy Skeffington papers in Cliona Murphy, *The Women's Suffrage Movement and Irish Society in the Twentieth Century* (New York and London, 1989), 221–4. See also Constance Rover, *Women's Suffrage and Party Politics in Britain, 1866–1914* (1967), 155.

[60] Letter from Francis Sheehy Skeffington to *Freeman's Journal*, 3 Mar. 1912.

prevented from entering.[61] Bitter public debates, family splits and the IWFL members' decision to smash UIL windows in 1913 destroyed what remained of a relationship between the IWFL and the Irish Party.[62]

Nationalist suffragists, even those who remained broadly loyal to the Party, developed an increasingly hostile critique of it, some questioning its definition of nationalism itself. 'Just as', one critic argued, 'the English Suffragists had to teach the Liberal Party and the Liberal Government the meaning of Liberalism, so will Irish Suffragists have to teach the Irish Party and their henchmen the essence of Nationalism.'[63] The 'essence of nationalism' was for many of these women located in Ireland's radical nationalist past and in a tradition which found its true expression in the Irish militant suffrage movement. They emphasised Ireland's tradition of political protest and stepped up their attempts to link it with their own.[64] Margaret Cousins of the IWFL, for example, argued that 'the whole recent militant movement' owed its inspiration to 'Charles Stewart Parnell and his policy of obstruction'.[65] Redmond's Party, they maintained, had betrayed this legacy. Reflecting on the imprisonment of Irish suffragettes, Hanna Sheehy Skeffington reminded John Redmond that 'there is a stronger and purer Nationalism in Mountjoy Prison at this moment than any of Mr Redmond's followers can boast'.[66]

While much of Redmondite nationalist Ireland appeared to disagree with the IWFL, advanced nationalists were often more sympathetic. As the Party actively turned women away, a number of new and vibrant organisations accepted their money and their membership happily. The most important of these 'other channels' as Sheehy Skeffington had termed them, were Sinn Fein and the Gaelic League, though a host of cultural organisations had opened their doors to women from the late nineteenth century. Cultural revivalism, especially in its politicised iterations, provided a particularly powerful platform for feminist nationalist women. It recognised women's power as domestic managers, educators, mothers and political activists. It provided thousands of nationalist women with practical and intellectual political education, and it allowed them to mix with like-minded collaborators.

The new cultural and political clubs and societies which sprang up in the late nineteenth century contributed to the 'new nationalism', a broad swathe of political and cultural organisations which largely operated

[61] *Votes for Women*, 5: 217 (3 May 1912), 482 and 491.
[62] Pašeta, *Irish Nationalist Women*, 69–90; *Report of the Executive Committee of the Irish Women's Franchise League for 1913* (Dublin, 1914), 5.
[63] *Freeman's Journal*, 3 Mar. 1912.
[64] *Ibid.*, 10 Apr. 1912.
[65] *Ibid.*, 22 Apr. 1912.
[66] *Irish Citizen*, July 1912; Leeann Lane, *Rosamund Jacob: Third Person Singular* (Dublin, 2010), 54.

outside the structures and remit of the Irish Party and in which female involvement was generally tolerated at the very least, openly encouraged at best. The men and women at its heart often described it as 'the movement', testifying to the excitement of this new phase of nationalist agitation.[67] The new nationalism was built on fresh ideas and new political impulses, but it also owed its development to older forms of political organisation, including the Ladies' Land League.

The radical republican women who organised as Inghinidhe na hÉireann from 1900 and Cumann na mBan from 1914 explicitly linked their own organisations to the Ladies' League, portraying themselves as its successors.[68] But the Ladies' League also served as a bridge between the Land War and cultural nationalism by setting in train a number of initiatives which expanded opportunities for nationalist women. They did so by, for example, politicising children through the Children's Land League, where boys and girls met weekly to learn about Irish history and culture.[69] Inghinidhe na hÉireann subsequently enthusiastically took up this crusade in the early twentieth century.[70]

A number of Ladies' Land Leaguers also turned to cultural activism including through the pioneering Southwark Junior Irish Literary Club and the 'Irish Fireside Club'. The Fireside Club became the most popular nationalist forum for children in nineteenth-century Ireland with a membership of around 25,000 by 1889.[71] Other members, such as Ellen O'Leary, became professional writers and editors in their own right and played a vital role in the admission of women into key literary societies including the Pan-Celtic Society, the National Literary Society and the Contemporary Club.[72] Such organisations served a vital role in providing intellectual and social outlets for the growing number of women who were eager to become more involved in the cultural and political life of their country. From its foundation in 1893, the Gaelic League became the most important of the many societies which accepted women members and made available to them invaluable training in organisation, education and politicisation. Although often romanticised, the notion that, as Jennie Wyse Power argued, the League 'rejected the false sex and class distinctions which were the result of English influence'

[67] Nic Shiubhlaigh, *Splendid Years*, 3–4.
[68] Cumann na mBan, *The Volunteers, the Women, and the Nation* (Dublin, 1914), National Library of Ireland, 161 (26), 1–2.
[69] *Nation*, 1 Oct. 1881.
[70] Pašeta, *Irish Nationalist Women*, 36–7; Ríona Nic Congáil, 'Young Ireland and the Nation: Nationalist Children's Culture in the Late Nineteenth Century, *Éire-Ireland*, 46 (2011), 52.
[71] Nic Congáil, 'Young Ireland', 56–7.
[72] National Literary Society Minute Book, 24 May 1892 and 20 Oct. 1892, National Library of Ireland, MS 645; Mary Macken, 'W. B. Yeats, John O'Leary and the Contemporary Club', *Studies*, 28 (1939), 137–9.

was important for women of her generation. So too was the fact that it was 'the first Irish national society which accepted women as members on the same terms as men'.[73]

It would be incorrect to argue that the Gaelic League provided a direct route into the more openly advanced nationalist Sinn Fein, but there is no doubt that many women members experienced the League as a kind of stepping stone to republican politics.[74] It would be equally incorrect to argue that Sinn Fein provided an unambiguously natural home for feminist women. But it was well in advance of the Irish Party in its opening of membership and executive positions to both sexes equally and in debating and supporting women's suffrage. Even the perennially distrustful Hanna Sheehy Skeffington admitted this.[75] One of the most striking, though little commented upon, features of the 'new nationalism' was its generally tolerant view on women's suffrage in particular. This was down to several factors including its appeal to middle-class, young and often urban members, as well its links to avant-garde literary and artistic circles. Unlike the Party, such societies rarely organised around the church, the pub or occupational and rural interests. More importantly, they rarely organised men and women separately.

Though lively, Ireland's radical nationalist and feminist circles were small and clannish. Activists tended to know one another well and to move in similar networks; this encouraged cooperation as well as loyalty. While the Irish Party seemed to be invincible, these political mavericks had little traction within nationalist Ireland. But, as the Party began to flounder under the stresses of unionist resistance to Home Rule, the Great War and the Easter Rising, radical ideas became less unthinkable and some of those on the margins of Irish political life moved closer to its centre. It was in this climate that nationalist women became more than merely symbolically or marginally important and came to play a vital role in the destruction of the Party which had rejected them.

Republican women including Maud Gonne rejoiced in the part they had played in the beginnings of openly hostility between the 'decaying' parliamentary movement and the rising Sinn Fein movement.[76] Hanna Sheehy Skeffington resigned in 1912 from the UIL in disgust at the Party's 'treachery' over women's suffrage.[77] Her friend, Patricia Hoey, resigned from the secretaryship of the Irish Parliament Branch of the UIL in the

---

[73] Jennie Wyse Power, 'The Political Influence of Women in Modern Ireland', in *The Voice of Ireland: A Survey of the Race and Nation from All Angles*, ed. W. G. Fitz-Gerald (Dublin, 1924), 158–61.

[74] Pašeta, *Irish Nationalist Women*, 24–6.

[75] *Bean na hÉireann*, no. 13, Apr. 1909, 6.

[76] Bureau of Military History, Dublin, Witness Statement 317: Maud Gonne MacBride.

[77] *Votes for Women*, 5: 435 (12 Apr. 1912), 438–40; Sheehy Skeffington papers, National Library of Ireland, MS 41,201/7.

same year.[78] She saw the Party's refusal to back women's suffrage as a personal insult and a repudiation of the very soul of Irish nationalism:

> There is a hard and even a bitter fight before us for many of us are fighting against our personal friends and lifelong associations – but with courage, determination and unity we can and we shall win. The Irish Parliamentary Party have betrayed us... So comrades let us forward in unison. We are not only working for women's suffrage but for the holy Cause of Ireland. The Irish Party are asking Home Rule for a section of Ireland – we are asking it for the whole of Ireland.[79]

Hoey would soon became active in Cumann na mBan and Sinn Fein.

Sheehy Skeffington and Hoey were exceptional in prioritising women's suffrage over Home Rule in 1912, but they would join the majority of women when they cast their votes in 1918. The reduced status of the Irish Party and its few women supporters was clear during the conscription crisis of 1917–18 when republican women largely swept aside the efforts of Home Rule women to coordinate opposition.[80] The extraordinary mobilisation of women through Sinn Fein and Cumann na mBan during the election campaigns of 1918 was utterly unmatched by their constitutional counterparts. The Party managed to win only 6 of the 105 available seats that year. The near annihilation of the Irish Party at that election could not have been possible without the voluntary work of female canvassers, lobbyists and election agents. Neither could it have happened without their votes as about 36 per cent of the new electorate was female, and women were in fact in the majority in some constituencies.[81]

Some republican feminists revelled in this extraordinary reversal in electoral fortunes. In late 1917, many of them gathered to chastise the Irish Party at two fiery public meetings at which the forthcoming Representation of the People Bill was discussed. Some argued that the Irish Party had attempted to secure the exclusion of Ireland from the new Franchise Bill, emphasising the Party's 'hostile' attitude towards women. This, they maintained, would cost it votes and contribute to its downfall at the next election.[82] Patricia Hoey, who was present at that meeting, argued that the Irish Party's lack of sympathy for women's suffrage was

[78] *Irish Citizen*, 8 June 1912.

[79] Patricia Hoey to Hanna Sheehy Skeffington, Sheehy Skeffington papers, National Library of Ireland, no date, MS 22,663(iv).

[80] Pašeta, *Irish Nationalist Women*, 242–6.

[81] John Coakley, 'The Election that Made the First Dáil', in *The Creation of the Dáil: A Volume of Essays from the Thomas Davis Lectures*, ed. Brian Farrell (Dublin, 1994), 35. They constituted about 40 per cent of the electorate in Dublin, 39 per cent in Belfast and just over 39 per cent in Cork; *Freeman's Journal*, 26 Nov. 1918.

[82] *Irish Independent*, 16 July 1917.

'instigated by the knowledge that the women would never follow their lead'.[83]

The Party's position on the enlarged franchise was much more complicated than these critics suggested, but there is no question that its failure to support women's suffrage and to cultivate a women's association was very harmful. While unionist and Sinn Fein women mobilised, canvassed and organised on behalf of their candidates, the Irish Party had no such support network to fall back on. Instead, its candidates faced an open campaign of feminist opposition from women who persisted in reminding it that 'women were more than lunatics and imbeciles; they were citizens of Ireland, and they had tenacious memories'.[84] Jennie Wyse Power concluded that the 'dying Parliamentary Party learned to its cost' that the woman voter had become a force to be reckoned with, and it is difficult to disagree with her assessment.[85] Irish women did not uniformly abandon the Party in 1918, but they clearly contributed to its comprehensive electoral defeat. The Party had created this situation by alienating politically active women over women's suffrage and, more catastrophically, by failing to tolerate, let alone welcome, women's participation in its constituency organisations and wider political machinery. Having pioneered women's political mobilisation in the late nineteenth century, its refusal to repeat the experiment in the early twentieth century helped to pave its path to political oblivion.

[83] *Ibid.*
[84] *Irish Independent*, 10 Dec. 1918.
[85] Wyse Power, 'The Political Influence of Women', 160.

Transactions of the RHS 27 (2017), pp. 211–232 © Royal Historical Society 2017
doi:10.1017/S008044011700010X

DEMOCRACY, SOVEREIGNTY AND UNIONIST POLITICAL THOUGHT DURING THE REVOLUTIONARY PERIOD IN IRELAND, *c.* 1912–1922*

By Colin W. Reid

READ 9 SEPTEMBER 2016

AT THE UNIVERSITY OF TEESSIDE

ABSTRACT. This paper examines ideas about democratic legitimacy and sovereignty within Ulster unionist political thought during the revolutionary period in Ireland (*c.* 1912–22). Confronted by Irish nationalists who claimed that Home Rule (and later, independence) enjoyed the support of the majority of people in Ireland, Ulster unionists deployed their own democratic idioms to rebuff such arguments. In asserting unionism's majority status, first, across the United Kingdom and, second, within the province of Ulster, unionists mined the language of democracy to legitimise their militant stand against Home Rule. The paper also probes the unionist conception of sovereignty by examining the establishment of the Provisional Government of Ulster in 1913, which was styled as a 'trustee' for the British constitution in Ireland after the coming of Home Rule. The imperial, economic and religious arguments articulated by unionists against Home Rule are well known, but the space given to constitutional rights and democratic legitimacy in the political language of unionism remain obscure. While the antagonisms at the heart of the revolutionary period in Ireland assumed the form of identity politics and sectarianism, the deployment of normative democratic language by unionists reveals that clashing ideals of representative government underpinned the conflict.

In 2002, the late Peter Hart made a clarion call for the revolutionary period in Ireland (*c.* 1912–22), then the subject of a historiography dominated by the drama of high politics, 'to be reconceptualised and to have all the myriad assumptions underlying its standard narratives interrogated'.[1] Historians have responded in kind, with an upsurge in innovative works that have charted the revolutionary process from a number of angles.[2]

* I am very grateful to Ultán Gillen, Matt Kelly, James McConnel, Caoimhe Nic Dháibhéid, Graham Walker and the two anonymous readers for their insightful reading of earlier drafts of this work.

[1] Peter Hart, 'Definition: Defining the Irish Revolution', in *The Irish Revolution, 1913–1923*, ed. Joost Augusteijn (Basingstoke, 2002), 30.

[2] See, for example, recent works by R. F. Foster, *Vivid Faces: The Revolutionary Generation in Ireland, 1890–1923* (2014); Fearghal McGarry, *The Rising: Ireland, Easter 1916* (Oxford, 2010);

However, the history of political thought during this turbulent decade, which opened with the Ulster crisis in 1912 and led to the partition of the island and the winning of independence for three-quarters of Ireland, remains obscure. This is partly explicable, as Ian McBride has observed, by the absence of a tradition of intellectual history in Irish historical writing, a trait particularly marked in the historiography of modern Ireland. Historians of Ireland have by and large displayed little interest in the rise of the 'Cambridge School' during the 1960s and 1970s, which, with different emphasises depending on the individual scholar, advocated a contextual approach to understanding political discourse.[3] In 1993, the editors of a volume on Irish political thought lamented that the history of ideas in Ireland 'is largely unwritten'.[4] This essentially remains the case. While more recent work has demonstrated an increasingly sophisticated and sensitive interpretation of political ideas within Irish life during the nineteenth and early twentieth centuries,[5] the chief emphases of the Cambridge School – understanding the range of political languages used in a society in the past, the spatial and temporal shifts in ideas, the role of ideas in legitimating action – remain at the fringes of Irish historiography. While scholarship identified as 'revisionist' has transformed the writing of Irish history by unshackling the past from nationalist and unionist pieties, we risk losing sight of the *meanings* of the polemics of the past. The point is not merely to bring historical fallacies to light; it is to understand *why* such beliefs permeated politics and culture, *what* meanings they carried and *how* contemporaries engaged with such activities. Languages evolved to articulate what was deemed legitimate in the realm of politics, and should be, thus, an important aspect of the work of political historians of Ireland.[6] Merely debunking the beliefs of historical actors will not result in understanding.

This article examines aspects of unionist political thought during the revolutionary period, when 'Ulster' firmly replaced 'Irish' before

Senia Pašeta, *Irish Nationalist Women, 1900–1918* (Cambridge, 2013); James McConnel, *The Irish Parliamentary Party and the Third Home Rule Crisis* (Dublin, 2013); Charles Townshend, *The Republic: The Fight for Irish Independence, 1918–1923* (2013).

[3] Ian McBride, 'The Edge of Enlightenment: Ireland and Scotland in the Eighteenth Century', *Modern Intellectual History*, 10 (2013), 135.

[4] D. George Boyce, Robert Eccleshall and Vincent Geoghegan, 'Introduction', in *Political Thought in Ireland since the Seventeenth Century*, ed. D. George Boyce, Robert Eccleshall and Vincent Geoghegan (1993), 1.

[5] See, for example, M. J. Kelly, *The Fenian Ideal and Irish Nationalism, 1882–1916* (Woodbridge, 2006); David Dwan, *The Great Community: Culture and Nationalism in Ireland* (Dublin, 2008); John Bew, *The Glory of Being Britons: Civic Unionism in Nineteenth-Century Belfast* (Dublin, 2009).

[6] Some of the best and most original work within Irish political history over the past decade is distinguished by an engagement with political languages and ideas: see the books mentioned in n. 5 and, especially, Richard Bourke, *Peace in Ireland: The War of Ideas* (2003).

the 'unionist' designation.[7] Ulster unionist political activism within the broader history of Ireland – from the apocryphal stories of Fred Crawford signing the Ulster Covenant of 1912 in his own blood, to Ian Paisley denouncing the pope as the anti-Christ in the European Parliament in 1988 – can appear as the triumph of hysteria over reason. Ulster unionists have been all too easy to caricature as 'irrational, backward and deviant'.[8] Yet this image has been challenged by scholars such as Paul Bew, Alvin Jackson and Graham Walker, who have probed the complexities of unionism from the nineteenth century to the present day, setting out the rationale of unionist politics.[9] The fine line between 'respectability and radical militancy' that Ulster unionists and their supporters balanced during the revolutionary period has been well illuminated.[10] Despite such advances in uncovering the militant and constitutional strategies embarked on by Ulster unionism, there remains, however, little work on unionist political ideas, particularly concerning democracy and sovereignty. Given the radicalising impact of the struggle against the third Home Rule Bill within unionism, the role of ideas, both in legitimising action and articulating alternatives, deserves more attention than it has hitherto received. Words are needed to justify action, particularly if that deed crosses the boundaries of normative constitutionalism. This is where Ulster unionists found themselves from 1912. Their militant stand against Home Rule, which led to the formation of an underground government and private army, demanded a political language to legitimise such a course. Tellingly, it was a democratic idiom that was developed to communicate the unionist case.

One of the most obvious features of unionist politics during the revolutionary period was the shift from an all-island political organisation and perspective to an Ulster-centric body. The partitioning of unionism, as a precursor to the partitioning of Ireland in 1921, has been charted by various scholars.[11] What remains obscure, however, is the language

[7] Jennifer Todd has provided an overview of unionist political thought after partition: 'Unionist Political Thought, 1920–72', in *Political Thought in Ireland*, ed. Boyce, Eccleshall and Geoghegan, 190–211.

[8] Ian McBride, 'Ulster and the British Problem', in *Unionism in Modern Ireland: New Perspectives on Politics and Culture*, ed. Graham Walker (Basingstoke, 1996), 1.

[9] Paul Bew, *Ideology and the Irish Question: Ulster Unionism and Irish Nationalism, 1912–1916* (Oxford, 1994); Alvin Jackson, *The Two Unions: Ireland, Scotland and the Survival of the United Kingdom, 1707–2007* (Oxford, 2012); Graham Walker, *A History of the Ulster Unionist Party: Protest, Pragmatism and Pessimism* (Manchester, 2004).

[10] Graham Walker, 'The Ulster Covenant and the Pulse of Protestant Ulster', *National Identities*, 18 (2015), 314. As well as *ibid.*, see, for example, Timothy Bowman, *Carson's Army: The Ulster Volunteer Force, 1910–22* (Manchester, 2007); Alvin Jackson, *Sir Edward Carson* (Dundalk, 1993).

[11] The classic works are Patrick Buckland, *Irish Unionism*, II: *Ulster Unionism and the Origins of Northern Ireland, 1886–1922* (Dublin, 1973), and Peter Gibbon, *The Origins of Ulster Unionism:*

that Ulster unionists deployed in making this transition. This is a serious omission in our understanding of unionism, as the transformation of unionist politics into a northern-focused fusion of constitutional and violent impulses was accompanied by the development of ideas relating to democratic rights and sovereign responsibility. This was not merely polemical rhetoric, but an attempt to reformulate the unionist position to suit the wider Edwardian political zeitgeist. From the late Victorian period, the wielding of power and the boundaries of legitimate action in the United Kingdom were increasingly tied to notions of democracy, both in terms of parliamentary politics and wider political culture.[12] As the result of what John Stuart Mill called 'controlled' expansions of the franchise during the nineteenth century, democratic sentiment during the Edwardian age largely shed the fears of the mid- and late Victorian generations.[13] Political discourse on the eve of the First World War, for example, shared little in common with the anti-democratic mood of Victorian intellectuals such as Sir Henry Sumner Maine, James Fitzjames Stephen and W. E. H. Lecky.[14] In 1896, Lecky, the most notable Irish unionist intellectual of the nineteenth century, condemned the notion of democratic equality as destructive to 'the balance of opinions, interests, and classes, on which constitutional liberty mainly depends'.[15] The most perfect constitution was, for Lecky, found in Britain between the Reform Bills of 1832 and 1867, which he believed successfully represented the competing 'interests and opinions of a great nation' while formally excluding the great majority of people from the franchise.[16] Despite Lecky's elevated status within Irish unionism, very few unionists of the Edwardian generation followed his lead in assaulting the principle of democratic representation. Indeed, the opposite occurred: unionists in Ulster embraced a particular democratic idiom to legitimise their stance against Home Rule. The unionist case against Home Rule in 1912 largely remained the same as it had done in 1886 and 1893; the difference was that opposition to Irish self-government was articulated in terms of normative democratic rights during the Edwardian period.

The Formation of Popular Protestant Politics and Ideology in Nineteenth-Century Ireland (Manchester, 1975), but see the important revisions by Alvin Jackson in *The Ulster Party: Irish Unionists in the House of Commons, 1884–1911* (Oxford, 1989), and *Ireland, 1798–1998: Politics and War* (Oxford, 1999).

[12] A fascinating approach to the (uneasy) Victorian transition to parliamentary democracy in Britain is found in Marc Baer, *The Rise and Fall of Radical Westminster, 1780–1890* (Basingstoke, 2012).

[13] Marc Mulholland, *Bourgeois Liberty and the Politics of Fear: From Absolutism to Neo-Conservatism* (Oxford, 2012), 84.

[14] Rodney Barker, *Political Ideas in Modern Britain: In and After the Twentieth Century*, 2nd edn (1997; first published 1978), 116.

[15] W. E. H. Lecky, *Democracy and Liberty* (2 vols., 1896), I, 212.

[16] *Ibid.*, 18.

While the revolutionary period was profoundly shaped by national and religious antagonisms, it was also a democratic tangle between competing interpretations of 'the will of the people'. Democratic discourse became intertwined with the unsettled national question: the enmity was heightened because there was considerable variation in what 'democracy' actually meant to contemporaries. In this sense, 'democracy' was a fluid concept, and this contributed to the intractability of the Irish problem. This was not a problem that was 'solved' by partition. Richard Bourke has made the distinction between the 'absence of a democratic state in Northern Ireland' after partition and the 'existence of a democratic government' based in Belfast. While Northern Ireland had the trappings of a democratic regime (elections, universal suffrage at the devolved level, press freedoms), the Catholic minority were permanently excluded from influencing the direction of sovereign power. Democracy, as it existed in Northern Ireland, Bourke notes, 'produced dissension, not cohesion, among its people'.[17] That said, unionists eagerly embraced the language of democracy to legitimise the maintenance of one-party rule after 1921. While republicans critiqued the 'fascist nature of unionist rule',[18] the dominance of the Ulster Unionist Party was rationalised by its advocates as an expression of majority (and thus democratic) opinion in Northern Ireland in favour of the union with Britain.[19] The origin of this unionist interpretation of democracy, which was firmly rooted in majoritarianism, is, however, found in the decade just before partition. Bourke's case for the centrality of democratic ideas within unionist political thought after partition can be extended back into the revolutionary period. During the Home Rule crisis of 1912–14, unionists appropriated the language of democracy, stressing their majority status within, first, the United Kingdom, and, second, within the province of Ulster, to counter the similar majoritarian arguments made by Home Rulers. What is striking, then, about political discourse in Ireland before, during and after the First World War is the widespread articulation of democratic arguments across the Irish political spectrum. The emergence of democracy as a legitimising idea, however, added to the rancour of the period, as majoritarianism – majority rule, with different conceptions of the design of the majority – underpinned the competing sovereign claims of unionism and nationalism.

I

J. W. Good was the literary editor of the pro-Home Rule newspaper, the *Freeman's Journal*, during its final years in the early 1920s. During that time, he penned two penetrating books on the nature of the 'Ulster

---

[17] Bourke, *Peace in Ireland*, 4.

[18] Gerry Adams, *Before the Dawn: An Autobiography* (Dingle, 2001; first published 1996), 91.

[19] See, for example, Terence O'Neill, *Ulster at the Crossroads* (1969), 11.

question' within Irish politics, *Ulster and Ireland* (1919) and *Irish Unionism* (1920). Good was implacably opposed to the Ulster separatism that emanated from the unionist leadership under Sir Edward Carson and Sir James Craig after 1912, but realised that, in the immediate aftermath of the First World War, circumstances had changed utterly. While he condemned the unionist campaign against Home Rule as an attempt to create a new Protestant Ascendency in Ireland, blocking the political will of the Catholic majority, Good wearily realised that unionism's appropriation of the language of separate political rights chimed with newly established international thinking. In August 1918, Carson issued a public letter to Woodrow Wilson, the president of the United States of America, depicting Ulster unionists as 'devoted adherents to the cause of democratic freedom'. The Irish problem, Carson informed Wilson, sprang from the Home Rulers' insistence on '"self-determination" for themselves, combined with coercive domination over us'.[20] Carson took to describing the Ulster unionist position in 1919 as marching 'hand in hand with the democracy of the Empire', the outgrowth of popular loyalism that spanned the imperial world.[21] But as will become clear, the political language of Ulster unionism at the onset of the Irish revolutionary period anticipated the democratic wave of the Wilsonian post-war milieu, which emphasised the rights of small nations seeking self-determination. This may have been accidental, as the original case against Home Rule was made to destroy the scheme for Irish self-government, not to politically split the island.[22] The unionist cause drew from many wells, imperial, national, economic and sectarian, but when articulated through democratic language, resistance to the island-wide jurisdiction of a Dublin parliament stumbled into self-determination. While it appeared logical for Éamon de Valera, the president of Sinn Féin, to cite Wilson's mantra that 'every people has a right to choose the sovereignty under which they shall live' in constructing the case for Irish independence, unionists were also able to tap into contemporaneous developments in political language.[23]

In reviewing the Irish situation in 1920, Good was all too aware of this. Reflecting on the 'emergence of the idea of self-determination', he wryly commented that it 'actually strengthened [the unionists'] case'. With the protection of democratic rights entrenched in the post-war environment and two political blocs in Ireland calling for 'self-determination', Good

[20] *Belfast News-Letter*, 23 Aug. 1918.

[21] *Belfast News-Letter*, 16 Jan. 1919.

[22] David W. Miller, *Queen's Rebels: Ulster Loyalism in Historical Perspective* (Dublin, 1978), 105.

[23] Éamon de Valera, *Ireland's Request to the Government of the United States of America for Recognition as a Sovereign Independent State* (Washington, DC, 1920), 5. Wilson's argument from 1916 can be found in *The Wisdom of Woodrow Wilson: Being Selections from his Thoughts and Comments on Political, Social and Moral Questions*, ed. Charles J. Herold (New York, 1919), 88.

grimly concluded that 'partition was inevitable'.[24] In this reading, the political conflict in Ireland transcended its ethnic, national and religious dimensions and became a democratic problem consisting of two competing, and mutually exclusive, rights. Good highlighted a distinct irony in this: he believed that the protracted unionist campaign against Home Rule was profoundly anti-democratic. In his previous book from 1919, Good's coverage of the remarkable events of 'Ulster Day' in September 1912, in which the Ulster Solemn League and Covenant was unveiled as a mass petition against Home Rule, was contained in a chapter entitled 'A Covenant against Democracy'. In opposing Home Rule, Good asserted that 'Sir Edward Carson linked opposition to Irish self-government with the general campaign against democracy.' Carson collaborated, according to Good, with British Conservative politicians to 'cripple democracy' and reaffirm oligarchic ruling principles in the wake of New Liberalism's socially progressive welfare reforms.[25]

For Good, Ulster unionism stood guilty of doublethink. Unionists were 'against democracy' in their opposition to Home Rule; their embrace of 'self-determination' was thus 'the crowning triumph of political hypocrisy'.[26] Indeed, he reasoned that the 'successes' of the unionist campaign under the leadership of Carson (most notably the traction it gained from the British Conservative Party) undermined the ethical rules of politics, draining the 'virtue . . . out of constitutionalism'.[27] Accusations that Carson's conception of democracy represented a form of 'Hibernian Caesarism' were made by other opponents.[28] As nationalists refused to consider Ulster as a separate political entity from the rest of Ireland, the appeal made by unionists carried little purchase in the south of the country; instead, the widespread belief was that Carson headed a subversive movement against the true democratic Irish sentiment in favour of Home Rule. The leader of the Irish Parliamentary Party, John Redmond, had set the tone in February 1912 by condemning the 'arrogant and intolerable claim on behalf of a small minority . . . to override the will of Ireland'.[29] Similar language was adopted by the Liberal prime minister, H. H. Asquith, during the second reading of the Home Rule Bill in 1913: 'we cannot admit, and we will not admit, the right of a minority of the people . . . to veto the verdict of the vast body of their countrymen'.[30] Home Rule was backed by numbers in Ireland, and this, according to a Redmondite–Asquithian reading, constituted a democratic

[24] J. W. Good, *Irish Unionism* (Dublin, 1920), 232–3.
[25] J. W. Good, *Ulster and Ireland* (Dublin, 1919), 200–1.
[26] Good, *Irish Unionism*, 235.
[27] *Ibid.*, 233.
[28] George Peel, *The Reign of Sir Edward Carson* (1914), 51.
[29] Quoted in Dermot Meleady, *John Redmond: The National Leader* (Dublin, 2014), 208.
[30] Quoted in Alan O'Day, *Irish Home Rule, 1867–1921* (Manchester, 1998), 248.

will, rendering unionism's resistance politically illegitimate. The logic of this interpretation of democracy – the equation of a majority with political supremacy – was not lost on unionists in the north of Ireland. Ulster unionists sculpted a democratic self-image and, in turn, deployed the language of democracy to challenge the nationalist monopoly over legitimate political rights. Crucially, this process began *before* the post-war democratic new world order was born.

II

In unionist folk memory, the Ulster Solemn League and Covenant holds a cherished place as a political creation myth.[31] The Covenant was publicly unveiled on 'Ulster Day', 28 September 1912. Thousands of people turned out in Belfast to witness the leader of unionism, Sir Edward Carson, sign the document in a ceremony replete with symbolic meaning. More than 218,000 men across Ulster followed Carson's lead in adding their signatures on the document, with almost 229,000 women committing to a separate declaration of support. The text of the Covenant, with its implicit threat of violence to resist the implementation of Home Rule, encapsulated the defiant 'radical populism' that sustained unionism during what became known as the Ulster crisis.[32] The popular activism that surrounded the signing of the Covenant made it akin to a unionist 'People's Charter', the founding document of the nineteenth-century Chartist movement.[33] Like the People's Charter, the Covenant was unveiled amidst much political theatre, and became the source of a widespread mass petition. Through the ritual of signing the document, the unionist population became tied to one another; the Covenant, and the subsequent mobilisation of unionism, gave the ordinary man and woman in the north of Ireland a taste of direct political participation.

The comparison with Chartism can be pushed further, especially regarding the nature of rights, duties and obligations. William Lovett, the intellectual architect of Chartism, pressed the point in 1840 that no amount of legislative coercion on the part of government would stymie those 'determined to obtain their just share of political right *at any sacrifice*'.[34] Justifications for unionist resistance in 1912 mirrored this sentiment; rather than *seeking* full political rights, however, unionism made the case that the implementation of Home Rule would corrupt *existing* constitutional rights, which were taken to be natural. Unionists believed that Home Rule would lead to the eventual separation of Ireland

---

[31] Alvin Jackson, 'Unionist Myths, 1912–1985', *Past and Present*, 136 (1992), 164.

[32] Walker, *History of the Ulster Unionist Party*, 35.

[33] Malcolm Chase, *Chartism: A New History* (Manchester, 2007), 7–10. Also see Liam Kennedy, *Unhappy the Land: The Most Oppressed People Ever, the Irish?* (Dublin, 2016), 132.

[34] William Lovett, *Chartism: A New Organization of the People* (1840), 2. Emphasis in original.

from the United Kingdom, and was, thus, according to the Covenant, 'destructive of our citizenship'.[35] This was a powerful component of the unionist case against Home Rule. Thomas Sinclair, who contributed to the wording of the Covenant, warned that the founding of a Dublin parliament implied the removal of enshrined rights and liberties from the imperial parliament. 'Ulstermen', Sinclair feared, 'would thus stand on a dangerously lower plane of civil privilege than their fellow-citizens in Great Britain.'[36] What is particularly striking about this argument was how, like the Chartist campaign for inclusion into the political nation, it was constructed with an emphasis on democratic sensibilities. The Covenant was deliberately styled to project the force of numbers behind it, providing unionism with an overtly popular backing. Sinclair made a virtue of the fusion between numbers and capitalist energy in his reading of democracy in the north of Ireland: the unionist population in the northern counties formed 'an unmistakable majority' in Ulster, who formed the backbone of the material prosperity of the province.[37] While a minority within Ireland, unionists stressed their majority status within the north of the country. That the unionist case against Home Rule was buttressed by a democratic aesthetic and logic, albeit from a radically revised interpretation of the national territory, highlights the pervasiveness of democracy as a key legitimising idea at this time. Appeals to the integrity of the United Kingdom and empire were not enough; the idea of maintaining (or, from a nationalist perspective, creating) representative government, underpinned by democratic sanction, was a vital dynamic in the Home Rule dispute.

The Covenant also emphasised the need for self-reliance within Ulster unionism – 'to stand by one another in defending, for ourselves and our children, our cherished position of equal citizenship in the United Kingdom' – to overcome the unfolding constitutional crisis.[38] Historically, Ulster Protestants have styled themselves as the first line of defence of the British interest against a perceived threat from the Catholic majority in Ireland. David Miller has profiled this mentality within Ulster Protestantism, which originated with the arrival of English and Scottish 'planters' in the north of Ireland in the early seventeenth century. During the Wars of the Three Kingdoms, the planters' security was undermined by an unsettling fluctuation in the power of the state in Ireland; the Ulster rebellion of 1641, staged by Catholics against the usurpers on

---

[35] 'Ulster Solemn League and Covenant' (1912). The document has been digitised by the National Library of Ireland: http://catalogue.nli.ie/Record/vtls000509452 (last accessed 28 Oct. 2016).

[36] Thomas Sinclair, 'The Position of Ulster', in *Against Home Rule: The Case for the Union*, ed. S. Rosenbaum (1912), 174.

[37] *Ibid.*, 170.

[38] 'Ulster Solemn League and Covenant' (1912).

their land in the province, reinforced the idea within the Protestant settlers in the north that 'public order derived in reality not from the sovereign authority . . . but from their own exertions on the ground'.[39] This led to the importing into Ulster of the Scottish covenanting tradition and, more potently, a culture of 'public banding',[40] most tellingly in the formation of armed militia groups (such as the Volunteers in 1778), ready to maintain order in the face of an Irish Catholic and/or Jacobite threat. This pattern reestablished itself during the Home Rule crisis. Carson declared in 1912 that '[t]he first law of nature with nations and governments, as with individuals, is self-preservation'.[41] A perception that the state had abandoned the union by siding with Irish nationalism lead to unionists mobilising in the name of 'self-preservation', most notably with the foundation of a mass militia in the form of the Ulster Volunteer Force (UVF). Unionism rationalised that war against a corrupt (and, from a unionist perspective, temporary) British government was preferable to nationalists exercising a measure of political power over Ulster.

The Covenant highlighted four main reasons why opposition to Home Rule was an imperative from a unionist standpoint: material well-being, civil and religious freedom, protection of citizenship and maintenance of the empire. To preserve the 'equal citizenship' enjoyed by unionists within the United Kingdom, the Covenant made an implicit threat of violence, suggesting that 'all means which may be found necessary to defeat the present conspiracy to set up a Home Rule Parliament in Ireland' should be deployed.[42] The beliefs uttered here were that the Liberal government, propped up by the votes of the Irish Party, behaved unconstitutionally in introducing Home Rule; that self-government for Ireland would create a repressive parliament in Dublin which would serve the interests of the Catholic church; and that devolution would pull a thread from the union, starting a process inevitably leading to the unravelling of the United Kingdom and empire. Such a disastrous chain of events lay at the heart of A. V. Dicey's influential politico-legal contributions to the anti-Home Rule cause since the 1880s, which gave unionism potent intellectual leverage within the realm of constitutional thought.[43] This line of argument had considerable purchase: champions of imperial union, such as Leo Amery, opposed Irish nationalist aspirations, fearing that 'Separatist Home Rule'

[39] Miller, *Queen's Rebels*, 16.

[40] Jacqueline Hill, 'Loyalty and the Monarchy in Ireland, *c.* 1660–1840', in *Loyalism and the Formation of the British World, 1775–1914*, ed. Allan Blackstock and Frank O'Gorman (Woodbridge, 2014), 89.

[41] Edward Carson, 'Introduction', in *Against Home Rule*, ed. Rosenbaum, 18.

[42] 'Ulster Solemn League and Covenant' (1912).

[43] A. V. Dicey, *A Fool's Paradise: Being a Constitutionalist's Criticism of the Home Rule Bill of 1912* (1913). Dicey made his name in unionist circles for his brilliant attack on the Home Rule Bill of 1886 in *England's Case against Home Rule* (1886).

would act as a constitutional wrecking ball to a wider scheme of inclusive federation across the empire.[44]

The Covenant thus represented a genuine set of fears – national, religious, economic, and imperial – in a context of immense constitutional uncertainty. Indeed, debates about Home Rule were complicated because it was framed as both a domestic and imperial question. Both unionists and Home Rulers conceded that Irish self-government would alter the constitutional fabric of Ireland, the United Kingdom and the empire, albeit with very different perceptions of the end result. But self-government in Ireland was also a democratic question. The Covenant's cry of protecting Ulster's 'equal citizenship in the United Kingdom' carried a hint of the precarious position that unionists, as a minority in Ireland, identified as a chief threat posed by Home Rule. The United Kingdom was a Protestant kingdom; the monarch was head of the Anglican church, and the dissenting denominations enjoyed every religious freedom. The perceived 'Popish' impulses of the Catholic majority in Ireland were, from a unionist perspective, tempered by Irish absorption into the United Kingdom, which was *the* sole legal polity that spanned the two islands. Home Rule threatened this arrangement by creating a second jurisdiction in Ireland, which Ulster unionists would be forced, by virtue of living on the smaller island, to recognise. Ireland under Home Rule was envisaged as a dystopia by unionists; while nationalists would formally wield power, the fear was widespread amongst Ulster Protestants that the true political master in a Dublin parliament would be the authoritarian Catholic church.[45] Unionism rejected nationalist claims to the contrary and, indeed, deployed the language of democracy to dispel the legitimacy of Home Rule. As the existing polity was the United Kingdom, unionists reasoned that the democratic mandate for major constitutional change should emanate from the two islands as a single bloc. That, from a unionist perspective, was lacking. The Home Rule Bill was introduced by a government that had failed to secure outright victory in two general elections in 1910, and found itself holding office only because it enjoyed the parliamentary support of John Redmond's Irish Party. Home Rule was not part of the Liberal manifesto at these elections. The unionist grievance intensified when it became clear that – as with Gladstone's handling of the Home Rule Bills of 1886 and 1892 – the Liberal government refused to recognise Ulster's arguments for special treatment.[46] 'Every argument used by Home Rulers for giving self-government to one Irish Nation', affirmed F. E. Smith, a leading English

---

[44] L. S. Amery, *The Case against Home Rule* (1912), 12.

[45] Ian Cawood, *The Liberal Unionist Party: A History* (2012), 56.

[46] Eugenio Biagini, *British Democracy and Irish Nationalism, 1876–1906* (Cambridge, 2007), 259–60.

Conservative advocate of Ulster unionism, 'can be used with equal validity to prove that the inhabitants of north-eastern Ulster should be allowed to retain the form of government that best suits them.'[47] This was an articulation of a double majority argument: if an appeal to the majority across the United Kingdom fell on deaf ears, then the argument should shift to another majority. In this case, it was the unionist majority in Ulster.

In many ways, Smith hit at the crux of the matter. The Ulster crisis (and, indeed, the fiercely contested Treaty settlement during 1922–3) was underpinned by drastically different interpretations of the 'will of the people', with the conflict being over *which* people should decide the constitutional future of Ireland.[48] A majoritarian mind-set was common across the political spectrum in Ireland, which saw the winning of power purely in terms of the weight of numbers, with scant regard for minority opinion. Home Rulers frequently pointed to the overwhelming electoral successes that the Irish Party had enjoyed since 1874 as an argument for self-government.[49] Republicans insisted they represented a suppressed sentiment of the Irish 'people' for political independence from the British.[50] Rather than rejecting the democratic arguments of their enemies, unionists in Ulster turned them on their head by appropriating a similar majoritarian language, albeit within a revised image of the national territory. At first, in responding to the Home Rule threat, unionist argument stressed the opposition to Irish self-government that emanated from the entire United Kingdom, as expressed through the ballot box.[51] But the ineffectiveness of this message ensured that the special circumstances of Ulster unionists, as a majority in the northern province of Ireland, soon came to dominate unionism's message.

This is clear from a reading of the most detailed account of the Ulster unionist position, which was given retrospectively by Ronald McNeill, a member of the Standing Committee of the Ulster Unionist Council (UUC). In 1922, he published *Ulster's Stand for Union*, which deployed a number of idioms – constitutional, national, historical, religious, and,

---

[47] F. E. Smith, *Unionist Policy and Other Essays* (1913), 105.

[48] For this angle during the Treaty controversy and resulting civil war, see Tom Garvin, *1922: The Birth of Irish Democracy* (Dublin, 1996); John M. Regan, *The Irish Counter-Revolution, 1921–1936* (Dublin, 2000); Jason Knirck, *Imagining Ireland's Independence: The Debates over the Anglo-Irish Treaty of 1921* (Plymouth, 2006); Bill Kissane, *The Politics of the Irish Civil War* (Cambridge, 2005); Gavin Foster, 'Res Publica na hÉireann?': Republican Liberty and the Irish Civil War', *New Hibernia Review*, 16 (2012), 20–42.

[49] Alvin Jackson, *Home Rule: An Irish History, 1800–2000* (2003), 61.

[50] See the illuminating series of essays in *Republicanism in Ireland: Confronting Theories and Traditions*, ed. Iseult Honohan (Manchester, 2008), which constitute a rare scholarly engagement with Irish republican ideas.

[51] See, for example, the speech of C. C. Craig in *Belfast News-Letter*, 27 Feb. 1913. For unionism within Great Britain, see Daniel M. Jackson, *Popular Opposition to Irish Home Rule in Edwardian Britain* (Liverpool, 2009).

above, all, democratic – to justify unionism's implicit and explicit threats of violence during the previous decade. In a key passage on competing national rights in Ireland, McNeill quoted from Sir Henry Sumner Maine's influential book from 1885, *Popular Government*: 'democracies are quite paralysed by the plea of Nationality. There is no more effective way of the majority to govern, but denying that the majority so entitled is the particular majority which claims the right.'[52] McNeill depicted the Irish question of 1912–14 as a microcosm of this national democratic problem. 'The will of the majority must prevail, certainly', he wrote. 'But what majority?'[53] When it became clear that the implementation of Home Rule would rest not on the will of the majority in the United Kingdom, as McNeill favoured, but within Ireland, unionists, using the same democratic arguments as nationalists, then stressed their own majority in *Ulster* as a buffer against self-government. The use of 'Ulster' as a political concept – something that McNeill emphasised in the opening line of his book – meant that the province (or, at least, most of it) could be reimagined as a solidly Protestant territory. This enabled unionists to employ a double majority argument, bringing together a powerful anti-Home Rule sentiment both in the northern counties of Ireland and the entire United Kingdom.[54] While Maine attacked both nationalism *and* democracy, McNeill's problem was solely with nationalism as a corrupter of democracy. McNeill wholeheartedly agreed with Maine's depiction of nationalists being the 'modern Irreconcilables' of political life, but he did not identify the Irish problem, as Maine might have, as one of 'popular government' itself.[55] Even the bitterest opponents of Home Rule maintained the importance of democratic legitimacy – in other words, asserting the backing of *a* majority – highlighting the intellectual distance travelled by Edwardian unionism from Maine's late Victorian sensibilities.

Unionist discourse transformed Protestants from a minority in Ireland into a majority in Ulster and the United Kingdom to project power and resist change. To build an effective case against Home Rule, unionists challenged the nationalist monopoly of a democratically expressed Irish 'will'. Redmond was frequently denounced in the unionist press as the 'dollar dictator' during the Home Rule crisis, 'the Irish autocrat with swollen moneybags from New York' after successful fund-raising trips in the United States.[56] The language chosen was deliberate: in pursuing the goal of Home Rule, Redmond, funded by American Fenianism, was

---

[52] Henry Sumner Maine, *Popular Government: Four Essays*, 2nd edn (1886; first published 1885), 28; Ronald McNeill, *Ulster's Stand for Union* (1922), 14–15.

[53] McNeill, *Ulster's Stand for Union*, 15.

[54] *Ibid.*, vi. McNeill explicitly deploys the double majority argument in 15.

[55] Maine, *Popular Government*, 27.

[56] Stephen Gwynn, *John Redmond's Last Years* (1919), 48–9.

subverting democracy. But the depiction of their nationalist enemies as undemocratic should not obscure the lengths to which unionism went to construct its own sense of democratic legitimacy. In 1911, a year before the introduction of the third Home Rule Bill in parliament, the Unionist Associations of Ireland published a short guide book for speakers on British platforms. Containing 'Unionist answers regarding Home Rule', the *Irish Unionist Pocket Book* explicitly rebuffed twenty-nine claims made by nationalists in favour of self-government, with the very first one being the 'majority argument': '"The majority in Ireland", it is said, "want Home Rule, and being the majority why should they not get it?"' Speakers were advised to demolish this assertion by pointing to the majority across the United Kingdom against Irish self-government. But, crucially, the demography of Ulster, where 'there is a large majority against Home Rule', was flagged as a significant additional counter-argument.[57] Representing a majority, in other words, was essential in asserting a sense of political legitimacy. During the second reading of the Home Rule Bill, T. P. O'Connor, the Irish Party MP for Liverpool, condemned the actions of 'the minority of the Irish people' who stood opposed to 'the primordial rights of the majority of Irishmen'.[58] Unionists responded in kind by transforming themselves from a minority into a majority, a shift of status which ensured they too should enjoy 'primordial rights'.

Ulster unionism was thus sensitive to the need to claim democratic legitimacy in the campaign against Home Rule; constitutional, economic or more overtly sectarian arguments were not enough. This is not to underestimate the importance of these impulses – they were vital in moulding the unionist mind-set[59] – but to assert the significance of unionism's appropriation of democratic values in making the case for excluding the north of Ireland from the jurisdiction of a Dublin parliament. The language of democracy was an essential part of unionism's toolkit during the revolutionary period; but the democratic norms championed by unionists were loaded with more established assumptions about the perils of Irish self-government, which drew on nineteenth-century precedent.[60] The crisis over the third Home Rule Bill differed from earlier episodes in the widespread deployment of democratic rationalisations by the major protagonists. The anti-Home Rule case articulated by unionists from 1912 was made with normative justification, which provided (they believed) legitimation for potentially militant action.

[57] *The Irish Unionist Pocket Book: Containing Radical Questions and Unionist Answers regarding Home Rule* (Dublin and Belfast, 1911), 7–8.

[58] *Hansard*, 9 June 1913, vol. 53, c. 1309

[59] Bew, *Ideology and the Irish Question*, 27–53.

[60] Walker, *History of the Ulster Unionist Party*, 30.

The Ulster crisis was, then, as much a conflict over numbers and majorities as an ethnic, national or religious dispute.

While asserting unionism's own majority status across the United Kingdom and within Ulster was a priority in constructing a democratic case against Home Rule, how did unionists conceptualise the term 'democracy'? There was an explicitly conservative slant on 'democracy' within unionist discourse, which mirrored the tendency by British Tories to accentuate the perceived anti-radical instincts of the 'people'.[61] 'Democracy' was thus imagined within late nineteenth- and twentieth-century conservative political thought as a potentially unifying force, the method by which to 'improve' the working class and counter the fracturing class conflict impulse of socialism. Similarly, Ulster unionists loaded the term 'democracy' with such a meaning, emphasising the cross-class appeal of their message. When the unionist candidate for West Belfast, Stewart Blacker Quin, declared in 1913 that 'there never was a greater democratic movement than the Ulster Unionist movement', he was referring to its cross-class appeal; cheers also greeted his promise to sponsor measures that led to the 'uplifting of the working classes'.[62] Indeed, the broadening of the class basis, and the geographical narrowing, of Edwardian unionism – from a gentry-dominated all-Ireland movement to a largely middle- and working-class northern-centred body – made Ulster's democratic credentials conceptually clearer than hitherto realised. The Ulster Unionist Labour Association, the overtly working-class wing of unionism, which was founded in 1918, claimed to represent 'the feelings of the democracy of Ulster'.[63] Carson spoke in paternalistic terms about the Protestant working classes of Belfast as 'the only true democracy in Ireland', the proletarian bulwark against revolutionary nationalism and socialism.[64] Indeed, Ulster unionism might be seen as a particularly regionalised form of nineteenth-century 'Tory democracy' – the means by which conservative principles such as patriotism, imperialism and veneration of property gained purchase from the 'respectable' working class – the political principle personified by Benjamin Disraeli, Randolph Churchill and, from an Irish unionist perspective, Standish O'Grady.[65]

[61] Robert Saunders, 'Democracy', in *Languages of Politics in Nineteenth-Century Britain*, ed. David Craig and James Thompson (Basingstoke, 2013), 162–3.

[62] *Belfast News-Letter*, 15 Mar. 1913.

[63] *Belfast News-Letter*, 10 Sept. 1918.

[64] Quoted in H. Montgomery Hyde, *Carson: The Life of Sir Edward Carson, Lord Carson of Duncairn* (1974; first published 1953), 315.

[65] Robert Eccleshall, *English Conservatism since the Restoration: An Introduction and Anthology* (1990), 118–31; Standish O'Grady, *Toryism and the Tory Democracy* (1886).

III

The most notable expression of Ulster unionism's embrace of democratic legitimacy was the declaration of a Provisional Government of Ulster in 1913. This body became a reality the following year, but was eclipsed by the outbreak of war in Europe in August 1914. There is only one surviving copy of the 'Ulster Provisional Government Proclamation', which is held in the Ulster Museum in Belfast. It was signed by six leading unionists, including Edward Carson, Lord Londonderry and Thomas Sinclair. Declaring that Ulstermen were 'Born into Possession of Full Rights and Privileges under ONE KING and ONE IMPERIAL PARLIAMENT', the Proclamation affirmed traditional unionist thinking on the ideas of citizenship and the intrinsically unitary nature of British sovereignty which Home Rule, by virtue of creating a parliament in Dublin, threatened to undermine. Given the imminent and perilous threat of Home Rule, and the Covenant's previous assertion that unionists would refuse to recognise the authority of a Dublin parliament, the Provisional Government of Ulster was established to fill the potential political vacuum in the North. If a Dublin parliament was created, this Provisional body would, according to the Proclamation, take over 'the Government of the Province IN TRUST for the British Nation'.[66]

The language of trustees of the nation would, of course, appear again in another, better-known proclamation by an Irish Provisional Government in 1916. The leaders of the Easter Rising embraced the form of the 'Provisional Government of the Irish Republic', made up of the seven signatories of the Proclamation of the Irish Republic. This Provisional Government was, according to the Proclamation of 1916, tasked with administering 'the civil and military affairs of the Republic in trust for the people', until a national government can be established.[67] The idea of a Provisional Government, a revolutionary administration proclaiming itself the true sovereign representative of the nation, is long established in Irish separatist history. Both the 1803 and 1867 risings were accompanied by proclamations from republican entities styling themselves as the 'Provisional Government of Ireland'.[68] The vanguard of the 1916 Rising were, however, as much inspired by the actions of the Provisional Government of Ulster as their own republican ancestors.

---

[66]'Ulster Provisional Government Proclamation' (1913): available at http://antiquesandartireland.com/2012/05/auction-ulster-proclamation/ (last accessed 4 Nov. 2016).

[67]'Proclamation of the Irish Republic' (1916): available at http://cain.ulst.ac.uk/issues/politics/docs/pir24416.htm (last accessed 4 Nov. 2016).

[68]The 1803 Proclamation was printed but never distributed: the text is reprinted in R. R. Madden, *The Life and Times of Robert Emmet* (Dublin, 1847), 303–17. For the text of the 1867 Proclamation, see *Freeman's Journal*, 8 Mar. 1867.

Patrick Pearse, who read the Proclamation of the Irish Republic aloud on the first day of the rebellion in Dublin, recorded his admiration for the audacity of the Provisional Government of Ulster in 1913. Pearse went as far as asking the unionist leaders to extend its remit to the rest of Ireland, as he recognised the potential for Ulster's underground state to subvert formal British sovereignty.[69]

This call for expansion was ignored by the unionist leadership, but the territorial claim of Ulster's Provisional Government remained fluid. The Proclamation of 1913 decreed a Provisional Government *within* rather than *of* the province of Ulster, a subtle but important distinction, until either Home Rule was abandoned or nationalists recognised the unionist right to self-determination. Carson was on record in claiming that the jurisdiction of a Provisional Government could not extend beyond 'those districts of which they had control', implying that its remit was limited to the mostly Protestant, eastern counties of Ulster.[70] Exclusion of a number of counties of Ulster from the jurisdiction of a Dublin parliament had been mooted since the appearance of the Home Rule legislation in 1912, but it did not become a prominent feature of unionist thought until 1913.[71] In framing the (limited) territorial extent of the Provisional Government of Ulster, unionists in essence adopted the argument aired by Thomas Agar-Robartes, a Liberal backbencher, who made an early (but rejected) amendment to the Home Rule Bill in 1912 to exclude four northern counties from the scheme on the basis of their Protestant majority.[72] The jettisoning of the western counties of Ulster was one of the most extraordinary acts by the unionist leadership during the revolutionary period; the virtue of 'Ulster' as a political entity was, for unionists, its very malleability. Indeed, when Alice Stopford Green, the nationalist historian, mocked the 'Council of the half-province' headed by Carson in 1918, she merely highlighted the ruthless pragmatism of unionism's leaders, while missing the democratic principle that they had followed.[73] The rationale behind the partitioning of Ulster was simple: as Protestants were in the majority in the eastern counties, they would gain political control in a new administration. Majoritarianism was a pressing instinct within unionism and the shedding of minority status within Ireland was imperative for political protection in the face of the Home Rule threat. If this meant that the historic province of Ulster was divided between two jurisdictions, then so be it; unionists reasoned this was a price worth

[69] Pádraic Pearse, *Collected Works of Pádraic H. Pearse: Political Writings and Speeches* (Dublin, [1922]), 187.

[70] McNeill, *Ulster's Stand for Union*, 51.

[71] Jackson, *Home Rule*, 124.

[72] Colin Reid, *The Lost Ireland of Stephen Gwynn: Irish Constitutional Nationalism and Cultural Politics, 1864–1950* (Manchester, 2011), 108–9.

[73] Alice Stopford Green, *Ourselves Alone in Ulster* (Dublin, 1918), 17.

paying for the maintenance of an unimpaired union for the majority of Protestants in the north of Ireland.

The Provisional Government of Ulster was unlike the Provisional Governments of Ireland declared in 1803, 1867 and 1916 in that it was more than a metaphysical entity. The Provisional Government of Ulster was in fact the UUC, transformed into what was called a 'Central Authority'. Various committees and boards were formed, prepared to take over the administrative departments of government and a scheme for a separate judiciary was drafted. While the language used to justify such an extraordinary step was rooted in a Burkean restoration of rights – the UUC resolved that the Provisional Government would remain in force until Ulster again resumed unimpaired her citizenship in the United Kingdom – a clear motivation underpinning the organisation of this audacious counter-state was fear of the perceived rupture to Irish life that Home Rule would bring.[74] As a motivating emotion, a means to galvanise a political campaign or providing the rationale to destroy one, the role of fear within Irish political thought has been underexplored. [75] Certainly, the fear of the loss of state authority, chiefly a threatened collapse of law and order, was a vital mobilising component of unionism's anti-Home Rule campaign. The logical end of the Home Rule crisis from the vantage point of 1913–14 was civil war in Ireland. The Provisional Government of Ulster was thus constituted as an authority to protect unionists in the north from the likely anarchy that would follow the establishment of a Dublin parliament. While unionists rejoiced at the near-mutiny of senior Army officials at the Curragh barracks in March 1914 – some from within the military elite let it be known that they would not enforce Home Rule in the north – the rupture in civil and military administration was a sign of dangerous times, with uncertain consequences. Indeed, the Curragh 'incident' did not stop unionists from importing some 25,000 rifles and three million rounds of ammunition into the north the following month, ensuring that the Provisional Government of Ulster – like a state – possessed coercive power.[76]

The language used by unionists was Hobbesian in channelling dystopian visions of a Home Rule Ireland, with echoes of a regression to the brutal state of nature. Vivid postcards were produced that depicted booming industrial and commercial towns in unionist heartlands, such as Belfast and Carrickfergus, falling into dilapidation under a Home Rule parliament.[77] Carson colourfully recorded in 1912 that 'Ulster

[74] McNeill, *Ulster's Stand for Union*, 145–6.

[75] Corey Robin's pioneering *Fear: The History of a Political Idea* (Oxford, 2004), which chiefly focuses on the United States, makes a number of suggestive points in this regard.

[76] Ronan Fanning, *Fatal Path: British Government and Irish Revolution, 1910–1922* (2013), 111–16.

[77] A number of these dystopian postcards have been digitised by the Linenhall Library in Belfast: www.postcardsireland.com/category/political (last accessed 4 Nov. 2016). Also

see[s] in Irish Nationalism a dark conspiracy, buttressed upon crime and incitement to outrage, maintained by ignorance and pandering to superstition.' [78] The perceived excesses of Parnellism from the 1880s were used to remind unionists of the dangers of Irish nationalism. In *Ulster's Stand for Union*, McNeill repeated the resolution adopted by the Ulster Convention of 1892, which was set up to resist Home Rule:

> That we express the devoted loyalty of Ulster Unionists to the Crown and Constitution of the United Kingdom . . . [and] we record our determination to have nothing to do with a Parliament certain to be controlled by men responsible for the crime and outrages of the Land League, the dishonesty of the Plan of Campaign, and the cruelties of boycotting . . . [W]e declare to the people of Great Britain our conviction that the attempt to set up such a Parliament in Ireland will inevitably result in disorder, violence, and bloodshed.[79]

The Ulster unionist fear in 1913 was that Home Rule was highly probable, meaning that political collapse and public disorder would follow. The Provisional Government of Ulster, underpinned by the guns of the UVF, was designed to counter the catastrophic breakdown of sovereign authority in the north in the face of a threatened Catholic 'takeover' of state power via Home Rule. In this sense, unionist militancy – with decided irony – was presented as the means by which to avoid public disorder.

David Miller has highlighted a potent contractarianism within the Ulster Protestant political psyche, which hinged on a steadfast relationship between political rights and the obligation of the state.[80] Certainly, unionists believed that they possessed a natural right, in a Lockean interpretation of the social contract, to resist a government that jeopardised the constitution and undermined their British privileges.[81] But the air of cataclysm within unionist discourse during the Home Rule debates chimes more with Hobbes's theory of rights and obligation. For Hobbes, writing in the context of the Wars of the Three Kingdoms, the one and only duty of the sovereign is the protection of those under its power; if the sovereign fails in this responsibility, the natural right to protection reverts back to the subjects.[82] As the legal authority – the British government – gravely undermined the safety of its subjects in Ireland through an embrace of Home Rule, unionists believed that government had made itself illegitimate. The constitutional obligation

see John Killen, *John Bull's Famous Circus: Ulster History through the Postcard, 1905–1985* (Dublin, 1985).
[78] Carson, 'Introduction', in *Against Home Rule*, ed. Rosenbaum, 25.
[79] McNeill, *Ulster's Stand for Union*, 33–4.
[80] Miller, *Queen's Rebels*, 28.
[81] John Locke, *Political Writings*, ed. David Wootton (Indianapolis, 2003), 88.
[82] Thomas Hobbes, *Leviathan*, ed. J. C. A. Gaskin (Oxford, 1996; first published 1651), 21.114.

facing unionists, they rationalised, was to continue a 'legitimate' form of British rule through the stewardship of the Provisional Government, as this represented the only method by which to avoid the loss of effective sovereign protection. By banding together as an underground government with its own citizen army, unionists aimed to fill the power vacuum threatened by the implementation of Home Rule. The stress on public order was an articulation of the precarious position of Ulster unionists: a minority who held onto strong folk memories of the 1641 massacres, who were surrounded by a perceived hostile majority and were cut off from the protection afforded by state.[83] There were thus special circumstances for unionists to enjoy what the *Belfast News-Letter* described as a 'love of law and order' in 1887.[84] Tellingly, the application form to join the UVF contained the subheading 'For the Preservation of the Peace': in joining the militia, volunteers committed to act 'for the mutual protection of all Loyalists, and generally to keep the Peace'.[85] The ironies of such unionist activity – resisting the state while upholding the constitution, running guns while preaching about the maintenance of the law – were obvious. But to dismiss the unionist rationale as paradoxical, or (in the words of one historian) a 'shameless appropriation of the clothing of lawful authority', is to miss the importance of long-established ideas concerning constitutional continuity, sovereign responsibility and the maintenance of law and order.[86] These had long been embedded into the political culture of unionism, but they were given their most forceful iteration during the years of the Ulster crisis. The UVF and the Provisional Government of Ulster were manifestations of these ideas in an era of immense political disturbance.

IV

In the aftermath of the Ulster crisis, unionist apologists made the case that the radical events of 1912–14 – from the Covenant to the formation of the Provisional Government, via the setting up of a paramilitary force – did not represent a rebellion, as unionists did not have revolutionary intent. One observer argued that the astonishing actions of unionists represented an 'effort to get back to the old and valued Government of the United Kingdom'.[87] Ronald McNeill believed that the actions of Ulster unionists in this regard were 'without precedent, a solitary

---

[83] Alvin Jackson, 'Irish Unionism', in *The Making of Modern Irish History: Revisionism and the Revisionist Controversy*, ed. D. George Boyce and Alan O'Day (1996), 130.

[84] *Belfast News-Letter*, 31 Dec. 1887.

[85] Application form to join the UVF, NLI: http://catalogue.nli.ie/Record/vtls000148771 (last accessed 28 Oct. 2016).

[86] Geoffrey Lewis, *Carson: The Man Who Divided Ireland* (2005), 114.

[87] 'A True Irishman', *Pampered Ireland: Fact, Not Fiction* (Belfast, 1919), 6.

instance in the history of mankind'. While rebellions have occurred since time immemorial to emancipate a people or overthrow a government, McNeill asked 'has there ever been a "rebellion" the object of which was to maintain the status quo?'[88] This sense of Irish exceptionalism permeated the mind-sets of contemporaries and indeed later historians; the events of the Irish revolutionary period seemed so extraordinary and thus defied comparison. Yet, this crisis was about competing interpretations of universal concepts such as political rights, democracy and sovereignty as much as a bewildering ancient 'ethnic' dispute. In this light, the dynamics of the Ulster problem appear less exceptional; rather than a sectarian-fuelled conflict over territory, the Home Rule struggle can be recast as a crisis of the idea of representative government. Unionist political thought was concerned with the maintenance of political and civil rights, which were underpinned by democratic backing, and the protection offered by sovereign authority. These principles were shaped in the context of a fractious political atmosphere, in which unionists believed they were forced to counter the seemingly inevitable coming of Home Rule for Ireland. The audacious proclamation of the Provisional Government of Ulster was a striking expression of unionism's conception of democratic sovereignty in action.

In the face of nationalist arguments based on a democratic demand for Home Rule, unionists appropriated their own version of the rights of a majority through a reimagining of the national territory. When appeals to majority opinion across the United Kingdom failed, an inward shift towards an Ulster perspective was prioritised. The emergence of 'Ulster' as a fluid political concept is one of the most striking features of the Irish revolutionary period. Unionists in the north were remarkably unsentimental in shedding their southern brethren, even within west and south Ulster, to create a viable political unit that stood apart from the rest of Ireland. That north-east Ulster had a majority of Protestants permitted unionism to articulate powerful democratic arguments against Home Rule. But herein lies the antagonism of the Ulster crisis. The English commentator, W. F. Monypenny, argued in 1913 that the Irish problem seemed so intractable because it was a 'clash of two rights'.[89] These rights were based on competing readings of democratic legitimacy. As both unionists and nationalists cited the support of majorities for mutually exclusive political programmes, the concept of democracy itself became a problem: there was no agreement across the political spectrum as to which majority was the legitimate self-determining 'people'. The overwhelming need to construct a majority to assert political power also ensured that the rights of minorities remained largely a side issue during the Irish

[88]McNeill, *Ulster's Stand for Union*, 140–1.
[89]W. F. Monypenny, *The Two Irish Nations: An Essay on Home Rule* (1913), 3.

revolutionary period as a whole. Democracy was simply interpreted by unionists and Home Rulers as majority opinion, which almost led to civil war in 1914. The violent targeting of minorities in Ulster and Munster during the early 1920s can arguably be framed as a normative offshoot of such majoritarianism; Catholics in the north and Protestants in the south were not accepted by all in their hinterlands to be part of 'the people', with lethal consequences.[90]

Unionists expressed a contractual interpretation of sovereignty based on social and political order, which implicitly included the right to rebel against the government to protect existing rights. With the sovereign power threatening to undermine social order in Ireland through the implementation of Home Rule, fear of a return to the state of nature – which Hobbes equated to 'this war of every man against every man'[91] – gripped Ulster unionism, and justified resistance against the state. The Provisional Government of Ulster, backed by the armed UVF, provided protection for unionists by maintaining sovereign authority as a counterweight to political collapse in Ireland. Given their precarious minority position within Ireland, law and order was a sacred principle within unionist political thought. The irony of rebelling against the British state to uphold British law was one identified by many contemporary observers and later historians, but it is important to locate the rationale for unionist action if we are to understand fully its dynamics. Home Rule was interpreted by unionists as the destruction of the fabric of civilised society, which rested on the maintenance of perceived British values of constitutional stability, sovereign obligation and democratic legitimacy. While the religious, imperial and economic strands of the unionist case against Home Rule are well known, rather less attention has been paid to unionism's assertion of democratic entitlement and the protection of the rights supposedly guaranteed by the British constitution. The Irish Revolution was thus as much about clashing ideals of representative government as it was a national, sectarian or ethnic conflict.

---

[90] T. K. Wilson, *Frontiers of Violence: Conflict and Identity in Ulster and Upper Silesia, 1918–1922* (Oxford, 2010); Peter Hart, *The IRA and its Enemies: Violence and Community in Cork, 1916–1923* (Oxford, 1998); Gemma Clarke, *Everyday Violence in the Irish Civil War* (Cambridge, 2014).
[91] Hobbes, *Leviathan*, 13.13.

Transactions of the RHS 27 (2017), pp. 233–251 © Royal Historical Society 2017
doi:10.1017/S0080440117000111

GLOBALISING AND LOCALISING
THE GREAT WAR

By Adrian Gregory

READ 26 OCTOBER 2016

AT THE UNIVERSITY OF LEEDS

ABSTRACT. This article is intended to suggest an approach to the global history of the
First World War that can provide a method of managing the potentially unwieldy
concept of global conflict by understanding it through the war's impact on localities.
By concentrating on four relatively small but significant cities; Oxford in England,
Halifax in Nova Scotia, Jerusalem in Palestine and Verdun in eastern France, which
experienced the war in very different ways, it looks at both the movement of people
and things and the symbolic interconnectivities that made the war a 'world war'.
This local focus helps challenge both the primacy of self-contained national history
and the focus on the violent interaction of the opposing sides which are the more
normal ways of narrating the war. It does not deny the usefulness of these traditional
structures of narration and explanation but suggests that there are different and
complementary ways the war can be viewed, which create different emphasis and
chronologies.

There could be few things more 'global' in 1914 than an Indian student
studying in Europe. There could be few things more self-consciously
'local' than a Pals battalion. Jogendra Sen was born in Chandernagore
in 1887. He studied for a Bachelor's degree in Engineering in Leeds from
1910 to 1913. After graduating, he worked as an engineer at the Leeds
Whitehall electrical station and continued extension studies. He sang at
the Mill Hill chapel and developed a relationship with Miss Mary Cicely
Newton. In September 1914, at the age of twenty-eight, he joined the
Leeds Pals with some of his friends and became a lance corporal in D
company of the 15th West Yorkshire Regiment. The regiment trained in
North Yorkshire and was shipped to Egypt in December 1915, and then
back to France in March 1918. On 22 May 1916, Sen was killed in action
on the Western Front. According to a letter from a comrade rediscovered
in 2001, he was apparently hit in the neck by shrapnel.[1] He is buried at
Sucerie cemetery. Two months later, his comrades came close to being
wiped out on 1 July 1916 on the Somme and most of those who had

---

[1] The best summary account of Sen's military service can be found on the Leeds
Pals website produced by Stephen and Sam Wood which also includes a letter from

enlisted with him were dead. As a result his story was largely lost until it was rediscovered in the early twentieth century.[2]

Sen's story throws light on many issues. It illustrates structural racisms in the British Empire. As a Bengali he was not considered one of the 'martial races' and would have found it hard to enlist as an infantryman in the Indian army. Yet at the same time, despite being highly educated, he was blocked from becoming an officer in the British army on account of his colour. Despite this experience of prejudice, he enlisted and was killed, and his family proudly preserved his memory which was displayed to the public in India. That his story came fully to light during the centenary period also tells us much about the interactions between academic history and public memory today.

This story then is one of two local histories, one in West Yorkshire and one in Bengal, and also of the global history of the British Empire. It is also a story within two 'national' histories, of the UK and India, but it fits only awkwardly into those, which is one reason that it was marginalised for so long. In a further twist, Chandernagore in 1914 was a tiny enclave in the suburbs of Calcutta that was actually part of French India. Technically, Sen was killed in action in 1916 on what was defined at the time as his 'home' soil. Does this story also belong to the history of France?

The 'Glocal' is a popular concept in certain academic circles. The origins of this idea are apparently in studies of Japan which suggested that global cultural and material forms became adapted in their use at a local level.[3] The term begins in the literature as descriptive although today it tends to be more prescriptive as an approved response to the pressures of globalisation.[4] Still, early use of the term which stressed the co-presence of universal and particularising tendencies may be useful to historians and even more so the suggestion that 'globalising' tendencies may not simply be best understood in their local manifestations but may in fact *only* be comprehensible in that fashion.

Global history has not generally dealt explicitly with world wars. Examining the *Journal of World History* reveals very few articles. The awkward relationship between global history and 'globalisation' has

---

Harry Burniston to his father describing Sen's death in some detail: www.leeds-pals.com/soldiers/jogendra-sen; www.leeds-pals.com/soldiers/harry-burniston, consulted 27 Sept. 2016. Burniston was himself killed on 1 July 1916.

[2] Most of the story was pieced together after Professor Santanu Das gave a lecture at Leeds University mentioning an exhibit of Sen's possessions in the Chadernagore museum. See *Yorkshire Post*, 6 Mar. 2015. I am indebted to Professor Das for bringing this story to my attention.

[3] For a useful overview of the emergence of the term, see C. K. Sharma, 'Emerging Dimensions of the Decentralization Debate', *Indian Journal of Federal Studies*, 19 (2009), 47–65.

[4] Globalisation is itself a deeply problematic concept. See M. Veseth, *Globaloney: Unravelling the Myths of Globalization* (Lanham, MD, 2005).

perhaps muddied the waters; the latter term is still somewhat freighted with unacknowledged 'Manchester School' assumptions about peaceful interactions.[5] By contrast, the historiography of the First World War has recently begun at least a modest global turn. There have been important articles by Hew Strachan and recently by Oliver Compagnon and Pierre Purseigle.[6] Two major synthetic overviews by William Storey and Lawrence Sondhaus have emphasised the global dimension.[7] There are also an increasing number of edited collections which are explicitly global in outlook.[8]

This paper will approach the global differently, by viewing it through the 'local' lens of four medium size cities. These cities are Oxford, Halifax in Nova Scotia, Jerusalem and Verdun. These were typical urban centres of the early twentieth century comparable in terms of size (Oxford had 53,000 population in 1914, Halifax about the same, Jerusalem 80,000 including suburbs, Verdun had a small civilian population in 1914 – about 13,000 – but a significant garrison of more than 25,000 and the Verdun fortified zone also included a dozen villages). They form opposed binaries. Two of these cities were well behind the lines as usually conceived and two were within the main theatres of operations, two were physically devastated by the war and two were mostly unscathed, two experienced traumatic suffering on the part of the civilian population and two less so, two were in Europe and two outside it. All of them have good documentation and were large enough to have interesting stories connected in multiple ways to the global history of the war.

I Oxford

The story of Jogendra Sen finds multiple mirrors in the experience of Oxford. This should not be surprising in a university town that saw itself as the intellectual hub of the imperial project. Non-white students seeking to enlist found themselves negotiating imperial prejudice with varying results. The New Zealand-educated Fijian Lala Sukuna studying

[5] See some scathing comments by David Bell, 'This Is What Happens When Historians Overuse the Idea of Network', *New Republic*, 26 Oct. 2013. In the generally excellent *The Prospect of Global History*, ed. J. Belich *et al.* (Oxford, 2016), the only index entry for 'war' is 'and market integration'.

[6] H. Strachan, 'The First World War as a Global War', *First World War Studies*, 1 (2010), 3–14; O. Compagnon and P. Purseigle, 'Geographies de mobilisation et territoires de belligerence durant la Premiere Guerre Mondiale', *Annales*, 71 (2016), 39–63.

[7] W. K. Storey, *The First World War: A Concise Global History* (Lanham, MD, 2009); L. Sondhaus, *World War, I: The Global Revolution* (Cambridge, 2011).

[8] *Re-visiting World War I*, ed. J. Suchoples and S. James (New York, 2016); *Bellicose Entanglements 1914: The Great War as Global War*, ed. M. Latkitsch, S. Reitmar and K. Seidel (Zurich, 2015). The new three-volume *Cambridge History of the First World War* (Cambridge, 2014) edited by Jay Winter has also been at least partially configured as global history.

History at Wadham was told that the enlistment of Pacific islanders into the British army was not considered responsible. As a result, he enlisted in the French Foreign Legion. After being wounded in combat and winning the Croix de Guerre, he returned to Fiji where he was allowed to join a Fijian labour battalion in 1916.[9]

Hardit Malik Singh, who had read History at Balliol, served with the French Red Cross in 1916 and then applied to join the French air service; his Oxford tutor, embarrassed by the situation, pulled strings for him to be allowed to join the British Royal Flying Corps. The Balliol archives have a picture of him in uniform visiting the college in 1918.[10] He won six victories and became the only Indian 'ace' to survive the First World War. He went on to be Indian ambassador to France after independence.

Perhaps most famous of all is Norman Manley. A Jamaican Rhodes Scholar studying law at Jesus he enlisted in the Royal Field Artillery at Deptford with his younger brother Roy. Roy was killed in action in front of Norman at the battle of Passchendaele; Norman went on to become the first prime minster of Jamaica.[11]

Of course, in crude numerical terms the overseas white scholars were far more significant. No less than nine of the Rhodesian Rhodes scholars were killed in the First World War out of a total of fifty-seven Rhodes scholars killed serving on both sides, including eight of the fifty-nine Germans. Of the US Rhodes Scholars in 1914, nineteen would join Belgian Relief, eighteen the American Ambulance Service, six the YMCA and two the Red Cross. More than 300 US Rhodes scholars served in the war either in the armed forces or civilian service or both.

Just as Oxford students from around the world enlisted to participate in the European struggle, so Oxford University students, past and current, participated in a global war. The first seven pages of the University Roll of Service list graduates serving at Gallipoli, Salonika, Italy, Mesopotamia, India, Egypt and Palestine and others serving in South, West and East Africa, Persia, Malta and the Hijaz. This is only A–C for a single college. Furthermore, whilst over 70 per cent of Oxford graduates did serve on the Western Front, a significant number did so serving with foreign, imperial and Dominion forces.

Two Oxford graduates were linked together in a murkier affair. In 1916, Prince Felix Yusopov, who had read English and Forestry at University College, and who had founded the Oxford University Russian Society prior to the First World War, claimed responsibility for the murder of Grigori Rasputin as a patriotic act to prevent Rasputin in conjunction

---

[9] D. Scarr, *Ratu Sukuna, Soldier Statesman, Man of Two Worlds* (1980).

[10] H. S. Malik, *A Little Work, a Little Play: The Autobiography of H. S. Malik* (New Delhi, 2010).

[11] S. Bourne, *Black Poppies: Britain's Black Communities and the First World War* (Stroud, 2014), 56–62.

with the Tsarina from undermining the Russian war effort. Yusopov was certainly in regular contact in Petrograd with his friend from Oxford Oswald Rayner (Oriel College) who was there with the British Secret Intelligence Service. Rumours that Rayner instigated or possibly even carried out the killing of Rasputin are undocumented but the Oxford connection is unquestionable.[12]

The most famous of all Oxford graduates in the global struggle was Thomas Edward Lawrence. Whilst planning operations in the Jordanian desert he mused, 'The special arts of tribal raiding and the details of food halts and pasturage . . . division of the spoils, feuds and march order were much outside the syllabus of the Oxford School of Modern History.'[13] This was only partly true: his undergraduate thesis on crusader castles had been what had first brought him to the region and begun his relationship with the Arabs. The wartime Arab Bureau was a very incestuous Oxford affair. David Hogarth, the acting director from 1916, was the keeper of the Ashmolean Museum, Kinahan Cornwallis, his deputy, had been president of the University Athletics Club, Gertrude Bell was a graduate of Lady Margaret Hall and Aubrey Herbert belonged to a circle of prominent Balliol men.

T. E. Lawrence had additional Oxford credentials: he was not only an alumnus of the university, he was a son of the town. His name appears on the Oxford Boys School Roll of Service, alongside the names of his two brothers who were killed in the war. This grammar school had been founded by T. H. Green as a service to the town. By 1914, it had become a vital part in the life of the Oxford bourgeoisie and even the aspiring working class. The Roll of Service traces the imperial and international destinations of the school's alumni in their wartime manifestations: nine old boys served as Indian army officers, eighteen in the Canadian forces, nine in the Australian, three in the South African and one each in the New Zealand and Rhodesian. There was also a major in the British West Indies Regiment and a lieutenant in the South African Native Labour Force. One old boy served as a doctor in the American army, two in the Belgian forces and another in the French Air Service. Two more were in the Calcutta local defence force and one in the Nigerian. And of course Lawrence served as a 'Colonel of the special reserve' attached to the Hashemite Arab army.[14] Together, these services in non-British forces made up just under 10 per cent of the total, similar overall to those who had served in the most local forces, the Oxfordshire and Buckinghamshire

---

[12] Chris Danziger, 'The Oxford Alumnus Who Helped to Assassinate Rasputin', *Oxford Today*, 12 Dec. 2016.

[13] T. E. Lawrence, *The Seven Pillars of Wisdom* (privately printed 1926; reprinted 2000), 368.

[14] The Roll of Service is today in the George Street building that houses the Oxford History Faculty.

Light Infantry and the Queen's Own Oxfordshire Hussars. But the 'Ox and Bucks' itself had a global war with battalions serving in Salonika, Mesopotamia and in the intervention in Russia. There are fifty-one men of the 'Ox and Bucks' buried at Kut el Amara where the 1st Battalion passed into captivity and many more would die without known graves on the subsequent death march.[15]

The school Roll of Service also includes those from the school who had served in a civil capacity. The most intriguing story is that of J. Arthur Salter. Salter was a figure embedded in the very heart of Oxford; his father was head of the prominent local boat building firm and had served as mayor of the city. Salter took a First in Literae Humiores at Brasenose in 1903. He joined the civil service and was posted to the transport department of the Admiralty and at the outbreak of war was recalled to become director of ship requisitioning. With the creation of a Ministry of Shipping, he became the key civil servant in managing a crucial part of the British Empire's global effort, and in 1917 he was sent to Washington to advise on the expansion of US merchant ship building. He ended the war in Paris where he chaired the Allied Maritime Transport executive, assisted by a young Jean Monnet.[16] Salter's global significance continued through the Peace Conference and beyond in helping to organise the maritime transport for the massive humanitarian efforts of 1919–20 and becoming the first head of the economic secretariat of the League of Nations. In Paris, he would have found himself potentially reunited with the younger OBS alumnus, Lawrence, who was present at the peace talks as an advisor to the Hashemites.

The existence of educational spaces and their underutilisation due to the enlistment of students prompted other developments. For example, Oxford became home to No. 2 School Military Aeronautics in 1916 in part because the University Museum on Parks Road was available for classrooms, and colleges could accommodate cadets. Best of all, it was in the vicinity of a suitable landing field on Port Meadow near Wolvercote. The initial cadets were from the UK and throughout the Dominions. Whilst billeted at Brasenose, Wilbert Gilroy from Winnipeg wrote to his sister on 9 October 1916 that 'the old colleges certainly have their peculiarities, all nooks and corners, one has to stoop to get thru the old passage ways . . . I am not terribly keen on it.'[17]

In September 1917, the Royal Flying Corps flyers were joined by fifty-three American cadets from the air branch of the National Guard who

---

[15] In total, 541 men of the 'Ox and Bucks' are listed on memorial registers in Iraq, many without known graves. http://www.cwcg.org/find-war-dead.aspx?

[16] D. Rickett, 'Salter (James) Arthur, Baron Salter', www.oxforddnb.com; J. A. Salter, *Allied Shipping Control: An Experiment in International Administration* (Oxford, 1921).

[17] www.canadianletters.ca/content/document-1437 W. H. Gilroy to Em. 9 Oct. 1916.

became the 1st American detachment; the 2nd American detachment, 151 strong, arrived a month later. In the second group were Laurence Callaghan, John McGavock Grider and Elliot White-Spring who would be immortalised in the classic interwar publication *War Birds*.[18] Perhaps less famously, a small number of cadets had been sent by Tsarist Russia for training in the UK; these men continued their training on behalf of the Provisional Government in 1917–18 and then ultimately were returned to Russia as aviators for the White forces.[19]

Even more significant was the use of university buildings as medical facilities. At the start of the war, the University Examination Schools were commandeered for use as a military hospital, the 3rd Southern General. The first wounded began to arrive before the end of 1914, not only British soldiers but also wounded Belgians, and by 1916 with the start of the battle of the Somme the hospital, by this point expanded to include Somerville College and the Town Hall, began to accommodate soldiers not just from the UK but from all of the British Dominions.[20] For example, large numbers of New Zealanders arrived in the aftermath of the battles of September and October 1916. An interesting relic of this Dominion presence can be found in the autograph book of Nurse Lily Green – several pages are the work of Dominion troops including a picture of a Kookaburra drawn by C. J. Macdonald of New South Wales in January 1917.[21]

Those who succumbed to their wounds or disease in the Oxford hospitals were buried at Botley cemetery just outside the city boundaries. The cemetery holds the graves of thirteen Canadians, nine New Zealanders, eight Australians, one South African, five Belgians and four Germans, these non-British graves making up nearly a quarter of all those buried in the cemetery. This is not a fully reliable guide to the proportion of those who were treated in the hospital or died there; the British dead were more likely to be claimed for burial by relatives. Nevertheless, it is still clear that a large and visible proportion of the wounded in Oxford were from overseas.

It was not only foreign soldiers but civilians who were swept by the tides of war to the banks of the Isis. As early as October 1914, 200 Belgian refugees had arrived in the city. More unusual was the presence of a large contingent of Serbians from May 1916. Survivors from the harrowing 1915 retreat across Albania were housed in Oxford due to the intervention of

---

[18] J. MacGravock Grider, *War Birds: Diary of an Unknown Aviator* (New York, 1926).
[19] P. Wright, *RFC in Oxfordshire* (pamphlet privately printed, Oxford 1985); I have benefited from conversations with Peter Smith of the Wolvercote WW1 Aerodrome Memorial project on this subject.
[20] M. Graham, *Oxford in the Great War* (Barnsley, 2014), 48–56.
[21] www.oxfordatwar.uk/items/show/3.

Sidney Ball of St John's College, head of the Serbian Relief Committee, housed at St John's, Wycliffe Hall and Lady Margaret Hall. In 1918, the Anglo-Catholics of St Stephen's house supported the establishment of a seminary there to train teenage Serbians for the Orthodox priesthood.[22]

The latter years of the war saw significant numbers of American and Dominion officers and soldiers attending training courses in the city. In the immediate aftermath of the war, an influx of American officers was allowed to study at the university before returning to the USA, amongst them the future novelist F. Scott Fitzgerald. The global nature of Oxford's war continued through to memorialisation. The largest donation for the funding for the Christ Church War Memorial Gardens was provided by King Vajiravudh of Siam. He had studied history and law at 'the House' between 1899 and 1901 although he never took a degree. The king had gone on to Sandhurst and served as an officer in the Durham Light Infantry. He subsequently played a crucial role in thinking through the kingdom's effective contribution to the allied war effort. His £500 gift in 1920 was more than four times that of the next nearest donation and one eighth of the total raised. It was crucial in allowing the project to proceed.[23]

II Halifax NS

The story of Oxford at war is in some respects undramatic: there is no single day that dominates the experience or the memory. By contrast, the wartime story of Halifax, Nova Scotia, is dominated by a single event. The Halifax harbour explosion of 6 December 1917 literally transformed the city. One of the largest non-nuclear explosions in human history, it generated shock waves, fires which destroyed a third of the city and a tsunami, which between them claimed 1,800 lives in a matter of minutes and left thousands more injured and homeless. Global history, perhaps betraying a residual Braudelianism, can have a weakness in dealing with 'events'. Yet treated correctly, events can be incredibly revealing of global connections and significance.[24]

The cause of the great explosion shows the significance of global maritime transport to wartime Europe. The ships that collided were two different examples of this. One, SS *Mont-Blanc*, was a French munition

---

[22] J. M. Winter, 'Oxford in the Great War', in *The History of the University of Oxford*, VIII: *The Twentieth Century*, ed. B. Harrison (Oxford, 1994), 1–25.

[23] I am grateful to Charles Bertlin of Balliol College for the reference to a letter from the Siamese Legation dated 1 Mar. 1920, Christ Church Archives, BR/1/1 GB XV. C3. It was accompanied by the king's personal cheque.

[24] W. H. Sewell, *The Logics of History* (Chicago, 2005). For an eccentric but clever use of 'events' to make 'global' points, see J. MacDougall, *Let the Sea Make a Noise: A History of the North Pacific from Magellan to Macarthur* (New York, 1993).

ship owned by the French state shipping service the CGT, loaded with a lethal quantity of volatile explosives. The other, SS *Imo*, was a Norwegian vessel that had been had been chartered by Belgian Relief and was still in ballast as it awaited permission to sail on to New York to pick up its cargo. Whatever individual decisions led to the fatal collision, the underlying cause was the increasing congestion of Halifax harbour as the U-Boat threat enforced the requirement of convoy assembly on Atlantic shipping.[25]

The victims of the explosion included the very local and the global as befitted a significant Atlantic port. Illustrating the local, the post-explosion tsunami obliterated the impoverished indigenous Miqmaq village on the Dartmouth shore, the last distinctive remnant of the First Nation presence in the area. On the global axis, amongst the dead was Matteo Ciccione, a twenty-five-year-old stevedore from Italy. Correspondence with his illiterate father, conducted in all probability through the good offices of the parish priest, revealed that Matteo had been sending remittances to his family in the old country and that they were therefore entitled to a share of the compensation.[26]

The explosion was briefly a global news story and this was reflected in a genuinely global outpouring of sympathy and charity. The Australian government donated $250,000 dollars to the relief effort, *The Times* in London raised the equivalent of 600,000 Canadian dollars and George V sent a personal donation of £5,000. Donations came from the West Indies and Latin America as well as all the Canadian provinces. Perhaps the most striking support came from the USA. The city of Chicago donated $125,000 but it was the city of Boston and the state of Massachusetts that led the effort with $750,000 in donations and a large volunteer effort by medical staff. Within a day of the explosion, medical teams were setting out from Boston for the city and the governor of Massachusetts had pledged all possible support.[27]

The explosion dramatically illustrated the importance of Halifax as the hub for a reconfigured network of Atlantic and global communications. On that same day, RMS *Olympic*, the sister ship of the *Titanic*, was further back in the Bedford Basin planning to load some 5,000 Chinese members of the Labour Corps. It was standard practice for the Chinese labourers recruited in Shandong to be shipped across the Pacific to British Columbia and then moved across Canada by train before embarking at Halifax for

---

[25] J. Kitz, *Shattered City: The Halifax Explosion and the Road to Recovery* (Halifax, NS, 2004). For context see Salter, *Allied Shipping*, 122–7, 144–7; M. B. Miller, http://encyclopedia. 1914-1918-online.net/article/sea_transport_and_supply.

[26] Kitz, *Shattered City*, 184–5.

[27] *Ibid.*, 82–95.

Europe. The total number moved in this fashion was 85,000, more than half the total of those sent to Europe.[28]

This in turn was one part of a far larger human movement. Halifax was a major port of embarkation for the Canadian Expeditionary Force, many of whom were returning migrants, and it was occasionally an assembly point for US forces. Estimates of the total number sent to Europe passing through the port are in excess of 350,000. Halifax was also infamously the inadvertent and disastrous destination for a contingent of Jamaican soldiers. In March 1916, the SS *Verdala* carrying over 1,000 men of the 3rd Jamaican contingent of the British West Indies Regiment bound for the UK was diverted north to Halifax after a U-Boat sighting. The men were wearing light tropical uniforms and by the time they arrived in Halifax hundreds were suffering from severe hypothermia.[29] One of them, Eugent Clarke, described the shock at arriving in a snow covered port. Frostbite led to 106 amputations amongst the Jamaicans.[30]

Whilst curtailed, civilian Atlantic travel did not cease. In April 1917, Halifax briefly played a part as an off stage locale in the unfolding Russian Revolution. Leon Trotsky, his wife and his two sons were sailing from New York exile to Norway with the intention of returning to Russia when he was stopped and interrogated by agents of the British security services when his ship put in to Halifax. Trotsky was sent to an internment camp in nearby Amherst whilst his family were held in the city. According to Trotsky, in his memoir even his two sons, nine and eleven years old, were kept under surveillance. The request to detain the well-known agitator on the far side of the Atlantic had come from the new Provisional Government, but it quickly backfired when the Petrograd Soviet, which idolised Trotsky for his role in 1905, began to protest publicly at the British action and demand that the government act on his behalf. George Buchanan, the British ambassador in Petrograd, initially responded that it was a lack of shipping that prevented Trotsky from returning but was allegedly swayed by the growth of anti-British feeling in the city, including threats to British businessmen, to pass on Miliukov's request for the release of Trotsky and his family.[31]

Perhaps the most striking contingent to pass through Halifax on their way to the theatre of war were the volunteers of the 39th Royal Fusiliers: the second battalion of the 'Jewish Legion'. Recruited in the USA and

---

[28] Guoqi Xu, *Strangers on the Western Front; Chinese Workers in the Great War* (Cambridge, MA, 2011).

[29] The official report by the Colonial Office from 29 June 1916 is The National Archives, CO 318/338/32.

[30] Bourne, *Black Poppies*, 66–9, citing a TV interview. Eugent Clarke survived to 108.

[31] A. D. Harvey, 'Trotsky at Halifax April 1917', *Archives*, 22 (1997), 170–4, presents key British government documents; http://ns1758.ca/quote/trotsky1917.html gathers the main memoir sources including Trotsky and Buchanan.

Canada, they also included a small number of Zionist settlers from Palestine who had travelled to the USA in 1915. One of these, David Ben Gurion, had initially intended to raise a Jewish Legion to fight on behalf of the Ottomans but had changed his plans after US entry into the war and the Balfour Declaration. The unit had originally been earmarked to train in Halifax but after the explosion the training camp was transferred to Windsor. Nevertheless, they spent some days pre-embarkation at the Halifax citadel in spring 1918, from which the Russian born settler Ben Zvi wrote to his wife:

> The hills and the bay remind me of the Bosphorous, near Constantinople, a multitude of ships go back and forth ... whenever I see the ships my heart expands within me, I gaze towards the East, across the ocean and in my mind's eye see my homeland, half of it redeemed and half of it enslaved.[32]

Within a few months, he would arrive in the half-redeemed 'homeland' along with other soldiers from every corner of the world.

III Jerusalem

The first man to fly the Star of David flag in Jerusalem was not a member of the Jewish Legion but a New Zealander serving in an Australian medical unit. Corporal Louis Isaac Salek, from a Jewish family in Wellington but enlisted in Melbourne, had commissioned a flag to be made whilst stationed in Alexandria from an Egyptian Jewish tailor. The flag only flew for a very short time from David's Tower before being taken down by British troops in order not to provoke the population.[33]

Jerusalem had a double existence as both a real and symbolic space at least as far back as St Augustine. The First World War did nothing to reduce this duality and in fact intensified it. Jerusalem is a particularly well-documented case-study for the interaction of the local and global due to the superb work of Abigail Jacobson, Roberto Mazza and Salim Tamari.

The permanent population of Jerusalem in 1913 was about 80,000, of which nearly two-thirds were Jews, many of whom had been born outside Palestine. The Arab Muslim and Christian population of the city were roughly equal parts of the remainder. The city also played host annually to upwards of 40,000 pilgrims, perhaps a third of whom were Russian subjects, and some 7,000 secular tourists. There were also perhaps a few thousand permanent foreign residents connected to the consulates, businesses, education and above all the churches.[34]

---

[32] Cited in G. J. J. Tulchinsky, *Taking Root: The Origins of the Canadian Jewish Community* (Hanover, NH, 1993), 194. Ben Zvi was born in Poltava and emigrated to Jaffa in 1911 but studied in Istanbul from 1912 to 1914. He was expelled from Palestine in 1915 and joined Ben Gurion in New York. He went on to become the second president of Israel.

[33] Louis Salek's official war record can be found at australiaremembers.net.au/anzacstories. For the flag, see *Haaretz*, 11 Dec. 2014.

[34] R. Mazza, *Jerusalem: From the Ottomans to the British* (2014), 37, 78–81.

The first impact of the war on Jerusalem was a conscious 'deglobalisation' of the city. Even before the formal outbreak of war, on 1 October 1914 the Ottoman governor announced the end of the capitulations, the formal agreements that had given the British, French and Russians substantial power and influence in the city and which played an important role in the local provision of health care and education.[35] This was soon followed by the expulsion of enemy aliens including 'foreign Zionists'. A city that had its rationale as a pilgrimage hub could not avoid social and economic damage from isolation. In 1915, the Spanish consul Ballobar noted in his diary that the procession of the Holy Fire was not as lively as normal due to the absence of foreign pilgrims.[36]

A particularly sad local effect was the requisition of the Anglican St George's College by the Ottoman military; the closure of the college playing fields removed what was the only real playground in the entire city from the children of Jerusalem.[37]

Yet by 1916, new outsiders were beginning to come to the city. Haggard survivors of the Armenian genocide were taking shelter in the Armenian quarter, doubling the Armenian population of the city, and German and Austrian troops arrived to support the Ottomans on the Sinai front. But it was the capture of the city by British imperial forces in December 1917 which did most to reconnect the city to the wider world.

Although the idea that the capture of Jerusalem as a 'Christmas present to the British people' preserving morale in the terrible winter of 1917 is overplayed, Justin Fantauzzo's survey of opinion on the capture of Jerusalem around the British Empire shows some very strong responses. In Toronto, Canon Gould lectured that the capture of Jerusalem, along with British control of Sinai and Mecca, would give the empire unprecedented prestige as the protector of the Holy Sites of the Abrahamic Faiths, whilst in New Zealand the canon of Otago looked forward to the conversion of Jerusalem's Muslims. Opinion in Ireland was divided: the moderate nationalist Freeman's journal rejoiced in the liberation of the Holy Sepulchre from the Turks and remarkably suggested that this one act would go a long way to erasing England's crimes, whilst the *Connaught Telegraph* shuddered at the idea of the Holy City falling to the Protestant heirs of Cromwell.[38]

The British control of the site did indeed cause some concern for the papacy. The capture of Jerusalem had been briefly marked by the

[35] R. Mazza, 'Churches at War: The Impact of the First World War on the Christian Institutions of Jerusalem 1914–20', *Middle East Studies*, 45 (2009), 207–27.

[36] Mazza, 'Churches at War', 214.

[37] Mazza, *Jerusalem*, 59.

[38] J. Fantauzzo, 'The Finest Feats of the War? The Captures of Baghdad and Jerusalem during the First World War and Public Opinion throughout the British Empire', *War in History*, 24 (2017), 64–86.

ringing of church bells and *Te Deums* in Rome, perhaps a required gesture towards Italy's ally (notably St Peter's was an exception). But the Balfour Declaration triggered a good deal of hostility, notwithstanding the clause about not interfering with existing religious rights. Benedict XV was deeply concerned that all existing Catholic privileges be upheld, but was ambivalent to the extraordinary proposal from Cardinal Mercier of Belgium that the best way to protect these would be for that devoutly Catholic nation to be awarded the League of Nations Mandate over Palestine.[39]

The sense of symbolic importance of the conquest of Jerusalem was not limited to the Christian nations. The *Hindustan* newspaper in Lahore described it as 'the greatest event in the history of the world' before taking aim at local Muslims who were calling for Palestine to be put under Muslim rule.[40] American Jewish opinion was galvanised by the combination of the recent Balfour Declaration with the extraordinary coincidence that Allenby had entered Jerusalem on the last day of Hanukkah, the Jewish festival dedicated to the liberation and cleansing of the city by the Maccabees.

The war brought the world to Jerusalem but also took Jerusalem residents to far-flung places. Aref Shehadeh, the middle son of a Jerusalem merchant family, had left prior to the war to edit a Constantinople newspaper. Just before the war, he had enlisted as an Ottoman military cadet. He was then captured by the Russians after the Ottoman defeat at Erzerum and sent to a POW camp in Krasnayorsk, deep in Siberia. Whilst in the camp, he was able to stay in touch with his family in Jerusalem courtesy of the Red Crescent. From them, he was kept informed about the deteriorating conditions in the city and he also became aware of the Arab revolt. In the camp, he helped edit an Arabic-language paper *Naqatu Allah* which served increasingly to differentiate Arab from Turkish Ottomans, and after the Bolshevik Revolution he set out with other Arab prisoners to join the Shariffian forces by a complicated Hejira via Manchuria, China, Japan, India and Egypt. Having literally travelled half-way around the world, he was able to return to his father's shop in Jerusalem, now under British control in 1918.[41]

From 1915 until 1918, Jerusalem was caught up in a wider humanitarian crisis in the region. One of the earliest major humanitarian interventions in the war was the shipment to Palestine of relief supplies by the American Jewish Joint Distribution Committee. Responding to an urgent appeal from the US ambassador in Constantinople, Henry Morgenthau,

---

[39] J. Pollard, *The Papacy in the Age of Totalitarianism 1914–1958* (Oxford, 2014), 88–9.

[40] A. Jarboe, *The War News in India: The Punjabi Press during World War I* (2016), 173.

[41] S. Tamari, *The Year of the Locust. A Soldier's Diary and the Erasure of Palestine's Ottoman Past* (Berkeley, 2011), 68–77.

a committee organised by the banker Jacob Schiff raised $50,000 in November 1914. In April 1915, just as famine conditions were first starting to emerge in the Ottoman Empire, the relief ship *Voulcan* arrived at Jaffa with 900 tons of food. Through a deal with the Ottoman authorities, the relief was distributed to each of the main communities, 55 per cent to the Jewish community and the rest to Christians and Muslims. 60 per cent of the aid to Jews and a significant amount of that to the others was delivered to Jerusalem where the American consul Dr Glazebrook oversaw the distribution.[42] American Jews were not the only Americans providing crucial assistance. The Orthodox churches had been cut off from their principle support from Russia and again it was Americans who stepped into the breach.

The conquest of the city by the British in December 1917 changed the international humanitarian landscape. The American Red Cross were able to reemerge as a major force and the Syrian and Palestine Relief Fund was finally able to operate in the territory for which it had been founded more than a year earlier.[43] The SPRF was a new, interdenominational relief fund with support across the British Dominions, as this extract from a New Zealand Diocesan Magazine from February 1918 makes clear:

> Our warmest sympathy must go out to our fellow Christians of the Greek Orthodox Church, the oldest church in the world. The Relief Fund administers relief to all of the oppressed utterly irrespective of creed... Apart from our sympathy and support from the point of view of Christian love and duty it is also to be considered what a great effect Christian charity and British charity will have upon the those Moslems and Jews who will be the recipients of it.[44]

Jerusalem would become a test case for the propaganda value of enlightened 'humanitarian imperialism' but rapidly became an embarrassing failure.[45]

IV Verdun

The Ottoman army group commander forced to abandon Jerusalem to the British in 1917 was Erich von Falkenhayn. He had found himself exiled to this perceived secondary theatre of war as a result of strategic failure in his post of chief of staff of the imperial German army. Verdun, the battle that doomed him, is my final site.

The classic locus of military history is the battlefield. In some ways, this is a highly obvious focal point for an attempt to globalise and localise. Battle lay at the end of the chains of global connections where they came

---

[42] A. Jacobson, *From Empire to Empire: Jerusalem between Ottoman and British Rule* (Syracuse, NY, 2011), 41–52.

[43] W. Canton, *Dawn in Palestine* (1918).

[44] *Waipu Church Gazette*, 8, 8 (1 Feb. 1918), 63. Digitised by NZLNA.

[45] See for example Jacobson, *From Empire*, 145–7.

into contact with local conditions. Some battlefields of the war had a very obviously global appearance: Ypres in particular saw almost every element of the French and British Empires pass through and the Salonica front was notoriously polyglot. But it is perhaps more interesting to test the concept on a less obvious case, to deliberately take a case that is generally understood through a strongly 'national' prism. Verdun was perhaps the most nationally mythic battle of the war, for France initially, then increasingly also for Germany and then ultimately as a site of Franco-German reconciliation which gave it a centrality in a Franco-German idea of Europe.[46] Despite its designation as a 'world capital of peace', Verdun is rarely considered as a global rather than a European battlefield.

The 'whitewashing' of the battle remains a live issue in French politics: the belated creation of a Muslim memorial on the battlefield met with resistance from the Front National. So did the proposal to include the French rapper Alpha Diallo 'Black M' in the centenary memorial programme. His performance was cancelled due to the perception that his 'anti-French' attitudes might 'offend veterans', even though he had greeted the original invitation by pointing out that he was proud his African grandfather had fought for France in the Second World War.[47]

Verdun was a battle which did draw in men (and some women) from vast distances. The final recapture of Fort Douamont in October 1916 was achieved in large part by the Moroccan Colonial Infantry Regiment, Tirailleurs Senegalaise, and even a small number of Somalis from Djibouti.[48] The aftermath of this attack was recorded by a member of another significant non-French contingent, the English nurses at the Red Cross urgent cases hospital at Revigny, 56 km behind the line. In their house magazine, *Faux Mirroir*, Sister S. M. Edwards described the casualties, 'from far off Brittany', 'from the heights of Savoy', 'from the sunny skies and orange groves of the Cote-Azure' but also 'Abdallah from far away Tunis and Bamboula from still farther Senegal'.[49]

Combat troops represented only one part of the equation. Verdun represented a global logistical revolution, the first time a major field army had been maintained by road transport and this itself represented

[46] For the mythic nature of Verdun for France, see I. Ousby, *The Road to Verdun: France, Nationalism and the First World War* (2002). For Germany, B. Hüppauf, 'Langemarck, Verdun and the Myth of a *New Man* in Germany after the First World War', *War and Society*, 6 (1988), 70–103. For insight into the politics of the famous Mitterrand/Kohl hand holding at Verdun in 1984, see www.mitterrand.org/Verdun-le-geste-Mitterrand-Kohl.html. For a long view, see S. Barcellini, 'Mémoire et mémoires de Verdun 1916–1996', *Guerres mondiales et conflits contemporains*, 182 (1996), 77–98.

[47] www.lefigaro.fr/musique/2016/07/13, 13 July 2016.

[48] M. Bekraoui, 'Les soldats marocains dans la bataille de Verdun', *Guerres mondiales et conflits comtemporains*, 182 (1996), 39–44; J. Lunn, *Memoirs of the Maelstrom: A Senegalese Oral History of the First World War* (Portsmouth, NH, 199), 121.

[49] Cited in M. Brown, *Verdun 1916* (Stroud, 1999), 154.

an achievement made possible by globalisation. Horses and fodder, trains and coal could be provided from western European resources but petroleum and lubrication for the internal combustion engines and rubber for tyres could not. On 8 July 1916, *Scientific American* published an article on 'supplying Verdun' illustrated with a picture of an 'American-made' truck being loaded with beef carcasses.

'Neutral' Americans were deeply involved at Verdun. The American Field Ambulance Service served right up to the front lines. One of the volunteers, Henry Beston, had visited the 'sleepy provincial city' before the war. In 1916, he vividly described the scene a few kilometres outside the citadel as the last civilians fled: 'Refugees tramped past in the darkness. By the spluttering light of a match I saw a woman go by with a cat in a canary cage . . . a smouldering in the sky told of the fires of Verdun.'[50]

The Lafayette Escadrille, the squadron of American volunteers in French service, was committed to the battle in May 1916 and it was at Verdun they suffered their first death in action. James McConnell in his 1917 memoir recounts how Horace Balsey was badly wounded and forced to crash land just behind the front line and was then rescued and treated in a hospital in one of the forts. Victor Chapman then flew on patrol with a bag of oranges to bring to Balsey, only to be jumped by a German patrol and shot down and killed near Douamont.[51] Another of the original volunteers Norman Prince would die later in the battle. Chapman's letters to his father were published in 1917 and became important propaganda at the time of the American entry to the war. The elite members of the Escadrille and the Ambulance were not the only Americans at Verdun. The African American boxer Eugene Bullard had enlisted in the Foreign Legion early in the war and in March 1916 was wounded at Verdun serving with the 170th Infantry in the Moroccan Division. Subsequently, he would transfer to the Escadrille.[52]

As well as global participants, the battle also had immediate global consequences. In particular, the French mobilisation of colonial labour and troops from Indochina to West Africa intensified oppression and galvanised resistance from Annam to Algeria and on to Benin.[53]

The global nature of the battle at Verdun from the French side functioned in terms of men and materiel but on the German side it is more connected to the issue of strategy. The German decision to attack

[50] H. Sheahan, *A Volunteer Poilu* (Boston, MA, 1916).

[51] J. McConnell, *Flying with the American Escadrille at Verdun* (New York, 1917), 42–4.

[52] *African American War Heroes*, ed. J. Martin (Santa Barbara, 2014), 33.

[53] C. Koller, 'The Recruitment of Colonial Troops in Africa and Asia and their Deployment in Europe during the First World War', *Immigrants and Minorities*, 26 (2008), 111–33; Lunn, *Memoires of the Maelstrom*, 46–9. For Algeria, see H. Strachan, *The First World War: To Arms* (Oxford, 2001), 764–6.

a fortress complex in eastern France in 1916 might not have occurred if the war being fought was purely a Franco-German one.

The problem Germany faced in late 1915 was that its most dangerous medium-term enemy was an off-shore island controlling access to global resources. Battlefield successes in the east had to date led nowhere decisive and were subject to diminishing returns as the German army advanced into the under-developed territory of the Baltics and Belarus. Falkenhayn's decision to attack Verdun in order to break France was the key element in a consciously *global* strategy to deal with the problem of fighting a war against the British Empire. It was based as much on assumptions about the British (and to a lesser extent about the Russians) as about the French. One does not have to accept the dubious and possibly retrospective version of strategy presented in the unverifiable 'Christmas Memorandum' to recognise the larger context in which the defeat of France (and the British armies in France) was intended to combine with the pressure of U-Boat warfare to force the British to accept a German victory.[54]

It was also the international dimension which derailed German strategy. The Habsburg plan to mount an attack against the Italians was kept from Falkenhayn. This in turn weakened their front against the Russians, creating the conditions that allowed Brusilov to mount his famous offensive, which was in turn enabled by the success of the Russians on the Caucasus front in spring 1916. Similarly, the turn to unrestricted submarine warfare was swiftly undermined by American protests after the sinking of the liner SS *Sussex* in the spring. Even before the Somme Offensive finally put paid to Falkenhayn's strategy, its failure had been determined by these distant forces.[55]

The sense of the battle as an epic struggle resonated globally. American involvement had created a particular interest there but it could be found much further away. In New Zealand, a boy born on 31 July 1916 was christened Verdun John Scott. He subsequently played test cricket for his country.[56] The town of Grunthal in South Australia, just outside Adelaide, was renamed under the South Australian Government Nomenclature Act of 1917 as Verdun.[57] Rue Verdun was a name that proliferated not only in

---

[54] Erich von Falkenhayn's problematic memoir *General Headquarters and its Critical Decisions*, trans. Anon. (1920), provides this wider context for the battle. See also R. Foley, *German Strategy and the Path to Verdun* (Cambridge, 2005); H. Afflerbach, *Falkenhayn. Politische Denken und Handeln im Kaiserreich* (Munich 1994); H. Herwig, *The First World War: Germany and Austria Hungary* (1997), 180–1.

[55] Herwig, *The First World War*, 206–11. See also Foley, *German Strategy*, 253.

[56] *Wisden Cricketer's Almanac* (2017), 445. I would like to thank Professor Graham Loud for drawing this to my attention.

[57] Officially announced in the *South Australian Government Gazette*, 10 Jan. 1918, 37. I would like to thank John Horne for alerting me.

France: the establishment of the French Syrian Mandate saw the name adopted for a main boulevard in Beirut.

The global resonance continued after the war. Whilst visiting France in September 1919, the Chinese foreign minister Lu Chengxiang authorised a donation of 50,000 French francs to the rebuilding of Verdun's schools.[58] Individual Americans played a central role in funding battlefield memorialisation. The memorial bell at the Ossuary was paid for by Anne Thornburn Van Buren in 1927 whilst George Rand had funded the memorial at the 'Trench of Bayonets' in 1920.

The last extraordinary twist in the global nature of the Verdun battle can be found in a long-term legacy. In 1919, under the aegis of the Fellowship of Reconciliation, British and American pacifists were able to meet their German counterparts at Bilthoven in Holland. At the end of the meeting, one of the German delegates mentioned that his brother was killed at Verdun and that he felt that the monument he wanted to raise would be the rebuilding of the ruins. This idea would resonate, and in 1920 the Swiss international secretary of the FOR, Pierre Ceresole, began to organise an international team to go to the battlefield to help with rebuilding. In November, a dozen Frenchmen were joined by Swiss, British, Germans, Hungarians and Austrians at the village of Esnes on the battlefield. The mayor welcomed them and they were able to rebuild the road and some homes. They also met hostility from the local head of a French relief organisation who objected to the presence of ex-enemies and after five months the international volunteer relief camp was disbanded. But Ceresole would not let the idea die and through the 1920s he began to organise other international volunteer work camps to provide aid after national disasters. In 1930, with the support of international contacts, including the Swiss Quaker and pacifist Jean Inebnit, Professor of French at Leeds University, he founded the international Association of Service Civil which in turn would give rise to Voluntary Service Overseas and the entire international volunteer youth service worldwide.[59]

V On metaphors and narratives

The dominant narrative of the First World War is still structured around the idea of the front. This suits a narrative which is linear and binary, focused on discrete and opposed units of analysis, above all nations and their armies. This is not wrong, but it is a partial description, as all descriptions have to be. The front does have the virtue of reflecting a language that emerged during the war, but it was also weighted with a

[58] P. Bailey, 'The Sino-French Connection and World War One', *Journal of the British Association for Chinese Studies*, 1 (2011), 16.

[59] A. Gillette, *One Million Volunteers. The Story of the Volunteer Youth Service* (Harmondsworth, 1968), 15–33; http://www.swiss-quakersd.ch/ge/history/doc/LetTheirLivesSpeak.

whole set of assumptions rooted in the power relations and norms of the early twentieth century which we can today recognise as concealing as much as they reveal. If we move away from the dominant metaphor of 'the front' and instead consider nodes and networks, we may gain new and different insights. Nodes and networks do not need to be invoked in the scientistic and quantified a manner of fashionable network theory. Each of these cases can be considered a node in a different sense, Oxford as a node of education and intellectual activity, Halifax as a transport node, Jerusalem as a diplomatic and religiously symbolic node, Verdun as a strategic node. The type of networks they generated naturally differed in style and significance. But interestingly, all of them develop a second shared nodal quality during the war as centres of international humanitarian networks; refugee reception and philanthropic activity in Oxford, disaster relief in Halifax, famine relief in Jerusalem and medical assistance during the war and reconstruction after the war at Verdun.[60]

On the face of it, this has been a picaresque ramble through the war, with Oxford archaeologists and Serbian seminarians, Italian stevedores and Russian revolutionaries, Chinese labourers and West Indian infantrymen, a New Zealand Zionist and a Palestinian POW in Siberia, assorted American aviators and even the king of Siam. But at the same time, the use of these places has shown simultaneously that the description of the war as a 'world war' was meaningful in these places and that at the same time what that meant was fundamentally framed and defined by local particularities. The war was everywhere a global event and everywhere the *way* in which it was global differed.

---

[60]See for example B. Cabanes, *The Great War and the Origins of Humanitarianism* (Cambridge, 2014).

Transactions of the RHS 27 (2017), pp. 253–269 © Royal Historical Society 2017
doi:10.1017/S0080440117000123

LANGUAGES OF FREEDOM IN DECOLONISING AFRICA*

By Emma Hunter

The Gladstone Prize Winner

ABSTRACT. The 'triumph of liberalism' in the mid-twentieth-century west is well known and much studied. But what has it meant for the way the decolonisation of Africa has been viewed, both at the time and since? In this paper, I suggest that it has quietly but effectively shaped our understanding of African political thinking in the 1950s to 1960s. Although the nationalist framing that once led historians to neglect those aspects of the political thinking of the period which did not move in the direction of a territorial nation-state has now been challenged, we still struggle with those aspects of political thinking that were, for instance, suspicious of a focus on the individual and profoundly opposed to egalitarian visions of a post-colonial future. I argue that to understand better the history of decolonisation in the African continent, both before and after independence, while also enabling comparative work with other times and places, we need to think more carefully and sensitively about how freedom and equality were understood and argued over in local contexts.

Gabriel Ruhumbika's 1969 novel *Village in Uhuru* tells the story of the rise of Tanzania's nationalist movement and the rocky first years after independence in 1961, as seen from the perspective of an island community living far from the capital Dar es Salaam. A striking moment in the novel comes when, in 1962, two government ministers visit the island to celebrate Saba Saba Day, a public holiday commemorating the founding of the nationalist party TANU. They hold a public meeting at which, Ruhumbika writes, they 'explained democracy, and the important Bill their Government had passed in conformity with its resolution and promise to democratise society, the Chiefs' Bill'.[1] The lesson that those who attended the meeting came away with was simple. It was that 'their *mtemi* [chief] was no longer *mtemi*. Even if he were to come back they were no longer supposed to send him the traditional presents.' In this time of *uhuru* (independence), 'all people were equal. Their *mtemi* had become an ordinary person like themselves.'[2]

---

* I am grateful to Charles West and the two anonymous reviewers for comments on earlier drafts of this paper.

[1] Gabriel Ruhumbika, *Village in Uhuru* (Harlow, 1969), 93.

[2] *Ibid.*, 94.

What are we to make of this encounter? On the face of it, the answer is simple. It is a familiar attempt by a modernising nationalist party in early post-colonial Africa to confront and to overcome the forces of tradition. In Ruhumbika's dramatic telling, we see party officials seeking to educate the citizens of the new state, to enable them to seize their new-found freedom with both hands and to discard old hierarchies. This was the moment when age-old tradition was swept away by the forces of progress and freedom: when the promises and dreams of independence were finally made a reality at the local level.

Ruhumbika's account is of course fictional, but encounters of this kind certainly did take place in African states as they gained independence and began building post-colonial states. And they rest at the heart of how historians generally assess the remarkable transformation of Africa in the mid-twentieth century, as it moved from a continent of empires to a continent of independent nation-states. At the moment of independence, nationalist parties in Africa typically rejected what they saw as outdated theories of society, defined by hierarchical bonds, in favour of a language of equality and of individual freedoms. In this sense, Ruhumbika's novel, and Africa's history more widely, seems to fit neatly into a global history of the twentieth century, in which the century's middle decades are defined by a 'triumph of liberalism' as a 'politico-intellectual tradition centred on individual freedom in the context of constitutional government'.[3]

If the basic outline of this transformation is not in doubt, in recent years the historiography of decolonisation in Africa has been dramatically rewritten. That historiography was once comfortably located within a nationalist framework which both took for granted that the outcome of post-war nationalist struggles would be a continent of nation-states, and tended to write the history of African independence from the perspective of the nationalist parties that eventually won power. In contrast, new work, much of it inspired by Frederick Cooper's analysis, has gone a long way towards reopening the sense of possibility which marked this period, and the many roads not taken.[4] The 1940s and 1950s are now understood to have been characterised by, in Cooper's terms, both 'possibility and constraint'.[5] Although a continent of nation-states came to be seen as inevitable, this future was not obvious to all in 1945.

At the same time, this new body of scholarship has reminded us that the thinking of the nationalist parties which took power at independence was itself only one aspect of a much broader spectrum of political

---

[3] Duncan Bell, *Reordering the World: Essays on Liberalism and Empire* (Princeton, 2016).

[4] David Armitage, *Foundations of Modern International Thought* (Cambridge, 2012); Frederick Cooper, *Africa since 1940: The Past of the Present* (Cambridge, 2002).

[5] Frederick Cooper, 'Possibility and Constraint: African Independence in Historical Perspective', *Journal of African History*, 49 (2008), 167–96.

thinking. Nationalist parties did not instantly capture the support of entire populations. Rather, they came to power as the result of a struggle which saw them marginalise alternatives. Some of those alternatives were based on political philosophies that would have been instantly recognisable to the nationalist parties which eventually triumphed, even if they disagreed on questions of emphasis.[6] But other people put forward sets of ideas that were more challenging to those principles. Some were suspicious of the focus on individual rights which characterised nationalist movements, and profoundly opposed egalitarian visions of a post-colonial future.[7]

While this latter group have increasingly attracted the attention of historians, they continue to fit uneasily into narratives of mid-twentieth-century Africa. They are sometimes described as conservatives, sometimes as ethnic patriots.[8] They were often older men, and the vision of society they promoted was a hierarchical and patriarchal one. The idioms which they used to make claims to power and influence are often unfamiliar. Yet the root concerns they had about society and the risks to it were often shared by nationalist parties, even if the remedies proposed were very different.

Early histories of the political thought of decolonisation in Africa were shaped by assumptions about the naturalness of nation-states which many historians shared with the subjects of their research. It is largely because historians have learned not to treat nation-states as natural and to shed the nationalist assumptions of an earlier generation that the last two decades have seen a radical rewriting of the history of decolonisation in Africa, as elsewhere. But moving outside nationalist frameworks has only taken us so far. It has led to a renewed recognition that there were other possibilities in 1945 beyond the territorial nation-states and nationalist regimes which eventually emerged.[9] But it remains hard to see where the growing power of a conservative vision of society after independence came from. It makes it hard, too, as the anthropologist Harri Englund has recently observed, to identify ways in which the exercise of power beyond agreed limits

---

[6] Giacomo Macola, *Liberal Nationalism in Central Africa: A Biography of Harry Mwaanga Nkumbula* (New York, 2010).

[7] Harri Englund has called on scholars to ask 'harder questions about the place that the liberal values of equality and freedom might have both among the instances being studied and in scholars' own commitments'. Harri Englund, 'Zambia at 50: The Rediscovery of Liberalism', *Africa: The Journal of the International African Institute*, 83 (2013), 670–89, at 685.

[8] Derek Peterson, *Ethnic Patriotism and the East African Revival: A History of Dissent c. 1935–1972* (Cambridge, 2012); Miles Larmer, *Rethinking African Politics: A History of Opposition in Zambia* (Farnham, 2011), 4.

[9] Summarising a body of new research in this vein, Harri Englund has described a 'rediscovery of liberalism' among historians. Englund, 'Zambia at 50'. Though at the same time, it is unclear how far other options were realistic possibilities. Samuel Moyn, 'Fantasies of Federalism', *Dissent*, 62 (2015), 145–51.

continued to be challenged even as political space was tightly constrained after independence, sometimes in unexpected ways.[10]

In this article, I want to suggest that to move the historiography of the decolonisation era forward, we need to go beyond simply provincialising nationalism. The first generation of scholars who wrote about nationalism in Africa certainly often did so within a nationalist framework. Yet, I would suggest, their vision was also shaped by the unspoken assumptions of a distinctively mid-twentieth-century liberalism. While we no longer view the political thought of the time through the prism of nationalism, we perhaps still have a tendency to view it through the prism of mid-twentieth-century liberalism, and therefore tacitly to privilege some voices above others. This means that while we understand the political thinking of decolonisation to have been concerned with 'freedom', we have not fully appreciated the diversity of thinking about what freedom meant to contemporaries. I would like to explore what happens if we historicise mid-twentieth-century liberalism and set the diverse political thinking of mid-twentieth-century Africa more firmly in its contemporary context.

To do so, I start by considering the ways in which mid-twentieth-century liberalism has shaped the scholarship of the history of decolonisation in Africa, and what it might mean to historicise it. I then turn to explore evidence from colonial Tanganyika in eastern Africa, which suggests that we can identify two broad families of political thinking in the 1950s, one making claims for equality and individual rights, the other making claims in idioms which explicitly recognised hierarchies. Putting both clearly into the same analytical framework helps us more effectively set the era of independence in context and, by allowing us to identify neglected continuities across the conventional dividing line of independence, helps us make better sense of post-colonial trajectories.

I Liberalism in context

When historians in the early twenty-first century looked back at the 1950s and 1960s, they were struck by the way in which it had become axiomatic that the basic building blocks of international society were nation-states.[11] Empires, which just a few decades before had dominated the globe, had been swept away, and come to be understood as an outdated and illegitimate form of political organisation. As Rupert Emerson wrote in 1960 in an evocative phrase which captures this transition, 'Empires have fallen on evil days and nations have risen to take their place.'[12]

---

[10] Englund, 'Zambia at 50'.

[11] For example, Jane Burbank and Frederick Cooper, *Empires in World History: Power and the Politics of Difference* (Princeton, 2010).

[12] Rupert Emerson, *From Empire to Nation: The Rise of Self-Assertion of Asian and African Peoples* (Cambridge, MA, 1960), 3.

For many people in the continent of Africa, this moment constituted a rejection of European domination, and a claim to equal standing in an emerging world order of nation-states. A new and powerful body of historical writing, often by scholars who shared the nationalist perspective of their subjects, was produced which told of and celebrated the struggles that led to African nationalist movements winning independence. But this moment in the history of international thought was not characterised only by the assumption that the international political order would and should be based on nation-states and not empires. It was also characterised by a set of assumptions about what kind of political society should be contained within the building blocks of nations, defined in terms of parliamentary democracy, representative government and individual rights.

These assumptions shaped the politics of the time. In post-colonial Ghana, for example, Nkrumah was forced to defend publicly his commitment to parliamentary democracy.[13] Those leaders, such as Kenneth Kaunda in Zambia and Julius Nyerere in Tanzania, who sought to move away from two-party systems had to take great care to show why, in their view, multi-party systems were inappropriate for their societies.[14] This anxiety was, of course, partly a product of the Cold War context. But also underlying it was, as the historian of political thought Duncan Bell has recently argued, an emerging hegemonic understanding of liberal democracy as the constitutive feature of western modernity. This was, Bell suggests, partly a consequence of a shift in thought which took place in the first half of the twentieth century and which saw a remaking of the definition of liberalism and a rewriting of the history of the liberal tradition.

For Bell, liberalism in this period 'increasingly figured as the dominant ideology of the West – its origins retrojected back into the early modern era, it came to denote virtually all nontotalitarian forms of politics as well as a partisan political perspective within societies'.[15] It was newly 'yoked' to democracy, a process which, Bell writes, 'automatically (and vastly) expanded the scope of those purportedly encompassed by liberalism, as supporters of "liberal democracy" were conscripted, however reluctantly, to the liberal tradition'. The consequence was that liberalism was 'transfigured from a term identifying a limited and contested position

---

[13] Richard Rathbone, 'Kwame Nkrumah and the Chiefs: The Fate of "Natural Rulers" under Nationalist Governments', *Transactions of the Royal Historical Society*, 10 (2000), 45–63, at 57.

[14] *Independence and Beyond: The Speeches of Kenneth Kaunda*, ed. Colin Legum (1966), 208–9; Julius Nyerere, 'Democracy and the Party System', in *Freedom and Unity*, ed. Julius Nyerere (1966), 195–203.

[15] Bell, *Reordering the World*, 87.

within political discourse to either the most authentic expression of the Western tradition or a constitutive feature of the West itself'.[16]

This mid-twentieth-century triumph of liberalism thereby gradually marginalised those modes of thinking which sat outwith liberal traditions. Yet it also marginalised ideas that had once sat more or less comfortably within a liberal tradition. As Michael Freeden has recently reminded us, rather than think in terms of liberalism in the singular, it might historically 'be more accurate to talk about *liberalisms* in the plural, all part of a broad family exhibiting both similarities and differences. Many members of the liberal family overlap in their characteristics, but some are hardly on speaking terms.'[17] But the mid-twentieth-century moment privileged some aspects of this tradition above others. The focus on the individual that characterised newly hegemonic understandings of liberalism eclipsed alternative modes of thinking about individual and community, equally embedded in a more expansive liberal tradition or traditions. In particular, it obscured the intellectual inheritance of the liberal idealism of the late nineteenth and early twentieth centuries with its emphasis on the individual as a member of a community, whose ability to flourish depended on social relationships within that community.[18] This was a vision of society which, through its adoption of familial metaphors, recognised hierarchies both within states and in the wider international order.[19] It was a way of thinking about society which was enormously influential in shaping the political thinking of the colonial officials and missionaries who governed Africa in the first half of the twentieth century.[20]

The mid-twentieth-century emergence of liberalism as the 'dominant ideology of the West', in Bell's terms, had, I would like to suggest, implications for the way that the decolonisation of Africa was viewed by observers, implications which have continued to influence more recent scholarship. Setting the scholarship of the time within its wider intellectual context, it is striking to see the echoes of a distinctively mid-twentieth-century set of assumptions about the naturalness of this definition of the liberal order. The belief that liberalism defined in these terms offered the best hope for individual flourishing under a just government proved a powerful one for those writing about African independence, as powerful perhaps as the assumption that Africa was destined to become a continent of nation-states.

[16] *Ibid.*

[17] Michael Freeden, *Liberalism: A Very Short Introduction* (Oxford, 2015), 1.

[18] Sandra M. Den Otter, *British Idealism and Social Explanation: A Study in Late Victorian Thought* (Oxford, 1996), 152.

[19] Jeanne Morefield, *Covenants without Swords: Idealist liberalism and the Spirit of Empire* (Princeton, 2005), 45.

[20] Emma Hunter, 'Dutiful Subjects, Patriotic Citizens, and the Concept of "Good Citizenship" in Twentieth-Century Tanzania', *Historical Journal*, 56 (2013), 257–77, at 259.

What this meant was that while a concern with freedom was understood to be central to the movements which powered the end of empire in Africa, freedom was understood as inextricably bound up with claims of equality. As John Lonsdale wrote in 1981, what had united the first scholars of African decolonisation, writing in the 1950s and 1960s, was a concern, at once moral and political, with freedom. As Lonsdale wrote, this was a definition of freedom 'based on Africans' claims for political and racial equality', in which '[i]ndividual self-realisation, political order, social freedom, and equity seemed destined to be joined together under the renewed sovereignties of independent Africa'.[21] The scholars of the 1950s and 1960s were far less interested in those who rejected this focus on the individual, social freedom and equality. Much of that body of thinking took place in the idiom of 'tribe', and as such seemed to be a backward-looking response to the forces of modernity, distant from the liberal tradition.

After the first flurry of scholarly writing in the 1950s and 1960s, the political arguments of Africa in the 1950s slowly slipped into the background of historians' attention. But this has changed dramatically in recent years, and there has been a new flourishing of research on that important decade. This growing body of scholarship has revealed two families of thinking present in this transitional moment. On the one hand, there were the nationalist movements who advocated a transformation in social relationships, breaking down old hierarchies and offering new opportunities to the young, women, trade unions and educated elites.[22] The political reforms they advocated were very familiar in a mid-twentieth-century context. They supported elections and universal suffrage, the abolition of chiefship and individual rights. Many were part of transnational networks, linked by socialism, organised labour and other elements of an emerging global civil society.[23]

Yet at the same time, others spoke a very different political language, less recognisable to onlookers today. In some contexts, this was a language of chiefship, but in other contexts, it was the chiefs who were the targets of criticism.[24] Particularly striking is the explicit recognition of and respect

[21] John Lonsdale, 'States and Social Processes in Africa: A Historiographical Survey', *African Studies Review*, 24 (1981), 139–225, at 143.

[22] Rathbone, 'Kwame Nkrumah and the Chiefs'.

[23] Recent work is starting to uncover the dynamism of these transnational networks, for example Leslie James, *George Padmore and Decolonization from Below: Pan-Africanism, the Cold War, and the End of Empire* (Basingstoke, 2015), and research groups such as Afro-Asian Networks, http://afroasiannetworks.com.

[24] Justin Willis, 'Chieftaincy', in *The Oxford Handbook of Modern African History*, ed. John Parker and Richard Reid (Oxford, 2013), 208–23; Cherry Leonardi and Chris Vaughan, '"We Are Oppressed and our Only Way Is to Write to Higher Authority": The Politics of Claim and Complaint in the Peripheries of Condominium Sudan', in *Citizenship, Belonging and Political Community in Africa: Dialogues between Past and Present*, ed. Emma Hunter (Athens, OH, 2016), 74–100.

for hierarchy, defended sometimes in a language of culture, and at other times in a language of tradition.[25]

The case of Ghana provides a particularly striking example of this contrast. Perhaps the most iconic figure of decolonising Africa is that of Kwame Nkrumah, who returned from studying in America to lead the Gold Coast to self-government in 1951 and then to independence as Ghana in 1957. Rejecting the gradualist approach of his predecessors, Nkrumah proclaimed that rather than wait for economic development, self-government must come first and development would follow afterwards. Yet while Nkrumah's success in binding together a nationalist movement and forcing the pace of decolonisation captured international imagination, politics at the local level in the 1950s were defined by a bruising battle between Nkrumah's Convention People's Party and local chiefs. These chiefs were presented at the time as forces of tradition, destined to be swept aside in modernising Africa. But as Richard Rathbone has shown, the battle was so bruising because of the power of chieftaincy, not its weakness. Indeed, what was really at stake was a battle between two contending visions: conservative nationalism on the one hand and Nkrumah's modernising socialism on the other.[26]

Nkrumah sought to remake society, and his radical anti-chief language was part of that wider project. On one level, then, this was a political battle whereby those with power in the colonial order sought to preserve it in the independent Ghana which was being created. But it was also a struggle over two different visions of society, in which questions about political relationships were part of a wider set of questions about what kind of society could and should be built.

On the other side of the continent in East Africa, the 1940s and 1950s saw the emergence not only of new nationalist movements, but also of new associations, often based on ethnicity, which, in Derek Peterson's words, 'sought to stitch society together in a hierarchical relationship of trust and dependence'.[27] Where nationalists were concerned with national self-determination, these groups were instead 'driven by the urgent need to find institutions that could protect civic virtues and define honourable conduct'.[28] For John Lonsdale, this is the realm of the 'deep politics' of 'moral ethnicity'.[29] Crucially, this sphere of debate assumed, as Harri Englund writes of modern day Malawi, that 'claims addressing

---

[25] Derek Peterson, 'Introduction', in *The Politics of Heritage in Africa: Economies, Histories, and Infrastructures*, ed. Derek Peterson (Cambridge, 2015), 1–36.

[26] Rathbone, 'Kwame Nkrumah and the Chiefs'.

[27] Peterson, *Ethnic Patriotism and the East African Revival*, 127–8.

[28] *Ibid.*, 16.

[29] John Lonsdale, 'KAU's Cultures: Imaginations of Community and Constructions of Leadership in Kenya after the Second World War', *Journal of African Cultural Studies*, 13 (2000), 107–24.

the wealthy and the powerful could be effective precisely when they left difference and hierarchy intact'.[30]

These groups, or those who wrote in these idioms, are often described as conservatives, but they were not simply trying to conserve. They often spoke explicitly about progress and how to manage it. They also had a lot to say about freedom – but did not necessarily link freedom with equality. What happens if, rather than attaching labels such as 'conservative' which fail to do full justice to their stated intellectual projects, we take these groups seriously when they say they were concerned with freedom, but freedom within society and existing social bonds rather than freedom as constituted through individual rights and the rejection of existing hierarchies? In the next section, I turn to show how evidence from 1950s Tanganyika might help us to reread local politics in terms of a contrast between two different modes of thinking about freedom.

II 1950s Kilimanjaro

In 1949, a new political movement which called itself the Kilimanjaro Chagga Citizens Union was created in the district of Moshi in north-eastern Tanganyika, on the slopes of Mount Kilimanjaro. At a time of rapid political change across the African continent, defined by a language of democratisation and self-government, this political movement seemed curiously at odds with the acknowledged trends of the times. While its leaders, Petro Njau and Joseph Merinyo, defined their project as defending the rights of 'free men', it was the threat to freedom posed by local chiefs that was the primary focus of their attention. They campaigned against a new local government structure which had created three new divisional chiefs, and instead called for an elected paramount chief of the Chagga. They demanded that clans, not chiefs, be recognised as the true basis of political authority in the district. Concerned that society was under threat from social, political and economic change, they argued for a patriarchal vision of society in which older land-holding males recognised, and fulfilled, their duties to the young.

While these ideas seemed to colonial officials and to many contemporaries to be out of step with contemporary developments, they had deep roots in local thinking about hierarchy and the location of legitimate social and political power, ideas that had in turn developed in response to the social and political change of the 1920s and 1930s. Far from being merely an unthinking hewing to tradition, this was a movement born of reflection and of a distinctive understanding of the historical past.

---

[30] Harri Englund, *Human Rights and the African Airwaves: Mediating Equality on the Chichewa Radio* (Bloomington, 2011), 224.

We can see traces of the historical writing which shaped this understanding in a 1950 document produced by the Kilimanjaro Chagga Citizens Union, entitled 'A History of the Customs of the Chagga'.[31] In it, the Union thanked those scholars, both insiders and outsiders, whose research helped provide the basis for their understanding of Chagga history. The person they probably had in mind when they wrote of Chagga researchers was a man called Nathaniel Mtui, a Christian convert and clerk. Born in 1892, Mtui met an untimely – and violent – death in 1927, but in his relatively short life he played a key role in researching and writing the history of the region. Amongst his works was a text which has become known as the *Nine Notebooks of Chagga History*, an English-language typescript translation of material originally prepared in the vernacular Chagga language. These *Notebooks* deal most comprehensively with the history of the Chiefdom of Marangu, on the mountain of Kilimanjaro. They describe both the earliest chiefs and those in power at the time of writing, between 1913 and 1916. In particular, the *Notebooks* deal with how chiefs came to power, their conflicts and the ways in which they lost power.

Mtui's *Notebooks* were produced for the Lutheran missionary Bruno Gutmann, a German missionary committed to the principle of evangelising through the institutions of society as currently constituted. Gutmann combined the role of the missionary with that of the ethnographer, because he believed that working through existing social institutions required first understanding them. Gutmann came to East Africa in 1902 from Europe, and his reading of Africa's present and its recent past was shaped by his experiences in Europe. He saw European history as characterised by corruption and decline. Individualism posed a threat, as he perceived it, to the social bonds that held society together, and he feared that this process was now spreading to Africa. Gutmann was also working in the context of a society under colonial rule, first German and then, after the First World War, British government under the supervision of the League of Nations. At the time when he commissioned Mtui to carry out this research, Gutmann was preparing to write his long ethnographic study, *Das Recht der Dschagga*, which served in part as a critique of social and political changes which he believed were taking place under German rule and in particular the strengthening of the power of chiefs, which he believed to rest on a fundamental misunderstanding of Chagga society.[32]

[31] Kilimanjaro Chagga Citizens Union, 'A History of the Mila ya Wachagga', Tanzania National Archives (TNA) 5/584, fo. 154.

[32] Emma Hunter, 'In Pursuit of the "Higher Medievalism": Local History and Politics in Kilimanjaro', in *Recasting the Past: History Writing and Political Work in Modern Africa*, ed. Derek Peterson and Giacomo Macola (Athens OH, 2009), 149–70.

Gutmann was particularly interested in the institution of the clan, as we can see from Mtui's text. At one point, Mtui breaks off his narrative to write:

> I now learn that you [Gutmann] are not interested in this material which I have collected about the clans except the notes on the method of offering sacrifices by the Nyange clan. You say you want to know about the careers of different clans and I can see that this is a job which needs patience and I will have to go into this account gradually. I have decided to postpone collecting material about the clans to get to the truth of the whole thing about them and how they were affected by the cruelties and richness.[33]

Influenced by the evidence he drew together with the help of informants such as Mtui, Gutmann's conclusion in *Das Recht der Dschagga* was that the core ties which knit Chagga society together were those of the clan. He argued that returning power to the clans would help restore social harmony and restore the social bonds which he felt were being destroyed by a too rapid transition into the modern world. He attempted to translate these prescriptions into practice, for example through the establishment of an advisory board of clan heads to promote Christian morality.[34] Gutmann's vision of society was profoundly hierarchical. In a 1935 article in the journal *Africa*, he wrote of the corrupting power of money, and the disasters caused by 'the confusion, the levelling down, and even complete abandonment of all difference in social position due to birth' which money inevitably caused.[35]

Gutmann's analysis and conclusions were not always shared by other missionaries and colonial officials. Charles Dundas, the British colonial official who similarly drew on Mtui's research but reached very different conclusions, argued, in line with the thinking which characterised interwar approaches to colonial governance in Africa and the policy of indirect rule, that the clan had long since been superseded by the institution of chiefship. But Dundas did not think that matters could be left there: rather, his point was that it was this institution that should form the basis of political progress.[36]

As Gutmann's and Dundas's writings suggest, the colonial officials and missionaries who worried about the impact of social change on society in the first half of the twentieth century were not simply seeking to repair and re-traditionalise social bonds that were being broken in order

---

[33] Nathaniel Mtui, *Nine Notebooks of Chagga History*, paragraph 160. A microfilm copy of a 1958–9 English translation is available in Leipzig University Library.

[34] Klaus Fiedler, *Christianity and African Culture: Conservative German Protestant Missionaries in Tanzania, 1900–1940* (Leiden, 1996), 42, 115.

[35] Bruno Gutmann, 'The African Standpoint', *Africa*, 8 (1935), 1–19, at 9–10.

[36] To see how the principles of indirect rule were explained by the government in Tanganyika, see for example: No author, 'Namna nci inavyotawaliwa', *Mambo Leo*, Dec. 1925, 265. Charles Dundas and his political thinking is discussed at greater length in Hunter, 'In Pursuit of the "Higher Medievalism"'.

to conserve; they were seeking rather to manage what they themselves termed 'progress' in a way that did not break society apart.[37] They were concerned with how to reconcile freedom with society and were often, as I have suggested elsewhere, inspired by late nineteenth-century liberal thought.[38] Where they disagreed with each other was in their interpretations of the societies they encountered: on their past, their present and their potential futures, and on whether growing individualism was perceived as an essential part of social and political 'progress' or as a threat to society.

Gutmann's concerns about society and social relationships, and his fears about the consequences of individualism, were certainly far from unique and seem to have tapped into and perhaps helped shape wider concerns in the region. We can trace similar anxieties through a wide array of written Swahili-language texts circulating at the time in the region, particularly in the Lutheran missionary periodical *Ufalme wa Mungu* and the periodical of the Kilimanjaro Native Cooperative Union, *Uremi*. In editorials, reports of church meetings and letters, we find a rich seam of discussion about society and social relationships, focusing in particular on the ways in which children were failing to obey their parents and were leaving the region to go to the coast in pursuit of work. As Ruben Moshi, a member of the Lutheran Church, complained in the pages of *Ufalme wa Mungu* in 1930, the youth 'like to dress in the European fashion, they wander about from place to place even as far as the coast and if they are prevented by their parents or church elders they do not listen' and were even 'arrogant towards them'.[39] If the complaints voiced by people such as Moshi were often similar, the answers that were proposed to the problems they identified varied. For Joseph Maliti, president of the local coffee cooperative, the answer lay in developing agriculture so that 'we profit from our country and can thus bring back our children who are lost and poor, going to the coast with an emptiness in body and soul'. Progress required working together and cooperation.[40]

At the same time, the pages of the Dar es Salaam newspaper *Kwetu*, colonial Tanganyika's only independent African newspaper in the 1930s

---

[37] It is important to emphasise this point. Karuna Matena's recent book has argued that indirect rule, the colonial practice of government through the framework of the 'tribe' and chief, was a response to the perceived failure of the liberal projects of the mid-nineteenth century and that in Africa it 'took on preemptive, and therefore more systematic, character', aiming to prevent the dissolution of social bonds before it was too late. Yet indirect rule in Africa was never simply a project of conservation and, as Duncan Bell has argued, reading it as a rejection of liberalism rests on a narrow definition of liberalism. Karuna Mantena, *Alibis of Empire: Henry Maine and the Ends of Liberal Imperialism* (Princeton, 2010), 173; Bell, *Reordering the World*, 57.

[38] Hunter, 'Dutiful Subjects', 259.

[39] Ruben Moshi, *Ufalme wa Mungu*, Jan. 1930, 8.

[40] Joseph Maliti, 'Letter from the President', *Uremi*, 3 June 1932, TNA 20984.

and 1940s, provided a forum for a vocal critique of Chagga chiefs who, it was said, were exceeding their powers and exacting too much from the population. The way forward was not however to strip chiefs of their authority, but to reinvigorate the traditions by which that authority had been controlled. By excluding wealthy elder men from a political role, it was argued, a key check on chiefly authority had been lost. In the past, wrote one correspondent in the pages of *Kwetu*, the rich could protect the poor, but these days 'any person who tries to help a person or two people with their problems, for example by lending money or slaughtering cows will find that people who try to help in this way are called agitators'.[41]

This context helps us make sense of the ideas of the Kilimanjaro Chagga Citizens Union, particularly in the 1950s. The Kilimanjaro Chagga Citizens Union put forward a hierarchical model of society, in which full citizenship was limited to land-holding men, who were responsible for providing for their children and poorer kinsmen.[42] They criticised chiefs as illegitimate, but when they called for a return of power to 'the people', their definition of 'the people' was a narrow one. Political rights were understood as being limited to land-holding males, and mediated through the Union itself.

Like the writers of the 1920s and 1930s, the Union's leader Petro Njau was concerned with the state of the moral order and convinced that trust had broken down. He called for the authority of clan elders to be resurrected, identifying the impact of the declining authority of clan elders in the rising 'price of bridewealth, lack of manners and respect' and 'dishonesty' in relation to property.[43] The cure would lie in clan elders reasserting their authority, and in all accepting the authority of the Kilimanjaro Chagga Citizens Union as a disciplinary body.[44]

Njau claimed to be concerned with freedom, and so he was: but this was freedom only for those who held membership cards for his organisation. Freedom came through membership of the Kilimanjaro Chagga Citizens Union, which for Njau was equated with belonging to a Chagga political community. To cite the historian Sean Stilwell, writing about a very different context, this was a definition of freedom not as 'the absence of obligations, dependence, or other ties that restrict or narrow an individual's right and ability to make decisions and act autonomously',

---

[41] Letter from S. M. Ngooly, 'Uzembe katika mabaraza ya wenyeji wa utawala wa Moshi', *Kwetu*, 8 Sept. 1939.

[42] This section draws on arguments made in Emma Hunter, *Political Thought and the Public Sphere in Tanzania: Freedom, Democracy and Citizenship in the Era of Decolonization* (Cambridge, 2015), ch. 4.

[43] 'Mkutano maalumu wa wanachama', 2 Feb. 1956, TNA 5/25/7, fo. 266.

[44] Kilimanjaro Chagga Citizens Union Pamphlet No. 4 of 1954, 'Urithi wa Wenyeji wa Nchi ni Mila, Iliyotokana na Wakale Wao', 26 July 1954, 5, TNA 5/25/7, fo. 221; 'Kilimanjaro Chagga Union amezaliwa Moshi', TNA 5/584, fo. 31.

but rather 'as the ability or right to belong'.[45] Crucially, this was an understanding of freedom which was entirely compatible with inequality and social subordination.

It is significant that Njau's project was briefly successful. He and his party managed both to convince the colonial administration of the need for a paramount chief, despite the administration's initial opposition, and to ensure that their candidate, Thomas Marealle, was elected. But over the course of the 1950s, Njau's increasingly conservative vision of society was challenged by a powerful alternative based on radical principles of social and political equality for men and women, young and old, and a rejection of social hierarchies. The district commissioner's response to Njau's attempt to limit rights to those who held membership cards was to charge him with 'complete ignorance of what democracy and freedom really mean' and to insist that the Union 'should also understand clearly that *all* Chagga have rights whether members of your "Union" or not'.[46] At the same time, the Union's exclusion of women was challenged by opponents in the Chagga Congress who set themselves apart by welcoming women members.[47] The demand of the paramount chief, Thomas Marealle, in 1955 that Chagga students studying at Makerere College in Uganda apologise after they had been critical of him in an article in the Makerere College magazine, and that they do so in a mode deemed to be in accordance with Chagga customs and traditions, provoked opposition from a younger generation unwilling to accept a humiliating insistence on deference of the young towards the old.[48]

Ultimately, Njau's opponents, first the Chagga Congress and then the Chagga Democratic Party, succeeded in arguing convincingly that there was no place in a democratising Tanganyika for a paramount chief and that he should be replaced by an elected president of the Chagga. A central theme in the opposition to the paramount chief was a concern that the position was out of step with democratic principles, particularly if it was now to be understood as for life and hereditary. As Joseph Merinyo wrote in 1958, articulating the case against hereditary chiefship and implicitly against the paramount chief whom he had previously helped to put into office, 'Many people would like there to be a vote every three years, especially these days. The people should be asked. The people are desperately waiting for the elections which will remove

[45] Sean Stilwell, *Slavery and Slaving in African History* (Cambridge, 2014), 8.

[46] District commissioner to secretary, Chagga Citizens Union, Oct. 1951, TNA 5/23/20, vol. 1, fo. 104. Emphasis in original.

[47] 'Minutes of the Meeting of the Chagga Congress which Met in the Welfare Centre on Saturday 30th January 1954', TNA 12844/4, fo. 538.

[48] 'Wanafunzi Wachagga wa Makerere wamejita', *Komkya*, Feb. 1955, 1; Kathleen Stahl, 'The Chagga', in *Tradition and Transition: Studies of the Tribal Element in the Modern Era* (Berkeley, 1969), 209–22, at 218.

imperialism and bring democracy to Uchaggani.'[49] Underlying this point was a conviction that political rights were the property of all. As one student, E. Alemyo, wrote in the pages of the Makerere College Chagga Students Magazine in 1959, God had not created some to rule and others to be ruled. All had a right and a duty to participate in government through regular elections.[50]

In the mid-twentieth century, these arguments were increasingly resonant, both locally and at a global level, and benefited from the support of TANU, Tanganyika's increasingly prominent nationalist movement committed to the same goals. Indeed, the Chagga Democratic Party and TANU were so closely linked as to be hard to distinguish. Eventually, a local referendum was held on 4 February 1960.[51] Of those eligible to vote, 44 per cent voted, and of those voters, 22,000 voted for a president, while only 5,000 voted for a continuation of the paramount chief, bringing the Kilimanjaro Union's project to an end.

Yet though the two intellectual projects we have discussed here were very different, with one based on the principle of social and political equality and the other on a hierarchical vision of society, they shared common roots in early and mid-twentieth-century thinking about progress, social change and society. Rather than casting one as 'modern' and the other as 'traditional', we might better see them as different wings of a broad spectrum of thought.

In post-colonial Tanzania, TANU's leader Julius Nyerere's conception of socialism, while radically opposed to Njau's thinking in that it was based on the principle of social equality, had its roots in a similar concern with how to reconcile progress with the maintaining and strengthening of social bonds.[52] Locally, the concerns raised by the Kilimanjaro Union, particularly around landlessness and gender and generational relations, did not disappear with their loss of local political power, but continued to be discussed in the pages of the local newspaper *Kusare* through the

[49] J. Merinyo to D. C., 'Tangazo Maalum kwa Wachagga la Tarehe 1st June 1958', TNA 5/23/20, fo. 149.

[50] E. Alemyo, 'Serikali ni Sisi', *Makerere College Chagga Society Magazine*, The National Archives (UK) (TNA UK), FCO 141/17864, fo. 10A.

[51] A. R. Denny, 'A Note on Chagga Tribal Politics Prior to Referendum in Jan. 1960', TNA UK, FCO 141/17864, 4 Jan. 1960, 3, fo. 55A.

[52] Emma Hunter, 'Economic Man in East Africa', in *The Moral Economies of Ethnic and Nationalist Claims*, ed. Bruce Berman, Andre Laliberté and Stephen Larin (Vancouver, 2016), 101–22. On the eclectic sources of Nyerere's thinking about society, see Tom Molony, *Nyerere: The Early Years* (Woodbridge, 2014). The term *ujamaa*, used by Nyerere to describe his policy of African socialism, was used in colonial didactic texts in the 1920s and 1930s to describe the choice of humans to live together rather than separately, and the responsibilities to each other which follow from that. This was, for the authors of the didactic primer *Uraia*, 'the basis of citizenship'. Emma Hunter, 'Languages of Politics in Twentieth-Century Kilimanjaro' (Ph.D. thesis, University of Cambridge, 2008), 231.

1960s.[53] Understanding their ideas, based as they were in a rich tradition of thinking about community and society, and interrogating them alongside ultimately more successful bodies of ideas in which freedom was bound up with equality, helps us better situate decolonising Africa in a longer framework of African history, and it is to these broader implications that I turn now.

III Conclusion

By stepping outside nationalist frameworks of analysis, historians of decolonisation have increasingly come to stress the possibilities open to political actors in the period after 1945. Although the final result was a continent of nation-states, historians have argued that it did not have to be this way. Yet while the recent flourishing of new histories of decolonisation to which we owe this insight has been very welcome, in some ways it has simply moved the moment at which political futures became fixed to a slightly later date. The moment of possibility was shortlived, and by 1960 it was increasingly clear that the territorial nation-state would dominate the immediate political future in Africa as elsewhere. The barriers to political federalism, perhaps the most widely talked about alternative to the nation-state, were too high.[54] While a critique of nationalist frameworks of analysis has, therefore, greatly enriched the historiography of decolonisation, it may be that we now need to look elsewhere to take the historiography forward.

Just as 'methodological nationalism' once shaped the way that decolonisation was understood, so, I have argued, has a kind of 'methodological liberalism'. Removing the prism of mid-twentieth-century liberalism reminds us that far from being always and necessarily constitutive of modernity, mid-twentieth-century liberalism was itself a distinctive ideology which responded to a distinctive moment. Provincialising this mode of thought opens up the possibility of exploring traditions of thinking which fit uncomfortably into that framework and rethinking what kinds of political possibilities were open in the era of decolonisation.

The political thinking of the period of decolonisation was, as those who first analysed it recognised, centrally concerned with the concept of

---

[53] A debate in the pages of *Kusare* in Mar. 1962 about chiefship and whether women could hold positions of local political authority is telling in this regard. See for example a letter from Makunduwira Kiwari, 'Umangi wa Ukoloni Hatutaki', *Kusare*, 26 Mar. 1962, 3. Letters to *Kusare* over the course of the 1960s also suggest that although local political associations could no longer be formed, this did not mean that all had reconciled themselves to the nationalist party, TANU. Letter from Abdullah S. Kweka, 'Wazee Waukaribisha Ujinga Mkoani Kilimanjaro', *Kusare*, 11 Sept. 1965, 3.

[54] Moyn, 'Fantasies of Federalism'.

freedom. Yet while for some freedom was inseparable from equality, for others it was conceivable that freedom could coexist with inequality and the reconstitution or maintenance of social and political hierarchies. Some of these conceptions drew on liberal ideologies, particularly the liberal idealism of the late nineteenth and early twentieth centuries which sought human flourishing through community, and could sit within a broadly defined liberal tradition. But others were incompatible with or directly challenged liberal ideologies. Exploring the ways freedom was thought about in its contemporary context means that we can take seriously the political thinking of those for whom freedom did not mean individual autonomy and did not presume social equality, as was the case for Petro Njau and the Kilimanjaro Chagga Citizens Union, who criticised chiefs while nevertheless seeking to defend the power of wealthy men and the authority of clan leaders.

To acknowledge this has implications for the way we approach the history of decolonisation in Africa, and what happened next. Focusing attention so heavily on those who argued for a conjoined package of '[i]ndividual self-realisation, political order, social freedom, and equity' has meant that the apparent rapid abandonment of these ideas after independence was a puzzle to be accounted for. It has usually been explained simply in terms of political necessity, as weak post-colonial states cracked down on perceived opponents in order to secure their position, employing colonial-era strategies of governance to do so.

But looking beyond the familiar, and putting the projects of the 'ethnic patriots' and 'conservatives' of the 1950s in the same analytical frame as those of the nationalist parties, allows us to think more carefully about the intellectual context in which post-colonial governments and their citizens were operating and the intellectual resources upon which they were able to draw. It reminds us to pay attention to those traditions of thinking about society and social relationships which were as strong, in some times and places, as the alternative radical tradition of individual rights and social equality that enjoyed a brief hegemony in the late 1950s. By doing so, we might better understand the intellectual roots of the conservative projects of post-colonial leaders. At the same time, we may also be able better to identify the ways in which, even as political rights were rolled back and political space closed down in the years after independence, moral claims and political critiques continued to be made, as they had been in earlier periods, both in recognisable and in more unfamiliar and even uncomfortable idioms.[55]

---

[55] Englund, 'Zambia at 50'; James Ferguson, 'Debating "the Rediscovery of Liberalism" in Zambia: Responses to Harri Englund', *Africa*, 84 (2014), 658–68, at 666.